# CONTENTS

# LIST OF FIGURES

# NOTES ON CONTRIBUTORS

**Charles N. Adams, Jr**. has been a practitioner and teacher of TIE methodologies since 1995, working for both universities and independent theatre companies. He completed his PhD at the University of Minnesota, focusing on theatre historiography, performance for social change, and critical pedagogies, and is currently the treasurer for the non-profit organisation Pedagogy and Theatre of the Oppressed.

**Steve Ball** is Associate Director at the Birmingham Repertory Theatre where he leads on learning, participation and community engagement. He worked for several children's theatre and TIE companies before moving to Birmingham in 1986 to found Language Alive! TIE company. He has also worked for BBC Education and was Head of Arts for Birmingham City Council 2001–3. Steve has an MA in Arts Management and a PhD in Drama (TIE), and is currently Chair of Theatre for Young Audiences England.

**Veronica Baxter** has taught theatre at South African and British higher education institutions, focusing on applied theatre, directing and South African theatre. Her research has involved Practice as Research projects on *inter alia* land legislation, health, the school curriculum and well-being. She has managed a youth theatre and theatre in education companies and has written and directed for the stage.

**Chris Cooper** has worked in TIE since 1988. He has been Artistic Director of Big Brum TIE Company, Birmingham, UK, since 1999. He is also a playwright and works in the UK and internationally as a freelance director, workshop leader, trainer of teachers and actors, and lecturer.

**Mary Cooper** is a writer for stage, radio and screen. She has written more than thirty commissioned plays and worked with companies throughout England and Wales including Asian Co-operative Theatre, Clean Break, Eastern Angles, Ludus Dance, M6 Theatre, Roundabout, Red Ladder, Sheffield Crucible, Theatr Powys, Theatr Clywd, Tutti Frutti, West Yorkshire Playhouse, Yorkshire Women and Z Arts.

**Lynn Hoare** specialises in Applied Theatre and runs the Theatre for Dialogue program (for the Counseling and Mental Health Center) at the University of Texas at Austin (UT) where she also teaches devising, facilitation and Theatre for Dialogue methods. She is co-founder of the Performing Justice Project, The Owl's Nest Retreat and Theatre Action Project where she served as Executive/Artistic Director. Lynn received her MFA in Drama and Theatre for Youth from UT Austin.

**Mary Ann Hunter** is Senior Lecturer in Drama Education at the University of Tasmania, Australia. She has worked in a range of academic, industry and school settings with a focus on young people's engagement in creative practice. She is currently researching in the areas of creative partnerships in education and arts-based peace building.

**Anthony Jackson** is Emeritus Professor of Educational Theatre at the University of Manchester. For his profile see Introduction, page 3.

**Wendy Lement** is Artistic Director of Theatre Espresso, which won a 2012 National Endowment for the Arts award and a New England Theatre Conference 2012 Regional Theatre Award for Excellence in Theatre. She is Producer of Wheelock Family Theatre in Boston. Prior to that she was a long-time Professor of Theatre at Regis College. She is co-author of *And Justice for Some: Exploring American Justice through Drama and Theatre* (2005).

**Peter O'Connor** is an Associate Professor and Director of the Critical Research Unit in Applied Theatre at the University of Auckland and co-director of Applied Theatre Consultants Ltd. He was named a New Zealander of the Year 2011 by *North and South Magazine* for his contributions in Christchurch following the earthquakes.

**David Pammenter** has been extensively involved in people's theatre, TfD, TIE and theatre-making, as a professional director, facilitator and trainer. He joined the Belgrade Theatre Coventry's TIE team in 1969, and was its Head, 1972–78. He has contributed to arts education programme development for the British Council and NGOs across the world, and was Principal Lecturer at Rose Bruford College and at the University of Winchester (UK). His theory and practice focus on the rights of the child and the development of a people-centred, theatre-based pedagogic arts praxis.

**Maya Krishna Rao** is a solo theatre performer. She devises her own shows, which range from dance theatre to stand-up comedy. She is a visiting faculty member at the National School of Drama, Delhi, where she teaches acting. For some years Maya's focus has been on designing syllabi and teaching drama in teacher education institutions and devising TIE programmes for children. In the 1980s, Maya was an actor-teacher with the Leeds Playhouse TIE Company.

**Chris Vine** is Academic Director of the MA in Applied Theatre at The City University of New York (CUNY). For his profile see Introduction, page 4.

**Helen Wheelock** joined The CUNY/Creative Arts Team as an actor-teacher in 1994 and was appointed director of the Early Learning Programme in 2008. She also directs CAT's partnership with United Arab Emirates University in Al Ain and serves as an adjunct faculty member at The CUNY School of Professional Studies.

# ACKNOWLEDGEMENTS

The editors gratefully acknowledge the invaluable co-operation received from all the individuals and theatre companies whose work is cited in the book, and their permission to include illustrations of their work, as follows:

Pit Prop Theatre (Wigan): *Brand of Freedom.* Photo: Arthur Thompson. From the Pit Prop Theatre Archives housed at the University of Manchester (Special Collections). Photo reproduced by courtesy of the University Librarian and Director, The John Rylands Library, The University of Manchester.

Y Touring (UK): *Starfish*. Photo: Nigel Townsend.

Theatre Company Blah Blah Blah (Leeds): *Hide and Seek*. Photo: Lizzie Coombes.

M6 Theatre (Rochdale): *Sonya's Garden*. Photo: Beate Mielemeier; and *Rare Earth* (Belgrade TIE, as restaged by M6 Theatre).

Big Brum TIE (Birmingham). *The Giant's Embrace.* Photo: Ceri Townsend.

Greenwich & Lewisham Young People's Theatre (UK): *Land Fit for Heroes.* Photo: John Daniel. Courtesy of GLYPT Archive.

Alex Mavrocordatos and cdcArts: The *Fountain of Hope* project. Photo: Alex Mavrocordatos.

Performance, Learning and Heritage Research Project (Manchester University) and Andrew Ashmore & Associates: *This Accursed Thing.* Photo courtesy of PLH archive.

Theatre for Dialogue (University of Texas Austin): *Get Sexy, Get Consent*. Photo: Andrew Mendoza.

The New Vic Theatre (Newcastle-under-Lyme): *Knutton's bothering us.* Photo: Julianna Skarżyńska.

National School of Drama TIE Company (New Delhi): *Pandita Ramabai*. Photos: S. Thyagarajan.

UBOM! Eastern Cape Drama Company (Grahamstown, South Africa) and Barefeet Theatre (Lusaka, Zambia): *Float*. Photo: Lindsay Callaghan; courtesy of *CuePix*.

arepp: Theatre for Life. (S. Africa): *About Us: Stepping Up.* Photo © Andrew Aitchison Photography. Courtesy of STARS Foundation.

Creative Arts Team (New York City): *Alphabet Keepers* and *Project CHANGE*. Photos: Krista Fogle.

Theatre Espresso (Boston, Mass.): *Uprising on King Street.* Photo by Sandy Kim; and *American Tapestry.*

Chris Vine offers his love and gratitude to Helen White for her help, understanding and unstinting support throughout the preparation of this book.

# INTRODUCTION

*Anthony Jackson and Chris Vine*

This is the second metamorphosis of a book that, since its first appearance in 1980, has striven to define, describe and debate the salient features of one of the most important – and radical – developments in contemporary theatre. (See Jackson 1980, 1993.) Theatre in education (TIE) may – at least in its 'classic' form – have had its heyday in the 1970s, 1980s and 1990s, but, in various permutations, and not always under the same name, continues to be a vital, innovative and inspiring practice for many concerned with the use of drama and theatre for educational purposes. Indeed, as one of the main precursors of what is now more widely termed 'applied theatre', it has become, in the view of the current editors, even more necessary to capture, promote and critically interrogate the qualities of TIE that have consistently been at the cutting edge of how the participatory arts contribute to the learning of young people – and, latterly, adults.

Interest in the subject has scarcely diminished since the last edition in 1993 (certainly if the number of reprints is anything to go by – fifteen at the last count), but of course the world has moved on since then. TIE has faced endless challenges and has itself changed in response to those challenges. In 1980 it was possible to celebrate fifteen years of what had become, in the UK at least, an identifiable movement in socially and educationally committed theatre, and to spend time and space advocating its wider use. By 1993, the fault lines had already become manifest: there had, in the UK, been severe funding cuts (in local authority education budgets and Arts Council budgets alike); more critical, reflective assessments of what TIE could do, and what it claimed to do; an acknowledgement that the lines between TIE and other forms of theatre had begun to blur noticeably (and not without good reason); and a widening of TIE practice globally. Now, at the time of writing (in 2012), that second edition has been overtaken by events in many respects. The shifts over the past twenty years have been seismic – technologically, economically and culturally. They have profoundly affected the realms of theatre and the arts, education provision and, even more broadly, the ways we think about 'learning' and the complex relations between learning, the arts and society at large. The relatively recent identification of a field of 'applied theatre' is just one symptom of these shifts.

While the descriptor 'applied theatre' has moved to the forefront, both in the academy and in professional practice, the roots of many of its diverse practices lie deep within a longer (if discontinuous) set of practices stretching back to the pioneering days of educational drama and creative dramatics, to the living newspapers of the 1930s and, perhaps most vibrantly, to the burgeoning of TIE from the late 1960s to the mid-1990s. In our view, TIE sits comfortably under the umbrella of applied theatre but at the same time can lay claim to playing a significant, if often unrecognised, part in shaping its various educational, social and political aspirations, its theoretical frameworks and its wide range of eclectic practices. For these reasons alone, the justification for a new edition is a compelling one. There is still in our view a need for a book that can:

- 'tell the story' of this vital art form
- offer insightful accounts of TIE (or TIE-related) practice in a variety of contexts
- theorise that practice in ways that are directly helpful – and stimulating – to practitioners, teachers and students in the present
- illuminate the central influence that TIE has had on the wide range of practices now broadly termed 'applied theatre', and
- generate debate on the value, usefulness and possible future shape of this work.

These in effect constitute our aims for the new edition. It endeavours to sustain a balance between the recent past and TIE and 'TIE-related' practice in the present. Just as the practice itself has altered, so our definition of TIE in the second decade of the twenty-first century has necessarily altered and widened in response to a changing world, and the marked cultural differences in how TIE – recognised or not – is used, adapted and developed in different parts of the globe. (Hence our frequent use of the 'TIE-related' qualifier.) But 'learning through theatre' remains the governing theme. Key TIE characteristics such as participatory engagement, social learning through role play, work with young people in both formal and informal educational settings, and the pivotal position of innovative theatrical forms within the process, continue to shape the content of the book as a whole; as do the concerns with social and personal change that TIE shares more broadly with other applied theatre practices.

## The genesis of the current volume

The genesis of this particular volume followed a similar pattern to that of the 1993 edition, which had begun simply as an attempt to update the first version of the book published in 1980: we were in a new decade; TIE had evolved; and time seemed ripe for a reassessment as well as a restatement of principles. However it soon became clear that a very different kind of book was needed. By the early 1990s, TIE was clearly no longer a British phenomenon. It was a vibrant and evolving practice in many countries beyond the British Isles. In some places there had clearly been a linear development from the British model; in others remarkably similar forms had emerged that appeared to owe no particular debt to British TIE, and were not called TIE, having grown out of curricular, social or cultural needs which lent themselves to theatrical treatment. Few would wish to engage in sterile debates about who thought of TIE first; what does bear scrutiny is the common ground and the differences between these various enterprises. This edition then continues the attempt made in 1993 to highlight practices in a selection of countries around the world. We make no pretence at comprehensive coverage; rather the attempt has been to represent just some of the developments, challenges and achievements in more than ten countries, with enough illustrative detail to give at least a flavour of the projects undertaken, problems encountered, directions pursued, and the differences and similarities between them, all demonstrating that TIE – or TIE-related – practice is still very much alive and kicking in the second decade of the new century.

This edition is co-edited by Anthony Jackson (The University of Manchester, UK) and Chris Vine (The City University of New York, USA) – a feature that we believe has helped to broaden the book's scope and cement its international relevance. Our aims, and reasons for embarking on this new edition, are closely shared, but arrived at from different starting points.

**Anthony Jackson,** the editor of the first two editions, is an academic, well versed in the history, theory and practice of modern theatre but with a long-standing interest in and enthusiasm for the uses of theatre as a medium of education. He pioneered the teaching of practical modules in TIE at Manchester University in the early 1970s, later widened out to include theatre as an educational medium in museums and historic sites. He served for many years as chair, now as board director, of M6 Theatre (a professional theatre for young people, based in Rochdale in Greater Manchester but with a national touring role) – itself one of many companies that, while having broadened the scope of its work considerably from its origins as a TIE team in neighbouring Bolton, has its roots and values in that early TIE experience.

**Chris Vine** is essentially a practitioner who entered the academic arena late in his career. He worked in TIE, professional community theatre and young people's theatre for over thirty years, was a founding member of Perspectives Theatre Company and Artistic Director of Greenwich Young People's Theatre (now known as Greenwich & Lewisham YPT), one of the pioneering British TIE companies. In 1984 he was instrumental in introducing Boal's Theatre of the Oppressed to the British TIE movement. In 1993 he moved to New York City to become Artistic and Education Director of The Creative Arts Team (CAT), the USA's first theatre company founded on principles and practices inspired by the British TIE movement. In 2004, CAT became a programme of The City University of New York (CUNY). Here, in collaboration with Helen White, he developed an MA in Applied Theatre at The CUNY School of Professional Studies, becoming its first Academic Program Director in 2008. A passionate believer in the transportative powers of participatory theatre and fascinated by its many forms, Vine's specialities include process drama, collectively devised theatre, Theatre of the Oppressed, and, of course, TIE.

## What is TIE, and why does it still matter?

The assertion made in the 1993 edition still holds true: this book is about a form of theatre that arguably represents one of the most significant developments to have emerged in British theatre in the second half of the twentieth century. TIE began as a *definable movement* in Britain in the mid-1960s in direct response to the needs of both theatres and schools. It originated as an initiative from within the professional theatre and soon became supported by regional arts boards and local education authorities in many parts of the country. For at least three decades it marked out for itself a territory that overlapped the domains of theatre and education in important and unusual ways. It has moreover been part of much wider developments that have taken place across the world especially in the latter decades of the twentieth century as the theatre looked for new audiences and new ways to speak to them. The emergence of TIE in the UK was not, then, an isolated event. It grew from a number of important changes in theatre and in education evident throughout the twentieth century: the movements to re-establish the theatre's roots in the community and in so doing broaden its social basis – manifested in the UK since the Second World War in the revival of regional theatre and the rapid growth of community, 'alternative' and children's theatre;[1] the theatre's search for a useful and effective role within society and an exploration especially of its potential both as an educational medium and as a force for social change – seen most notably in the work of Bertolt Brecht and Augusto Boal and in the wide spectrum of activity ranging from children's theatre to political theatre; and, in education, the recognition during the 1960s and 1970s of the importance of the arts in the school curriculum, together with the increasing stress given to the *functional* role that the arts can play in helping children to understand, and operate in, the world in which they live.[2] The influences upon TIE have been many and some are discussed in more detail later in the book. Within the context of those larger developments, however, the role of TIE has been a distinct one.

If it no longer survives as an identifiable *movement*, its practices, methods and driving principles still inform, influence and indeed inspire a wide range of 'socially committed', 'developmental' and 'applied' theatre practice in the present – not only in schools but in museums, prisons, in building-based theatres, and in countries across the globe, as later chapters will demonstrate. Interest in TIE and, more broadly, applied theatre, and debate about their aims and methodologies, have also gained significance in a further important respect. Over the past two decades, TIE and applied theatre have appeared increasingly as subjects on theatre and education syllabuses in higher education, offering a valuable way in, practically and theoretically, to the study of fundamental questions about the role of theatre in society. TIE has never been shy of addressing such questions.

Essentially TIE seeks to harness the techniques and imaginative potency of theatre in the service of education. The aim is to provide an experience for young people (and, increasingly, adult populations) that will be intensely absorbing, challenging, often provocative, and an unrivalled stimulus for further investigation of the chosen subject in and out of school. Subjects dealt with have ranged from the environment, racism and local history to language learning, science and health. But it is the *formal* innovations that have given TIE its special quality and made its appearance upon the British 'alternative theatre' scene so significant. One of the major and most effective features of TIE is the structured active participation of the young people in the drama. Frequently placed *within* a dramatic fiction, they become caught up in its events, interact with a range of characters and have to make decisions in the midst of 'crisis'; or are invited to challenge or advise characters from a play they have just witnessed, sometimes being incorporated into its action. This practice incidentally pre-dates Boal's *Theatre of the Oppressed* by some years.[3] What most TIE and TIE-related projects share is a commitment to placing their audiences at the centre of their own learning, pressing home challenges while simultaneously communicating the belief – and trust – that they are sufficiently intelligent and sensitive (and 'intelligently feeling'[4]) to think and act autonomously to find their own solutions.

The essays that follow give vivid and stimulating accounts that illuminate the different ways practitioners are seeking to undertake this. In so doing, they identify many of the current strengths – and problems – of TIE practice, describing achievements, posing questions and issuing challenges. Taken as a whole they paint a fascinating, if inevitably partial, picture of the development of TIE around the globe. An overview of the genealogy of TIE is offered in chapter 1; now, however, we look briefly at some of the defining characteristics of TIE as it emerged, flourished and reinvented itself in Britain, in order to foreground some of the themes and further clarify the rationale for this new edition.

The most important innovation in what we might term 'classic' TIE was undoubtedly the concept of the TIE 'programme', and it is this element that has distinguished TIE most obviously from other kinds of young people's theatre. The TIE programme is not a performance in schools of a self-contained play, a 'one-off' event that is here today and gone tomorrow, but a coordinated and carefully structured pattern of activities, often devised and researched by the company, around a topic of relevance both to the school curriculum and to the young people's own lives, presented in school by the company and involving the audience directly in an *experience* of the situations and problems that the topic highlights. It generally utilises elements, in a variety of permutations, of traditional theatre (actors in role and the use of scripted dialogue, costume and often scenic and sound effects); educational drama (active participation of the students, in or out of role, in improvised drama activities in which images and ideas are explored at the students' own level); and simulation (highly structured role-play and decision-making exercises within simulated 'real life' situations). There is, however, no set formula. The shape, style and length of the programme vary enormously depending upon the subject tackled, the age range catered for and the institutional setting.

Thus, to take just four TIE programmes from the past four decades, not to represent TIE but at least to suggest something of that variety: *It Fits* (Perspectives Theatre Company, 1976) was a fully interactive programme about mathematics and problem-solving for five- to seven-year-olds; it involved two clown-like characters and a colourful array of lightweight 'bricks' (cubes, cuboids, cylinders and prisms), and took place almost entirely in the school hall in the space of one hour.

*Brand of Freedom* (Pit Prop Theatre, 1984) was a three-part programme for nine- to eleven-year-olds dealing with the Lancashire Cotton Famine of the 1860s and relating local history to the American Civil War and the struggle for freedom by slaves in the South. It consisted, over a three-week span, of a short play, directed project work in collaboration with teachers, and a full-scale participation event in which the children 'became' the cotton operatives at a Lancashire mill who had to cope with the pressures of unemployment and the conflicting demands of various characters from mill owner to escaped slave.

*The Longest Road* (Greenwich Young People's Theatre, 1990) was a full-day programme for ten- to eleven-year-olds that explored complex

*Figure 0.1* *Brand of Freedom* by Neil Duffield (Pit Prop Theatre, Wigan, 1984). Participatory programme for 9–11-year-olds. In the oakum-picking room, a group of children in role as mill workers discuss their next course of action. Actors: Ray Meredith, Flo Wilson. Director: Cora Williams. Photo: Arthur Thompson. Reproduced by courtesy of the John Rylands Library, The University of Manchester.

questions about the way we live together. The programme's inspiration was Brecht's poem, 'The Children's Crusade, 1939'. Students were enrolled in an environmental drama as a group of Polish children, fleeing war-torn homes in search of safety and lost families. They encountered many challenges as they attempted to organise themselves and deal with the adults they met (played by actors). Choices were genuinely open and different decisions reverberated with different consequences. The final, individual dilemmas asked whether or not they should abandon their searches and flee Europe for an orphan's life in America.

*Starfish* (Y Touring Theatre Company, 2009/10) is one of Y Touring's series of 'Theatre of Debate' programmes, each of which explores themes and questions that will shape young people's futures, aiming to use 'a rich mix of live performance and digital technology to engage audiences in an informed debate around the outcomes of the latest scientific research' (Y Touring website). *Starfish* consisted of a play followed by a live debate between the actors in character and the audience supported by the use of electronic voting, and further enhanced by extensive online resources. It addressed the importance and ethical implications of clinical trials through the stories of four characters, one of whom suffers from 'social phobia'. In the course of the drama she gains confidence through visits to the virtual online world 'Second Life', and as a result is able to reconsider the option of taking part in the testing of treatments for her debilitating syndrome. The programme was developed in partnership with several medical research charities and Central YMCA, with a set of tailored follow-up lessons provided by *Centre of the Cell*, a national science education project.

The event in the school (or in the theatre-studio to which the students have been brought) is not the be-all and end-all of the exercise. The TIE 'programme', as the word suggests, will usually involve a fully conceived programme of work with the theatrical event, or a set of theatrical moments, as the central stimulus for a deeper and richer learning process than the 'one-off' play (or indeed most other teaching methods) could possibly hope to offer. The pattern adopted by most British TIE teams from 1965 through to the early 1990s (but to a diminishing extent since) was to provide, first, an introductory teachers' workshop for all teachers whose classes would receive the programme, the purpose of which was to explain fully the aim and method of the project and the teacher's role; second, a project pack or teachers' notes which contained relevant research material and suggestions for 'follow-up' to aid the teacher's subsequent work with the class; the programme visits themselves; and finally, some form of

*Figure 0.2* *Starfish* by Judith Johnson (Y Touring, London, 2010). Shannon (played by Susannah Freeman) 'enters' the virtual world, Second Life, as her avatar. Photo: Nigel Townsend.

'feedback' mechanism (often a questionnaire to be filled in by teachers after the programme ended, sometimes an open forum for both teachers and performers) through which the teachers could offer constructive criticism and the team glean some idea of the effectiveness or otherwise of their efforts. Close liaison between company and teachers was thus essential. Ideally, it remains so. In practice, it has become much harder to implement and sustain, given the increased pressures from funding constraints and changes in the organisation of education. (Y Touring's concerted move into interactive online resources is just one innovation designed to mitigate those limitations – and to enhance 'real time' engagement through new technologies with which young people are likely to be increasingly familiar.) Such constraints exist not just in the UK but also in most countries where TIE has managed to gain a foothold. Demands for cost-effectiveness and measurable outcomes severely limit the nature and quality – if not always the duration – of in-class partnerships. Intertwined with this is the varying degree to which the funders determine the form and content of the work, calling into question its formerly radical nature as it is co-opted to serve mainstream agendas. These issues provide some of the recurring themes of this book – exemplified perhaps most vividly in the chapters by Mary Cooper, Veronica Baxter and Helen Wheelock.

## TIE and related areas of work

By now it should be clear that TIE as a term implies a kind of theatre markedly different from most other kinds of young people's theatre, with characteristics that also distinguish it from many similar applied theatre practices. Unfortunately the term is *still* all too often confused with those denoting other forms. Because it is used here in a very specific sense it may be helpful to indicate broadly the other terms that are in general use in this and related areas of work. The distinctions are important, and need to be made if TIE is to be fully understood – although in so doing, it is not our intention in any way to deny the validity or importance of those other forms of theatre or to suggest that the forms do not frequently overlap. In practice today there are very few companies that do not engage in a wider range of theatre activities than TIE alone. The terms most commonly in use, then, are as follows:

**Applied Theatre** is a broad umbrella term, developed in the 1990s to describe 'a wide range of participatory, socially engaged, often politically inspired, non-traditional theatre practices' (see Vine, chapter 3), usually conducted in spaces not designed for theatre, with and for populations that would not typically constitute mainstream audiences. The term is often used to describe a variety of companies and practices that display many of the characteristics of TIE without invoking its name. In some cases the term TIE has been deliberately replaced by Applied Theatre to blur boundaries for the purpose of inclusion.[5] (See recent studies by Nicholson (2005), Prendergast and Saxton (2009), Prentki and Preston (2008), Taylor (2003) and Thompson (2003).)

**Theatre for Development (TfD)** refers to the use of theatre and drama workshop techniques for developmental purposes, most commonly (but not exclusively) deployed by non-governmental organisations (charities such as 'Save the Children' for example) operating in Third World countries. While much of the work is overtly instructive, even propagandist, promoting specific health or lifestyle changes (especially in relation to HIV/AIDS education), increasingly practices have become oriented more towards participation – a 'bottom-up' rather than 'top-down' approach – in the belief that active involvement and 'co-authorship' will more likely encourage a sense of ownership of the material and embed the messages more effectively. (See Pammenter's chapter for a fuller discussion of TfD practices and the crossovers with TIE.)

**Theatre of the Oppressed (TO)** is a system of participatory theatre methodology developed by the Brazilian director and activist Augusto

Boal. At its heart is the aim of changing the passive spectator into a 'spect-actor', a protagonist, first in the theatre fiction and then in the real world. In Boal's own words it is a 'rehearsal for revolution' (Boal 1979: 122). Its different forms include image theatre, forum theatre and 'Rainbow of Desire' techniques used to address individual, internal oppression. Boal's philosophy, first outlined in his seminal book, *Theatre of the Oppressed* (1979), was significantly influenced by the work of Brecht and the educationalist, Paulo Freire, author of *Pedagogy of the Oppressed* (1970).

**Educational Theatre** is another 'catch-all' term, frequently used in the United States, to describe theatre that is played for explicitly educational purposes, usually for young audiences. The term can embrace equally performances that might be considered as TYA (see below) and those, with an interactive component, that would fall more nearly under the heading of TIE. A number of universities offer programmes in educational theatre that might include a wide range of the drama and theatre practices noted here.

**Young People's Theatre (YPT)** is yet another broad umbrella term, intended to cover all forms of professional theatre for children and young people, including TIE; it is often used more specifically to cover play performances for the older age range, usually between twelve and eighteen (or over).

**Children's Theatre and Theatre for Young Audiences (TYA)** are both terms that refer to the professional performance (in theatres or in schools) of self-contained plays for young audiences. Children's Theatre typically caters for the younger audiences (up to about twelve or thirteen years of age) while TYA frequently embraces the teenage years. This category includes the work of national touring companies, productions by local repertory or TIE companies, and those of the building-based children's theatres (of which there are woefully few in the UK but considerably more in the USA).

**Youth Theatre** generally denotes non-professional theatre work[6] involving young people in the preparation and performance of group-devised or scripted plays. Often theatre companies, including former TIE companies, will employ a youth organiser responsible for initiating and fostering this kind of activity. Schools also offer youth theatre as part of their extra-curricular provision but independent youth theatres are increasingly common, dedicated to broader policies of youth development through the theatre arts.

**Theatre Education**. There are no universally recognised terms to apply to this area of work, indeed it is sometimes, confusingly, also referred to as 'theatre in education'. It typically covers three aspects of work very often considered a normal part of the responsibility of a repertory or (in the US) a children's theatre, that is, establishing links with schools, youth clubs, etc., in order (a) to impart a more informed awareness of what theatre is and how it works, sometimes also teaching theatre skills, (b) to offer play appreciation before theatre visits (see below), and (c) to build new audiences for tomorrow. These aims are generally fulfilled through lectures, backstage tours, open rehearsals, demonstrations, classroom residencies, and the performance of short plays or play extracts both in schools and in the theatre itself.

**Set play 'workshops' or 'play days'** are frequently run by the more enlightened repertory companies, and often by the larger YPT companies, on the plays being studied as a set part of the syllabus in schools in their area. These sessions will often consist of a series of extracts from the play in question linked by a commentary that stresses the play's contemporary relevance and its theatrical dimension, the options available to the director in rehearsal, and how final interpretations are arrived at.

**Museum Theatre** is the use of theatre and theatrical techniques as 'a means of mediating knowledge and understanding in the context of museum education' (Jackson and Rees Leahy 2005: 304). It is generally presented by professional actors and/or interpreters in museums or at historic sites and may range from performances of short plays and monologues based on historical events or on-site exhibitions, to interactive events using 'first person' interpretation or role-play (often drawing directly on TIE methodology). It may be designed for the curriculum needs of visiting schoolchildren or for family groups and/or the independent visitor. (See Jackson and Kidd 2011: 4.)

There is then a good deal of professional theatre work taken into schools and other educational settings, but much of it is not TIE although it may appear or even purport to be. This is not to say that such work is of inferior quality in theatrical terms. Sometimes it may consist of an excellently researched documentary piece or indeed a fine example of contemporary playwriting on a contemporary issue. Sometimes it may be merely well-intentioned, lacking the rigorous application of educational criteria in its preparation and the skills needed to engage with (rather than patronise) the given age group. In both cases the 'programme' concept will be absent and though the 'one-off' performances may well be educational in the broadest sense, the distinction from TIE is an important one to draw.

The **theatre professionals** who implement this kind of work and the set play workshops are often, and increasingly, in the USA at least, called 'teaching artists'. 'Actor-teacher' (or 'teacher-actor' in some places), traditionally reserved for the TIE actor, is rapidly disappearing as a recognised title. Applied theatre practitioners tend to favour the generic 'facilitator' or sometimes 'actor-facilitator'. There is an understandable resistance to titles that appear to align practitioners with institutionalised education. In museum theatre, the terms are even more varied – from 'actor-interpreter', 'costumed interpreter', 'presenter' and 'enactor' to, simply, 'actor' – all depending as much upon the policy preferences of the museum or site as upon the nature of the work undertaken.

Finally there are three key areas closely connected with TIE but outside the professional theatre arena:

**Process Drama or Drama in Education (DIE)** is drama as taught in schools, sometimes with a theatrical bias, involving the preparation of a play for public presentation and learning about theatre styles and techniques; but more usually concerned with the exploration of themes and problems through role play and improvisation, with emphasis upon developing the child's imagination, self-awareness and expressiveness and upon the social skills involved in group work. The emphasis, as 'process drama' suggests, is on the process of an unrepeatable 'lived-through' experience with no intention to present to an external audience. DIE differs from TIE primarily in its reliance upon a teacher who meets the children regularly and knows their particular needs; in the relative 'open-endedness' of the experience offered; and in the absence of the full theatre resources (characters, costume, set) available to the TIE company. (Chris Cooper explores some of the differences and common ground in chapter 2.)

**Dramatherapy** evolved in Britain in the 1960s from drama in education, remedial drama and TIE. Definitions are fraught and much argued over, but it is generally agreed that it involves the application of drama and theatre techniques to promote mental and physical health. Creative, drama-based interventions are employed with clients, with whom there should be an explicit contract, to bring about interpersonal, intrapersonal and behavioural change. It is related to the psychotherapies: healing is the primary goal. In many places there is an expectation that practitioners will be trained, qualified and licensed, but this is far from universally the case. There is often confusion around the distinctions between therapeutic processes and therapy, and an ongoing debate as to whether or not dramatherapy should come under the umbrella of applied theatre.

**Simulation gaming** is an educational technique that grew rapidly in the 1970s, developed for use both in schools and in management training schemes. (See Taylor and Walford 1972.) Such games generally offer a carefully packaged and highly structured (if not rigid) programme of activity in which students explore 'real life' situations, solve problems and make decisions in roles that are predetermined but never require acting skill. The simulation technique is one that closely parallels some TIE participation formats and has often been adapted as an integral part of a TIE programme. Most simulations however, especially those in published form, do not make use of the added stimulus, flexibility and imaginative possibilities achieved by the use of skilled actors in role.

## The present volume and organisation of chapters

The broad aim in this edition has, then, been to introduce important aspects of Theatre in Education, its development, its theory, its practice and its international dimension. The chapters are designed to appeal both to those who have little or no experience of the subject but who are interested in the educational possibilities of theatre, and to those experienced in some but not all of its various manifestations and who would like to know more. But our intentions go further.

The almost fifty-year period of TIE's existence has been marked by the extraordinary determination, belief, enterprise, imagination and skill of its pioneers, often in the face of immense obstacles. Its history has been marked too by some confusion of aims and counter-productive struggles for the ideological high ground on the part of some of its practitioners. TIE today, in its various manifestations, is still subject to the changing tides in education and theatre, tides that can easily disguise or submerge its real value and achievement. The achievement, and indeed the potential, is undeniable. But reassessment is needed – now, just as much as in 1993 – to help pinpoint and clarify the nature of that achievement and the essentials of its working methods; to make TIE and its potential more widely understood in educational and theatrical circles and beyond; and to help distinguish effective TIE from ineffective (or, worse, counter-productive) TIE.

This book is intended to make a positive contribution to such a reassessment by drawing on practitioners and theorists from some ten countries who are not only distinguished in their own field but bring to this subject, between them, a width of experience, a variety of skills and expertise and a diversity of critical standpoints. The book deliberately does not attempt to make any final, unified, definitive statement about TIE, which is of its very nature complex, dynamic and evolving, but rather aims to promote a lively, intelligent debate that will at least clarify the issues and suggest some of the most fruitful ways forward. Emphasis has therefore been placed on highlighting the already considerable achievement of TIE, on articulating some of the major governing principles that drive the practice, on demonstrating the *how* as well as the *why* of TIE work, as well as locating its practices within an historical perspective, and posing, we hope, some provocative challenges to practitioners, theorists and critics alike.

The approach has been as far as possible to integrate theory with practice, and historical and social context with working examples of TIE practice sufficiently detailed to offer genuine insight. The essays are grouped in sections to aid the reader in finding his or her way around the material as easily as possible, each of which is preceded by its own short editorial introduction. Those sections are as follows:

- *Identifying TIE* is about histories, developments and definitions, offering a range of perspectives on the emergence and manifestations of the genre and its philosophical, aesthetic and pedagogic implications.
- In *Ways of Working*, different working practices in TIE are examined, together with the principles that, in the view of the authors, underpin that practice. Essays from the different perspectives of deviser, writer and performer/facilitator are complemented by essays that consider relevant acting theory and innovative practice in rapidly changing cultural contexts.
- *Global Perspectives* offers insights into an extraordinary range of practices across the world, from India to Australia, southern Africa and the United States. Recognising the near-impossibility of providing genuinely comprehensive coverage, we have included a chapter which offers a number of shorter 'snapshots' of TIE practice in countries and locations elsewhere, and serves, we hope, to complement the more detailed analyses.

- Finally, the essays in *Issues and Challenges* pursue many of the themes that have resonated throughout the book – TIE's unique ability to address issues of the present through stories from the past; to engage with profound matters of personal and collective distress through the power of metaphor; and to generate a critical pedagogy through processes that are simultaneously co-intentional and aesthetic. Each essay in its own way captures and provides insights into moments of extraordinary achievement and illuminates TIE's ongoing potential.

## Notes

1 For a useful general account of these developments see Bradby and McCormick (1978), though their survey oddly includes no reference to young people's theatre; also Rowell and Jackson (1984) on TIE in relation to regional theatre; Jackson (2007) and Nicholson (2011) for developments in theatre as an educational medium through the twentieth century.

2 For a discussion of trends in arts education from the 1970s onwards, see (among others) Bolton (1984, 1998), Hornbrook (1989), Nicholson (2011), Ross (1978), Somers (1994) and Witkin (1974).

3 Boal's most prominent audience intervention techniques were developed in the 1970s, beginning, most notably, during his participation in the Freire-inspired ALFIN (literacy) project in Peru in 1973. His work was not introduced to the UK TIE movement until 1984, followed by his first working visit to the UK in 1985. The beginning of his major influence in the USA can be dated a few years later, to the end of the 1980s.

4 Robert Witkin's *The Intelligence of Feeling* (1974) is a persuasive argument against the dichotomising of rationality and emotion, particularly in the educational arena.

5 For instance, in 2008, the American Alliance of Theatre and Education (AATE) redesignated its TIE Network as the Applied Theatre Network. Companies previously working under the TIE nomenclature have happily adopted the applied theatre label; companies that were not sure if they were TIE or not have entered the fold; and new companies have emerged that were never aware of the distinctions. Generally, this is a positive development. The downside is that the loss of the term TIE is sometimes accompanied by a loss of knowledge and the disappearance of specific practices.

6 To add to the confusion, in some countries, the USA being a prime example, the term is sometimes used interchangeably with TYA, to describe professional performances *for* young people.

## Works cited

Boal, Augusto (1979), *Theatre of the Oppressed*. London: Pluto Press.

Bolton, Gavin (1984), *Drama as Education: an argument for placing drama at the centre of the curriculum*. London: Longman.

——(1998), *Acting in Classroom Drama: a critical analysis.* Stoke on Trent: Trentham Books.

Bradby, D. and McCormick, J. (1978), *People's Theatre.* London: Croom Helm.

Freire, Paulo (1970), *Pedagogy of the Oppressed.* New York: Continuum Books.

Hornbrook, D. (1989), *Education and Dramatic Art.* Oxford: Blackwell.

Jackson, Anthony (2007), *Theatre, Education and the Making of Meanings: art or instrument?* Manchester: Manchester University Press.

——, Tony (1980), *Learning through Theatre: essays and casebooks on theatre in education*, 1st edn. Manchester: Manchester University Press.

——(1993), *Learning through Theatre: new perspectives on theatre in education*, 2nd edn. London and New York: Routledge.

Jackson, A. and Kidd, J., eds. (2011), *Performing Heritage: research, practice and innovation in museum theatre and live interpretation.* Manchester: Manchester University Press.

Jackson, A. and Rees Leahy, H. (2005), '"Seeing it for real?": authenticity, theatre and learning in museums', *Research in Drama Education*, 10.3: 303–25.

Nicholson, Helen (2005), *Applied Drama: the gift of theatre.* Basingstoke: Palgrave Macmillan.

——(2011), *Theatre, Education and Performance.* Basingstoke: Palgrave Macmillan.

Prendergast, Monica and Saxton, Juliana, eds. (2009), *Applied Theatre: International Case Studies and Challenges for Practice.* Bristol: Intellect Books.

Prentki, Tim and Preston, Sheila, eds. (2008), *An Applied Theatre Reader.* London: Routledge.

Ross, M. (1978), *The Creative Arts.* London: Heinemann.

Rowell, G. and Jackson, A. (1984), *The Repertory Movement: a history of regional theatre in Britain.* Cambridge: Cambridge University Press.

Somers, John (1994), *Drama in the Curriculum.* London: Cassell.

Taylor, J. and Walford, R. (1972), *Simulation in the Classroom.* London: Penguin.

Taylor, Philip (2003), *Applied Theatre: creating transformative encounters in the community.* Portsmouth, NH: Heinemann.

Thompson, James (2003), *Applied Theatre – bewilderment and beyond.* Bern: Peter Lang.

Witkin, R. (1974), *The Intelligence of Feeling.* London: Heinemann.

Y Touring: www.theatreofdebate.com/TheatreofDebate/YTouring.html (last accessed 2 August 2012).

# Part I

# IDENTIFYING THEATRE IN EDUCATION

## Introduction

This section is about histories, developments and definitions. The aim here is, first, to provide an overview of TIE as it has evolved in Britain, identifying some of the key shifts in its development, and, second, to offer a more explorative and reflective account of the nature of TIE and TIE-related practice.

In 'Education or Theatre?' (a revised and expanded version of the 1993 essay), Jackson traces in outline the history of the TIE movement in Britain, from its emergence in 1965 to the present, and relates its uneven growth and precarious existence to the perennial problems of how it has been both perceived and funded. The British experience has been seminal, providing a model which has been followed in many other countries, and suggesting interesting parallels and points of contrast with practice elsewhere with roots in different cultural, educational and political contexts. It therefore aims to set the scene for, and anticipates some of the themes that will emerge in, many of the subsequent chapters. It may also, perhaps, offer pointers to recurring challenges in the future.

Chris Cooper's chapter is a response to, and a contemporary rethinking of, Gavin Bolton's essay in the second edition, 'Drama in Education and TIE – a comparison'. As Cooper argues, Bolton, an internationally known theorist and practitioner of educational drama, has had a major and continuing impact upon the thinking and practice of many TIE teams; here, Cooper examines Bolton's legacy and uses it as a starting point for reflecting on the current state of TIE and DIE and the principles that might drive the work forward in the new century.

Chris Vine's chapter on the influence Boal's work has had on TIE – again a reworking of his 1993 chapter – considers not only the ways in which that practice was necessarily adapted to British contexts in the 1980s and 1990s but the questions it raises about the function and purpose of TIE in the present. Vine was one of the first to see the importance of Boal's work for British TIE and, while director of Greenwich Young People's Theatre, did much to promote and adapt Boal's theory and practice. Here he assesses not only Boal's influence but, just as importantly, those areas of difference between Boal's practice and that of many TIE companies.

While no simple watertight definition of TIE is possible, or desirable, it is hoped that these chapters will provide the reader with some useful orientation points in the process of understanding the background to TIE, the routes by which it emerged and changed, and some of the theoretical implications. The later chapters will, in various ways, put more flesh on the bones. Although the focus here is primarily upon the British experience, the parallels, connections and differences with TIE experience elsewhere will, we believe, quickly emerge.

# 1

# EDUCATION OR THEATRE?

## The development of TIE in Britain

*Anthony Jackson*

The story of the development of TIE in Britain is one that oscillates between surges of enthusiasm and rapid growth at one extreme and periods of cutbacks, gloom and despondency at the other, intermixed with phases of rediscovery, reinvention and experiment. The trajectory has of course never been even or free of anxiety: struggle for survival has rarely been far from its practitioners' minds. TIE is indeed one of theatre's most vital yet most vulnerable forms. At the time of writing, in 2012, it is undergoing yet another episode of challenge, this time one that might be described as a search for redefinition against a backdrop of much broader 'applied theatre' practice. Yet, as I surmised in 1993, when TIE faced a severe threat from the ramifications of the most radical shake-up of the education system for fifty years, 'survive it will even if in different shapes and more varied and more fluid permutations' (Jackson 1993: 17). Just as a number of TIE teams fell prey to the economic axe wielded by beleaguered repertory companies or education authorities and as some discussed the imminent demise of TIE in Britain, so new companies formed (if with different briefs and even less secure futures) and interest in TIE across the world was increasing (not always modelled on the British pattern). Why this bumpy ride? Why has TIE's place within our cultural and educational infrastructure been so insecure? Why, on the other hand, despite predictions of terminal decline, does it still continue to resonate and influence contemporary practice?

The history and sustainability of TIE are of course inextricably tied up with how it is and has been funded – which in turn reflects uneasy philosophical tensions and debates about the function and purpose of the arts in education more generally. This may seem axiomatic but it applies more closely to TIE than to any other form of theatre practice.

TIE tends to be labour intensive: at its most effective, and certainly in its 'classic' form (of which more later), it usually operates with one or at most two classes of children at a time (i.e. between thirty and sixty) since a close rapport and interaction with its audience are central to the experience. Even when circumstances demand performances to larger audiences, the attempt is normally made to involve them actively at some point and in some way. Moreover, its audiences are not, and more important should not be, required to pay for the service it provides. Its *raison d'être* lies in its function, first, as a method of education and therefore with a justifiable claim to be seen as an educational resource within the school system, and, second, as an art form in its own right but one that is peculiarly suited to its specific audience and age range. However, to say that TIE is an educational resource and therefore belongs in schools and other educational settings is not to say that TIE should be wholly funded and controlled by a local education authority (LEA), let alone by central government. Direct funding and oversight by an LEA has occasionally been the most appropriate arrangement but not always – and historically TIE teams have cherished the strong degree of independence from the school system which is reflected in and reinforced by their funding from more than one source. As David Pammenter argued in the 1993 edition of this book (Pammenter 1993: 55–56), it is significant that TIE was born and nurtured in the theatre. And its characteristic contribution to school-based education does perhaps derive from its roots outside the system.

## Early developments: the first phase

TIE emerged from the new thinking and atmosphere of experiment that characterised the British theatre of the mid-1960s, and from the developments in educational drama in schools that were taking place at the same time. Beginning first as a project of the Belgrade Theatre in Coventry in 1965, TIE quickly took shape as a unique method of expanding the role of theatre companies who sought to develop proactive relationships with the broader community.[1] At Coventry, the unit of four 'actor-teachers', funded jointly by the theatre and the city, and touring schools with programmes of work that embraced both performance and drama 'workshop', set a pattern that was soon followed by theatres in Bolton, Edinburgh, Greenwich, Leeds, and Watford. Before long there were companies offering regular TIE performances in rural and metropolitan communities across the country. They quickly proved themselves to be a valuable educational resource, and the participation format, designed for class-size rather than auditorium-size groups, became from the start the key identifying feature of TIE, clearly distinguishing it from more conventional children's theatre. The format also reflected a philosophical as well as an educational stance. 'Theatre for social change' rather than 'Building audiences for the future' was the way that most practitioners preferred to see their work, allying themselves with – and often in the vanguard of – the progressive movements in both theatre and education.

From its inception, and until the mid-1990s, TIE has generally relied upon two main sources for its income: (1) the Arts Council (including the Regional Arts Boards who for several decades took on devolved responsibility for funding arts work of a specifically local or regional kind); and (2) the Local Authorities, especially (though not necessarily) LEAs. Thus at Coventry the money for the first project came from a specific allocation of funds from the city authorities supplemented by money from the Arts Council via the theatre's board of management. This was a pattern that seemed to work well and, with some modifications, was applied to companies formed elsewhere during the following few years. Being based at a theatre, the TIE company was able both to make use of the theatre's resources (stage management, set and props construction, and so on) and to establish for itself a healthy measure of independence, organisationally, from the education authority. On the other hand, as a separate department of the theatre with funds earmarked for work in local schools, it was afforded the opportunity to build up close liaison with the schools themselves – aided by the appointment of personnel whose background was at least in part in education. When many of the early members of the Coventry company left to set up new companies in Bolton (Roger Chapman and Cora Williams), Edinburgh (Gordon Wiseman) and, later, Leeds (Roger Chapman again) and Nottingham (Sue Birtwhistle), not surprisingly it was the Coventry model on which those companies were based. The only main difference was that in some cases revenue came from the LEA rather than direct from the authority itself. The establishment of those first companies, funded on a similar basis in each case, constitutes in effect the first phase of TIE's development. Accompanying those pioneering ventures was a significant shift in the policy of the Arts Council towards theatre for young people.

### *The Arts Council*

The Arts Council of Great Britain (ACGB), and its successors Arts Council England, Arts Council Wales and the Scottish Arts Council, operate with funds from central government and exist mainly 'to develop and improve the knowledge, understanding and practice of the arts', and 'to increase the accessibility of the arts to the public throughout Great Britain' (ACGB 1986: 12). Given these objectives, it was something of an anomaly that until 1966 theatre for young people had been explicitly excluded from Arts Council support. The anomaly was recognised and corrected when, as a result of increasing pressure from many quarters, the Arts Council set up in 1965 a committee 'to enquire into the present provision of theatre for children and young people in the widest terms, to make recommendations for future development and in particular to advise on the participation of the Arts Council in such work' (ACGB 1967: 7). The opening paragraph of their 1966 report is worth quoting at some length for the clarity with which it sums up the difficulties faced in the mid-1960s and the interrelationship between the work done and its sources and level of revenue:

> When the Arts Council originally elected, as a matter of policy, to exclude Children's Theatre Companies from its circle of beneficiaries, it unconsciously set a pattern which has influenced the development of theatre for young people ever since. The amount of subsidy then available for distribution to the Arts generally was very small; here, it was felt, was a sphere in which the education authorities, national and local, might give sustenance and guidance. The result, however, has been a failure of responsibility, with help and patronage on a meagre basis and to no particular pattern. It is surprising that so much has been achieved ... With some local education authorities, Drama suffers from old puritanical overtones. Music, Poetry, Literature, Art: all are 'respectable'. The Drama is not quite yet – even in 1966. And in the ever growing number of enlightened quarters where it is accepted and welcomed, it is still too often regarded as a luxury and an 'extra' in children's education and not, as this Committee believes it to be, a necessity.
>
> (ibid.)

During the course of its enquiry the committee travelled to Coventry where 'the unique Theatre in Education team of the Belgrade Theatre was presenting a programme' (ibid.: 8) which ensured that TIE became included in the scope of enquiry. The conclusions and recommendations of the committee were many and wide-ranging. For the purpose of this brief survey the most significant was that financial help should be given both to enable the larger regional theatre companies to establish second companies to play specifically to young people and also to support recommended new young people's theatre companies. The report was seminal: it was acted upon by the Arts Council and provided a major boost for those who saw the potential of TIE and for repertory theatres that would now be eligible for additional funds to provide young people's theatre on a regular basis. Hence the developments at Bolton, Leeds, Edinburgh, Greenwich (all between 1968 and 1970), and before long Nottingham and Peterborough (1973) and Lancaster (1975). What the report did above all was assert in no uncertain terms the value of theatre work for young people, including TIE, and the paramount need to subsidise it if there were to be any hope of its flourishing, experimenting, developing and gaining the status it deserved. It also suggested strongly, though it could not insist, that LEAs should finance the work that was done on school premises and in school hours. Not a wholly unreasonable suggestion one might think. But this, the question of who should pay for TIE in schools, was a bone of contention that plagued the growth of TIE in many areas of the country, and the issue has continued to be a stumbling block ever since. At root, was this work education or theatre?

Responsibility for education provision in the regions and cities of Britain has generally lain with the LEAs – at least until the early 1990s, when, increasingly, powers and budgets were devolved to individual school governing bodies. Policy has varied considerably from one part of the country to the next and LEAs accordingly varied in the extent to which, if at all, they supported professional theatre in schools. The 1944 Education Act certainly empowered them to do so if they wished. There were still many, however, who expected the individual school to finance an incoming company (whether TIE or children's theatre), either out of its own limited 'capitation' allowance or by requiring the children themselves to pay. Other authorities took a more enlightened and imaginative view and either allocated substantial funds to an independent or theatre-based company (as at Greenwich) or set up their own TIE or Drama in Education teams. The Inner London Education Authority (ILEA) did both.

## The second phase: the 1970s

It is perhaps from around 1971, with the formation of the Cockpit and Curtain TIE teams by ILEA, that one can see the emergence of a second phase of TIE's development – characterised by closer interest in TIE among a growing number of LEAs and by some considerable strides forward in the work produced in terms of both form and content. TIE had clearly become a definable movement, even in some respects a bandwagon.

By the end of the decade the situation looked decidedly encouraging. By and large some form of TIE even if on an infrequent basis was available in most of the major centres of population, and in many rural areas as well. There had been, since the early 1970s, not only expansion but diversification. Many companies, especially those which had widened their brief to include community and young people's work generally, chose to go independent, setting themselves up as limited liability companies with non-profit-making (charitable) status and receiving grant aid direct from the local authority and the Arts Council, or increasingly from the regional arts boards. This gave them a much greater degree of autonomy and control over their work than would have been the case were they attached to a main theatre. In several places (such as at Wakefield in Yorkshire), authorities established Drama in Education (DIE) teams consisting of peripatetic drama teachers who from time to time worked together as TIE units. Moreover, taking the country as a whole, it was possible to say that TIE companies now covered the complete educational spectrum: from infant schools to further education colleges, from youth clubs to special schools for those with learning disabilities, from summer play schemes to work on A-level examination texts. Several companies also explored ways of using the same material both for their school programmes and for their adult shows – part of a widening out from TIE to educational theatre for the community at large.

Some of the most innovative TIE work dates from this period – work that might now be termed 'classic', in the sense that it marked out patterns of participation and performance that became benchmarks for much future TIE practice. From 'straightforward' involvement of children in a story, in which they meet and talk with characters and actively become part of the narrative, programmes were developed that put children right at the heart of the events with responsibility to investigate, interrogate and make decisions that had repercussions for the characters involved – as in *Pow Wow* (about the contentious history of the American Indian: Coventry 1973), *Poverty Knocks* (on the Chartist movement of the 1840s: Bolton Octagon TIE, 1973), and *Marches* (about racism in the 1930s, designed for older students: London Cockpit TIE, 1977).[2] Experiments with theatrical form led to 'adventure programmes' such as *Ifan's Valley* (Belgrade TIE, 1973), which involved a school field trip to nearby countryside with children meeting characters en route, and to such complex pieces as *Rare Earth* (Belgrade TIE, 1973), a three-part programme about the environment that included an interactive simulation and a powerful play *Drink the Mercury* which drew on Japanese Noh and Kabuki Theatre for its stylised presentation including, most strikingly, the personified depiction of the deadly mercury-emitting factory in Minamata Bay.

A further important step was taken in 1975 when the Gulbenkian Foundation supported the establishment of the Standing Conference of Young People's Theatre (SCYPT) to represent the interests of TIE and young people's theatre to funding bodies and also, perhaps more importantly at that time, to promote debate, the sharing of ideas and experiences and the furthering of the general aims of the movement. This also signalled the growing politicization of the movement, which had already been evident in the foregrounding of contemporary social issues in many programmes from the early 1970s onwards.

TIE companies have always been among the most socially conscious of theatre groups, consistently choosing to examine issues they believe to be of direct relevance to the lives of the children with whom they work. Their work has often been motivated by a strong sense of the injustices that prevail in society at large, and many companies saw it as part of their responsibility to contribute in some way to the making of a better world. Marxist analyses of social processes, and the educational philosophies of such as John Holt, Ivan Illich and Paulo Freire, generated not only heated debate about the need for 'alternative' approaches within the state system but also a vital atmosphere of experiment with form, with ways of engaging children actively in their own learning. Inevitably there were mistakes made and blind alleys rushed into: for some groups the idealism slid all too easily into misconceptions about the capacity of TIE to act as a medium for direct social change (and indeed about the desirability of such a role). Theatre may influence attitudes and thus contribute *indirectly* to social changes, but to expect it to transform on its own and 'overnight' would of course be naive in the extreme. Significantly, though, despite the rhetoric that often emanated from the highly charged political debates at SCYPT conferences, remarkably few TIE programmes of the many hundreds produced actually portrayed society in the simplistic terms common to the overt campaigning of some of the political 'agit-prop' theatre groups of the time. The demands made by the nature of the work to relate one's script constantly to clear educational objectives undoubtedly enabled TIE companies to achieve a greater degree of realism about, and insight into, the medium and consequently to avoid the temptation to oversimplify for the sake of quick but superficial solutions to societal ills.

As TIE activity increased on all fronts there was also, perhaps inevitably, some fragmentation of aims and dissipation of energies. A few theatres placed their priority on building new audiences, on promoting an appreciation of what adult theatre had to offer, rather than providing theatre for young people in their own right. And some actors saw the expansion of job opportunities in the field simply as stepping stones to employment in the 'real' (adult) theatre. At the other end of the spectrum, and accompanying the increased confidence in TIE of its practitioners during this expansive phase, it was possible to detect, among a handful of companies, a somewhat condescending attitude to schools. This grew from a belief (conscious or not) that TIE was somehow vested with a monopoly of wisdom *because* it was outside the school system. Again, fortunately, this was not widespread, and the major companies were notable for the immense efforts they put into developing close contact and mutual understanding with teachers.

But there was bound to be some tension and misunderstanding between TIE companies and those who controlled, or taught within, institutions that tended to be inherently conservative. In 1976, a group of Schools Inspectors undertook an official survey of the work of theatre companies in schools and published a positive, highly encouraging report called *Actors in Schools* (DES 1976). Two years later, the principal author of the report, Bert Parnaby, assessed the developments and changes since the survey and noted that the biggest shift of emphasis, 'especially in areas where companies have not been fully used or appreciated by schools, by the LEA, or both', had been a move into the community (Parnaby 1978: 20). While this was welcomed (provided that the school 'is realistically regarded as part of that same community'), he was concerned at the lack of any evidence of schools making positive use of TIE as part of the general rethinking of their role and their curriculum, especially in the area of political, social and moral education, that was so acutely needed. And he concluded that, if such were the case, 'the actors' move into community work must be seen as a move out of schools because of indifference and lack of understanding of the work, often by those most closely concerned with curriculum planning' (ibid.).

By 1980 the picture was not as bright as it might have appeared on the surface. Thus, citing the number of companies in existence (twenty-one fully-fledged TIE teams plus another sixty or so who claimed to undertake TIE work on a less regular basis) disguises the very considerable losses and gains that had taken place in the late

1970s and the fact that many of those gains were due to the use made of government-funded job creation schemes which, by their very nature, were only temporary measures and largely dependent upon the will of the particular government in office. Inevitably, many of those schemes, and hence the TIE personnel involved, soon disappeared from view.

## The third phase: the 1980s – crisis and change in a cool climate

By the early 1980s, with inflation rampant and a squeeze being applied to the funds available from both central and local government, TIE, generally run on the most minimal of 'shoestring' budgets, was already looking vulnerable. And it was the participation format – so long the key distinguishing feature of TIE – that took the brunt of the new pressures.

Two contrasting trends in the formats of programmes became evident during the subsequent decade:

(1) a shift away from participation-programmes to performance-only pieces (*Raj*, about the last days of British rule in India, being a good example of such a 'TIE play': Leeds TIE Company, 1984) which were only occasionally followed by discussion or workshop; accompanied by a reduction in the overall volume of new work; and
(2) the redevelopment of participation-programmes among a handful of the more firmly established companies, but in different guises and with different emphases.

The reasons for the trend towards performance-only work are many. TIE was unable to escape the rapid and far-reaching social, economic and cultural changes that came to the fore in the 1980s: the decline in the public funding of the arts; the changed, more censorious political atmosphere of Thatcherite Britain; the structural changes being introduced into the education system, involving a new National Curriculum and an emphasis upon skills and training often at the expense of the arts;[3] and the general promotion of an 'enterprise culture' based on the short-term values of the market place. Financial pressures led to more and more companies looking for increased 'cost-effectiveness': performance-only pieces meant that larger groups of children could be played to per performance. Companies had to reduce the number of their personnel and spend an increased amount of time in administration, negotiating continually to retain the most minimal of funding. Less time was available for newly devised, and especially collectively devised, work. It was easier and quicker to contract a writer to produce a self-contained play, or to use extant scripts. Some excellent work was still done (*Raj* being just one example; see also Mary Cooper's discussion in chapter 5), but against greater odds.

There was also some loss of confidence in the participation method. Many TIE actors with a conventional theatre training felt that participation work was better handled by teachers, others found it simply exhausting, while still others became frustrated by activating children towards decisions and understandings about the need for change in society but then walking away, leaving them in the hands of the institution, resulting in little or no change. Surely, it was argued, actors should play to their strengths: could not theatre be powerful through performance alone, through sharper imagery and more controlled, resonant narrative, which too much TIE was ignoring or handling carelessly? If you have to walk away, better to leave children with the memory of a powerful theatre performance that might continue to resonate, beneath the surface. TIE was, in the view of many, therefore, failing to provide enough of an *artistic* experience.

But the trend among some companies in the opposite direction was equally salutary. The ideas and methodology of such DIE practitioners as Dorothy Heathcote and Gavin Bolton became more widely known in TIE circles through the 1980s, and their approach – which stressed the pedagogic value of drama and the development of such strategies as teacher-in-role (itself a technique close to the notion of the actor-teacher) – notably insisted upon much greater structured opportunity for *reflection* by children in classroom drama work. Many in TIE found this methodology highly applicable to their own work. In part this was a response to the sense many had that TIE was too often guilty of pushing children through a programme, gesturing towards participation on the surface but controlling and manipulating their involvement such that outcomes were wholly predictable and participation of the most superficial kind. Likewise, debate and actual practice were greatly stimulated by the work (and visits) of Augusto Boal which offered methods that enabled young people to exert yet more control over the problem-solving process. (Boal's methodology is discussed in more detail by Chris Vine in chapter 3.)

Such approaches drew a number of companies towards a different kind of participation format. In this new variation, performance was often punctuated by halting the action ('freeze-framing') or re-running scenes for closer investigation, and encouraging more detached discussion and reflection, out of situation, out of role, with usually at least one actor as facilitator: this would then inform how pupils viewed, and perhaps influenced, the next stage of the drama. (Examples of this approach are Greenwich Young People's Theatre's *School on the Green* (1985), which looked at ideas about education, and M6 Theatre's *Trappin'* (by Frances McNeil, 1991), a play about oppression within a marriage, culminating in a 'forum theatre' workshop. Further examples are described in later chapters.)

A closing of the gap between the practices of the DIE teacher and the TIE team was an evident outcome in many locations. At the same time there was an opening of the gap between those companies committed to the participation format and those who increasingly offered plays with just a nod (or not even that) towards participatory follow-up work.

## The fourth phase: the 1990s to the present – new threats, new directions, new forms

As the National Curriculum and the diminishing role of the LEAs began to 'bite', all companies – no matter how strongly they resented the undermining of the long-held principle of state-funded arts provision within schools – now had to look increasingly towards other sources of income to supplement and, before long, replace grants from the LEAs. Many faced extinction if they failed, for the arts funding bodies, national and local, were unwilling and unable to become sole providers.

A number of new teams, seeing opportunities open up in the wake of growing public concern over such phenomena as child abuse and the spread of HIV/AIDS, managed to obtain project funding to serve the requirements of particular agencies involved with young people – such as the Health Education Council or the National Society for the Prevention of Cruelty to Children. Heritage organisations also started to employ groups of actors, based at a number of major centres of historical interest, whose task was to 'bring history alive' for both tourists and organised parties of schoolchildren – a trend that was, initially at least, viewed with suspicion by some in the TIE movement. Many such groups thrived through the 1990s and well into the new century – ranging from the impressive Young National Trust Theatre, a sizable professional company that presented full-scale participatory TIE projects for schools in various National Trust properties around the country, to the smaller team based at Wigan Pier whose task was to enliven the industrial museum's turn-of-the-century theme ('the way we were'), often for visiting school parties, but just as much for the casual visitor, and to the team of actor-interpreters and demonstrators at the Royal Armouries Museum in Leeds. Those teams have since been disbanded while others, especially those based in and around London, continue to survive and thrive.[4]

Diversification has been evident for some decades now at all levels – ideological, dramaturgical, financial and organisational. It is no longer possible to speak of a TIE *movement*, and SCYPT, once the voice of that movement, has long ceased to exist. Instead, new groupings emerged at national and international levels to represent those changing interests, demands and alliances.[5] Perhaps most significant has been the emergence from the early 1990s of 'applied theatre', not as a 'movement' but as a broad umbrella term that encompassed a variety of participatory drama practices, including not only TIE but prison theatre, theatre for development, community theatre and museum theatre. Initiated from within the academy to encompass the burgeoning number of modules and degree programmes dealing with, and in many cases training future practitioners for, this multiplicity of practices, the term has since gained currency in the professional field too. Such changes are welcome, and often necessary – so long as dialogue between those groupings exists to foster the sharing of good practice and innovation and to promote and defend the work whenever necessary.

## TIE – education or theatre?

One of the reasons for TIE's particular vulnerability at times of economic gloom has been its precarious position poised between two main sources of funding. While in some areas and at less financially fraught times the dual system functioned perfectly well, in a spirit of genuine partnership, there was a very real sense of bewilderment, frustration and above all, insecurity felt by many companies who found themselves accountable to two very different bodies and often judged against very different criteria. Moreover, inherent in that dual system of funding and the seemingly endless arguments over who should really pay for TIE, there lay a deeper tension – and that was the debate about whether TIE was really theatre or education. Ideally the terms should not be mutually exclusive, but in practice they often tended to be in the eyes of bureaucrats, politicians and even fellow educationalists and theatre professionals. Thus while the Arts Council preferred not to fund work undertaken in school hours, many LEAs, school governors and head teachers saw any activity undertaken by a professional theatre company as 'entertainment', the 'icing on the cake', not educational, and not a priority for grant-aid.

While in the 1980s and early 1990s one of the major tasks facing the TIE movement was wider dissemination of what TIE meant, what it did and how it could be used, now the need is perhaps more for redefinition and for fuller debate about the ways TIE methodologies underpin a range of applied theatre work. But resistance to the notion of theatre as a teaching instrument seems deeply ingrained in institutional attitudes – as Parnaby implied in 1978. One does not have to agree totally with the pessimistic analyses of institutionalised education by Illich, Holt and others to recognise that such diagnoses contain more than a grain of truth – that the education offered is all too often dictated by organisational needs, that syllabuses and teaching methods are driven by examinations and government targets, rather than the other way round. TIE, because it offers through the art form a vibrant and alternative way of looking at things, therefore has an important role to play as a necessary 'gingerer' within the system, and also as a vital link between the school and the larger community and its concerns. However, the likelihood of teams being able to persuade institutions, let alone funding bodies, of this function became immeasurably more constrained with the delivery of a narrowly conceived and examination-orientated National Curriculum at the forefront of teachers' minds. In addition to which, the devolved budgets have meant that, separately and with much narrower horizons, schools have placed the buying-in of an expensive TIE visit as an optional extra rather than a necessity.

It has been argued, in more philosophical vein, that TIE is a hybrid form that represents a disturbing trend in the arts generally towards diluting the quality of artistic experience with dubious and extrinsic social or educational objectives. Is TIE education or theatre or both? Does theatre make the education offered superficial, transitory, untrustworthy? As I have argued elsewhere (1993, 2007), we must be wary of seeing theatre and education as totally different commodities whose mingling together is surprising, suspicious and even damaging. Indeed, as Wooster (2007) argues, hybridity can be seen as a strength. The words of Bertolt Brecht, when faced with a not dissimilar resistance to his own experiments with 'teaching plays' in the 1930s, still have relevance for the twenty-first century:

> Generally there is felt to be a very sharp distinction between learning and amusing oneself. The first may be useful, but only the second is pleasant ... Well, all that can be said is that

> the contrast between learning and amusing oneself is not laid down by divine rule; it is not one that has always been and must continue to be … Theatre remains theatre, even when it is instructive theatre, and in so far as it is good theatre it will amuse.
>
> (Brecht 1974: 72–73)

TIE at its best has shown, in perhaps the most complete way yet, that theatre and learning need not be incompatible bedfellows. It is possible to learn through theatre.

Part of the problem, for those who worry about such notions, no doubt stems from the fact that we often confuse 'education' with school, with institutionalised state education, and they are not necessarily the same thing. (See Charles Adams' discussion of this in chapter 16.) Education can take place in an enormous variety of ways – not least through the medium of the arts. Any good theatre will of itself be educational – that is, when it initiates or extends a questioning process in its audience, when it makes us look again, freshly, at the world, its institutions and conventions and at our own place in that world, when it expands our notion of who we are, of the feelings and thoughts of which we are capable, and of our connection with the lives of others.

One of the main assertions of an Arts Council working party, set up in 1977 to make recommendations on the provision of theatre for children, was that children's theatre, including TIE, is an *art*, an 'imaginative event using actors', and should be funded as such wherever and whenever it may occur – preferably by the Arts Council so that the independent function of the art might be preserved. Despite the Council's valiant support for children's theatre during the previous decade and a half, it was not until 1986 that it finally produced *A Policy for Theatre for Young People*, which did give some renewed impetus and recognition (if not the level of funding many had sought) to the use of theatre as both an artistic and an educational medium.

Nonetheless, through the 1990s, the Arts Council maintained a wary distance from TIE, and, as partnerships between arts and education funders became increasingly fragile, it already seemed apt in 1993 to wonder whether, in the event that local government funding for TIE should disappear, and schools separately should find themselves unable to pay for a full-scale TIE service, the work would survive at all. Would TIE increasingly have to go down the road of servicing the requirements of agencies whose major concerns were social amelioration rather than educational provision? While TIE must respond to the rapidly changing needs of the social world, it would surely be a tragic misuse of the skills, imagination and theatrical potential of TIE were it to be wholly appropriated for the purposes of 'crisis management'. Its roots lie in the theatre and its strength in its independence from direct state (or state agencies') control. It must of course be accountable and responsive and it must work through fullest collaboration with schools and other organisations, but ultimately it is an *aesthetic* enterprise and those who wish to see it contribute energetically and effectively to young people's education in the broadest sense must acknowledge that fact.

In fact, despite recurring governmental pressures to make arts organisations increasingly reliant upon commercial sponsorship and other non-governmental funding, the outcomes have, over the past two decades, proved more complex than might have been expected. Partnerships have been initiated through publicly funded schemes (Creative Partnerships, Sure Start and the like) and through charitable trusts (M6 Theatre's three-year partnership in 2002–5 with the Nationwide Foundation, with a remit to produce TIE programmes dealing with teenage health and well-being, being one example). But they have tended to be constrained by limited-term contracts or curtailed in response to austerity cutbacks: many such programmes have flourished then vanished or been replaced by new but equally short-term initiatives.

By 2008, there were signs of a more holistic approach emerging. In that year, the McMaster Report was published. Commissioned by government to help shape future arts funding policy, it proved influential. McMaster noted that there had been, for many years, a tension between the intrinsic value of the arts and the instrumentalist arguments that the arts play a socially useful role in, for example, diverting people from crime, contributing to people's well-being and promoting social cohesion. McMaster attempted to reposition some of this thinking and to consider *excellence* as core to any artistic endeavour. Indeed, his definition of excellence was unequivocal: excellence in culture occurs when an experience affects and changes an individual (McMaster 2008: 9). Subsequently, faced with the contradictory pulls of McMaster's call for a philosophical shift in the discourse of arts funding on the one hand and diminishing funds from government on the other, as the world lurched into economic crisis, ACE has attempted to forge, in an era of austerity, and against much opposition, new models of funding fewer arts organisations better. Some companies (large and small) have benefitted from promotion to 'National Portfolio Organisations' (NPOs) while for others the contractual demands proved insurmountable, resulting in yet further closures. As a result, the landscape for 'classic' TIE has become for the most part unsustainable, at least for professional companies; student-devised work at universities, in a handful of drama and education departments, is not so constrained, allowing the form to continue if intermittently. While some fully fledged TIE companies such as Big Brum (Birmingham), Blah Blah Blah (Leeds) and Y Touring (London, national tours and online) continue, the dominant trajectory has been for TIE practice to become absorbed and integrated into (some would say submerged under) other forms of theatre work for young people – touring YPT, participatory youth theatre, and outreach and community-oriented work in building-based theatres.

M6 Theatre is a case in point. As one of the longest-lasting educational theatre companies in the UK, having its roots in the Bolton Octagon TIE Company before re-forming as an independent TIE/YPT company in 1977 with a remit to tour communities throughout the north-west of England (defined initially by the route of the M6 Motorway), it has survived innumerable funding crises and adapted its strategy accordingly, still maintaining its long-standing commitment to 'ignite the imagination' and 'challenge the mind' (M6 Theatre 2011). Recently awarded NPO status, it is now one of the leading companies

*Figure 1.1* *Hide and Seek* – the Story of the Gunpowder Plot (Theatre Company Blah Blah Blah, 2011/12). Participatory programme for 9–12-year-olds. Brigshaw High School and Language College, Leeds. Photo: Lizzie Coombes.

*Figure 1.2* *Sonya's Garden* by Dot Wood (M6 Theatre, 2004). A programme about friendship for 3–6-year-olds. Puppeteers: Gilly Baskeyfield and Lizzie Hughes. Photo: Beate Mielemeier.

specialising in theatre for the very young, small-scale TIE for older teenagers (monologues on contemporary issues used as a stimulus for debate and exploration) and participatory theatre projects with young people. It tours its work for the three- to seven-year-old age range nationally and internationally (demand for this area of work in recent years has grown hugely), while its participatory youth work is geared mainly to those in the economically distressed areas of Rochdale and nearby boroughs.

Ironically, while participatory TIE may have become difficult to sustain in its classic form, the value of the 'participatory arts' more broadly has gained currency, not least in the eyes of ACE. It is now interpreted, however, as the provision of opportunity for potential audiences, and the young especially, to become actively involved in arts events and processes. Youth theatre in its various manifestations, when led by professional artists and at the same time involving a degree of 'co-authorship', was one of the fields to be prioritised. This has coincided with, and been largely contingent upon, the emergence of a range of 'applied theatre' companies and freelance practitioners working in schools, prisons and young offender institutions, using participatory arts approaches. There are of course many reasons why participation has been embraced as an important ingredient in educational theatre. Although running counter to examination-oriented policies, there has been a shift away from the traditional 'one-way traffic' models of education, rooted in positivist notions of epistemology. This has been accompanied by the increased application of constructivist theories of learning and of 'experiential learning' approaches (Kolb 1985) and the further development of participatory models of education. Likewise, the growth of interest in aesthetic theory and reception studies, emphasising the audience's role in making meaning (see Jackson 2007), has helped to create a more receptive climate for participatory theatre.

While TIE companies have been an integral part of this development, and have adapted accordingly, it is perhaps less well understood that the current prioritisation of the participatory arts has built on those early experiments with audience participation pioneered by TIE companies in previous decades. The debt to TIE is undeniable. The challenge now must be to ensure that the particular qualities and characteristics of that earlier practice – above all, the harnessing of the art form to progressive notions of learning, and resisting their all-too easy separation – continue not only to survive but to nurture and sustain new forms of TIE and TIE-related applied theatre practices in the future.

## Notes

1 For a detailed account of the early days of TIE see Vallins (1980) and Redington (1983); also Pammenter's account of TIE and 'child-centred' education (1993).

2 *Poverty Knocks* and *Marches: from Jarrow to Cable Street* are unpublished but appear in scenario/case study form in Jackson (1980).

3 In 1988 the Education Reform Act ushered in a sweeping series of changes to the structure and content of education in Britain. A National Curriculum was instituted for the first time consisting of three core subjects (English, Maths and Science) and ten 'foundation' subjects (which did not include Drama or Dance; Drama as a teaching method was included under English, but could be taught separately as an optional extra). At the same time, Local Management of Schools gave schools increasing control over the budget allocated by the LEA. Most LEAs that grant-aided TIE companies had done so from those (now redistributed) central funds. More recently, governments of various persuasions have offered financial incentives to schools to opt out altogether from the LEA and assume 'academy' status, receiving budget allocations direct from central government alongside sponsorship from private donors. The implications of all these changes for the funding of TIE companies were far-reaching, and led to a constant, ever-widening search for alternative and complementary sources of income.

4 Freelance companies continuing to operate include Past Pleasures (working mainly at the Historic Royal Palaces, including the Tower of London);

Spectrum (at several major London museums such as the National Maritime Museum and the Science Museum); Andrew Ashmore & Associates (at various sites and museums in London and occasionally in the regions); and Platform 4 (at the Railway Museum, York). For a fuller discussion of theatre in museums and 'live interpretation' see Jackson and Kidd (2011), and Jackson (2007).

5 Notable examples include: TYA-UK, the British Centre for ASSITEJ: the International Association of Theatre for Children and Young People (see www.tya-uk.org/); IMTAL-Europe: the International Museum Theatre Alliance (see www.imtal-europe.org); and IDEA: the International Drama/Theatre & Education Association (see www.idea-org.net/en/).

## Works cited


Arts Council of Great Britain (ACGB) (1967), *The Provision of Theatre for Young People in Great Britain*. London: HMSO.

——(1986), *A policy for theatre for young people*. London: Arts Council.

Boal, Augusto (1979), *Theatre of the Oppressed*. London: Pluto Press.

Brecht, B. (1974), 'Theatre for pleasure or theatre for instruction', reprinted in J. Willett, ed. (1974), *Brecht on Theatre*. London: Methuen, pp. 69–76. First published 1936.

Department of Education and Science (1976), *Education Survey 22: Actors in Schools* London: HMSO.

Freire, Paulo (1993), *Pedagogy of the Oppressed*. London: Penguin.

Holt, John (1965), *How Children Fail*. London: Pitman.

Illich, Ivan (1970), *De-schooling Society*. New York: Penguin.

Jackson, Tony, ed. (1980), *Learning through Theatre: essays and casebooks on theatre in education*, 1st edn. Manchester: Manchester University Press.

——, ed. (1993), *Learning through Theatre: new perspectives on theatre in education*, 2nd edn. London: Routledge.

——, Anthony (2007), *Theatre, Education and the Making of Meanings*. Manchester: Manchester University Press.

Jackson, A. and Kidd, J., eds. (2011), *Performing Heritage: research, practice and innovation in museum theatre and live interpretation*. Manchester: Manchester University Press.

Kolb, David (1985), *Experiential Learning*. Englewood Cliffs, NJ: Prentice-Hall.

M6 Theatre: www.m6theatre.co.uk/about/what-we-do/ (accessed 30 Sept. 2011).

McMaster, Sir Brian (2008), *Supporting Excellence in the Arts: from Measurement to Judgement* (The McMaster Report). London: Department for Culture, Media and Sport (HM Government) Also online at: www.culture.gov.uk/reference_library/publications/3577.aspx (last accessed 30/4/12).

Pammenter, D. (1993), 'Devising for TIE', in Jackson, ed., *Learning through Theatre*, 2nd edn. London: Routledge, pp. 53–70.

Parnaby, B. (1978), '*Actors in Schools* and after', in *Trends in Education* vol. 4. London: HMSO, pp. 17–21.

Redington, C. (1983), *Can Theatre Teach?* London: Pergamon Press.

Vallins, G. (1980), 'The Beginnings of TIE', in Jackson, ed., *Learning through Theatre*, 1st edn. Manchester: Manchester University Press.

Wooster, Roger (2007), *Contemporary Theatre in Education*. Bristol: Intellect Books.

## Published TIE programmes referred to

Dates given below are dates of publication; dates in the text are those of first performance

Belgrade TIE Team, *Pow Wow* and *Ifans' Valley* in Schweitzer, P., ed. (1980), *Theatre in Education*, vol. 1. London: Methuen.

——(1976), *Rare Earth*. London: Methuen.

Greenwich Young People's Theatre, *School on the Green* in Redington, C. ed. (1987), *Six TIE Programmes*. London: Methuen.

Leeds TIE Company (1984), *Raj*. London: Amber Lane Press.

McNeil, Frances (1991), *Trappin'*, in *Ask Me Out*, ed. R. Robinson. London: Hodder & Stoughton.

Pit Prop Theatre (1984), *Brand of Freedom*. On DVD with accompanying notes. Manchester: Manchester University Media Services.

# 2

# THE IMAGINATION IN ACTION

## TIE and its relationship to Drama in Education today

*Chris Cooper*

Since Gavin Bolton wrote 'Drama in Education and TIE: A comparison' for the first edition of *Learning through Theatre* in 1980 (and indeed the revised 1993 edition), there have of course been enormously significant changes in the field of arts education, changes that make a comparison today very difficult if not impossible. These changes relate to social, economic and political developments as well as to form and content, which are of course inextricably linked. The above could be the subject of a substantial book in itself, but revisiting Bolton's chapter serves as a useful starting point for anyone wishing to understand the historical 'kinship' between Drama in Education (DIE) and TIE and the current state of both today. What, however, does Bolton mean by 'kinship'? In some of his later writings he makes this absolutely explicit:

> I want to suggest that what we have all been doing is indeed theatre and that it is about time we acknowledged it more fully. … [T]he work from Newcastle and Durham Universities … became known as 'Drama in Education', a term that in fact first appeared in print in 1921 but in the '60s & '70s became associated with the use of teacher-in-role and whole class 'living through' dramatic activity. Dorothy Heathcote always claimed that she was working in 'theatre', a view I used to find very difficult to swallow, but she never got round to changing the

> name of her courses to 'teaching teachers to use theatre', because it would certainly have been misunderstood.
>
> (Bolton 2010: 164)

While I agree that 'it's all theatre' in terms of form, I would paradoxically argue that as far as content is concerned, it's all actually drama, but more of that later.

'DIE and TIE are concerned with dramatic art and pedagogy, but in recent years political and economic expediency have had a reductive effect' (Bolton 1993: 39). This is truer today than it was in 1993. DIE as defined by Bolton, Heathcote and many others has become increasingly marginalised in schools, while TIE practised as the complex and discrete art form that grew out of the Belgrade Theatre, Coventry, in 1965 has virtually ceased to exist.

The need for DIE and TIE that bring about a 'change in understanding' (ibid.) in participants, about themselves and the world they live in, has never been more pressing. The year in which I write this, 2012, is a time of profound social, political and cultural crisis throughout the world deepened by the worst recession since the 1930s. Once again young people (along with the most vulnerable) will bear the brunt of it. A banking crisis has been turned into a crisis for public spending and the cuts to public services, including the arts, and 'reforms' to state education are proving as brutal and damaging as, if not worse than, those implemented by the Thatcher government.[1] We live in a society that has lost its moral compass. All the measured educational 'standards' in the world will not make our increasingly incoherent society flourish and grow. We live at a time when education needs to serve more than the requirements of the world markets and be part of creating a vision of a society worth living in with shared convictions about the kind of people we want to be. Education, as with all social and civic institutions, needs human values. And if DIE and TIE are about anything, they are about the 'self', society and human values.

What follows is not so much a comparison between DIE and TIE, but rather an attempt to take the reader on a journey from Bolton's 1993 chapter to the present. Along the way I will outline briefly the main developments in DIE, define TIE, and following in Bolton's footsteps look at *mode, structure, purpose* and *engagement in meaning* to demonstrate how some of the most important developments in the field of DIE continue to shape TIE. I will also identify some key ways in which the theory and practice of playwright Edward Bond have influenced the thinking of Big Brum (the TIE company which I direct) and which I believe can be of use to the development of both DIE and TIE today.

## DIE

The DIE Bolton argued for in *Learning through Theatre*, and which generations of drama teachers have since fought for and provided, was already under attack at the time he was updating his chapter for the second edition, as a result of the introduction of the national curriculum. The intellectual justification for complying with the new curriculum followed. Peter Abbs and David Hornbrook were at the forefront of the criticisms of DIE. Hornbrook's *Education and Dramatic Art* (1989) compared the work of Bolton and Heathcote to that of the seventeenth-century religious sect, the Muggletonians, and the people they trained as drama teachers to a cult following that led children into a 'narcissistic wilderness' (Hornbrook 1989: 67). There is not the space here to refute this; I highly recommend Bolton himself in 'Have a Heart' (Bolton 2010). Hornbrook, whilst decrying the practice of DIE developed by Bolton and Heathcote, was advocating the reduction of drama to a subject whose study was theatre arts. In my opinion there is no substance to their argument that DIE neglected the art form, but the accusation supported the reductionist thinking behind the present drama curriculum: one that is largely vacuous and almost totally focused on skills paradoxically undermining of the art form of theatre itself. This skills-based approach to examination-level drama in British schools separates form and content. It's important to note that many teachers recognise that form and content are interdependent and make meaningful drama with their students despite the curriculum, but the constraints it places on teachers are profound.

Dorothy Heathcote devoted a great part of her working life, right up to her death, developing Mantle of the Expert as a specific approach to drama while also developing a broader philosophy of education (see Heathcote and Bolton 1995). This was a significant development that has flourished internationally. During this same period, Bolton continued to develop his interest in 'lived through' drama. His book, significantly called *Acting in Classroom Drama* (Bolton 1998), built on this rich body of work.[2] Cecily O'Neill notes that the ongoing development of the 'lived through' drama of DIE is now widely referred to by drama educators throughout the world as Process Drama (a term that appeared in the late 1980s): 'Process drama is a complex dramatic encounter. Like other theatre events, it evokes an immediate dramatic world bounded in space and time, a world that depends on the consensus of all those present for its existence' (O'Neill 1995: xiii). She also notes that process drama was influenced by developments in contemporary theatre in the 1960s as much as it was by educational drama, with its emphasis on 'presence and immediacy, process and transformation' (ibid.) filtering into the work of drama teachers. It is in the development of process drama that the cross-fertilisation with TIE practice is still to be found. Before looking more closely at this relationship, however, it is worth explaining my own understanding of TIE.

## TIE

> TIE lets children come to know themselves and their world and their relation to it. That is the only way that they can know who they are and accept responsibility for themselves. TIE is carrying out the injunction of the Greeks who founded our democracy and our theatre: they said know yourself – otherwise you are a mere consumer of time, space, air and fodder.
>
> (Bond 1994: 37)

TIE, as I understand and practise it, developed in the UK through peer-led theoretical and practical experimentation and collaboration; crucially through its national association (Standing Conference of Young Peoples Theatre), sadly now defunct. As cuts to the funding of TIE companies destroyed the material base for this TIE movement, it has been gradually replaced by a diversity of practice that, whilst sustaining a quantity of work for young people, is often (in Bolton's terms) utterly reductive. Often what passes for or is labelled TIE bears little relation to the actual art form. I say theatre in education, not theatre for young people or young audiences, or children's theatre or different approaches to work with young people that are perfectly valid and some of it, without doubt, of high quality.

I agree with Bolton that 'drama has a great deal to do with pedagogy *because* it is an art form' (Bolton 1993: 39). I interpret the term pedagogy to mean educational methodology that takes a holistic approach to personal and socialised learning. TIE is not a theatre of instruction for the transmission of a 'message' to the audience. There is no message. The aim is to use the dramatic art of theatre to explore values, by dramatising the human condition and behaviour so that the audience makes meaning through experience.

> Art is not a 'cure'. It provides patterns of reason and tension which organise our experience and give meaning to life – and thus purpose … All important drama has shown that there are no 'cures' for the problem of being human. Just as there

> are no 'facts' which constitute 'knowledge'. ... Art must always pass responsibility back to the spectator. The artist is creative in order to make the audience self-creative. That is, neither 'cure' nor mere propaganda.
>
> (Bond 1995)

Passing responsibility back to the audience is necessary because, as Geoff Gillham noted,

> We cannot 'give' someone our understanding. Real understanding is felt. Only if the understanding is felt can it be integrated into children's minds, or anyone's. Resonance is the starting point of the integration process. The resonance of something engages us powerfully; that is, affectively. But, significantly, it also engages us indirectly with that which it resonates. Resonance is not authoritarian; yet it's an offer you cannot refuse!
>
> (Gillham 1994: 5)

## TIE and DIE

### *The common feature*

The most distinctive feature of TIE as an art form, and the most significant common feature of the kinship between TIE and DIE/Process Drama, is participation, which historically in TIE has involved one class at a time in order to ensure the highest possible actor-teacher/participant ratio. Critical to the development of participatory work has been the contribution of the actor-teacher, a unique hybrid of skills that the title suggests. (See also discussion in chapter 7.) All the key developments in TIE theory and practice have come about as a result of the continuity that comes with employing actor-teachers as full-time staff. Big Brum currently employs three full-time actor-teachers and a designer, which is of critical importance to the drive to consolidate progress, develop and explore new territory. In all of our work the theatre or performance element is a part of a whole programme – there is usually work before a performance, in between scenes and episodes and/or after (which also includes provision of teaching resource materials). The participatory element is sometimes integrated even further into the structure with a much more fluid boundary between the two different modes of audience and active participant. The aim is always to engage the young people in direct participation in the art form – often through role play or dramatisation. Each participant is consciously framed.[3] Participation will sometimes relate to the use of a role and there is always a central task, a purpose to it, for the class. The task is a way of encoding our new insights and understandings based on experience. Frame, role, task and enacting moments or dramatic situations enable the participants to bring their whole selves to the TIE programme, it matters to them because they are *in* it and they experience a *felt* understanding, this is something that cannot be handed over, it has to be experienced. But by utilising the safety that fiction provides, the participants are protected *into* the material. Physical participation, the manipulation of time and space in a TIE programme, has many of the characteristics of learning in real life.

> The TIE experience, like drama in education, is lived like 'ordinary life' and is at the same time 'not life' but fiction. This dialectical characteristic enables children to 'learn right' – not learn right answers, but 'learn right' in the sense of – learn to become more human not less.
>
> (Gillham 1994: 5)

### *A significant distinction*

The most significant distinction between TIE and DIE (leaving aside the obvious difference that TIE is performance-based with professional actors) is that the former tends to be a one-occasion event while the latter gives the teacher much more freedom to discover the centre of each drama with the students and the flexibility to pursue in subsequent drama sessions the interests that arise through the doing of it.[4]

The flexibility afforded the classroom teacher, however, does not in itself guarantee internal or external coherence. As Bolton pointed out (1993), whenever the teacher (or TIE company) interacts with the child/group there are always two plays going on simultaneously. This is the tension between what Geoff Gillham (cited in Bolton 1993: 41) termed the play for the children (what interests them) and the play for the teacher (what the teacher/company wants the children to explore) and is ever present in any interaction.

TIE, therefore, requires structures that have a rigidity which keeps the participants focused on the matter under consideration and dramatised in a play, but that are also flexible enough for the class to take ownership of their own learning. On tour the same material is tried and tested daily with a new group of young people. To remain authentic, it requires constant attention and development of structure in order to avoid any tendency to fix things and fall back on what 'works' rather than what meets the needs, or takes account of 'their play', for the particular group on each particular day. TIE practitioner Tag McEntegart once (in conversation) coined the phrase 'don't teach yesterday's kids today'; it has become an indispensable rule of thumb in our work.

So in the absence of continuous engagement over a number of weeks and months with a class of young people, TIE has to take full advantage of the signing system that theatre offers. This is TIE's strength. As Heathcote points out,

> actual living and theatre, which is a depiction of living conditions, both use the same network of signs and their medium of communication; namely the human being signalling across time and space, in immediate time, to and with others, each reading and signalling simultaneously within the action of each passing moment.
>
> (Heathcote 1981: 18)

This makes theatre form very efficient: young people can be brought into relationship with the heart of the situation very quickly.

But in the drive to develop TIE, the kinship with DIE remains a strong bond. Of course this is most evident in the participatory elements of the TIE programmes, but at a deeper level the bond is formed by a shared philosophy and pedagogy. It is also a question of struggling for continuity and innovation, a synthesis of the old and the new which historically has been characteristic of both art forms.

I want to illustrate how, in some key aspects, what has been learned from DIE continues to shape TIE. So, to return to the footsteps of Bolton.

## Mode of engagement

Bolton noted that the greatest kinship between DIE and TIE is the mode of engagement contained in 'whole group experiencing' (Bolton 1993: 40). To my mind some of the most powerful and dramatic art in classroom drama emerged through 'lived through' drama.

> What is drama? When is drama, drama? When does educational drama go straight to the heart of drama? ... it seems to me that possibly an answer to this is, when it is composed of those elements that are common to both children's play and

> to theatre, when the aims are to help children learn about those feelings, attitudes and preconditions that, before the drama was experienced, were too implicit for them to be aware of [so that they are] helped to face facts and to interpret them without prejudice; so that they develop a range and degree of identification with other people, so that they develop a set of principles, a set of consistent principles, by which they are going to live.
>
> (Bolton 2010: xv)

Companies, such as The Dukes TIE, The Belgrade, Theatr Powys and Big Brum amongst others, have developed work that has sought to capture the freedom and flexibility of this lived-through whole-group experience by blurring the boundary between participation and performance, shifting quickly and directly from theatre moments to spontaneous dramatisation and lived-through engagement with young people (often in role themselves). This has brought us closer to how theatre works, as an event.

*Separation Wall*, for example, devised for years 5 and 6 (ages 9–11) by Big Brum in 2005, was set in a fictitious country divided by a wall. The students were in role as the parents of the community whose access to work, water, electricity – their lives in fact – was controlled by the people on the other side. The children of the community were endangering their own lives by walking a yellow line two metres away from the wall; anyone, children included, crossing the yellow line was immediately fired on by guards in watch towers. This 'playing by the wall' had become an elaborate and terrifying game of 'chicken' which was also an act of youthful resistance. The programme began with a ten-minute piece of theatre where the participants watched actors in the role of children playing. Very soon they were engaged by the children's mother appealing to the community to help stop her eldest child, and any other child (including their own), from playing the 'game'. There were elements of the programme that were fixed as part of the sequencing of the programme.[5] There were other non-negotiables such as getting the parents to experience standing in a queue, waiting and hoping to be picked for work, and the first community meeting. But the rest of the programme unfolded depending upon how the class we were working with each day engaged with the problem of protecting their children. The actor-teachers were guided by what lay at the centre of the programme: an exploration of 'what is home?' and 'what separates us from ourselves and each other?' The challenge was to work in the moment with the class in a drama that could draw on a bank of pre-prepared theatre moments (not always drawn on), or dramatise moments using objects and situations that related to the centre of the programme (our play) and converged with what the young people were exploring (their play).

Big Brum developed this work further, drawing more explicitly on the relationship to children's play in *The Giant's Embrace*, devised for years 1–3 (ages 5–8) in 2006. The centre of the programme was an exploration of deferred gratification, sustainability and responsibility, and took the form of a fairy tale. The children were framed as fellow storymakers by the actor-teachers who had an emergency on their hands: an unfinished story! The storymakers were asked to finish Tom's story (the central task) because he was in terrible trouble. The story concerns a world where a Giant (played by an actor-teacher) with an insatiable appetite is literally devouring every living thing on the planet. Tom (a small puppet), who has made his way into the

*Figure 2.1 The Giant's Embrace* (Big Brum TIE, 2006). Afraid to die, young hopeless Tom offers his Mother and Brother to the Giant instead. Giant played by Richard Holmes. Photo: Ceri Townsend.

heart of the dying forest in search of food to feed his mother and (ever crying) baby brother, is captured by the Giant and, at the point of being devoured, offers his mother and baby brother in exchange for his own life. The Giant agrees, telling Tom to return with his dinner the next day. Tom is too afraid and ashamed to go home, and hides amongst the trees sobbing in despair. The animals (also puppets) that he has befriended through previous acts of kindness watch over him.

At this point in the programme the children were taken into the forest (stepping onto the set) where as fellow storymakers they set about creating an ending with the actor-teachers. This involved trying to work out solutions enactively (thinking through doing, rather than thinking then doing what you already know), manipulating Tom and the animal puppets, and the objects in the story, speaking with their voices and directly engaging with the terrifying Giant who towered over poor Tom and his animal friends. The relationship here between the whole group experience as theatre and children's play is obvious, the results were immensely powerful. The children were endlessly inventive in their play. A teacher from Kings Norton, Birmingham, recorded one class's ending:

> Paint the knife orange, disguise it as a carrot.
>
> Ask ladle to check if the giant has a heart, then put knife in it. When giant eats knife it kills him as it goes in his heart. It stabs him 10 times. Shouting don't kill people, don't eat children, don't eat animals …
>
> He falls to the ground where a hole has been dug and then Tom buries him.
>
> Out of his body 10 rivers of blood which are different colours – the colours he has taken out of the ground. The rivers are rivers of truth,
>
> 10 rivers of truth are: Life, care, family, expensive things, world, joy, taking care of the environment, luck, love, health.
>
> Out of the ground deep underground the trees grew and the world was repaired.
>
> Tom ran home as fast as he could to his family and they all lived happily ever after!!
>
> (Big Brum archive)

This ending has all the authenticity of a real fairy tale and is as epic as any Greek myth. The play for the children varied but the structure of the programme could make this tension productive because there was a very powerful angle of connection and rich secondary symbolism[6] for the children.

The angle of connection (Bolton 1979: 60) is the link between the material of the TIE programme and the lives of the children that enables them to connect with what is on offer affectively. Poor Tom was an embodiment of this. He was a reluctant hero who felt responsible for (and resentful of) both his crying baby brother and his crisis-ridden mother and he was guilty, at the point the children met his story, of betraying them. But this was feelingly understood by the children at the beginning of the programme. When the children were asked 'have you ever done something you knew you shouldn't have done but couldn't really help it?', it was answered with a forest of arms. The secondary symbolism (Piaget 1972) in both *Separation Wall* and *The Giant's Embrace* powerfully engaged the children's unconscious self; being in role as parents making decisions as active members of an adult community and being able to determine the outcome of a story gave them a freedom and power in dramatic action that they are denied but hunger for in real life.

Through the angle of connection and secondary symbolism, the mode of engagement becomes an affective whole-group experience because it relates to the life experiences of the participants.

## Structure: teacher and actor-in-role

> When a teacher takes on a role as part of class drama s/he is, at a fictitious level, joining with them, but at an educational or aesthetic level is working ahead of them.
>
> (Bolton 1993: 41)

The work described above relies heavily on teacher-in-role (TiR) or, as we term it, the actor-in-role (AiR) who is usually fully costumed as a character from a play. Left to themselves the children will be dominated by what happens next in the story at the expense of the drama. TiR/AiR, however, becomes playwright to the emerging experience to build what Bolton names as the main elements of drama – focus, tension, constraint, ritual, contrast and symbolisation (ibid.: 42). By symbolisation he means action that resonates more than its literal meaning would suggest. I would add action, images and the (use of) objects that resonate beyond their literal meaning *but* are coherent *within* the logic of the situation. This logic is important because it is the logic of the situation that Edward Bond has called (in conversation) 'the relationship between the kitchen table and the universe'. In

*Separation Wall* the opening ten minutes of theatre revolved around a family dividing a tomato into three parts and eating it. The resonance can only go beyond its literal meaning if the way it is done is coherent within the logic of the situation.

The capacity to be with and ahead of the class simultaneously makes AiR a versatile tool that is under-used in TIE – engaging the children in both word and deed. 'The point being the actor can move from a mode of work within the action of the play to a mode without the action of the play almost seamlessly: maintaining and developing the implications of the learning process' (Yeoman 1995: 36). Hot-seating is a poor comparison to this.

## Purpose

> I believe that DIE is concerned with change in understanding, but it is a mistake to isolate this objective by treating it as a commodity separate from form. I suggested that such tunnel vision leads to extreme views of drama as either functional role-play or 'theatre' studies.
>
> (Bolton 1993: 44)

The unity of form and content to bring about change in understanding remains the function of theatre and drama in society. The imagination is the foundation for that change in understanding. Edward Bond has much to offer us in this respect. Since 1995, Big Brum has been working in collaboration with this great British playwright. He is not only the writer of over fifty plays but also a pioneering theoretician on drama and theatre with a radical aesthetic. Bond argues that it is the imagination that makes us human and that it is the source of value because reason without imagination divorces us from being human, or humanness. A corrupted imagination (and values) results in atrocities; the history of the twentieth century is littered with barbaric examples.

> When we reason imaginatively we cannot be cold and detached because the self is engaged or dramatised. Because imagination animates the 'other' it makes us socially engaged. In this way we take personal political responsibility.
>
> (Katafiasz 2005: 211)

This is not the same as imposing your values upon the young people. The change in understanding we are looking for from the Bondian perspective is driven by the need for justice that is in all of us, a need that ideology obscures.

> The Greeks created the first democracy. They did this not because they had a public assembly and law courts, but because they created the first public drama. Courts and assemblies give only the law, but drama gives justice. We are the dramatic species and drama is deep in our psyches. It is the only means we have of unravelling and reweaving our complex contradictions and visions. Our society thinks in terms of cures, punishment and gadgets. The Greeks *relished* their problems and made them creative in the profound liberty of tragedy. We are not restricted to their ideological solutions, but we have the same problems of self-and-society. After two thousand years their drama towers over our stage.
>
> (Bond 2009)

Because we are the dramatic species I think that the future development of TIE and DIE depends upon making it all about *drama* – rather than theatre. While I embrace Bolton's assertion that 'it's all theatre' in a fundamental sense, because drama uses theatrical form and conventions without which there is no art form or relationship between form and content, I feel that it is also important to distinguish between Theatre and Drama in the way that Bond does. Drama as an act of 'self'-creation is close to reality because it is as if in drama reality, through the self, is seeing itself. Theatre avoids looking at reality. Theatre, in Bond's terms, is ideologically distorted by sentimentality, or catharsis, because it does not address the human problem of the need for justice. It is focused on using theatricality – set, lights and sound etc. – for an *effect* that is designed to entertain us, or manipulate the audience/participant by determining the meaning for them; in the past he has compared a public execution, or Nazi rally, to theatre. At its most obvious is the use of music or lights which tells the audience that what is happening is 'sad' or 'chilling', but it is also true of a lot of writing and acting which wants to explain meaning for us. There are no gaps for the audience or participants to fill for themselves. Drama, on the other hand, uses theatricality to create *event*. The word originates from the Greek word 'Dro' or 'Dran', meaning I do, or act, in order to influence (*Triantafyllidis* online dictionary). And it is this active 'doing' in drama as opposed to the seeing of theatre (which also comes from the Greek: *theatron – a place of seeing*) that is significant for Bond. Greek drama put all the great problems of what it is to be human on the stage creating a conflict (*agon*) that is enacted both in the play *and* in the mind (the imaginations) of the audience. The contradiction between what is on stage and simultaneously in the mind of the audience is a challenge to our values and demands we actively make meaning of it.

In what Bond characterises as the profound 'liberty of tragedy', dramatising events necessitates activating the imagination of the audience or participant so that they have choices and decisions to make. This also creates a space to bring our own understanding of our lives into the equation, and in doing so we create our selves, which is what makes drama an act of self-creation that, because we are socially engaged, changes reality. The choices and decisions are real and dramatists have to allow for the freedom to choose, not to manipulate the audience towards the 'correct' answer, or to what we think. This is what Bond means when referring to humanness and in drama our choices, just like the choices of the characters in a play, make us less or more human. I believe that Bond has developed an approach to acting (see also chapter 7) and a range of theatrical devices such as the 'site' and the 'drama event' that can be explored and adapted in order to develop new approaches to classroom drama.[7]

## Engagement with meaning

> There is a symbiotic dependency between the particularity of 'contextual meanings' and the generality of 'universal meanings'. If the drama is working as art, the participants' or audience's response will be a holistic one: attention will not be given to one or other level of meaning, but to each in the other.'
>
> (Bolton 1993: 47)

Theatre, as noted, is the most efficient sign system because it can be used to create drama in which the ontological cohabits with the existential – the kitchen table and the universe.

> The TIE company has a huge advantage over the teacher in respect of the contextual meaning. The actors create, three dimensionally and with immediacy, a believable context that arrests attention and interest and, above all, creates the potential for a multi-level experience.
>
> (ibid.)

If drama has a great deal to do with pedagogy precisely because it is art, this multi-level experience is also a pedagogical question. TIE and DIE have a lot to thank Bolton for, not least his interest in the work of Lev Vygotsky and Jerome Bruner. Vygotsky recognised that in play children are dealing principally with the *meaning* (or concepts) of things: 'In fundamental, everyday situations a child's behaviour is the opposite of his behaviour in play. In play, action is subordinated to meaning, but in real life, of course, action dominates meaning' (Vygotsky 1978: 79). He also observed that in play, where meaning dominates action, a child stands a 'head taller than himself' because s/he is working in the Zone of Proximal Development which:

> defines those functions that have not yet matured but are in the process of maturation, functions that will mature tomorrow but are currently in an embryonic state. These functions could be termed the 'buds' or 'flowers' of development rather than the 'fruits' of development. The actual development level characterises mental development retrospectively, while the zone of proximal development [ZPD] characterises mental development prospectively.
>
> (ibid.: 86)

Imagination represents a specifically human form of conscious activity that can lead the child towards the development of the higher psychological and mental functions. The conscious ability of the child to move into an imaginary situation from the real world represents a new stage of development. The use of the imagination both individually and socially can enrich the ZPD. Through the imagination we are able to know the world in a different way. We can reach beyond the present moment and our actual daily lives to envisage possible worlds. To be imaginative is not something distinct from being rational, but rather it is what gives reason flexibility, energy, creativity and human value. At a later stage of development Vygotsky noted that the imagination in older children and adolescents, because it is internalised, is play without action; yet the role of the imagination remains the same. Bond has stated that it is the imagination – the ability to recognise the 'other' – that makes us human; it creates human value. This is because in drama and theatre, as in imaginative play, action is also subordinated to meaning. Theatre and drama have the same attributes as play, creating fictional situations in which real action takes place. Through its movement in the field of meaning, then, what is true about play is true of theatre and drama, which in this sense is the imagination in action: a social act of meaning making in which participants and audience members can also be said to stand a head taller than themselves in terms of both thought and indeed action, which can have implications for real life.

The Vygotskian model of developmental psychology views the child as an active seeker of knowledge: the child and environment interact together enabling cognitive development in a culturally adaptive way; the mind is socially constructed; development occurs as a direct result of contact with the environment. There is a strong connection here between Vygotsky's thinking and the Socratic tradition, or what Dorothy Heathcote usefully coined the 'crucible paradigm', whereby students and teachers or more capable adults and peers stir knowledge around together in order to gain insight, experience and new knowledge. It has to be the dominant paradigm for interaction between the drama or actor-teacher and the participant if engagement in meaning is going to be achieved both individually and collectively for the participants.

Vygotsky also emphasised the importance of objects in play, and DIE and TIE have always made great use of objects. The multi-level experience Bolton refers to in theatre, however, also relates to the objects 'signalling across time and space' in the immediate three-dimensional context. Here we can indentify a powerful connection between the Vygotskyian ZPD and Bond's dramatic use of objects in his plays.

Bond, in order to release the potential of the object in the dramatic site, creates what he calls a drama event (DE), where the object is 'cathexed' (see Davis 2005: 203). When an object is cathexed, it retains its use value but it is also invested with emotional attachment, its grammar is changed and it accrues new values as it journeys through the play creating a productive tension. In *The Broken Bowl* (Big Brum, 2012; see also chapter 7), a young girl insists on bringing a bowl to the table, much to her Father's annoyance, to feed her imaginary friend. As the play progresses the tension between the values invested in the bowl by the girl (her emotional attachment) and her father's relationship to it (how it *should* be used) grows. The Father's response to his child is a totally ideologically governed perception of reality. At one point, as the title suggests, he brutally smashes the bowl with a hammer to stop her play. The smashing is literal and metaphorical and in a most important sense metonymical. The way the bowl is used, cathexed and de-cathexed creates a gap for a new meaning that can radically shift our thinking: the domestic comes into relationship with the universe through the use of the bowl and projects the children into their ZPD. During the TIE programme when asked 'What got smashed when the bowl was broken?' a nine-year-old child responded by saying:

> He crushed the daughter's imagination. She uses her imagination to be fearless and not to be scared by what's going on outside.

This was developed by another child:

> The bowl is the heart of the family. When he broke it he broke the family – their connection.
>
> (Big Brum archive)

They were talking on a multiplicity of levels – those of the contextual and universal meanings – and deepening each other's understanding of the implications for the familial relationships and the implications of starving the girl's imagination for the girl and for themselves.

Sustaining and developing both DIE/Process Drama and TIE in the UK today is a serious challenge, mainly because of the constraints of the curriculum and ever dwindling funding. Big Brum constantly has to readdress the question of what TIE is. For example, working with one class at a time (no more than forty students) is becoming increasingly difficult to sustain because value is increasingly measured monetarily rather than educationally and artistically in schools. Furthermore, the future survival of drama as a discrete subject in UK schools is increasingly insecure, while the need to focus on theatre skills demanded by the curriculum means that drama teachers now lack the training to become DIE/Process Drama practitioners with their students. The need for this work, however, is more pressing than before because the learning through theatre and drama that this work embodies has profound implications for individual and societal development. We may have to find different contexts, or pretexts, for working in schools, but the necessity to build on the legacy of Bolton and Heathcote, their successors' work, and nearly fifty years of TIE, is in my opinion beyond doubt, and the drive to ensure it continues to develop will perhaps see it described in a fourth edition of *Learning through Theatre.*

## Notes

1 The 1988 Education Reform Act (see also p. 38 n. 3) brought about a shift in education based on delivering the new national curriculum and teaching to pass tests, the reductive approach to education mourned by Bolton. Today the acceleration of an academy system and the introduction of 'free' schools will, to my mind, open the door to widespread privatisation of state education and once again systematise class-based educational inequality that the great 1944 Education Act was designed to bring to an end. In the latest curriculum review, Drama only appears under the generic title of 'the arts' at Key Stage 4 (15–17 years).

2 See 'Re-interpretations of Dorothy Heathcote's "living through" drama' and 'Towards a conceptual framework for classroom acting behaviour' in Bolton (1998).

3 'Frame' denotes both a role function for the participants in a dramatic event, a degree of distance from the actual event, and a certain viewpoint through which the event is explored. Frame gives participants a heightened consciousness of the significance, implication and understanding of the event. It is also a means for providing dramatic tension.
4 Time to explore meaning with the students is increasingly limited for the TIE Company. Since 2008 Big Brum has produced only half-day TIE programmes because it is impossible to get the students off the curriculum for a whole day. The loss to the future development of the work is immeasurable.
5 Sequencing is a term Heathcote used to describe the ordering of processes, not events, required to ensure participants always have the experience they need in order to progress to the next stage of their drama work.
6 Davis explains Bolton's approach to secondary symbolism thus:

> Drawing on Piaget (1972) he uses the example of a child who, in play, may use a doll to represent a person, the primary level of symbolism, but also, subconsciously, to represent his or her annoying new baby brother who needs to be sent on a very long journey. This became a crucial element of his drama as he tried to read the other, hidden levels of significance in the roles his pupils chose to play.
>
> (Davis, in Bolton 2010: vxi)

7 See also Bond (2000) and Davis (2005).

## Works cited

Bolton, Gavin (1979), *Towards a Theory of Drama in Education*. London: Longman.

——(1993), 'Drama in education and TIE: a comparison', in Jackson, ed., *Learning through Theatre*, 2nd edn. London: Routledge, pp. 39–47.

——(1998), *Acting in Classroom Drama*. Stoke on Trent: Trentham.

——(2010), *Gavin Bolton: Essential Writings*, ed. David Davis. Stoke: Trentham.

Bond, Edward (1994), 'The Importance of Belgrade TIE', *SCYPT Journal* 27, pp. 36–38.

——(1995), A Preliminary Note for a Play for Young People (in grant submission to the Arts Council). Big Brum Archives.

——(2000), *The Hidden Plot*. London: Methuen.

——(2009), Programme notes for his play *A Window* commissioned by Big Brum. Big Brum Archives.

Davis, David, ed. (2005), *Edward Bond and the Dramatic Child*. Stoke: Trentham.

Gillham, Geoff (1994), 'What is TIE?' *SCYPT Journal* 27, pp. 4–12.

Heathcote, Dorothy (1981), 'Signs and Portents', *SCYPT Journal* 9, pp. 18–28.

Heathcote, Dorothy and Bolton, Gavin (1995), *Drama for Learning: Dorothy Heathcote's Mantle of the Expert Approach to Education*. Portsmouth, NH: Heinemann.

Hornbrook, David (1989), *Education and Dramatic Art*. Oxford: Blackwell.

Katafiasz, Kate (2005), 'Addendum to Glossary of Terms', in Davis, ed., *Edward Bond and the Dramatic Child.*

O'Neill, Cecily (1995), *Drama Worlds.* Portsmouth, NH: Heinemann.

Piaget, Jean (1972), *Play, Dreams and Imitation in Childhood.* London: Routledge, Kegan Paul.

*Triantafyllidis* online dictionary: http://www.greek-language.gr/greekLang/modern_greek/tools/lexica/triantafyllides/index.html (accessed 1 July 2012).

Vygotsky, Lev (1978), *Mind in Society.* Cambridge, MA: Harvard.

Yeoman, Ian (1995), 'The Actor in Role', *SCYPT Journal* 30, pp. 28–36.

# 3

# 'TIE AND THE THEATRE OF THE OPPRESSED' REVISITED

*Chris Vine*

## Foreword

Re-reading my original chapter twenty years on, I was surprised by how relevant it remains. On the surface it may appear only to record a specific artistic journey undertaken at a particular time, offering along the way an historical account of how one company integrated Theatre of the Oppressed (TO) methodology into its practice, and how, subsequently, it entered the British TIE mainstream. However the chapter actually does more than this and I have chosen to leave it more or less intact, opting to draw out and re-emphasize some of what I consider to be its more universal, and certainly still current, themes.

Of course many things have changed in the intervening years since the chapter was first written. During this period Boal – sadly no longer with us[1] – worked tirelessly, travelling the world to spread and develop his practice while also adding to his body of written work. (See Boal 1995, 1998, 2006.) He implemented projects, led workshops and presented at conferences. Indeed, in the US, The Pedagogy and Theatre of the Oppressed Conference (PTO) was established[2] specifically to propagate his work and its Freirean connections. As a result of these efforts his influence spread exponentially with an ever-increasing number of individual theatre artists and companies adopting and adapting his techniques (if not always his theory and activist intentions); entire movements and centres, such as that founded by Janasanskriti in India, sprung up, embracing his theory and practice; many publications appeared popularizing or interrogating his methods; and increasingly his work showed up as a staple ingredient of theatre courses in colleges world-wide.

This proliferation of TO activity coincided with the emergence, in the late 1990s, of the term 'applied theatre', that was increasingly used to describe a wide range of participatory, socially engaged, often politically inspired, non-traditional theatre practices. (See Introduction, p. 10.) This coincidence was so marked and the association between TO and applied theatre so strong, that in some quarters the terms have become almost synonymous: certainly, many so-called applied theatre practices seem to rely almost entirely on games, techniques and strategies drawn from the TO 'arsenal'.

This same period saw a sharp decline in TIE (and DIE) practices, as exemplified by the demise of a number of the original, influential companies and the closure of educational drama courses in the UK, mainly as a result of changes in the patterns of funding to both the arts and education, and the erosion at the public policy level of those values that had first encouraged and then sustained them. This decline, as other contributors point out, was not confined to the UK. Global monetarist policies and cost-driven, outcomes-led, utilitarian approaches to education rapidly marginalized student-centred, labour-intensive practices that were not readily susceptible to testing and finite measurement. Increasingly, it appeared that TIE had had its day and, as a genre, was rapidly becoming a theatre history footnote. Fortunately, appearances can be deceptive.

New terminology and definitions sometimes conspire to obscure the substance and continued resilience of older theories and practices whose efficacy is not diminished by changing trends or the emergence of more fashionable concepts. Indeed, these trends support the rationale for reproducing much of the original chapter, with the explicit purpose of highlighting some of its original themes from a new perspective in our changed reality.

These themes include the demands the different forms place upon the actor-teacher, as interactive actor or facilitator (the Joker in Boal's terminology); the challenges of working as an educator from *within* the art form of theatre; the challenges of Freirean pedagogy and the concomitant dangers of abandoning his dialectical method in favour of a theatre of 'alternatives' (Boal 1992: 247); and the value of integrating TO practices with the older, eclectic and arguably more flexible participatory methodology developed by the early TIE companies and DIE practitioners such as Heathcote, Bolton and, later, O'Neill (see also Chris Cooper's discussion in chapter 2).

Today these themes are no less pertinent. Many accomplished practitioners have developed potent variations of Boal's original processes, arguing that they are staying true to the original spirit and intentions of his work when tasked to defend themselves in the face of purist objections to their perceived methodological and ideological political heresies.[3] Others, perhaps less sure of their ground, have frequently suffered frustration, as they struggle to adapt the dichotomized forms of TO – that pit the oppressed against the oppressor – to address more diffuse needs that require more complex and nuanced interactions than traditional TO forms can support.[4] Many of these practitioners, working under the umbrella of applied theatre, are unaware of the available wealth of conventions, developed by the DIE/TIE pioneers, that could free them from the frequently restrictive shackles of the TO *forms* and obviate the need to reinvent the wheel – all without any loss of pedagogical efficacy or political integrity!

I hope this revised chapter will foreground these themes and practical concerns, introducing newcomers to the rich history of the intermingled *genres* – TIE and TO – while encouraging novices and veterans alike to reassess and explore the considerable range of conventions and strategies available to them. I hope it will encourage practitioners to consider most carefully the relationship between their intentions and chosen methods. ('Theatre of the Oppressed' is so named for very specific reasons. Can we, should we, reduce it to a collection of techniques? Does it, *de facto*, become something else if we cease to use it to address oppression? Does it matter?) Finally, I hope the thoughts herein might help to halt the tendency of applied theatre to drift towards 'an exclusionary discourse' (Ackroyd 2007) that divorces it from the complex network of its diverse roots, most specifically the nourishment to be acquired from the still-fertile ground of TIE and DIE.

## Beginnings

In 1982 the Greenwich Young People's Theatre (GYPT) began integrating the methodology of the Brazilian director Augusto Boal into its existing TIE practice. It was the first British TIE company to do so, and those early tentative steps marked the beginning of an experiment which was not only to enrich its own work for the next decade but to spread the influence of Boal throughout the TIE movement and to presage the introduction of the Theatre of the Oppressed to a wider constituency of practitioners and teachers in many reaches of the British theatre world. This chapter will examine the reasons for Boal's work proving so peculiarly appropriate for translation to a TIE context and providing such an enduring source of inspiration; it will also highlight the significant changes and developments made by the GYPT company in the process of adapting his methodology to its own usage.

In order to appreciate the potential relevance of Boal's work within a British TIE context, it is important to remind ourselves of some key features of TIE itself: that its prime motivation lies in its explicit educational purpose and that its distinctive formal feature is its use of active audience participation. Central to the work, in all its variety of theatre forms and educational strategies, are the twin convictions that human behaviour and institutions are formed through social activity and can therefore be changed, and that audiences, as potential agents for change, should be active participants in their own learning.

It was within this TIE mainstream that GYPT was working when it first encountered the ideas of Augusto Boal: their relevance to its own practice was immediately apparent. The GYPT Company had a long tradition of innovatory participation work: from the early 1970s it had given particular prominence to the development of complex forms involving the audience working alongside the actors in a theatrical context, often framed within elaborate theatrical environments. This practice was part of a conscious attempt to enhance the cognitive and affective experience of the audience by combining the power of the theatrical experience with techniques developed in DIE. GYPT, like many companies, was subject to a wide variety of influences; inspiration was to be found in diverse quarters including the theatre of Brecht, the DIE work of Gavin Bolton and Dorothy Heathcote and the pedagogy of Paulo Freire. But this eclecticism was tempered by a determination to build a progressive practice within a coherent theoretical framework. At this time GYPT was working to develop a dialectical and materialist practice through which its audiences could be actively engaged as the *subjects* in the learning process but simultaneously be challenged to take a critically *objective* view of their experience, recognizing themselves as part of the same social reality from which the contents of the TIE programmes were drawn.

The central educational concern of the Company was to find ways of reuniting feelings, thoughts and actions in its audiences, and thus create a *praxis* in direct opposition to those practices in both theatre and education that tend to keep them separated.

The company's first encounter with Boal's ideas was through his book *Theatre of the Oppressed*. The connections to its current concerns were immediately apparent:

> In order to understand the poetics of the oppressed one must keep in mind its main objective: to change the people – spectators – passive beings in the theatrical phenomenon – into subjects, into actors, transformers of the dramatic action. … Aristotle proposes a poetics in which the spectator delegates

> power to the dramatic character so that the latter may act and think for him. Brecht proposes a poetics in which the spectator delegates power to the character who thus acts in his place but the spectator reserves the right to think for himself … In the first case a 'catharsis' occurs; in the second an awakening of critical consciousness. But the poetics of the oppressed focuses on the action itself: the spectator delegates no power to the character (or actor) either to act or to think in his place; on the contrary, he himself assumes the protagonic role, changes the dramatic action, tries out solutions, discusses plans for change – in short, trains himself for real action. In this case, perhaps the theatre is not revolutionary in itself, but is surely a rehearsal for the revolution. The liberated spectator, as a whole person, launches into action.
>
> (Boal 1979: 122)

Here was the most coherent theory of the relationship between the actor and the audience (including a view of the social responsibility of the artist) to be propounded since Brecht. In his struggle to make his work increasingly relevant and effective as a tool for liberation, Boal had come to the conclusion that traditional forms needed reworking and, specifically, that the relationship between the actor and the audience must be changed. He believed that feelings as well as the intellect were critical to the development of people's perceptions and understandings and saw in the language of theatre the means to help them think with their whole being – not passively but 'in action'. For him theatre was a dialectical process concerned with the movement of people and matter: 'Theatre is change and not simple presentation of what exists: it is becoming and not being' (ibid.: 28).

It was no coincidence that a crucial stage in the development of Boal's work occurred while he was working in Peru in 1973 on a literacy project derived from the methods of Paulo Freire. Freire believed education should be an active process in the service of social change:

> Teachers and students (leadership and people) co-intent on reality, are both Subjects, not only in the task of unveiling that reality, and thereby coming to know it critically, but in the task of re-creating that knowledge. As they attain this knowledge of reality through common reflection and action (praxis) they discover themselves as its permanent re-creators. In this way, the presence of the oppressed in the struggle for their

> liberation will be what it should be: *not pseudo-participation but committed involvement.*
>
> (Freire 1972: 44; my italics)

Both Freire and Boal espoused the cause of human liberation, and Boal, like Freire, came to realize that the process of liberation begins with our own critically active responses to our experiences of the world. These responses must be authentic; they should not be dictated to us by others – be they teachers, political leaders or actors – defining the nature of our problems, much less *telling* us how to solve them!

It was not surprising, given the pedagogical concerns of the GYPT Company, that the *Theatre of the Oppressed* created so much interest. A real sense of excitement was generated both by its theory and by the descriptions of Boal's methods, particularly his use of image and forum theatre, forms which encourage the spectators to intervene directly, in the first to 'speak' through images made with the actors' bodies[5] and in the second to 'act' in the place of the main protagonists. The company sensed that these methods could add an important new dimension to its work but they remained insufficiently clear to be translated into practice.

Then, by fortunate coincidence, an opportunity arose in 1982 for three company members to attend an international workshop run by Boal in Austria under the auspices of the International Amateur Theatre Association (IATA).

At that time the Company was remounting a full-day high school programme, *Land Fit for Heroes*, that counted among its key objectives an exploration of the relationship between experience, thought and action. At the heart of the programme was an extended, 'lived through' role play drama (a fusion of simulation techniques with what today we would describe as process drama). This took as its starting point the historical events of the 1926 British General Strike. The students were carefully inducted to a variety of roles chosen to reflect a cross-section of society in a provincial industrial town of the period. The roles included coal miners, railway workers, shopkeepers, landowners and powerful industrialists. One group of students was in role as journalists and actually produced editions of a newspaper that reported, in real time, on the unfolding events of the drama. The different socio-economic interests of the groups (e.g. the railway workers and small business owners) were cross-threaded with individual family and class loyalties. Once in their roles, the students worked alongside the actor-teachers, also in role and costumed, within a carefully designed theatrical environment. Although the drama was structured to produce a number of predetermined initial conflicts between groups (based upon the social conflicts of the period), there were no predetermined outcomes. Once the action began, the students were free to respond to events as they thought best, based on their groups' wants and needs. In turn, the actor-teachers' choices and actions proceeded in response to those of the students. No two 'performances' were ever the same, and the finishing point was determined solely by the strictures of time.

The whole undertaking was extremely complex, but we knew from previous experiments with the form and structure that it was very effective for revealing the discrepancies that arise between what people *say* they will do (in theory) and what they *actually do* when confronted with the immediacy of a situation (their practice). The students always became actively involved, immersed in the escalating action of the drama but still able to reflect upon their own behaviours *during* the event itself, frequently stepping in and out of role of their own volition, or 'twilighting' (switching frames back and forth from moment to moment to speak both as themselves *and* through their roles) to comment on what was happening even as they made it happen. The company never paused the action for any reason, only asking for formal reflection once the drama concluded.

*Figure 3.1 Land Fit for Heroes* (Greenwich Young People's Theatre, 1982). Students confront railway magnate Sir Robert during the role-play sequence. Director: Chris Vine. Photo: John Daniel. Courtesy of Greenwich & Lewisham Young People's Theatre Archive.

The drama operated at a very high level of emotional intensity as a 'lived through' experience in real time. Afterwards, the students' initial reflections always focused on their surprise at what they had just done. They recognized the many contradictions between prior expressed intent and actual behaviour but found it hard to analyse the causes. The educational challenge lay in trying to find a method to help them to examine, more objectively, the forces which had been at work on them and which had conditioned many of their responses, but we seemed unable to capitalize on the energy and emotions we had stimulated. The second session of the day was often anti-climactic. What was needed was a new approach that would both maintain the students' emotional engagement, and at the same time provide them with the cognitive space to reflect upon and analyse their recent, charged responses and actions. We were still struggling with this problem when three of us attended Boal's workshop in Austria. The methods he introduced to us were new but not alien. We could see the connections: they resonated with possibility. On our return we decided to experiment with the use of a new form, forum theatre.

## First steps

Working from improvisations the actors created a short play containing conflicts that mirrored many of the dilemmas the students had faced individually and in groups during the earlier drama. The piece ended with the central character, a female railway employee, facing a difficult choice: should she comply with the oppressive demands of her employer and derive considerable benefit for herself and children, but at the expense of her brother and workmates; or should she maintain solidarity, refuse to cooperate and risk the promised security for herself and family?

As the students watched this scenario unfold they recognized a series of dilemmas similar to those they had encountered in the earlier drama. Indeed the main antagonist was Sir Robert, a character they had already encountered face-to-face! When the play ended they were asked what they thought the main *protagonist could* do. They discussed the possible options open to her and speculated on their ramifications *based on their earlier experiences.* The many different suggestions were noted. Then we shifted gear and asked what *they would* do if they were in that situation. More suggestions were offered and there were now some strong disagreements – again informed by their earlier experiences in the drama. After the different opinions had been clarified, the next stage began.

Individual students were now invited to step into the shoes of the central character to test out their ideas. The results were impressive. Hardly ever did the students consciously 'perform'. They wrestled with the problems as they arose, sometimes were devious, sometimes became very angry, often ended up doing the opposite of what they had intended – but seldom gave up. Sometimes they worked alone and sometimes they drew other students into the drama as their friends or workmates. The audience was spellbound. Not only were the students 'watching a performance', they were weighing the chances of their own proposals against the results of the other proposals being tested in front of them. Interestingly, there were still disagreements but seldom a sense of competition: the focus was on helping the protagonist – and defeating the oppressor.

Between interventions the students were asked to give their analysis of what happened. As a group they became the sounding board for objective reflections on the continuing action. Often a student who had just intervened would say, 'I did such and such … the problem is solved', and the others would say, 'No it isn't … ' and predict a consequence. Conversely, some students stepped out saying they had failed to make a difference, only to be contradicted by many positive comments. When disagreements persisted, divergent opinions could be explored by stepping back into the drama. In this way students worked as a whole group, tackling the problems *collectively.*

## Artistic and pedagogical demands

This method of working placed particular demands on the actors, requiring an interesting new orientation of the synthesis between their acting and teaching skills in a way not normally needed in role-play situations where there is not the same element of performance to an audience. The actors needed to be very clear about the motivation of their characters and pursue their objectives truthfully; at the same time they needed to reveal those motivations as subtly as possible and make clear the means, both social and personal, that were available to help the characters achieve their objectives. Only by doing this could they begin to show both their strengths and weaknesses and demonstrate, in the Brechtian sense, the truth of their characters' actions as social beings, rather than individual psyches. But this was happening in improvisations with non-actors and needed orchestrating physically and vocally, in the moment, to make them as accessible and engaging as possible for the rest of the audience.

In addition the actors were also working pedagogically: they needed to give the participants the maximum support and allow them time to explore their ideas and actions. They had to provide them with options to pursue, offer questions that would challenge them, help them to clarify their ideas and spur them on to struggle with the problems they were confronting. It was crucial that the pressures on them were truthfully maintained with no easy or 'magic' solutions allowed, but, at the same time, it was counter-productive, both theatrically and educationally, to overwhelm them with the full force of the character's (or actor's) powers. The aim was to enable the students to think and act, not to defeat and paralyse them. They could only do this in an informed manner if they were able to recognize the truth of the situation. The task of the actors was paradoxical: they had to reveal the reality through distortion, not obscure it by simply reproducing its 'realistic' outward appearance.

A key figure in the forum process is the 'Joker'. The Joker is the facilitator, the direct link between the audience and the dramatic action; she or he has the responsibility for orchestrating the whole event. The Joker must encourage and enable the spectators (or 'spect-actors' as Boal calls them) to intervene. We discovered that this entailed taking time to clarify student suggestions to make sure that students who wished to intervene were clear about the situation, and their intentions within it, before the intervention began. It was also important to ensure the actors understood what a participant wanted, where the intervention was to begin, which characters were present, and so on.

After each intervention, the Joker was responsible for developing – but not imposing – the analysis of what had happened. A careful questioning process was used to elicit contributions, beginning with the individual who had intervened and then opening it to those who had been watching: Did you achieve what you intended?' Why? Why not? What helped you? What stopped you? What did you *feel* while this was happening? What effect did your feelings have on your actions? What have you discovered about the situation – and the other people? What did the audience see? What was achieved? What has been discovered? What do you think he (the antagonist) will do next? What power does he have? What power does our central character have? What else could be done? And so on, helping the group to develop a deeper analysis of the situation and formulate new ideas for further dramatic interventions.

The role of the Joker proved particularly exacting. No two performances of the forum ever followed the same course and it was impossible to predict all the suggestions the audience was likely to make. In rehearsal the actor-teachers had prepared for as many different kinds of interventions as they could anticipate; they were used to responding 'in the moment', through drama, to the demands of young people, and were confident they would be equal to the task as each intervention arose. In the event this proved a great deal more difficult than anyone had foreseen, demanding intense concentration and continuous reassessment of educational and theatrical strategies. For the Joker the challenges were even greater. She or he (in our early experiments two actor-teachers alternated in the role, supporting and learning from each other) was responsible for the ultimate success or failure of the whole forum. We discovered the functions were numerous.

In the first place the Joker must make the aims and procedures of the forum clear, and then set the process in motion. At all times she must be responsive to the desires of the spectators, listening carefully and enabling them, individually and collectively, to pursue their journeys of exploration, without imposing 'solutions' or the analysis of the company upon them.

At the same time, choices have to be made: not all interventions are equally productive and not all suggestions can be pursued. The Joker has to judge when to move from one line of enquiry to another, when to stop pursuing one action and its consequences and allow someone else to open up a new possibility: she must keep the audience focused on the central problems, select the appropriate questions to further the dramatic debate, support the spectators and the actors, *challenge* the spectators, know when to listen, when to speak and when to insist on action ('Don't tell me, show me!'). At all times the Joker must transmit energy, excitement and an enthusiasm for tackling the problems, combined with a genuine interest in all the contributions from the audience. But above all else, the Joker must carry the overall responsibility for structuring and deepening the learning experience as it is unfolding.

For the experienced actor-teacher many of these skills were not in themselves new: what was new was their convergence and concentration upon one individual in a single event. Although the Joker was still part of a team, the focusing of demands on that individual reminded us most sharply of the responsibility and skills required of the drama teacher leading a 'lived through' process drama who, working alone, strives from moment to moment to structure the drama as a dramaturg, while simultaneously deepening the learning of the group and each individual student within it.

It was an important realization that inspired us to re-examine and refurbish the range and depth of our education and theatre skills. It also raised a number of questions about the function of the Joker as originally conceived by Boal. The answers began to emerge as we discovered more details of Boal's actual practice.

## Learning, leading and developing

The first experiment with Theatre of the Oppressed techniques was an extremely exciting and powerful experience. The Company was in no doubt that it wished to explore them further, experimenting with the use of both image and forum theatre, and extending their use into its work with younger students and to students with special educational needs. Over the next few years the process of experimentation and adaptation was rapid and thorough. As it progressed, other companies and individuals began to see the potential of the Theatre of the Oppressed techniques in the TIE context, recognizing the similarities, both in intention and in the skills required, between the two genres. This snowballing interest had a number of effects that further encouraged the development of the work at GYPT. Almost by happenstance we were thrust into a TO leadership role within the TIE movement.

More practitioners wanted first-hand exposure to Boal and his ideas and a small group, led by GYPT actors, attended his workshops in France and Holland. Then in 1984 GYPT presented a *Theatre – and Pedagogy – of the Oppressed* workshop for the Standing Conference of Young People's Theatre (SCYPT); understanding Boal without Freire was unthinkable. Following the interest this generated, in March 1985 the Rose Bruford College of Speech and Drama, Goldsmiths College and the GYPT Company collaborated to organize the first-ever workshops to be led by Boal, with his French company, Le Cetitade, in the UK.

As Boal's ideas spread, different companies and individuals adopted his methods in tune with their own needs. In the GYPT Company, experimentation continued, but it was now more thoroughly informed by knowledge of Boal's own intentions and processes and one thing became rapidly apparent: we had previously misunderstood the structure of forum theatre and misapplied the techniques in a number of particulars.

In its early use of the Theatre of the Oppressed techniques, the GYPT Company would invite the audience to intervene at a predetermined, intense moment of decision and choice (as described above); the actors never completed the play. The audience had to determine the next steps. This approach was similar to Boal's early technique of simultaneous dramaturgy in which he stopped the action at a crisis point and asked the audience to advise the characters – the actors on stage – what to do next. The actors would then enact the various suggestions *on behalf* of the audience. It was during one of these sessions that he famously discovered it was more potent for the spectators to come on stage and do it for themselves!

Boal's classic 'anti-model' does not work like this. In a fully developed forum, the actors present a complete play in which the main protagonist falls victim to his or her oppressor or oppressors, failing to overcome the obstacles they present: the movement, as in a classical tragedy, is from fortune to misfortune, happiness to despair, success – or anticipated success – to defeat and failure. The audience sees the whole story and is invited to consider whether or not the outcome could have been different if the protagonist had made other choices, taken other actions; the play is then replayed and the audience invited to stop it at any moment it feels a crucial mistake is being made by the main protagonist. At this point individuals or groups can intervene to do things differently and try to alter the course of events.

One of the merits of this approach is that it objectifies a complete experience (as portrayed through the play) and asks how we might generalize from the particular, learning from the experiences of others and reapplying those lessons to produce different outcomes in our own lives. It therefore also conveys the implicit belief that outcomes and futures are not predetermined; we are simultaneously the products and creators of our own history.

GYPT decided to explore the method in its original form; it found the perfect vehicle in a one-woman show entitled *No Going Back*, a short play originally devised by the Coventry Belgrade TIE Team. It is set in a women's refuge. The central character, a woman physically abused by her husband, tells her story. She describes her relationship from her early courtship, through her marriage and the birth of her children. She tells how her husband first assaulted her, how the attacks increased in regularity and severity, how others, like her parents, refused to take it seriously, how she kept forgiving him, and even after leaving him would always go back, convincing herself he would eventually change. Now, she says, she will never make those mistakes again, she will never return to him. As she finishes her story, the telephone rings; it is her husband begging her to go home. She agrees and leaves.

Under the direction of Lynne Suffolk (now Clark), the play was produced with the characters from the woman's life peopling the stage as she spoke to them: it was no longer a one-woman play, although none of the other characters ever spoke. The spectators showed no such restraint. As she left the stage, even before the official participation had begun, the female audiences[6] were already calling out to her in exasperation.

Two of Boal's techniques were applied to this programme. Before the play, audience members were asked to make still-images, sharing their visions of romantic dreams (the 'ideal') and the everyday reality of relationships. In this way the area of exploration was delineated in a very concrete manner. The audience was asked to consider what prevents people from changing their circumstances even when they are extremely unhappy. It then watched the play.

Afterwards, there was a short discussion about the behaviour of the woman. The play was then re-presented as forum theatre. The spect-actors were able to stop it and intervene whenever they thought the woman should have taken a different course of action. During the interventions, the other characters (the husband, parents, police and others) *did* now speak, responding directly to the participants.

By contrast to the approach used in *Land Fit for Heroes*, this method did not focus on one moment of choice and decision, but allowed the audiences to examine a number of key incidents in the woman's life, over a period of time. Some focused on the early attitudes of the woman to the man, before they were married, and began questioning social attitudes to gender roles. Others were more interested in the responses of the police or the parents to intimations of violence, and began to examine how society often encourages its victims to believe they are the ones at fault. By experiencing this directly, through the drama, they were able to analyse the complexities and contradictions of people's responses in such situations and – frequently – by reapplying this awareness, display the new strength and persistence they realized was necessary to change them. On several occasions, knowing the teachers had a responsibility to take it further, students told them that these things happened in their families: for them, speaking out for the first time was perhaps the first step towards changing their reality.

The model first employed in *Land Fit for Heroes* had helped the Company to focus very precisely on a single moment of choice that contained in embryo a world of personal and political perspectives, understandings, misunderstandings and illusions. In *No Going Back*, the emphasis was on examining how people become victims, unravelling how they allow their emotions to be distorted and unwittingly collude in their own oppression. In this instance it was essential to examine the early choices and influences on the characters. To focus solely on the moment at the end of the play when the woman decided to return to her husband would not have illuminated the causes of the problem. Everyone could agree that she should not have gone back, but only by exploring the earlier subtle and more insidious pressures did we begin to understand why she did so, and begin to reflect on the importance of those apparently insignificant responses and choices which, in their cumulative effect, predispose us to collude in our own oppression. It also drew attention to the role of the bystander, the person who can choose to turn away, thus tacitly supporting the oppression, or can be persuaded to step forward to become an ally in the fight against it.

## Critique and reassessment

The increasing familiarity with Boal's own working processes led to a reappraisal of a number of the practices which GYPT had originally, and mistakenly, attributed to him. This new awareness also produced a more critical perspective on his theory and practice as it was now clearly emerging. In some instances Boal's original techniques were applied with impressive results, but in other cases variations, like the Company's first mistaken use of intervention at the point of crisis, were deliberately developed and embedded in its approach or further adapted to suit the needs of specific groups such as young adults with moderate and severe learning difficulties.[7] The Company also began to look more closely at Boal's work in relation to other influences and the now well-established range of TIE and DIE practices.

During this period the Company experimented with different variations on the techniques for different age-groups, but whatever the nature of the audience or the fictional context, one revision to Boal's methods remained constant: this was the insistence on analysing the results and implications of the various interventions *as they occurred*. This meant there was rigorous discussion as the work progressed. By contrast, Boal consistently insisted that the Theatre of the Oppressed is about action not words, maintaining that over-analysis disrupts the dynamic of the theatre and the nature of the 'theatrical' debate. He preferred to let the audience's experience, individual and collective, speak for itself, and warned of the dangers of the actors imposing their own solutions upon the spectators. There is much merit in these cautionary impulses: all 'teachers', actors or not, should be aware of the fine line between challenging the views of spect-actors and imposing their own upon them. But there is an important pedagogical distinction between the imposition of a dogma, which closes debate and inhibits thought, and a dialectical process which recognizes bias, highlights disagreements, acknowledges the conflict of opposites and challenges fixed positions.

For many TIE companies, following Freire's lead in 'problematizing reality' was a priority. Indeed, the overt challenging of received truths and accepted norms was seen as an essential step towards encouraging students to deepen their own thinking. The view of the Company was therefore very clear: forum should not be allowed to develop its own momentum, moving from one intervention to the next, without comment. Were it to do so, it would rapidly become a theatre of alternatives that failed to offer any criteria for choosing between them. Each individual would be left to draw his or her own conclusions and might well attribute the success or failure of the various interventions to the individual qualities of the participants rather than to the intrinsic effectiveness of those actions based on an understanding of the forces at work in society. All actions could be applauded as equally good efforts without any objective analysis of their efficacy. A side effect of this could be that our existing judgements of ourselves (often derived from other people's opinions of us) as more or less intelligent and competent individuals would be perpetuated: 'My idea didn't work because I'm not very smart. It's my fault.'

If on the other hand the Joker was prepared to intervene in order to challenge the perceptions of the audience and help them towards an analysis of the inherent contradictions of the real world, then a less comfortable but more profound learning process would become a possibility. This approach did not merely raise a question of technique: it isolated important philosophical differences between the Company's view of education (and the concomitant responsibility of the artist-educator) and Boal's own view of the role and function of his theatre and his actors.

Our view was that the audience members should be encouraged to reflect upon their actions as a group, articulating thoughts and feelings, challenging and being challenged by each other and by the Joker. The Joker should not impose her views but should most certainly accept the pedagogical responsibility to challenge assumptions, highlight contradictions and pursue disagreements. What is at stake is not only the possibility of taking different courses of action, but an understanding of the merits of those actions in relation to what people are trying to achieve, and the material circumstances in which they are trying to achieve it.

Even more important is the question of the *real* nature of the problem. Is it a question of our *individual* qualities or is something deeper at work? Is the problem my inadequacy or the oppressor's unreasonableness? Or does he have more power? Perhaps systemic oppressions and inequalities rooted in race, class, gender or sexual orientation, for example, are at play? Who *does* have power and where does it come from?

Only if difficult questions are posed and different perspectives articulated and made openly available for debate can shared learning begin. If they are not, the danger is that the whole experience is at best therapeutic and at worst depressingly negative, circumscribed by the strengths and weaknesses of each individual's *isolated* attempt to solve what may be a misapprehended problem. The intended strength of starting from the experiences and perceptions of each individual becomes a fatal weakness if these are not drawn into the social framework provided by the forum and reappraised collectively under guidance derived from a progressive pedagogy – a pedagogy that recognizes that many of our received beliefs and perceptions are in fact false. The collective task is to distinguish truth from falsehood in our present reality in order that we may better construct our future reality.

These views do not imply that the educators should know the answers in advance or ignore the need for others to find their own solutions. But they do mean that we should abandon that position which says all points of view are equally valid and the (neutral) artist should only help generate an ever-growing list of alternatives. It is one of the fallacies of social democracy that choice itself is beneficial. Unless people are equipped to understand the true nature of the choices, and can create their own possibilities if they don't like the choices they are *given*, the mere existence of 'alternatives' is meaningless.

Much of Boal's work seemed, wittingly or unwittingly, to have ignored this problem. As time passed this became more explicit. In the concluding paragraph of the English version of *Games for Actors and Non-Actors* he proclaims, 'Let us be democratic and ask our audiences to tell us their desires, and let us show them alternatives' (Boal 1992: 247). This is a long way from the 'rehearsal for the revolution' and the language of dialectics to be found in the original *Theatre of the Oppressed*. Indeed, he seemed to be increasingly at pains to avoid being labelled or identified with any recognized ideology, perhaps in an attempt to avoid being pre-judged or constrained by expectation, or perhaps as a result of the political uncertainties besetting so many people in a rapidly changing world. In his practice his insistence upon the importance of personal experience appeared to turn much of his interventionist theatre towards a theatre of alternatives at the cognitive level and a theatre of therapy at the affective level.

## Coming full circle

At GYPT, the Company, still excited to mine Boal's rich seam of inspiration,[8] was mindful to do so judiciously. The early pedagogical reservations, as discussed above, were accompanied by other theoretical concerns in which pedagogical and ideological questions were entwined. At the heart of these lay the problem of TO's binary juxtaposition of oppressor and oppressed, compounded by the difficulties of trying to explore *systemic* social oppression through the lens of the individual. None of these problems were insurmountable, but we perceived the power of the work was derived from its original intention of combating oppression and thought it important that any adaptations we made did not separate it from this purpose, thereby reducing it to a collection of conventions no longer deserving of the title 'Theatre of the *Oppressed*'. We were certainly not TO purists: innovation and adaptation were always a part of the TIE tradition, but whenever we made changes, we had to ask ourselves, 'What are we trying to achieve and how does it relate to the strengths and purpose of TO?' Or to look at it another way, 'Are the intentions and methodology of TO appropriate to our educational and artistic goals?'

The TIE/DIE canon (I think of the terms as denoting an interrelated continuum of practices) contains a wealth of conventions and strategies appropriate for the exploration of complex material and nuanced relationships that may not be best served by a dichotomous oppressor–oppressed analysis. One of the strengths of TIE is its ability to engage audiences in an interactive 'heteroglossic[9] dialogue between characters and between views of the world' (Jackson 2007: 16), highlighting contradictions, challenging easy definitions of right and wrong, good and bad, and requiring an active search for new meanings. This does not readily align with a Manichean view of human relationships to which TO *can* be susceptible.

I am not suggesting that we were constantly changing our pedagogical or ideological hats. Indeed we prided ourselves on the consistency of our Freirean-infused theoretical framework and the importance of grounding our work in a rigorous socio-political analysis. But we were working in an art form and the best of our already considerable TIE heritage reminded us of the power and importance of intuition, unconfined creativity, our non-linear and illogical interior worlds, the infinite variety of human relationships and, above all, the vast wealth of stories – real and imagined, past and present – we have to draw upon.

This linked to our aesthetic concerns. Working with spect-actors within the framework of forum theatre makes it hard to counteract the vice of realism and avoid the 'talking heads' syndrome. Also, although it undoubtedly promotes dialogue, unlike many forms of participation (such as group role-play), it limits the number of participants who can actually engage *within the fiction* focusing on the few individuals who step forward to intervene. It was important therefore not to confine ourselves to a dominant methodology that limited, or even negated, the full power and potential of the art form.[10]

Thus we came full circle, tempering our enthusiasm for TO with an analytical appraisal of the strengths and weaknesses of the genre, reappraising our own roots and traditions and trying to approach our work more holistically, based upon the needs of our audiences.

## A second look

In the early 1990s my work brought me to the Creative Arts Team (CAT) in New York City. CAT was already acquainted with Boal's work, but to a far lesser degree than the TIE movement in Britain. Boal himself was only just beginning to make an impact in the US and his methods were still incompletely understood. Here was a familiar scenario. This time around, however, I was equipped to match methods with needs – and context. For example, in New York City high schools, it was rare to have more than forty-five minutes with a class at any one time, and very unusual to have a space other than a classroom. Also, CAT actor-teachers seldom worked in teams larger than two! This made mounting a full-blown forum very difficult. However, simultaneous dramaturgy offered many possibilities. Without moving from their seats, students could stop the action and demand that characters 'rewrite' their behaviours to achieve better outcomes. This kind of encounter became even more dynamic when combined with a variation on hot-seating. Instead of a facilitator mediating between audience and actor, the protagonist, still in role, would respond directly to the students, often problematizing the situation by, initially, resisting suggestions and challenging them to explain why they wanted to change things. If convinced, the character would comply and consequences be subsequently explored.

At the other end of the age range, kindergarten classroom residencies offered an ideal opportunity to experiment. Could the very young be motivated by the forum dynamic to step forward, articulate needs, take control and solve problems? At first it seemed unlikely, but the then Program Director, Karina Naumer, hit upon the idea of having the children intervene with, and speak through, puppets. Under her guidance there gradually emerged an intriguing blend of methods that she named 'puppet intervention' (Dishy and Naumer 2010: 17). In these ways, yet again, TIE and TO have proved compatible bed fellows.

Latterly, when I was given the opportunity to create a new MA in Applied Theatre (the first of its kind in the US) there was no question but that TIE and TO should be required components. Separately and together they now provide key planks of practice with diverse audiences in a wide range of venues at home and abroad, including ongoing drama education with student teachers in Rwanda. New generations of artists and teachers are being enthused by the power, potential and challenges of these complementary genres.

## Conclusion

TIE practitioners have always taken responsibility for selecting and shaping the material for their audiences in such a way as to help them make connections and deepen their understanding of their own experiences and other experiences that may *appear* to be very remote to them. While elements of Theatre of the Oppressed can be used to this end they will continue to be employed and developed within the TIE framework, hopefully adhering to Boal's initial *intentions*, though perhaps diverging from some of his more restrictive practices. Whatever the future holds, my personal debt to Augusto Boal for inspiring over three decades of experimentation, debate, development – and change – remains incalculable.

Perhaps this can be a two-way street. Perhaps the wider field of applied theatre can also learn from these experiences, not to 'demote' Boal or diminish his considerable achievement but to refocus and reinvigorate his work by applying it where and when it is really effective, while exploring and incorporating a plurality of less prominent, older but equally effective practices that stand in danger of being lost to new generations of committed, socially engaged theatre practitioners.

## Notes

1 Augusto Boal died on 2 May 2009 at the age of 78.
2 Inaugurated in 1995 at the University of Nebraska, Omaha, with Boal in attendance. It has become a national organization.
3 For an example of the controversies that beset the TO fraternity see Paterson (2011).
4 At a recent conference of the *American Alliance of Theatre & Education* (AATE) I listened to a colleague explain her frustration at how hard it is

to use TO to explore relationship conflicts without demonizing one or other party as an oppressor! Her concern prompted me to observe that a monkey wrench is useless when you need a screwdriver! Can we acquire the right tools for the job rather than make do with the only ones we have?

5 This was different from but resonated and connected with Dorothy Heathcote's use of the sculptor and, variously, images, effigies, waxworks and depictions.

6 The piece played mainly to female upper secondary school students but also to some female adult audiences, including some in women's refuges.

7 For more details see earlier version of this chapter in 2nd edition of *Learning through Theatre* (1993).

8 Among other developments it devised a dance-based forum, created forums *for* the elementary age range and TO models *with* young unemployed adults, and inserted mini-forums and other TO strategies into process drama based TIE projects.

9 Mikhail Bakhtin coined the term 'heteroglossia' to describe a multifaceted diversity of voices, perspectives and feelings interacting within an artistic framework (Bakhtin 1994: 113).

10 It was for these reasons that we experimented with staging (playing in the round, thrust and traverse) dance/movement and the use of concrete symbols (e.g. a long swathe of silky fabric was the only 'prop' in *No Going Back*).

## Works cited

Ackroyd, J. (2007), 'Applied Theatre: An Exclusionary Discourse?', *Applied Theatre Researcher/IDEA Journal*, No. 8. Online at www.griffith.edu.au/–data/assets/pdf_file/0005/52889/01-ackroyd-final.pdf.

Bakhtin, M. (1994), *The Bakhtin Reader*, ed. Pam Morris. London: Edward Arnold.

Boal, A. (1979), *Theatre of the Oppressed*. London: Pluto Press.

——(1992), *Games for Actors and Non-Actors*, trans. Adrian Jackson. London: Routledge.

——(1995), *The Rainbow of Desire*. London: Routledge.

——(1998), *Legislative Theatre*. London: Routledge.

——(2001), *Hamlet and the Baker's Son*. London: Routledge.

——(2006), *The Aesthetics of the Oppressed*. London: Routledge.

Dishy, A. and Naumer, K. (2010), 'Puppet Intervention in the Early Childhood Classroom: Augusto Boal's Influences and Beyond', in *Youth and Theatre of the Oppressed*, ed. Peter Duffy and Elinor Vettraino. New York: Palgrave Macmillan, pp. 17–43.

Freire, P. (1972), *The Pedagogy of the Oppressed*. London: Penguin.

Jackson, A. (2007), *Theatre, Education and the Making of Meanings*. Manchester: Manchester University Press.

Paterson, D. (2011), 'Putting the Pro in Protagonist', in '*Come Closer': Critical Perspectives on Theatre of the Oppressed*, ed. Toby Emert and Ellie Friedland. New York: Peter Lang Publishing, pp. 9–20.

# Part II

# WAYS OF WORKING

## Introduction

The chapters that follow examine different working practices in TIE and the principles that, in the view of the authors, underpin that practice. David Pammenter's essay draws on, but substantially develops, his original chapter (1980, revised 1993), itself a classic statement of what was at the centre of the TIE process since its inception: devising. Recognising the more complex challenges faced by applied theatre practitioners in the early twenty-first century, Pammenter offers not a how-to-do-it essay on devising, rather a reflection on the philosophical, ideological and political questions that must underpin the creation of any new TIE programme or the closely related practice commonly known as 'theatre for development' (TfD). Pammenter brings to bear both his extensive experience as a TIE practitioner through the 1970s and 1980s and his more recent TfD experience – as tutor and as practitioner in sub-Saharan Africa. Indeed the fundamental questions he raises about the function of education in relation to devising seem just as pertinent now as they did in 1980 and 1993.

Mary Cooper offers a complementary and, in many ways, a counter-view of the creation of TIE programmes: while she shares many of Pammenter's philosophical assumptions about the purpose of TIE, she argues forcefully for a far more prominent role for the writer as artist in his or her own right. In part, as she explains, this derives from the particular experiences and pressures of working to commission in the very different economic climate of twenty-first-century Britain and across a variety of theatre contexts, from TIE through to community drama. Her view is also reflective of the trend away from collective devising that has taken place since the late 1990s in most TIE and YPT companies in Britain and elsewhere.

Yet further angles on the creative processes involved in TIE work are offered in three shorter essays dealing with the performance of TIE (chapters 6, 7 and 8). Jackson begins by examining the broad challenges faced by the TIE actor working in both 'classic' TIE and 'museum theatre', and draws on elements of acting theory to identify some of the key – and interconnected – qualities and skills required. Two practitioners, Chris Cooper and Lynn Hoare, each from very different working contexts, then tackle, variously, questions of performance and facilitation. In discussing the 'TIE Performer' (otherwise known as 'actor-teacher'), Cooper interrogates a distinguishing feature of much TIE practice: the duality of the TIE actor as theatre artist (embodying the theatrical narrative and highlighting significance) and educator, intent on encouraging audience members to excavate their own meanings, both individual and social. In a provocative essay, he draws upon the work and theories of the playwright Edward Bond to propose that a new approach to acting (or 'enacting') – one that creates both a 'site' and a 'gap' for the audience to fill with meaning – is essential to the genuinely educative and enriching experience that TIE can provide.

In contrast, Lynn Hoare explores the function and processes of the TIE actor as facilitator, sometimes working in role, but often leaving the character behind to communicate with the audience unmediated by the mask of fiction or dramatic 'distance'. The role of the facilitator has emerged as perhaps the pivotal role in contemporary TIE and applied theatre practice more generally. Hoare, drawing on her experience of creating programmes that deal directly with issues of sexual health and relationships, examines the facilitator's challenges and requisite skills, and proposes a framework for training and development.

Finally, Steve Ball – a contributor to the 1993 edition, in which he discussed theatre in health education – reports here on recent developments in building-based theatres, offering examples of how 'mainstream' repertory theatres, where once attached TIE companies may have thrived, are now reconceiving their educational outreach missions. As former TIE practitioners, like himself, assume new roles in the theatre establishment, is the influence of TIE still discernible in the emerging practices and principles?

# 4

# THEATRE AS EDUCATION AND A RESOURCE OF HOPE

## Reflections on the devising of participatory theatre[1]

*David Pammenter*

### Introduction

This chapter is about devising and constructing theatre projects as forms of pedagogic and counter-cultural action. Though sometimes bleak in perspective, the chapter is driven by the need to develop creative 'resources of hope'. I should make it clear from the outset that I am concerned with devising theatre in education (TIE) as an art form that examines, questions and represents the realities of our current human condition and makes new meanings in pursuit of progressive change and positive human development. I am not concerned with the use of theatre in education to support the current dominant cultural, educational and political orthodoxies, or as a 'bandage' to cover cultural wounds without diagnosing their causes and trying to heal them. There is no single way to devise participatory theatre. New creations will take many forms and draw upon many methods and processes. Different cultural contexts will require different kinds of interaction and innovation. However, making meaningful theatre should always be a contextually specific, audience-centred, dialectical process that strives to deepen our understanding of the world and ourselves so that we can change those things that diminish our humanity.

As part of my argument, I will explore some of the common ground between TIE and Theatre for Development (TfD). This will inevitably be connected to my own journey, but its intention is not personal. It is to assist us in the creation of the new work that meets the needs, wants ns of the young people and adults we serve: it will order crossings.

rofound, the work of TIE, Drama in Education (DIE) dresses questions of identity and action, so perhaps we should gin with reflections on who, what and where we – our audiences and ourselves – are. What is our individual and collective sense of our own being and becoming? Are we the subjects of our own world or the objects in somebody else's? These are fundamental questions about how we see and understand each other and the world we inhabit. I believe our human concerns should dictate that as artists – devisors, writers, directors, actors or facilitators – we engage our audiences in the pursuit of freedom. Our theatre practices, whatever we call them, should promote an exploration of the true meaning of our experiences as social beings. We either contribute to the struggle for human rights, including the rights of the child, or we become the cultural tools of the prevailing political and economic forces that demand subservience to the profit motive above all human needs.

In order to devise a socially relevant theatre of action, we need to consider some key questions. What is theatre? Who is it for and what does it say? How does it work, and in whose interests? Theatre, at its best, is a collective action and an exploration of human experience; it is a forum for examining our values: social, political, moral and ethical. It is concerned with the interaction of these values at the emotional and intellectual levels. It is a medium for collective and individual reflection. I say 'at its best' because much of what passes for theatre these days has little to do with any of the above.

TIE, defined both as an artistic medium for the communication and questioning of human experience, and as an educational force in the service of individual and social change is, and always has been, primarily concerned with the development of our human values. It can help us probe our 'being' and prefigure our 'becoming'. Our TIE praxis[2] should 'disturb' our audiences. It should help them make and remake meaning from out of that disturbance. It should help them reassess the way they perceive the world and their roles within it. If we truly believe in the humanising power of theatre, then as theatre artists we must, by extension, be concerned with concrete issues of justice, rights and responsibilities. This holds true whether we are creating the theatre, presenting it, observing it or participating in it. Our theatre must be about the amplification of voices and the revelation of experiences that cause us to question our perceptions, assumptions, beliefs and actions. Thus, the devising process itself is a form of cultural action.

According to Renato Constantino,

> the culture of a people may be defined as the organisation of shared experience which includes values and standards for perceiving, judging and acting within a specific social milieu at a definite historical stage … [P]atterns of behaviour and thought, concepts, standards and values encompass the economic, political, social and aesthetic areas of human life and society … [B]oth culture as patterns of thought, concepts, standards and values, and culture as aesthetics are shaped by material life. In turn, culture by shaping human consciousness and defining the self-view of the people and their view of the world also influences the development of material conditions.
>
> (Constantino 1985: 14)

Culture is the product of a distillation of social experience as people cope with existential realities: it requires effective social communication. Communication itself is crucial to society's development because, essentially, it shapes social relationships:

> At an early stage of social development, communication was a bond among equals but, as society developed and stratified, the means of communication became privately owned and controlled and were used by its owners as a medium for reproducing the types of society favoured by ruling groups. As such, communication was transformed into a channel of domination.
>
> (ibid.: 15)

Communication, what it contains and how it occurs, is crucial in terms of both the context and process of education. Education and communication are central cultural components on which human groups have always been dependent for their sense of identity and history. As I have argued elsewhere (Pammenter 2006: 199), the way a social group sees itself, the way it promotes its ideas, values, ethics, rights and responsibilities, is embedded in its systems of education. The ownership of the means of communication determines the interests it serves. For example, there is a huge difference between knowledge and information. We inhabit a world where the constant flow of information replaces thinking, conditions our perceptions of reality and defines truth. Indeed, information is increasingly seen as synonymous with knowledge and understanding. The information we are fed seems to obviate the need for further inquiry; it erodes our imaginations and capacities for critical thinking. These practices within the neo-liberal paradigm are largely under the control of transnational corporations and are consciously intended to constrain or prevent our imaginations from nourishing our humanity.

True learning springs from the need to know. The best TIE has always focused on this need. In turn, this focus has historically provoked the questions: What is learning? What is knowledge? How is it constructed? How does it occur? What should be the contribution of the student? Today, worldwide, the notion of learner-centred education, starting with the students' experiences, has largely been abandoned or marginalised – along, of course, with any interest in the students' personal histories. This marginalisation of real peoples' histories in our culture and schooling is one of the prerequisites of the process of de-historicisation. If we lose our owned sense of our histories we become dislocated from our collective identities. The individual, social and cultural sense of who we are, what we have done and what we might yet achieve, becomes fragmented and thus we come to believe the prevailing narratives about what we can and can't do, what is good for us – and who should decide.

Little has changed since the advent of mass education. Broadly speaking, during the nineteenth century there were two types of 'schooling' in the UK. Neither had much to do with real education. Neither saw their function as helping the child to fulfil his or her potential but each had its own curriculum to suit the purposes defined for it by the ruling elite. There were the public[3] or grammar schools for the sons of 'gentlemen' destined for leadership, and there was an elementary school tradition to equip the masses with just sufficient skills to work as needed to keep society running in such a way as to maintain the status quo. In short, they were taught to be of use but to know their place and, to that end, forms of social communication, laws, rituals, systems and orthodoxies of social order and religion had their role to play in ensuring the unchangeable order of things. Occasionally, exceptional talents were recognised and individuals were able to transcend their class origins. These were the exceptions that proved the rule. During the period of colonialism these orthodoxies began to envelop most of the world.

The questions to be confronted in the twenty-first century are as stark now as they were almost two hundred years ago. What is the purpose of education? Who is it for and what should it say and do? Is it system-centred or child-centred? Should it adapt students to fit the world or equip them to change it?

By and large, schooling has dictated the value generally placed upon our forms of cultural expression, including our social rituals and forms of representation such as literature, theatre, television, film and the visual arts. Quality has been separated from taste, high art from popular culture. Similarly, our personal narratives have been shaped by curriculum choices that have crucially impacted our understanding of ourselves as historical beings. We have internalised a distorted view of our place in the order of things and in so doing have helped to confirm the distorted meta-narratives that contradict our lived experience. Our education system, with some welcome exceptions, has little to do with critical thinking and authentic human development. It has everything to do with the demands of a post-industrial and technological society and the economic imperatives of a neo-liberal New World Order.

## Examples of practice in TIE

If this analysis is correct, what can we as artist-educators do about it? Perhaps we can look to the future by developing a form of theatre-making, a theatre *as* education, drawn from our experiences in TfD, TIE and DIE – all of which recognise the interconnectivity of research and creativity that are central to the devising process and which themselves can take us, the devisors, on a significant educational journey. The experimentation and analysis embedded in the action of theatre-making, and the subsequent testing and development in light of audience responses, exemplify the pedagogical process of praxis which is at the heart of our work.

Let me take as an example of what I mean a programme from the early period of TIE. *The Price of Coal* was devised in 1973, in Coventry, as a response to the media misrepresentation of the miners' strike and political vilification of the miners and their communities. We devised a two-part, two-visit programme for older elementary school children (9–11 years) in order that the hidden histories and social realities of the miners might surface and be understood by the children of Coventry at a time when the media and political machinery sought to prevent it. It was a programme that placed the children in role as miners in the 1840s concerned with their working conditions. The narrative action of this participatory programme could not proceed without real decisions from the children, both in and out of role. However, informed decisions would not have been possible without the living 'research' opportunities that the in-role, fictional experiences provided. In turn, the validity of those decisions could only be tested in action. How successful were the actions to which the decisions led?

In part two of the programme, following the death of the central character (and after much preparation work with the teacher between visits) the children voiced the historical concerns of the now long dead real miners at a 'Royal Commission of Inquiry'. (The actual historical event of 1842 led to extensive reform in the coal mining industry.) The children took over all the character roles and the actors receded into the background. At this stage the piece was entirely owned by the children. They were writing, performing and evaluating, both as characters and as themselves, the consequences of their own decisions and actions.

This kind of participatory ownership developed in much of our early work in Coventry. In the *Rare Earth Trilogy*, for example, all the elements of this three-visit programme were very different in both form and content but were all concerned with human progress and the environment. In the first visit, the form used was a combination of comedy and documentary as the archetypal Ramsbottom family from England colonised, stole and developed America at the expense of the indigenous peoples. In part two, the play, *Drink the Mercury*, dealt with industrial pollution. The piece drew upon traditional Noh and Kabuki theatre forms. It told the true story of the death of a child living on the shores of Minamata Bay in Japan: one of many people

*Figure 4.1* *Rare Earth* (David Holman and Belgrade TIE, 1973/restaged by M6 Theatre, 1981). The mercury-emitting Chisso Factory. Photo courtesy of M6 Theatre.

who suffered as the result of mercury poisoning from the industrial practices of the Chisso Fertiliser Company. The play raised questions about power, greed, responsibility, care of the environment and the attempt to silence the truth.

Part three was an entirely participatory drama/simulation about the distribution and allocation of the world's natural resources. All the action was initiated and undertaken by the children. This child-centred work drew upon the newly encountered pedagogy of Paulo Freire and other educational theorists concerned with child-centred practices of teaching and learning. Freirean pedagogy and, later, the Freirean-inspired practices of Augusto Boal, were also evident in the work of Greenwich Young People's Theatre (GYPT) in its programmes about racism (*Race against Time*), history (*The Great Illusion*), education (*School on the Green*) and processes of change (*Circles of Fire*). There were similar developments and achievements across the country in Bolton, Leeds, Nottingham, Lancaster, London and elsewhere. The companies employed many different forms and structures for their programmes, but all placed the twin ideas of student ownership and participation high on their educational and artistic agendas.

The power of these practices was recognised surprisingly quickly and spread rapidly to many parts of the world from Africa to Australasia, Scandinavia to Asia, Latin America, the Philippines and the Middle East. As time has passed, names and terms have changed. TIE practice and its influence, often unrecognised, has been integrated into Theatre for Development (TfD) and other applied theatre practices, but the significance of the early work still remains as a powerful example of a response and resistance to monological, disempowering and coercive educational and cultural practices.

In a very few years, TIE managed to articulate a coherent counter-cultural alternative to the dominant education and theatre practices of the time. Not only was it pedagogically dissident in its embrace of student-centred teaching and learning but it was also structurally provocative, attempting to work from the bottom up rather than the top down, built upon grass-roots, sustainable partnerships with classroom teachers in local schools. It gave rise to relationships wherein both parties could engage in pedagogical and artistic discussions, learning from each other and developing innovative, co-intentional practices that frequently addressed the same challenges from different perspectives, using different but complementary methods. Unfortunately, the more control that was exercised over teachers by prescribed curriculum demands, and over companies by funder-driven outcomes expectations, the less viable the progressive relationships became.

Within the theatre industry itself, TIE represented a very conscious challenge – and threat – to traditional hierarchies and artistic orthodoxies. The companies themselves were largely non-hierarchical. Many operated formally as collectives; many others, even when subject to traditional management structures, were non-hierarchical and cooperative in spirit if not always in fact. Artistic authority was recognised where needed (in the roles of director, writer, musician stage manager etc.), but companies frequently challenged the autonomy of the director as sole arbiter of company policy, artistic standards and employment practices. (The TIE movement even managed to negotiate its own specialised contract within British Equity, the actors' union.) Of course, in turn, the traditional relationship with a passive audience was also disrupted as new forms were developed that invited untutored 'amateurs' into the previously privileged preserve of the professional artist!

On all fronts, individuals – children/audience members, teachers, theatre artists – were empowered to ask questions, exercise choices and make new, often subversive, meanings that had previously been denied to them. All of this ran counter to the philosophy of centralised, top-down, curriculum-centred, outcomes-driven and funder-controlled projects that had previously dominated education and the arts. It is these counter-cultural values and progressive practices that need to be vigorously reasserted in the face of the prevailing coercive trends that emphasise conformity but deride collectivism, promote individualism but stifle critical thinking, and seek to measure standardised achievement, all in deference to the profit motive and financial bottom line. The way forward may lie in the reconceiving of TIE as a form of participatory devising or, put another way, theatre-making *as* education.

## From TIE to TfD: new conceptual frames of reference

Let us begin this section with the premise that all people are artists. We all shape and tell stories. We use them to make sense of the world. When we hear vivid stories, either real or imagined, we are entertained, intrigued, perhaps disturbed by them. If so, we have to reflect on them to make sense of them and that means we must engage in our own journey of discovery in recognising the old and responding to the new. This is the beginning of a process of conscientisation.[4] We have to ask questions about the stories but our first questions raise more questions. They require analysis, judgments of what is useful or not useful, right or wrong. In making sense of the 'd what happens to others – the people in the stories – we sider their reality. If we are allowed to participate in the s as we do in participatory theatre, we might want to o perspectives, suggest ways forward or solutions to the prob do so we first need to understand them, and we have to recognise that the 'other' participants might have different views from ours.

We have to listen, hear what others say and either justify or change our own position. We are drawn into dialogue. In the search for solutions we have to collaborate and communicate with others. We have to take leaps into the unknown, to be open to the processes of adaptation, to use our imagination, which is the source of our creativity. It is our imagination that fuels our power to adapt, and adaptation – of ideas, opinions, replacing old beliefs with new facts – is the basis of education. Our imagination drives our ethical, human development. It distinguishes us from other animals. Without it we cannot develop except as de-humanised objects in the hands of the de-humanisers. As Edward Bond puts it:

> Imagination makes us human but may also make us inhuman. Imagination is basically the desire – the need – to be at home in the world. But our societies are unjust. When we try to make ourselves at home in injustice we corrupt our imagination. We deny our deepest need. We become angry and destructive … Imagination seeks justice. Fear may corrupt imagination so that it seeks violence and destruction. The structure of imagination is drama. From this it follows that imagination is the basis of our humanness and secures or destroys our place in reality … The strength of a society's search for justice is always reflected in the state of its drama.
>
> (Bond 2000: 57–58)

If imagination is the source of our values, which interact with our ideas of self and otherness, then in devising our theatre programmes we must consciously avoid the dominant ideological influences, but we must also avoid the construction and imposition of our own ideologies, orthodoxies or dogmas. We must be concerned with the development of our audiences' critical thinking.

It is perhaps helpful here to look at past practices in TIE and TfD. Typically, we tried to sharpen contradictions, to present irreconcilable views and 'awkward' perspectives, not explain them. Not surprisingly, we were frequently accused of political and pedagogical bias but understood that it came from those who were afraid that knowledge was a dangerous thing, who were opposed to student-centred pedagogy and who sought to control the generation of knowledge and access to it.

In what we were devising, we sought to create a disturbance, through our images, our metaphors, our dramatic juxtapositions, and, by implicating our audiences, encourage them to intervene in role, and require them to make difficult choices, usually in the face of irreconcilable demands and opposing actions. It was therefore crucial also to create space for critical reflection. Ours was not a theatre of message transmission and we did not see that our task as storytellers included imposing conclusions. Rather we were concerned with questions about the politics and poetics of representation which are often in opposition to the normative concerns of inclusion and conformity. We were concerned with creating contradictions so the child might ask 'why?' – with creating a theatre that supported children's capacities to *imagine* their own solutions. Other theatre practices had done this before; we see it in the work of Brecht, of Meyerhold, of the *jongleur* from the third century, and more recently in the art of Dario Fo.

The actor-teacher, in common with the jongleur, street performer, clown or storyteller of old, was concerned to engage, surprise, ask questions, make demands, show contradictions, provoke laughter, induce discomfort, arouse emotions and stimulate intellectual reflection. The actor-teacher wanted to create an existential 'feeling' experience for the participant, but also to induce critical reflection on what they were experiencing. We offered contemporary stories but also drew upon different times and places in order to connect our identities to those of others near and far. We moved from personal, specific perceptions to a broader critical understanding and social contextualisation of our individual responses.

Our theatre often worked through metaphor. Theatre, like the art of storytelling, has a long history of the use of metaphor as a means to challenge audiences to make new meanings from apparently familiar material, to speak of things that they might otherwise find hard to name. Metaphor allows audiences to speak of things that politically, socially or culturally they are expected to avoid. Metaphor helps create an aesthetic distance that allows us to reflect upon experiences that a documentary approach to our own everyday reality may obscure. This does not mean that we ignore real life – quite the contrary – but we approach it differently by distorting it, through the fiction, so that it can be seen, analysed and reflected upon more clearly. This is the paradox of art.

Many of these insights, developed in the work of TIE and DIE, were shared in common with emergent, people-centred TfD practices; hardly surprising when you understand that much early TfD was implemented by practitioners steeped in TIE/DIE methodologies or in similar cultural and educational perspectives. However, unlike TIE, early TfD was soon appropriated for message transmission, largely in the service of non-governmental organisations (NGOs) that had outcome-led agendas designed to meet utilitarian objectives. Although this was understandable in the face of the perceived urgency of the situations they needed to address, it meant the work tended to be normative in intention and, we can claim with the wisdom of hindsight, not very effective. There were many examples of content shaped into propagandist warnings such as, 'Sex without a condom can kill' or thinly disguised invocations to 'do what the experts in the NGOs tell you as they know best!' Although there were frequently local forms of expression to hand – storytelling, puppetry, dance, music, ritual celebrations and traditions of community education to name a few – these forms, and their potential as media for learning, were often ignored and the question of affective pedagogy seldom broached. Not surprisingly, it became increasingly clear that these generalised practices were ineffective. The work either failed to recognise the specific challenges of the local cultural context or assumed an alienating didactic stance that ignored the need for people to recognise their own needs and solve their own problems. (Compare Veronica Baxter's discussion of similar challenges faced in South Africa, chapter 12.)

The marginalised, disenfranchised and oppressed are the best people to articulate their needs, born from their profoundly understood histories and current realities. When they are asked to tell their own stories, unexpected preoccupations emerge. They may appear not to have any answers but usually no one has asked. They are often acutely aware of their silent complicity in their own oppression and, offered the chance, eager to explore the alternatives: 'What if we had not accepted that outcome as inevitable but had done something different? What would that be like?'

We have many creative tools that can be used to explore such questions: improvisation, storytelling, sculpting still images, making physical 'machines', drawing pictures, writing poems, singing and dancing. By sharing histories and identifying common experiences, using these methods, we found people could assert their identities and define their collective needs. If these ideas were given theatrical form, by refining, shaping and rehearsing them in order to re-present them to an external audience, their significance was further deepened. The definition of theatrical objectives – 'What do we want to say to our audience? Why and how?' – and the actions of repetition and refinement that are the essence of devising and rehearsal, continually produce new insights. It is then just a short step from enacting present realities to imagining future possibilities – and asking an audience to do the same. This could be thought of as the people's process of devising. In many ways it is similar to the process of devising common to TIE in its heyday.

Many of us working in the TfD field began to see how participants in 'consciousness-raising' workshops frequently wanted to share their discoveries with others through performance, working as facilitators and actors themselves, ready to test their new perceptions in the public domain. The original workshop participants were transitioning to something akin to a cross between actor-teachers and peer educators as they shared their new knowledge with others.

Thus, the functions of the 'invading'[5] TfD team could now be placed in the hands of the original participants. They became the cultural creators who were consciously making their own meaning in pursuit of change in their own lives. This was a dialectical process of reclaiming ownership and autonomy. It does not of itself create revolution on a national or international stage, but it begins the process of

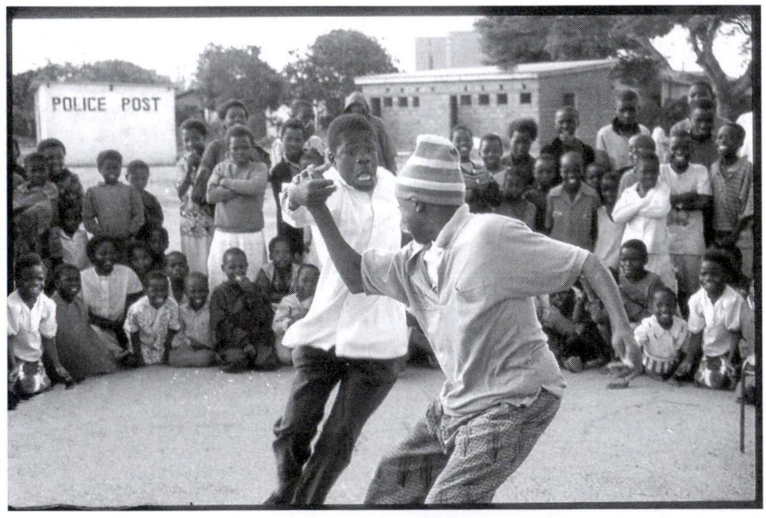


*Figure 4.2* The *Fountain of Hope* project (collaborative TfD project with cdcArts, 1999). Zambian street children perform a devised play about their experiences of prejudice. Facilitators: David Pammenter and Alex Mavrocordatos. Photo and copyright: Alex Mavrocordatos.

conscientisation, through imagination and creativity, that may lead to a people-centred practice of self-development.

## The new paradigm: a closer look

It might be useful at this point to examine what I have been suggesting by taking a closer look at a specific project. I was working in Zambia in 2000 on a number of TfD projects, one of which was concerned with street children. The project took place in the north of the country with the small non-government organisation (NGO) called Safe T Child.

The participants were all street children, aged between six and thirteen. They were all at the bottom of the social hierarchy, which impacted heavily on their self-image. Many of their stories were about the consequences of being at the base of the social pyramid – in the family, when they were still in one, and later, on the street, when they were not.

Their collective experience, which became the source of the theatre they made, was of living in a world where everyone was 'doing them a favour'. They felt they were obliged to accept their whole existence because of the 'goodness' of somebody else: a cousin, an uncle, or perhaps an NGO worker. As a result they were continually reacting to coercion or oppression that they internalised as a form of silent acquiescence and self-marginalisation.

They all had low status in relation to those around them. In the family, in cases where a family had taken them in after the loss of their own parents, they were the ones who were required to do the menial tasks. They had to demonstrate their gratitude and accept their place in relation to the family group. In most cases they were obliged by those in control to pray a lot and to thank God and their benefactors for their survival! To them fell the tasks of gathering the wood, fetching and carrying, cleaning the yard, doing the washing, while of course being last in line for everything they needed, including food. They had to acknowledge their status as being placed below the 'real' children of the family in terms of importance, acceptance, respect or even recognition. Many were abused physically, psychologically and sexually. Most had run away and become street children to avoid this kind of bonded slavery.

Our project was conducted with around twenty children. We started with the usual introductory icebreakers and early exercises designed to help us get to know each other and begin building relationships. Then we began to facilitate the telling of their stories and the identification of the common experiences between them.

One of the most useful processes in this kind of theatre work uses letter 'writing'[6] as a way to relocate the self in relation to one's own history and in the context of one's own family. In this case, our participants were asked to make their own life maps, which were depictions of their journeys, showing significant events, including memories from their homes. They created coloured drawings, moving or still images, sculptures and environments. Sometimes they made fragmented maps and diagrams. The focus was not on the spoken word but on the visual, audio and kinaesthetic feelings and memories. Words came later as still images were brought to life or themes enacted through improvisations.

It was not a quick exercise. It spanned several workshops over a period of time. As it progressed participants wrote letters to their deceased parents and grandparents. Then they wrote letters out of the past *from* their parents and grandparents. The exercise asked them to imagine what the hopes and dreams from specific family members could have been. These were imagined journeys to the location of their *own* becoming rather than reinflicted versions of their weaknesses and failure to achieve imposed upon them from the dominant ideology. These life-maps and letters helped build collective stories of their 'arrival' and experiences in the present. They required a re-consideration of their common sense of injustice and the possibility of change: 'What do you recognise in each other's stories? What made you happy or unhappy? What did you do? Did you speak about it? Who to? Did you ever confront the people causing you problems? Could you? Why? Why not? What do you think the other figures in your stories need to think about? What should they do? What would your parents or grandparents have wanted you to do? How do you decide what action you could take? How do you take it?' The problematising, over time, went deep.

These exploratory workshops were based on the need of the children to find their collective voice. They were about revealing hidden connections. They were rooted in the children's 'need to know', their need to rediscover and talk about their lives. They were, in the Freirean sense, 'unveiling reality' (Freire 1993: 51) and looking for ways in which they could demand that others confront it with them.

Having used these techniques to research themselves, the next step was to decide what to share with an audience, and how to share it in such a way that the audience members would not remain passive but would be required to think critically as citizens implicated in the young people's stories. This then was the journey from researching to devising to performance. It entailed an exploration of the available forms of presentation and participation that a theatre event might use.

Our job as theatre facilitators and co-intentional devisers was to pose questions to the young people to continue developing their critical thinking abilities. It was also, at this point, to work on building their practical theatre skills, and their understanding of theatre forms, both of which would enable them to honour and illuminate their stories and to challenge their audience to engage with the issues. There were many questions requiring practical answers: What form should our stories take? How should we construct them? What journey should we take our audience on? Who are they and what do we want them to think about? How can we help them to understand us? Where might the rhythm of the piece be flexible to adjust to audience responses? Which indigenous forms can best 'hook' the audience and create a strong focus? What other forms will suit our purpose? What, when and how do we want the audience as participants to feel, think and reflect? How do we create time and space for the audience to reflect? Where, when and how can we sharpen the contradictions in the audience's perceptions of our and their experiences? Where and how do we wish to give them the opportunity to question themselves about their feelings, views and responsibilities?

These are the same questions which any deviser or writer working in the TIE genre is obliged to ask when creating models that allow for genuine participation and the opportunity for audiences to discover new meanings. By posing them to the marginalised young people in their roles as co-creators we entered the co-intentional process of educational dialogue of which Freire speaks. We began to resist the silencing of the self that is imposed by the orthodoxies of the powerful. We were not preoccupied with theatre literacy or skills – though these were important. We did not offer introductory improvisation classes or run voice classes: rather we were concerned with a commitment to collective creativity, the collective imagination, critical thinking and action for change. When the desire to express oneself is as strong as it was for the young people, clearly the processes of creating, shaping and presenting the material go hand in hand. Distinctions between the generation of text and its rehearsal are largely superfluous. We devised co-intentionally a theatre event that was a reflection on and of our experiences but which was also designed as an intervention to 'disturb' the perceptions of others, the audience members, who were also part of the same reality that the street children inhabited. We were simultaneously creating and participating in a process of transformation.

This process of simultaneous devising and rehearsal resulted in the use and re-creation of indigenous forms drawn from the local culture. These forms were evaluated in terms of their potential for audience engagement. We did not choose to use in their entirety any of the extant models of participatory theatre with which we, as experienced facilitators, were familiar. We chose instead to incorporate, eclectically, any elements that supported audience engagement, and the storytelling and skill levels of the young actors. We constantly changed frames for the audience, moving backwards and forwards in time between past and present, shifting place as well as time, changing styles, drawing on a range of African and European forms and improvising new dialogue in response to audience reactions.

The performances took place on a patch of land by the side of a road in front of the base of Safe T Child which the children had decorated with painted cloths and a few tables and chairs. As people arrived, the children greeted them with songs of welcome and moved among their guests introducing themselves, shaking hands and telling their guests what the event was going to be about. The children then performed their song of introduction followed by their scenes.

There were four pieces of theatre each lasting around ten to fifteen minutes. All the scenes invited audience participation at some point. The scenes showed many elements of the journeys we had explored in the workshops: journeys that encapsulated the collective lived experiences of the children. Some were simple narratives based on the story of a central character, showing key turning points on his or her journey to disenfranchisement. Two of the pieces used a freeze-frame technique, stopping the action to allow the audience members to question what was being depicted, discuss the causes of the events they were seeing, and debate the decisions and actions of the characters. These discussions were followed by the audience being asked to suggest alternative ways for the characters to deal with the contradictions and problems they were facing. Audience members were then invited to replace the child actors and show how they thought resolution could be found. In this playful form of participatory theatre the real children were the facilitators and jongleurs. The actors wore quickly changeable costume pieces, used a lot of mime and worked with humour. Much of the performance was improvised, based on established scenarios but not scripted, and all the pieces were punctuated with strong images, movement and sound. The pieces used easily recognisable indigenous roles and situations along with familiar songs and music supported by a vibrant use of percussion.

Three scenes depicted the death of parents and the break-up of the family. Two dealt with the kind of abuse the children received at the hands of extended family members or carers. Some were performed as complete semi-naturalistic 'journey' stories showing groups of travelling children finding food, stealing, and escaping police or adult authority figures. In one story the plot led to the death of a child who was running away after violent and sexual abuse from her guardian. After her death friends sought help to bury her. They were chased away and threatened. What were they to do? They sought advice from the audience, took it and tested it; but the audience solution was unsatisfactory as it depended entirely on other people being 'charitable' to them and this was not their experience of the world. This scene was based on a true story. It struck a chord and provoked a lot of discussion with the audience.

In all their pieces the children depicted problems which, because of their marginalised status, led them to find solutions in ways which were not approved of by the communities in which they found themselves. At best, the children's only real courses of action were frowned upon as unorthodox, and at worst their actions were viewed as criminal.

The performance was both powerful and disturbing. The audience had to listen and hear things of which they had thought little. They had to look at the 'other'. The process provoked genuine dialogue between the children and their audience. After the performance the children brought out food and drink and offered it to audience members moving amongst them to talk about what they had witnessed. The children were the hosts and spoke with the adults as equals.

The event successfully raised the questions the children had intended and posed the central, underlying question, 'What is to be done?' In considering that question, the street children and audience entered a collaborative process in search of solutions to specific problems. This was in itself an action of social transformation. In some cases the adults were obliged to reconsider their attitudes and behaviour whilst the children grew in confidence to speak, to demand change in the behaviour of others, to refuse to be silenced by fear, and to hope, dream and begin to fight for a more human existence. They gained an individual and collective strength and began to lose their fear of those with power. The creative work was the start of their journey; the performance was a potential awakening for many in the audience. The collective work had become a form of Cultural Action as Social Transformation.

What should we call this process? Is it TIE, TfD, DIE, community theatre, political theatre, applied theatre? Does it really matter what we call it? Does it really matter where it came from? Ownership and knowledge of its historical purpose and past practices is important and useful, but they should never of themselves translate into a 'correct' or imposed orthodoxy. The need is for creative social transformation. The process of transformation begins with the self. It is about breaking the silence, claiming our rights and constructing our own futures. It is about understanding, and rejecting, the control of the dominant ideology, moving beyond its coercive reach to determine for ourselves the destination of the journey we are embarked upon. It is about trusting our selves, and assuming responsibility for constantly re-examining our values and actions. It is about trusting our imaginations, our creativity, our art, our critical faculties, our judgments, and our capacity to reconstruct what is broken in our world. Above all, it is about understanding and changing those parts of reality that deny our true humanity.

The work in Zambia was a 'disturbance' for all who participated. It demanded that we all make sense of it in some way. That is change in action. It may be small; it may not be permanent, but it is change. This kind of work is not easily classified. In its purpose and pedagogical processes the work has much in common with classic TIE and DIE, but in its practice perhaps it points us towards more fluid forms of theatre interventions and facilitator–actor–audience relationships. Hopefully, it raises important questions about the time, place, space and economics of our work and about the nature of education, art and cultural action.

## Conclusion

As teachers, directors, facilitators, actor-teachers, teaching artists – or whatever other labels we bear – we must ask whether or not we are content to support the status quo or reassert our true roles, like the pioneering TIE workers did, as counter-cultural artist-educators. Are our schools, as currently constituted, any longer of use or value? If not, how must they be changed or reinvented? Are our theatre institutions any longer relevant? If they are not, then how do we make them so? If they are not capable of being transformed, then should we move beyond them and work outside their sphere of influence? What are the constraints on our capacity to build the counter-culture into a world of our own making? How might we break them? Indeed, 'What is to be done?'

Let me be absolutely clear about what is and is not being proposed. This chapter is not a recommendation for prescribed models of working, old or new; still less does it seek to set the virtues of some forms or genres against the shortcomings of others. This is not a question of

TIE versus TfD. I have focussed primarily on the past successes and future potential of participatory theatre because it is effective (and more participation is required in all spheres of civic life) but I do not want to isolate or separate it from the performance traditions of our work. They are what give it its unique power. I have tried to continue the exploration of what it means to practise student-centred education through the process of theatre. There is no single model by which to achieve this purpose. There is no guarantee of success. However, there are principles we can invoke and defend. The bedrock of our progressive theatre practices is the dialectical encounter between the lived experience of our participants and the unconstrained world of the imagination. It is this aesthetic experience that enables them to see afresh, and to understand more clearly, but more optimistically, the historical moment in which they are living. What was 'right' yesterday may be of limited use today and irrelevant tomorrow. However, this meeting, this negotiation between experience and imagination, is enriched by the recognition of past achievements and future possibilities. In attempting to resist the life-denying culture of the dominant ideology we need every weapon at our disposal.

Our urgent challenge is to develop a people-centred, 'theatre *as* education' pedagogy, based upon the very best practices of TIE and TfD. We must also find new ways to implement it. If the apparatchiks and functionaries of governance, of education systems and of arts councils and other funding bodies fail to recognise the right of the child to proper child-centred theatre as education, they must, politely or not, be shown the door. If they are not, and if our practice becomes one of complicity with the dominant orthodoxies, we will stand accused of the betrayal of the young people we claim to serve. We will, and should be, held accountable. It is our co-intentional vision, with and for our young people, that is the main source of a new pedagogy of hope. 'Terrible is the temptation to do good', Brecht warns us in *The Caucasian Chalk Circle* (Brecht 1976: scene 2). Perhaps it is time to stop doing what we are told is 'good' and start doing what we know is good. It is only through a reappraisal and development of our own practices as 'resources of hope' that we can truly answer the pressing contemporary question of 'What is to be done?' Perhaps this is what Marx meant when he coined his phrase 'the negation of the negation' (Marx 1977: 487). It is time to say 'no' to a world that denies the humanising power of the imagination, and 'yes' to our young as they struggle to make a future world that they can happily choose to inhabit. We must act now – lest in our graves we inherit the wrath of those who, through our complicity, we have betrayed.

## Notes

1 This chapter is dedicated to the memory, achievements and contributions to people-centred theatre of Romy Baskerville and Noel Greig who died in 2012 and 2009 respectively.

2 Paulo Freire adopted the term praxis to describe the cyclical process of reflection and action, uniting theory and practice as a key part of his emancipatory educational process (1993). In reference to our theatre process, particularly devising, it describes a spiralling process in which we take creative action, reflect upon the results, modify subsequent actions and so on. By implication, the theatre practice is usually explicitly committed to the cause of progressive social change.

3 Paradoxically, in the English system, a 'public school' is actually an expensive, elite private school.

4 Conscientisation (*conscientização*) is the term coined by Freire to describe a two-phase process consisting of the raising of awareness about social, political and economic structures and contradictions, followed by the taking of action, as a consequence of the new awareness, against the 'oppressive elements of reality' (1993: 17). One of the phases without the other does not constitute conscientisation.

5 This is a reference to Freire's concept of 'cultural invasion' (1993) whereby educators, who are not a part of the community they serve, frequently impose alien cultural values on their students, good intentions notwithstanding.

6 There are of course many forms and ways of 'writing' regardless of literacy levels.

## Works cited

Bond, Edward (2000), *The Hidden Plot*. London: Methuen.

Brecht, Bertolt (1976), *The Caucasian Chalk Circle*, trans. S. Brecht. London: Eyre Methuen.

Constantino, Renato (1985), *Synthetic Culture and Development*. Manila: Foundation for Nationalist Studies.

Freire, Paulo (1993), *Pedagogy of the Oppressed*. Harmondsworth, UK: Penguin Books.

Marx, Karl (1977), *Selected Writings*, ed. David McLellan. Oxford: Oxford University Press.

Pammenter, D. (2006), 'On the Making of Journeys: Young People's Theatre in Zambia'. In M. Banham, J. Gibbs, and F. Osofisan (eds), and M. Etherton (guest ed.), *African Theatre: Youth*. Oxford: James Currey, pp. 189–201.

# 5

# THE PLAYWRIGHT IN TIE

*Mary Cooper*

In the 1993 edition of *Learning through Theatre*, Dave Pammenter in his chapter on devising for TIE stated:

> The TIE movement, during its short history, has had to rely almost entirely on its practitioners for its material. Its whole history has been one of self-devised work either with or without writers, so the central activity of most teams has been devising.
>
> (Pammenter 1993: 53)

In 2012, this is no longer the case: few companies have either the time or the 'team' to devise; and most of the material, though still likely to be bespoke rather than extant, is written by an individual who may be within the company or a commissioned freelance writer.

In this chapter I will examine the development of the role of the dedicated writer in TIE; trace the current strands of work in which writers are commissioned; and acknowledge common pitfalls which writers might encounter en route to producing high-quality work. And to address these challenges, I will present a methodology – not as gospel or panacea but as a framework, a pattern to be used or departed from as required by the task.

## From full-time to freelance

In 1986, as an aspiring writer working towards my MA at the Workshop Theatre, Leeds University, I had the startling realisation that the magical, dreamlike event at my primary school in York in the 1970s, which had transformed the school hall and left a lasting visual and emotional imprint, had been a piece of TIE. As an adult my study of the form left me inspired, knowing 'that's what I want to do'. At the time, however, there seemed to be little scope for the would-be writer – in my case, neither an actor nor a trained teacher, but a former journalist – to participate in the world of TIE.

Most of the well-established TIE companies were teams of actor-teachers who devised their work collectively and seemed cautious, even suspicious, about the idea that a writer, separate from the team, might create their scripts apart from the devising process. However, it was exactly at this time that the collective devising model of TIE was beginning to change.

The Education Reform Act of 1988 meant that the management of schools' budgets was devolved to individual schools, which resulted in local education authorities being less able to provide TIE provision across the whole of their area. Services that had hitherto been provided free within a local authority were now charged to the schools themselves. The same Act introduced the National Curriculum; consequently teachers had less autonomy and flexibility in both the content and delivery of their lessons. League tables meant that schools were required to measure their success by uniform and prescribed quantitative criteria rather than the qualitative reports of governors, teachers, parents and pupils. Head-teachers were forced to ask themselves how they could evaluate the benefits of a visit from a TIE team when it was no longer assumed to be a good thing in itself.

These political, artistic and financial pressures squeezed the full-time teams of actor-teachers and forged a company model more likely to comprise a full-time director, an administrator/company manager, possibly with a production manager/stage manager, and whatever freelancers were appropriate to the company's current project. The director would decide on the nature of the programme, or increasingly 'the show', to be created, the target audience and very often the form of the piece. Increasingly the director's choice of material would arise from a brief provided by a statutory authority, or be built around an aspect of the National Curriculum. A writer, not infrequently also the director, would be commissioned to create the script and the production would be rehearsed over a two- to four-week period by a team of specially employed actors, who were unlikely also to be teachers.

While these financial and political developments were undeniably important in the changing approach to the writing of the TIE script, there was also a realisation that theatre created by group devising might not always result in the best possible work. The competing ideologies and different skills of company members, coupled with the desire to sustain the inclusive and egalitarian nature of the work, at times overrode the quest for artistic focus and quality.

As the TIE company changed, many now frequently commissioned writers for young people emerged from the TIE teams of the 1970s and 1980s. Neil Duffield, Mike Kenny, Kevin Dyer, Charles Way, Julie Wilkinson and Brendan Murray, all former members of TIE or young people's theatre companies, took the opportunity to bring a writer's focus to the creation of new work.

Mike Kenny, who worked as an actor for Leeds TIE Company for many years and was part of the team which devised *Raj* (1983) and *Flags and Bandages* (1985), commented that he chose to leave the company in 1987 partly because 'I like the well-made play. The company was returning to a participation-based, open-ended workshop method of working while I wanted to explore the artistic and educational possibilities of the carefully constructed script' (Kenny 2011).

Kevin Dyer, who worked as an actor with a number of leading TIE teams including Derby Playhouse TIE, Northampton Royal TIE, Avon Touring, and Roundabout at Nottingham Playhouse, observed that in devised work, artistic and theatrical considerations could be subsumed by the need to convey political or educational messages:

> The first time I saw a TIE play in the eighties I thought it was the worst piece of theatre I'd ever seen. The actors kept stopping the action and explaining the learning points through a narrator. They knew exactly what they wanted to convey and they were going to make sure no one missed it. Many TIE companies at the time were anti-establishment and their objective was, overtly or surreptitiously, to create political awareness in children and bring about a revolution. I was left-wing too but I also liked quality theatre. While there was some excellent work produced, when it was well-written, there was a great deal that was not. Good stories were often marred by poor structuring, unfinished plotting and by a devising team lacking those skills which a writer can bring.
>
> (Dyer 2011)

So while the decline of the devising company of actor-teachers was hardly to be celebrated, it did create a role for the dedicated, usually freelance, writer – often emerging from a TIE company, but in my own case the informed outsider, eager to become involved in the exciting possibilities of creating challenging and stimulating, socially engaged theatre for young people.

## The journeyman writer in TIE

The constraints of the National Curriculum post 1988 meant that the space in schools which had previously been available for TIE shrank – and the funding which had supported the labour-intensive process of devising was reduced. TIE companies had to look for both different educational spaces to inhabit and different sources of funding.

From the early 1990s there have been three prevalent strands of development for TIE and young people's theatre: the personal, social and health education (PSHE) curriculum; plays for early years and Key Stage One, especially the adaptation of well-known children's fiction; and the 'voicing of the voiceless' – often working in educational settings outside mainstream education, for example with disabled or special needs groups, mental health service users, within the criminal justice system and with young people in care or in the youth service.

A fourth area of expansion has taken TIE teams away from working with young people entirely, and into using theatre for training – for example, for health professionals, charities and in corporate settings. How does the playwright function within these strands – and strive to produce the best possible work?

### *A healthy relationship? TIE and the Personal, Social and Health Education curriculum*

The exclusion of drama from the National Curriculum and the increasingly prescribed English and History syllabi left TIE companies looking for different 'entry points' to mainstream education. One part of the curriculum which seemed to offer a welcome was Personal, Social and Health Education.

While this strategy might have seemed merely expedient it nevertheless reflected a broader political shift from class-based politics to personal politics. At the dissident margins this meant a shift from an analysis of economic inequalities to an analysis of the power inequalities of gender, race and disability; an increasing interest in individual change through therapy and the personal growth movement; and engagement with environmental issues. Proponents believed personal change could lead to social change; 'revolution' would happen through the sum of individual actions, rather than organised collective action.

In the mainstream, this shift towards individualism meant the elevation of freedom of choice, of personal responsibility rather than social responsibility, and an emphasis on changing the individual 'lifestyle' or indeed the physical body, rather than changing personal or social relationships.

What both the mainstream and the margins agreed upon, from their different perspectives, was that the power of theatre could be enlisted to influence, and possibly even change, the behaviour of individuals, whether that be in questioning or conforming to social norms. And while this shared acknowledgement of the power of theatre to influence thinking and behaviour encouraged an increasingly instrumental approach to TIE, it, arguably, ensured its survival.

Public bodies, with specific 'public information' requirements commissioned theatre companies to undertake that brief on their behalf, providing funding and a lifeline for many companies – and a *raison d'être* for others. As particular issues have hit the headlines, the resulting tremors of concern have brought public funding to companies when other sources were slipping away – so there have been waves of TIE plays about child abuse, bullying, drug use, HIV and AIDS, young people and alcohol, bereavement, teenage pregnancy, road safety, knife crime, gun crime, gang culture and, most recently, social networking and internet pornography.

For the freelance writer commissioned in one of these areas, the process is likely to have involved an approach from a TIE company charged by a public body to 'deliver' a particular information brief. So, for example, in 2000, M6 Theatre Company commissioned me to write *Forever*, a play for high school audiences funded by the Nationwide Foundation with support from the local Teenage Pregnancy Unit. It is possible, however, for writers to instigate this process themselves. Seeing for myself the growing problem of the use of heroin among young people in South Yorkshire in the mid-1990s, I was able to interest the charity, Turning Point, and the local education authority in helping to create and fund *Head On*, a drugs education programme, before approaching West Yorkshire Playhouse Touring to act as the producing company.

The artistic impact of accepting this funding, with its contractual obligations to convey specified information or encourage certain behaviour, is debatable. For myself, I feel it is often possible to work within these briefs to produce work of genuine artistic merit and integrity. However, work produced through this kind of commissioning process has been referred to disparagingly as 'issue-based drama'; implicit in the use of this term is the assumption that it is little more than a living leaflet, having limited theatrical aspirations, simplistic characterisation and schematic plotting, a good dollop of informational exposition and a conformist message: the twenty-first-century version of cautionary tales.

Kevin Dyer referred to this strand of work critically as 'drug-money shows'. He defined TIE in the 1970s and 1980s as serious in its intentions, focused on learning and attempting to produce work of the highest artistic quality, while children's theatre

> was often non-unionised, usually took no political or ethical position and frequently had poor production values. But now, partly because of the number of drug-money shows out there, I think it's turned right around, so that the companies calling themselves TIE often do not pay Equity rates, have no political or ethical position, and are producing poor-quality, issue-based work.
>
> (Dyer 2011)

He believes it is companies which call themselves children's theatre companies, and theatres for young people, that are now striving to produce high-quality work which is serious in its intentions, though not necessarily in its style, and educational in the broadest sense of the term.

So what does this mean for TIE? Has the term itself become an insult? How is it possible for a writer to make a 'drug-money show' which is serious in its intentions, focused on learning and of the highest artistic quality?

### *Theatre for education – or entertainment?*

The growth of theatre for children as young as two – and even for babies – has been a particular phenomenon of the past fifteen years. Mike Kenny wrote his first pre-school play *The Lost Child* in 1989 for Sheffield Crucible TIE.

> Theatre in Education didn't do work for the very young – and only occasionally for children with special needs. But the changes in the National Curriculum meant that these areas were now much more accessible than the usual TIE audiences in primary and secondary schools.
>
> (Kenny 2011)

Since then he has gone on to write fifteen plays for young children, many based on traditional folk or fairy tales. He rejected the idea that the retelling of an old tale might be purely 'entertainment':

> Everything I write is serious work; it's about stuff. Whether it's Pinocchio or an original play for young children it should be like Miller, Chekhov or Ibsen, about the world we live in and why we act as we do. Just because it's a fairy tale doesn't mean it's empty.
>
> (Kenny 2011)

Charles Way and Neil Duffield too, both writers noted for their work in TIE in the 1970s and 1980s, have gone on to adapt traditional stories for family audiences and young children. But how as a writer do you ensure that, for example, an adaptation of *The Gingerbread Man* or *Cinderella* is 'about the world we live in and why we act as we do', and not simply an animated retelling of the story?

### *Voicing the voiceless: writing with, rather than writing for*

TIE in the 1970s and 1980s was engaged in revealing and analysing oppression and inequality. In many ways the work of contemporary TIE companies with groups deemed to be 'hard to reach', 'vulnerable' or 'socially excluded' is a continuation of this political impetus. TIE-inspired projects have given voice to marginalised groups with a number of different objectives: perhaps as a means to bring greater attention to their special difficulties; to bring about greater social understanding; to reflect back to these groups their own experiences and so to provide validation; to enable such groups to understand, analyse and change their own circumstances; or to provide a record of remarkable lives which might otherwise go unrecorded.

Since 1988 I have created TIE-inspired projects with people with learning difficulties, the physically disabled, the elderly, young offenders, refugees, women with mental health problems, women who have experienced traumatic childbirth, young carers, parents of drug-users, women offenders and young Bangladeshi women. The challenge of producing work for and with these groups lies in ensuring that the play communicates not only within their 'ghetto' but to the world at large. Too often, it can fail to make the all-important transition from the specific to the universal. The play might be an effective mirror to those whose experience it reflects, but how does the writer avoid it becoming of only voyeuristic interest to the audience beyond?

## Following the money without selling out

Since accepting the invitation to write this chapter I have been asking myself whether, as a freelance writer, I approach writing a play for

TIE any differently from any other commission. The truth, I think, is that I don't. I'm always trying to write the best possible script for the intended audience – and a good script is a good script. But what may be characteristically different is the instrumental nature of the TIE brief. Not only is the writer attempting to fulfil all the aesthetic and artistic requirements of the 'good script' but, within this, they are delegated to create an instrument of education. Of course, one could argue that all good scripts will be educational in the broadest sense of the term, but the TIE script is usually explicitly so. The writer's brief for TIE is likely to be far more specific in content and function than, for example, a radio play, or a play for a theatre company playing to mainstream adult audiences. The challenge for the writer, then, is how to meet the prescribed educational brief while still producing work of high artistic and theatrical quality. How to get from Road Safety for five-year-olds to art?

Whatever the commissioned content my thought process is always, 'Yes, the content is x – but what is the drama *really* about?' By this I mean, what is the universal question which underlies the specific issue, the old tale or the marginalised area of experience? So, for example, a commission about road safety for five-year-olds might really be asking the question, 'How can I feel safe in a world which seems unpredictably hostile?' For me it is this search for the universal theme, and its successful exploration through theatre, which is the key to avoiding the common pitfalls I've outlined above. If the play is genuinely exploring a universal question it can never be simply living-leaflet, issue-based work, an animated but empty retelling of old tales, or a curiosity piece which fails to resonate beyond its specific setting.

Mike Kenny echoes this thought: 'Whatever the play, I have to make a personal journey, as well as an objective exploration of the subject, and I have to know what the play is about for me' (Kenny 2011).

### *From the specific to the universal*

The process of discovering what the commission is 'really about', and of suffusing the play with this theme, for me, has four stages:

(1) Examining, defining and confirming the brief.
(2) Researching the field.
(3) Developing the scenario.
(4) Writing the first draft. And rewriting.

While for the sake of analysis I have separated out these stages, there will always be an overlap. I may do some preliminary research even before I have effectively defined the brief; I will still be researching while I am developing the scenario, and even when I'm writing and rewriting. And it is often only at the end of the first draft that the writer becomes fully conscious of the play's themes and how they can be best explored.

### *Examining, defining and confirming the brief*

Mike Kenny, when asked what his first step was on receiving a commission said, 'I listen a lot. I listen to what is being said – and to what is *not* being said. I try to understand what they're expecting – but I let them know that I am the one writing the play' (Kenny 2011). Kevin Dyer commented, 'I devise and write plays with, not for, companies and that ensures that we get the brief clear' (Dyer 2011).

For myself, clarifying the brief is a continuing dialogue between commissioner and writer, rather than the handing down of an edict. Whatever the nature of the commission, the writer first needs to grasp its concrete requirements. What is the specified length of show, cast size, the nature of the venue(s) and the age range of the intended audience? Is there any flexibility on any of these? Could this change as the project develops? Though apparently straightforward, even these stipulations need to be defined. Is the 'length of show' determined or is the commission for a given slot of time which would be better divided between, for example, a performance and a workshop? Does the venue – or venues – have a rake, blackout and lighting, and any other limitations, peculiarities or strengths? What is the likely size of the audience: a small group, a whole class, a whole school, a whole theatre? What is the likely ethnicity of the audience? What languages do they speak? What are the expectations of the commissioners in terms of a workshop and/or supporting materials?

Second, besides these more obvious questions, the writer needs to understand the more amorphous demands, the subtext of the brief, which the commissioners themselves may have yet to articulate. If at all possible, I try to meet with the primary commissioners to investigate their needs and expectations. The producing theatre company may be the primary commissioners – or they may have been funded by an external body to produce the play. This is particularly likely to be the case where a theatre company has taken on a public information or training brief. While superficially this might be straightforward, for example, a thirty-minute play about knife crime for Key Stage Three pupils in High Schools in Rochdale commissioned by the local police force, it is vital to investigate what this means to the commissioners themselves.

So, for the example above, what exactly are the commissioners hoping the play will do? Give information about the penalties for carrying weapons? Deter young people from carrying knives? Help young people feel safer on the streets? Provoke discussion about the gang culture? Address issues around identity and masculinity? Reduce knife crime? Or all of these things? What expectations do they have in their minds about the nature of the show and what it can achieve, which they may not be able to articulate fully, but which will impinge upon their reaction to the script?

An organisation which is new to commissioning may feel that it needs to control the process. It is up to the writer and the theatre company to gain their trust and to educate them about what theatre can and can't do well. In particular they need to understand that theatre works through a process of provoking relevant questions in the audience, not by providing answers; that it may not necessarily present large amounts of information but should stimulate the audience to *need* that information, to understand that it is relevant to themselves and their world, and that effective theatre invites young people to enter into a debate in which they can make better-informed judgements for themselves, rather than being told what to think or how to act. Theatre relates to education in the original etymological sense of the word, that of 'drawing or bringing out', rather than in the didactic tradition of imparting wisdom.

Ultimately the writer is aiming to take the audience on a journey of questioning.

*Who is that person? Why are they behaving in that way? What's going to happen to them? What if that person were me? How would I behave in those circumstances? And, if that were me, what would I need to know in order to decide how to act? And, if that person were me, in the light of that information, what would I think and feel, how would I act? And, finally, in the light of that information, if I am faced with a similar situation in the future, what will I think and feel, and how will I act?*

However, this process of questioning, searching for answers and making decisions on the basis of that learning will only happen if the audience are engaged with the characters and the story – both intellectually and emotionally. In other words, the commissioners must see that the play has to work first and foremost as a piece of theatre if it is to achieve its 'learning objectives'. This may mean that information which commissioners imagined would be incorporated into the performance will be offered during a post-show workshop or through supporting teaching materials.

By the end of this process the writer, theatre company and commissioners should have a shared understanding of what the commission is aiming to address educationally and how it will be ap[illegible] artistically.

In the case of a commission for young children, whether [illegible] or adaptation, the defining conversation is more likely to happen between writer and director, but here too there is often unarticulated subtext. In the case of an 'old tale', the writer needs to know why the theatre company is choosing to retell this story *now*. And why this *particular* audience? What relevance do they believe it has for their intended audience? In the case of an adaptation of a contemporary children's book, the writer will additionally need to investigate why the company believe the story should be retold as drama. What can a dramatic retelling add to the story? What does the company hope live performance will illuminate and deepen?

When working with marginalised groups, defining the brief is likely to be a much more organic and fluid process, often happening after, rather than before, the research phase. By definition, if you're 'voicing the voiceless' the writer needs to discover what there is to be said, before defining how it should be done. For example, when I was asked by Yorkshire Women's Theatre to 'use drama as a tool for learning English' with young Bangladeshi women in Harehills, Leeds, I had little idea that a bilingual play would eventually emerge.

### *Researching the field*

'Write about what you know', is a writers' cliché, but like most clichés it is based on a truth and underlines the need for authenticity and research. To this I would add a warning against assuming or pretending knowledge, both about the audience and about the commissioned content. Research is as much about shedding preconceptions, especially those which involve a moral judgement, and being open to surprise, as it is about acquiring knowledge and understanding.

In general I would identify five kinds of research: *Observing*: spending time with your intended audience and simply watching and absorbing. *Experiencing*: this might mean, for example, exploring a particular place you have in mind as the setting of your drama or making a journey undertaken by your central character. *Listening*: talking to people about their relevant experiences, ideas and opinions. *Reading*: this can be a directed process, absorbing the major published material on your subject, or more free-form in which one source can lead to another. *Imagining*: this is internal research. You may not, for example, be the Bangladeshi father of a fifteen-year-old girl growing up in Britain – but what would it feel like if you were? This kind of imaginative research is a lot easier if you've already done the other kinds of research. It also requires courage and honesty.

Initially my research will involve casting the net wide, in terms of developing my understanding of both the audience and the subject matter. Particularly for a 'public information' brief, I will work from several different perspectives at once. In the case of a play about young people and drug use, such as *Head On*, this meant hearing about the experiences and understanding of a broad range of young people in relation to their own drug use, or lack of it, as well as researching social trends in drug use, the chemical effects of drugs, the perspective of drug agencies and other 'specialists' such as long-term drug users and dealers, the police, doctors, psychologists and social commentators.

In the case of an adaptation, besides studying the various versions of the text, I will focus on the audience, examining the interconnection between their lives and the material. What can an adaptation of *Pinocchio*, a novel written for children in mid-nineteenth-century Italy, offer a family audience in Hulme in Manchester in the twenty-first century?

For work commissioned to voice the voiceless, the research phase is crucial and will define the brief as well as the scenario and the drama itself. Here the research is likely to involve listening, observing and experiencing; finding ways to access, and enable the articulation of, the lives and world of the marginalised group, perhaps through the practice of drama but, certainly, through the building of relationships and through in-depth interviews. So, in the case of the young Bangladeshi women in Harehills, some of whom had never been to school either in Bangladesh or in Britain, I worked through games and group conversation for a number of weeks, getting to know them, before finding a way towards creating drama and producing writing.

Then I began to encourage the girls to improvise both from their own lives and from stories, fictional or factual, moving freely from English to their mother tongue. The scenes were transcribed – in both phonetic and literate versions – as those who spoke Sylheti or Bengali did not write necessarily write it. I also made audio recordings, since those who spoke English, Sylheti or Bengali did not necessarily read or write any of those languages. I supported the improvisations with writing and story-telling exercises and gradually began to shape the material into scenes. As the scenes began to build towards a play I guided the improvisations more specifically, though always in consultation with the girls. The resulting script was a seamless mix of the two languages. *Ridhoy Neye Khala* or *Heartgame* was given a rehearsed reading at the Crucible Theatre, Sheffield and eventually developed into a production at the Soho Theatre, London, by Asian Co-operative Theatre (1989) as well as being published by Methuen (Cooper 1990). It incorporated as much of the girls' input as possible, but, without a writer selecting, focusing, deepening and shaping the material, it would have remained a series of superficial sketches. The girls, however, still felt they had ownership of the script and closely guarded the authenticity of the characters' voices and the storyline.

A further devised project with second-generation Bangladeshi girls in Beeston, who spoke mainly English outside of the home and Sylheti within the home, went on to form the basis of the Red Ladder production, *Consequences* (1991), and toured to Asian girls groups nationally.

Whatever the nature of the commission, in the research phase of the writing, I am attempting to find out what the audience(s) believe, know or assume about the commissioned subject matter, be it drugs, road safety, refugees, the ancient Greeks or Pinocchio, and what they might need to know. And while I'm casting the net of research wide, I'm simultaneously filtering my 'catch', looking for patterns, noting particular recurring phrases or experiences, identifying major tensions, debates and paradoxes in the field, and forming my own ideas and approach to the material.

Above all I am trawling for the dramatist's treasure: a specific moment, character, event or image which has the potential to bind together the drama and hold the research, while seeming to do nothing other than tell a story. So, for example, in the play *Missing Out* (2009) discussed below, it was an aside by an interviewee about her cellmate absconding to see her child, and to prevent the child's adoption, that proved to be the key to the drama.

### *Developing the scenario*

This process of immersion and distillation will gradually lead to the development of a scenario. A protagonist, world, plot, notion of style and a preliminary understanding of the play's theme will begin to emerge until, instead of the research developing the scenario, the scenario begins to direct the research.

The play's protagonist will start from a similar perspective to the intended audience, but will not necessarily mirror them; rather, she or he will present a point of emotional connection – a character with whom the audience are prepared to go on a journey. The identification of the protagonist and their world will provoke a series of questions leading to the creation of subsidiary characters. What are their significant relationships? Who loves them? Who hates them? With whom are they in conflict? I tend to avoid the concept of 'an antagonist' as this presupposes that conflict in the play operates in a single dimension. I will always try to absorb different levels of conflict: from conflict with self/conscience, through conflict within the character's immediate circle of peers and family, to conflict beyond the immediate circle, perhaps at work or school, and finally, the fourth level of conflict, with wider authorities such as the law or the state.

Subsidiary characters also provide an opportunity to engage with the range of audience members and to present a variety of perspectives on the emerging theme. Even when a play is commissioned for a specific age group in a specific city, the writer will be addressing audience members who differ in values, experiences and assumptions and, having understood these differences, the writer may attempt to create subsidiary characters which reflect this.

Usually I will write a biography of my major character(s), including a timeline of events. I will do this whether or not the setting is contemporary, historical or fantastical. If I'm working in a real-world setting, this may go back as much as two generations. The creation of a character biography inevitably begs the question of how the story of the protagonist's life will be translated into the plot of a drama. Where and when, in the unfolding life of the protagonist, will the drama begin and end? In what way will the dramatic arc of the play span events in the character's life?

During the research I will be trawling for the inciting incident: the event which triggers the action of the drama and clarifies the protagonist's goal. So, for example, in a play about women prisoners, it might be the moment when the protagonist is threatened with the loss of her child. The plot of the drama then arises from imagining various strategies that the character might employ to secure access to her child despite being in prison. To what lengths will she go to retain that relationship – and what will be the consequences of those actions? This imaginative exploration, fuelled by research, creates the major events of the drama and moves the protagonist through increasing complications to a crisis, a moment when they will be forced to make a crucial choice, which will propel them into the climactic action of the drama.

In a conventionally structured drama, the climax would lead to a resolution and the audience would discover whether or not the character achieves their goal. However, in a drama which has educational objectives, it may be more effective to draw the protagonist to a climactic moment and leave the audience to examine the possible consequences of the character's actions and create their own resolution. So the writer is striving for a dramatic arc which is begun by the script but is completed in the minds of each member of the audience as they find their own resolution.

Particularly in the case of a public information brief, the protagonist will be taken on a journey in which change is presented as necessary, and possible, but exactly how, and if, that change is achieved is not determined in the drama, but left with the audience to resolve, both for the character, and by implication, for themselves.

So, in *Head On*, mentioned earlier, which took the form of a series of six monologues, the audience meet the protagonists in the midst of their involvement with drugs, and journey with them through the drama to a climactic moment. But it is left to the audience in a workshop to determine how the character's journey might be resolved, for better or worse. For example, in one of the monologues, *Cooling Off*, the young protagonist is attempting unsuccessfully to find a way of reconciling with his father; while in the workshop the audience are invited to help him write a letter to his father and, if they choose, to improvise the meeting between them. While the writer does not dictate the workshop form, her creation of an unresolved ending will provide, or hook into, a particular set of questions which will drive the post-show exploration by the company and the audience. Ideally these questions will have been discussed and crystallised in collaboration with the commissioning company, and a skilled facilitator will have been employed to fashion a workshop enabling their full and complex investigation.

The unresolved ending is also likely to be a feature of TIE-inspired drama working with marginalised groups. Their experiences are being articulated and revealed, at least in part, so that their difficulties might be better understood and addressed by the groups themselves, as well as by the mainstream. The audience are implicitly invited to be part of a resolution in the real world, rather than watching a fictitious resolution on stage.

*Missing Out* (2009), aimed at women prisoners, their families and relevant professionals, and commissioned by Action for Prisoners' Families (APF) and Clean Break Theatre, showed the protagonist pleading with her mother to take custody of her youngest child and so prevent his adoption while she was imprisoned. The drama finished leaving her question unanswered – and therefore open to debate by the audience. Should the child be adopted? Should he be brought up by his ageing and over-burdened grandmother? What action is in the best interests of the child, the grandmother, or the prisoner? How could this situation be avoided in the future? How might prisoners, professionals and families act differently?

The close collaboration with the commissioning organisation and the producing company is vital, but it is also important for the writer to retain their independence and their adherence to the complex truth revealed by their research. In the case of *Missing Out*, the two commissioning organisations did not necessarily have the same agenda. Clean Break works mainly with women in the criminal justice system, while APF works mainly with their families; and, inevitably, sometimes the sympathies of these two groups are in conflict. But the writer's responsibility is to create sympathetic characters who, through the compelling action of the drama, can embody the complexities and the sometimes unpalatable truths revealed by research. For myself, I will always be asking, 'Are all my characters complex and authentic?' 'Is the action of the play truthful?' 'Is it good theatre?' 'Will it engage the intended audience?' Rather than, 'Will the commissioners be happy?' Playwrights must work with their commissioners while remembering they are not writing advertising copy.

While arriving at the plot outline I will, at the same time, be considering questions of style: what is the best way to tell the story? And while content gives rise to form, the generation of form will deepen my understanding of the content. I will be asking myself questions about chronology, movement, language, use of sound and music, the tone of the drama, imagery and motifs – both visual and verbal, staging and dramatic conventions. Crucially, I will be asking myself why this story needs to be told through *theatre* and reminding myself of the many possibilities of the form, beyond televisual naturalism.

Of the many stylistic questions faced by the writer of drama for young people, perhaps the most often raised relates to character voice. Should the drama reflect the argot, dialect or language of the young people in the audience? For me the struggle is always to find a balance between authenticity and accessibility; the voice of the specific character must feel authentic while at the same time being universally accessible. This was particularly true in the case of *Heartgame/Ridhoy Neye Khala* mentioned above. The bilingual mix of English and Sylheti I arrived at is a theatrical construct accessible to the whole audience which nevertheless reflects the authentic merging of languages especially common in second-generation migrant communities.

And it is this same journey, from the specific to the universal, that the writer is attempting in arriving at the theme of the drama, in deciding what the play is 'really about' and allowing that to suffuse the writing of the play.

*Writing the first draft – and rewriting the play*

Creating a play is a balance of planning and discovery, and while the discovery of research may lead to the plan of scenario, the process of writing the first draft will launch the writer further into discovery, particularly in relation to the play's universal theme. So whether writing the first draft is swift or slow – it will always be the *first* draft. Through both self-critique and feedback from the commissioning company, the script will be analysed and redrafted, perhaps several times, before being taken into rehearsal. There it will change again, and even when in front of its intended audience, the writer should be prepared to redraft – not just in order that it better meets the commissioner's brief but to make it the best possible theatrical experience it can be. I want to write theatre for the ears and eyes, the head and heart, theatre that is visually and aurally engaging, theatre that makes you think and feel; theatre that can be successful both educationally and artistically.

Looking again at the last edition of *Learning through Theatre* I begin to question how different are my artistic and educational aims from the devising teams of the 1960s, 1970s and 1980s. Yes, as a writer I bring a single sensibility to the creation of theatre, but fundamentally I undertake the same process for similar reasons. In association with the commissioning company I focus the educational objectives, carry out the research, explore and discover character, world, story, style and theme and refine and rewrite in order that the play authentically connects with its audience and fully addresses its objectives. And, like them, I aim to write plays which provoke the audience to crave a better understanding of the society they live in, and the people they live with, and by doing so to make their world a better place.

## Works cited

Cooper, Mary (1990), *Heartgame*, in Mary Remant (ed.), *Plays by Women: Eight*. London and New York: Methuen.

Dyer, Kevin (2011), Personal interview. 10 October 2011. Manchester.

Jackson, Tony, ed. (1993), *Learning through Theatre*. London: Routledge.

Kenny, Mike (2011), Personal interview. 15 September 2011. Leeds.

Pammenter, D. (1993), 'Devising for TIE', in Jackson (ed.), *Learning through Theatre*, 2nd edn. London: Routledge, pp. 53–70.

And it has been used to further the development of 'the museum as forum', fostering debate about museum collections, their origins and their contemporary relevance. Again, it operates in an 'in between' setting, its potential not always understood or adequately exploited. Its actors are not only faced with similar challenges to those of the TIE company in school, but must also deal with an extraordinary variety of audiences, often unpredictable in number, age, social background and extent of prior knowledge, many of whom have no intention of being audiences until the very moment that a performance begins. What is shared with TIE in general and Y Touring in particular is the dedication, first, to using drama to highlight and illuminate issues of relevance to contemporary audiences, and, second, to an interactive process that will generate, directly or indirectly, debate.

One way of trying to get a handle on what actors working in this broad and varied field do, is to see how far acting theory might be used as a template for what in so many respects goes beyond the call of the conventional skill of the actor. The American academic Bert O. States developed in the mid-1980s a useful theorisation of the modes in which the actor operates. According to his phenomenological approach, he argues that theatre can usefully be understood as 'an act of speech'; and that this idea 'allows us to see how an actor's relationship to the audience may shift "keys" during a performance' (States 1983: 360). The actor has, he says, 'three pronominal modes in which he may speak to the audience'. These modes can be summarised as:

- the **representational** – here the emphasis is on the pronoun 'he' or 'she', the character being played, and on the actor's function as a vehicle of signification, that is, on his/her ability to communicate and sustain the world of the play and to 'be' that character;
- the **collaborative** – here the emphasis is on 'you', the audience, that is, the actor's direct interaction or communication with the audience (States is thinking primarily of such examples as Shakespearean direct address, comic asides or Brechtian epic acting – he does not mention the more open forms of interaction characteristic of so much TIE work); and
- the **self-expressive** – here the emphasis is on the 'I', the actor, that is, the actor as actor, where the performance itself becomes the primary focus of attention, with the audience more conscious of the skill, inventiveness and virtuosity of the performer than of the character she may be playing; this is 'See what I can do' (as States puts it, *ibid.*: 361) rather than 'Let me convince you that I am the character I play'.

As States goes on to explain, these are not exclusive categories; indeed it is possible for an actor to operate in all three modes at different points within the one performance and sometimes in more than one mode at any one time. My argument is that in TIE (in which I include Y Touring) and museum theatre, such simultaneity of mode is not just a common occurrence but actually fundamental to this kind of performance.

So how far and in what ways might States's formulation of those three 'pronominal modes' of performance apply to the work of the Y Touring actor-teacher or the museum performer? And in what ways can these modes be said to operate – and intersect – from moment to moment? I will refer to two very different but, on one level at least, closely related examples of professional practice – to Y Touring's *Breathing Country* (2009–10) and to a production devised for performance at the Manchester Museum, one which I observed closely for research purposes: *This Accursed Thing* (2007–8) which dealt with the abolition of the slave trade, and was first presented as part of the series of commemorative events in 2007 that marked the 200th anniversary of the passing of the Abolition Act in the British Parliament.

First, the mode that is most commonly associated with conventional theatre: the **Representational Mode**. This is the acting mode that we perhaps most take for granted – the actor in role as a 'character', inhabiting a world depicted by the playwright in a well-crafted script, in which the people on stage, the objects they handle and the actions they pursue are all signifiers for a world 'out there' (the 'real' world of mid-twentieth-century America in Arthur Miller's plays, say, or of Shakespeare's historical reimagining of events in English history). In relation to museum theatre, we might suggest that – *in situ* – in the setting of the sprawling kitchen of an historic seventeenth-century manor house, that world may be a relatively easy one to conjure up: the 'set' and the heavy texture and drape of the (more or less) authentic costumes are constant and powerful reminders of that world. In a school hall or museum gallery, however, it's much more difficult, especially so in museums. Costumes will be paramount for historical pieces, but the stage set rarely corresponds to the world being depicted, while the objects that might serve as signifiers are often in glass cases or behind roped-off barriers. In the plays devised for Y Touring, set in the immediate present, or an imagined future, one that young audiences will recognise as their own, the costumes and sets will tend towards the everyday, with attire used to signify status, profession or age, while objects and furniture will likewise provide the briefest of signifiers of location and occupational necessity. In

*Breathing Country*, the scenes set in the family home or the researcher's office are deftly and rapidly conjured into being by the presence, and use, of an easy-chair or a desk. Given the need for portability and for quick get-ins and get-outs, especially when touring schools, screens and drapes generally frame the action and attention to small detail, characteristic of full-frontal naturalism, is shunned.

But creating a plausible illusion of that world, by whatever means, is one vital way of drawing the audience into a world and a narrative recognisable enough for them to connect with and then, it is hoped, take something from – insights, ideas, understandings about unfamiliar subject-matter, a curiosity to discover more, making fresh links with their own lives. Engaging them in debate is then more likely to follow. And, in the circumstances of the school hall, the onus is on the actor, not the set, to sustain that plausibility.

In *This Accursed Thing*, the challenge of representation, especially of a world in which the slave trade flourished, was huge. A promenade performance at the Manchester Museum,[3] it lasted about an hour, two actors played six characters, and each scene was played in a different location in the museum. Before the performance began, a short introduction was given by the two actors out of role, and, at the end, a fifteen-minute debriefing took place at which the audience were able to ask questions of the actors again out of role – about the performance, the research, and of course the subject-matter of slavery and the slave trade. Finding a dramatic vehicle with which to say something useful and purposeful about such a sensitive and controversial subject carried both opportunity and considerable risk. It required not only in-depth research but immense care in how the factual knowledge was translated into drama – avoiding the twin-barbed charge of 'dumbing-down' on the one hand and appearing to condone the views of advocates of slavery on the other. As well as the use of period costume and props, the introductory briefing provided an essential framing for the drama, indicating the factual basis for the characters, actions and dialogue that were to follow, and making it crystal clear that the words spoken, some of which would now seem offensive, were based on those used at the time. The pre-show induction was also necessitated by the commitment to producing an interactive drama that would promote genuine dialogue. In fact, the generation of debate was as important an aim here as it has been for most Y Touring programmes, despite the otherwise marked differences in approach.

The **Collaborative Mode**. Across the spectrum of applied theatre, from 'forum theatre' and Y Touring-style 'theatre of debate' to 'museum theatre', this is the mode that is generally to the fore. There will of

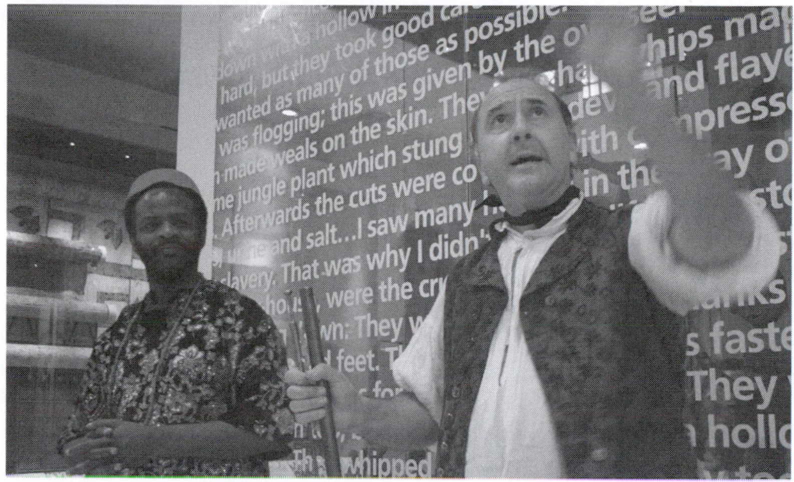


*Figure 6.1* *This Accursed Thing* (Andrew Ashmore/Performance, Learning and Heritage Research Project, 2007/8). Promenade performance at The Manchester Museum. The traders barter over slaves. Performers: Paul Etuka and Andrew Ashmore (Ashmore & Associates). Photo courtesy of PLH archive (Manchester University).

course be widely different kinds of performer–audience relationship and different demands made on the audience by the performers, but blurring the clear dividing lines between 'stage' and 'auditorium' is invariably central to the purpose of the exercise. The actor shifts into collaborative mode most overtly when the audience is addressed directly and invited to contribute actively to the investigation of the issues dramatised.

The out-of-role induction and debriefing sequences that introduced and closed the performance of *This Accursed Thing* were designed to free up the drama sufficiently to allow for moments of interaction and genuine challenge *within* the performance, accompanied by the tacit permission given to the audience to opt in and out at any point. Audience involvement was designed to be incremental as the drama progressed through the galleries, through history and through the intellectual and emotional challenges proffered by the narrative. In part the induction sequence was also about finding ways of trying to equalise the power relations at work, reducing vulnerability and so enabling people to engage voluntarily and in their own way, without at the same time feeling patronised. Expectations matter greatly, and will often condition the responsiveness of the audience.

Y Touring are equally very clear about the 'rules of engagement'. *Breathing Country* began with a sustained introductory sequence, establishing a relaxed but focused atmosphere in which the workshop leader-cum-scene setter was able to introduce the subject-matter, its potential relevance to the audience and the *modus operandi* of the following play and culminating workshop. The use of live electronic voting also created opportunities to test pre- (and later post-) performance attitudes to sharing personal information through digital media. But the question in the title of this essay perhaps also implies that, irrespective of the explicitness of that introduction, the student's doubts and confusions remained unresolved. Was there a need for a fuller induction to the programme and its interweaving of drama, fact and debate? Based on research findings elsewhere (see *PLH: Final Report* 2008), the answer is probably not: an even more extensive induction – making yet more explicit the rules and the way drama was going to feed into the process – would not have eliminated all puzzlement. Drama often is, perhaps should be, unsettling. It may be fiction but it also can illuminate and reveal in ways that other media cannot, and in the process is likely to leave question marks over the precise relationship between the fiction witnessed and the real-world implications that the workshop and ensuing debate address. There is also much to be said for work that confounds expectations, where surprise is a strong part of the very enjoyment and educational impact, and for the 'wow factor' which by definition should not be explained in advance.

In *This Accursed Thing*, probably the most challenging and unsettling sequence – for actors and audience alike – came during and immediately after a scene between a black African slave trader and his white (British) counterpart, here to do a deal over the next batch of slaves to be brought to the trading post. The audience begin as witnesses but then find themselves faced by a disconcerting confrontation. The white slave trader turns to them, sees their critical looks and challenges them to tell him what he's doing wrong. Some engage immediately, others (for whatever reasons) avoid his eyes and hope this is only a rhetorical question; for many there is a sense that to remain silent is either to offer tacit consent, to be complicit in the trade, or at the very least to accept its validity in the context of its time. Young children sometimes jumped in without hesitation to accuse the trader of unfairness; older children and many adults became increasingly frustrated at the trader's apparent ability to find a justification for his trade whatever the objection. For some, it was only in the relative safety of the final question-and-answer session at the very end, with the actors now out of role, that they felt empowered to express their reasoned analyses of the evils of the trade or, for others, their anger at its existence, or for others still, their perception of the close parallels with modern forms of slavery.

Of course, the need to challenge, to unsettle, surprise, stimulate, has to be balanced against the counter-productive risks of embarrassing, confusing, demotivating, angering and ultimately disempowering the visitor who has not yet agreed to 'buy in' to the process. That in a nutshell is one of the main challenges for the performer: how to unsettle and take your audience with you.

The final mode States discusses is one that is least talked about in TIE and museum theatre, but which is just as vital to the successful implementation of theatre that aims at a powerful and lasting impact. The **Self-Expressive Mode** refers to the kind of performance in which the virtuosity of the actor predominates, and where the audience tend to be most conscious of the actor as actor. In museum theatre, no matter how close you intend to stay to the period and the narrative articulation of the subject-matter, in the end the success of the performance will hang first and foremost on the skill and persuasiveness of the performer – often operating in challenging and distracting environments and needing every ounce of performative skill to arouse the onlookers' curiosity, engage their attention and concentration, and sustain interest through to the end. The world being created and the theme being explored will not be supported by the atmospherics possible in a hushed auditorium. In the museum the actor is often on his own, is intensely vulnerable and relies on a wealth of experience, a well-researched and richly dramatised script, an in-depth knowledge of the background to the narrative, and a teacher's ears and eyes and a politician's – or stand-up comedian's – ability to handle heckles and banter. Her closeness to her audience allows for no hiding-place, no masking of any loss of focus – she must be in the moment throughout, on top of her role and alert to audience response second by second.

The slave trader sequence mentioned earlier offers a useful illustration of all three modes in operation, both sequentially and, for a time, simultaneously. During the debate initiated by the white slave trader, the actor operates mostly but not exclusively in collaborative (i.e. interactive) mode, while in the slave trading scene that precedes it he is mostly in representational mode. The scene represents the kind of trade deals that would have been done and is located precisely in 1807, just after the Abolition Act came into force – demonstrating that impact on the ground was minimal. But the representational mode also underpins and colours what happens in the interactive sequence that follows – the course of history can't be changed and the trader can never be persuaded to stop trading no matter how interactive the dialogue, nor how persuasive the audience's objections. The nature of that dialogue is inevitably conditioned by the audience's awareness of the doubleness of the action they witness. But also, at another level, the actor's ability to sustain that 'world' draws hugely from the self-expressive or virtuoso mode – that of the actor as actor. Many audience members commented afterwards on their frustration at, accompanied by reluctant admiration for, the character's (actor's) ability to have seemingly plausible answers for every objection they raised.

In Y Touring's *Breathing Country*, the clearest example of the simultaneity of these modes comes when the narrative section of the play ends (on a note of crisis as it's revealed that the memory stick containing vital, confidential and highly personal patient records has been lost) and the audience are invited to investigate further the issues raised, first by questioning the characters directly. As Marlene Winfield has explained (Winfield 2010), each of the four cast members had to answer questions in role from the audience and be sufficiently prepared for 'all the directions the debate might take'. It was, for the purposes of the exercise, vital that the actors remained wholly and believably in role, answering from the necessarily limited perspective of their own character – sharing their insights, confusions and beliefs with their questioners, but equally resisting any temptation to yield too readily to advice from the audience. In collaborative mode, they have to listen with care and explain with clarity – but not cave in! Only by grasping the validity and plausibility of the distinctively different positions offered by the teenage girl, her boyfriend, her father and the researcher, will the student audience be able to appreciate fully the complexity and importance of the issues at stake. But of course such ability, to retain character and yet to respond to often challenging questions in ways that help move the debate forward, requires considerable virtuosity. The concluding workshop – all too often tacked on in lesser TIE productions as a gesture towards 'participation' – was key to the effectiveness of the debate that ensued. And it required of the actors an ability to operate in all three modes, often at one and the same time: to be both in, and sometimes beyond, the kind of theatre to which our student questioner seemed to allude.

## Conclusion

Given the open, fluid and (in Michael Kirby's words, 1969) 'non-matrixed' performance conditions found in the average school hall, museum gallery or historic site, the challenges for actors in this field, the skills required of them, and indeed the institutional obligations upon them, are immense. And they all converge, in my view, in the ability not only to operate effectively in each of States's three modes but to sustain a performance in which, often, all three must be in play simultaneously. It is what any actor needs to be able to do *plus* a commitment to detailed research into the subject-matter, and to working with unpredictability; he or she must know how to 'read' and engage their audience (when to listen and watch as well as when to provoke) and know when and how to reassert the unyielding reality of the world they represent – as a corrective to easy mis- or pre-conceptions or as a stimulus to understanding that world more complexly. At its worst, acting in such settings can be an embarrassment, especially when undertaken in the mistaken belief that this is a diluted form of 'real theatre'. At its best it constitutes an acting skill of enormous impressiveness, and one that too often gets unrecognised and under-estimated. Y Touring has demonstrated a commitment to a theatre that can generate debate precisely because it stimulates the need for such debate *through* not despite the theatre. And the company's ceaseless exploration, over more than twenty years, of ways to renew and progress such theatrical forms, and to open up productive links with the electronic media, stands as something of a beacon in an educational landscape all too lacking in experiment and the willingness to work with uncertainty. Likewise, museum theatre at its best will always seek to provoke curiosity and a reassessment of historic events and scientific endeavours that we tend to take for granted but that still impact our lives in the immediate present and imminent future. In that endeavour, the actor's multifaceted range of skills and understandings is pivotal.

## Notes

1 Some elements of this discussion previously appeared in Jackson (2010a) (*This Accursed Thing*) and Jackson (2010b) (*Breathing Country*).

2 A number of other companies have also explored the possibilities of mixing live performance and digital media, most notably C&T, based in Worcestershire, UK – originally the 'Collar & Tie' TIE company. See www.candt.org.

3 The play was commissioned by the 'Performance, Learning and Heritage' research team at Manchester University and developed in partnership with the theatre company (Andrew Ashmore & Associates) and the museum curators and education staff. Further discussion can be found in Jackson (2010a), also Jackson and Kidd (2008).

## Works cited

Jackson, A. (2010a), 'Visitors becoming audiences: negotiating spectatorship in museum performance', *About Performance* 10, pp. 163–85.

——(2010b), '"So are you really a theatre company then?" – Y Touring and participatory theatre in the UK' at www.theatreofdebate.com/ytouring21/Blog/Blog.php (last accessed 31 January 2012).

Jackson, A. and Kidd, J. (2008), *Performance, Learning and Heritage: Final Report*. Online at www.plh.manchester.ac.uk (last accessed 31 July 2012).

Kirby, Michael (1969), *The Art of Time: Essays on the Avant-Garde*. New York: E. P. Dutton.

States, Bert O. (1983), 'The Actor's Presence: Three Phenomenal Modes', *Theatre Journal*, 35, pp. 359–75. (Reprinted in *Acting [Re]Considered*, ed. Phillip B. Zarrilli, Routledge, 1994.)

Winfield, Marlene (2010), 'Breathing Country: a breath of fresh air' at www.theatreofdebate.com/ytouring21/Authors/Authors/MarleneWinfield.html (accessed 31 January 2012).

Y Touring: Theatre of Debate. Online at www.theatreofdebate.com (accessed 31 January 2012).

# 7

# THE PERFORMER IN TIE

*Chris Cooper*

In the second edition of *Learning through Theatre* Cora Williams eloquently outlined the development of the actor in theatre in education ('The Theatre in Education Actor' 1993: 91–3). The relationship of the actor to the TIE company and the artistic process points to something both radical and unique in the history of British theatre. Since the inception of TIE the term actor-teacher 'encapsulate[d] the very nature of the then new theatre form, a hybrid, one species emanating from educational drama, the other from a traditional British theatre background' (ibid.: 91). Today, because of a lack of funding and training, that species stands on the edge of extinction. That is the subject of another essay, but the challenge for the actor, I believe, whether working in educational theatre with young people or on the 'main stage' of our theatres, remains fundamentally the same: to engage the audience's creativity.

In this essay I would like to focus on playwright Edward Bond's collaboration with Big Brum Theatre-in-Education Company and how this has developed the company's approach to acting – or as Bond calls it 'enactment', which is not about 'acting' at all. I will concentrate on some of the key aspects of this approach, in the hope that it will identify something new in the relationship between the audience and the actor which may be of interest and use to other performers – and especially to those working in TIE or TIE-related practice.

The work of the actor-teacher described by Williams is an extraordinarily dynamic one that was made possible by having a permanent company of actors in a TIE company. In 1993 there were dozens of TIE companies employing three to five full-time actor-teachers, something that is extremely rare today. This is a factor that makes it even more imperative to look for new ways of thinking about the actor-teacher (or performer) in TIE and how to engage the audience creatively. The advantages of having full-time actor-teachers are obvious because the TIE actor must constantly develop the TIE programme and performance, so that the interaction with the audience is continually renewed and refreshed. The relationship to audience in TIE is unique because the audience is also participant. 'TIE is the irregular sphere which invites and needs the audience to perfect it' (Williams 1993: 102).

In TIE the young people are invited to interact, intervene and manipulate time and space with and alongside the actor-teacher. But I believe that the theatre exists to connect with the audience in a way that brings it, if not physically, then imaginatively, into the performance space in order to seek what Bond calls our humanness. To do this in drama is an act of self-creation. As David Davis puts it:

> In drama, whatever happens on stage happens also in the self of the audience. They are not mere spectators. This is because the self must always seek meaning. This is simply the result of the way in which the self is created by the early infant. The audience is not just 'on stage', they *are* in a sense the stage.
>
> (Davis 2009: xli)

This requires an approach to acting that creates both a 'site' and a 'gap' for the audience/participant to fill with meaning.

## The site

If Stanislavskian theatre is distinguished by the foregrounding of character, and Brechtian theatre by the *Verfremdungseffekt*, then Bondian drama is distinguished by the concept of the site. Sites are used in Bond's drama primarily to establish the dramatic logic of the situation in order to illuminate our social reality and forge the direct connection between the play and the experience of the audience. The site is a tool for practice and analysis that can enrich all drama work. There are many sites in drama but we can identify four main categories based on Bond's own definitions (Bond 2000: 10).

Site A – the social sites, our ec[illegible]n.
Site B – the specific sites of the drama/play through which the story is told.
Site C – the action, images and objects that activate sites A and B in site D.
Site D – the audience/participant *as* the site of the imagination – the source of human value and meaning, humanness.

Each site is dialectically interconnected or contained in the other. Each site is specific and in playing the play it is the responsibility of the actor to resist both *generalising* 'joy', 'anger' or 'fear', and *commenting on* the situation they are enacting. (In this way a distinction may be drawn between the Bondian approach and that of Brecht who advocated actors capable of commenting, at least implicitly, on the dramatic action.)

In Bond's *The Broken Bowl*, commissioned by Big Brum in 2012 for 9–12-year-olds,[1] our social site, the world of 2012 (Site A), is present in the dysfunctional future society, described outside the front door of the family home, that is tearing the family apart. It is a world of social, economic and ecological crisis which resonates with our lived experience and is therefore present in us. The specific site of the play (Site B) is a room in which the family lives. The story is enacted in Site B and conveys the play's centre to the audience/participant through Site C – the dramatic action, images and objects. Site C is distinct from Site B because Site C conveys not the story but the potential meanings contained within the story to the participant/audience. Site D is not simply the audience passively receiving but the site of the imagination, actively engaging with the other sites in order to make meaning and become a source of value through what Bond calls the gap. This is an act of 'self'-creation.

## The gap

Just as the site is more than a place, the Bondian Gap means much more than an absence. In a way it is also a site that exists in order to be filled, imaginatively 'inhabited', or brought to life in many ways. As explained by Bas and Hankins (2005: 207):

> Bond writes of the gap as 'the space between the material world and the self.' Its essential nature is at once individual (psychological and ethical) and collective (indeed *communal*). Above all, it is an essentially ontological dimension, made up of our 'being': *we are the gap.* And, just as it can be contaminated or corrupted, so the gap has the authority to produce Value and Meaning, to be the site of Humanness.

Creating the gap with 'the authority to produce Value and Meaning' requires shifting from a transmission- or message-based paradigm to using the dramatic art of theatre to explore the human condition so that we come to know ourselves and the world we live in better. There is no right answer to how we do this. It is perhaps the difference between creating a piece of theatre about the impact of bullying that locates the problem in individuals and creating a drama which exposes the coercion and violence that saturates our culture and manifests itself in individuals; or creating dramas that complicate the situation whereby the actor can enable the audience to see themselves in the perpetrator of an abuse rather than just the victim. To do that requires that the actor leaves comment in the rehearsal room and judgement to the audience.

## The centre

The task for the actor then is to stay in the logic of the situation (the site) and create the gap for the audience to inhabit. (It is worth noting here that many plays do not make it possible for the actor to achieve this potential by virtue of having too little or conversely too much to say.) There is ground work that can be done in rehearsal to facilitate this connection with the audience.

One of the most useful tools for the actor-teacher working both on the text and facilitating the TIE programme as a whole is to establish a *centre* for each production: the core of what the production, and programme as a whole, are exploring and creating with the audience/participants. The centre of a TIE programme or drama workshop for young people, then, refers to the particular aspects or areas we are exploring for learning with the participants. The centre of a *text* is reflected in the play's main metaphors, similes and metonyms. Its patterns or structures are extended from the centre and contained within all the sites.

In the rehearsal or devising of a TIE programme the centre is defined and tested and redefined throughout the process. There is an overall centre but also the centre of each scene and central images, actions and objects. For the participatory elements of the TIE programme the centre can be defined and developed through questions and tasks that will open the gap further for the participants. It's important to state that, in order to access the full potential of the sites, the centre of any play or programme has to be defined for each production at the particular moment in time of its production. It is not an attempt to define a text for all time. For example a production of Hamlet will explore a different centre depending on the company, the audience/participants and that specific moment in history. But the centre can't be simply whatever we want it to be, because it is usefully constrained by the logic of *Hamlet*, the logic of the given dramatic situation.

In my experience, working with the centre changes the way the actor goes about her work, thinking not about foregrounding a character's individual psychology over the social situation but how her part relates to the whole site and the centre being excavated within it. The actor focuses on how the centre is reflected in what she is doing.

The sites and the centre define each other because the site provides the specific logic of the situation while the centre provides a thematic, conceptual or ontological framework for the actor. Together they provide the basis of 'our play' (the company's exploration) in order to connect with the audience and create space for them to engage in 'their play' – their life experience and the meaning of what occurs on stage for themselves.

## Exploring the situation

To take *The Broken Bowl* as an example: the site and the centre were used to define the performance of the play and the TIE programme as a whole. To understand the text the Company began identifying the concepts within it by exploring what was outside the room (Site B) but never seen in the street. The actors were then asked to explore the objects that appear in the play and identify what they tell us about both Sites A and B. We identified that there was a lot of hunger in the play that could be centred on the bowls, connecting the street with the room, but that the Girl, the Mother and the Father are hungry for different things and so the bowls acquire different values for each of them – for the Mother it contains routine family life, for the Father a means of survival, for the Girl it is a means of feeding the imagination. We then began to look at the text using these insights and identified a central speech for the play, and also central lines, actions and images connecting these different hungers in each scene. We were doing this in order to build the scaffolding for the enactment of the play. Over time we defined the centre we decided to work with as an exploration of how fear and isolation impacts on our perception of the real and the imagined. This became the centre of 'our play' and the starting point from which to build a programme to which the children could bring their own life and meanings. The TIE programme was then structured accordingly.

Before the play started, we established a frame for the children by asking them if they had ever been frightened and invited them to share their experiences in pairs. Then they were asked to look at the living room carefully and explore what they could see, before being asked if they could see or sense any fear in it – if so, where exactly? After sharing what had been discerned the facilitator explained, 'We want to share a story with you, a story we need to understand, about a Girl your age. A Girl who … [here the facilitator would reflect back what they had said about the room and fear]. Like life, it is a difficult, complicated story. We need to understand it. Will you help us do that?'

Invitation accepted, the programme moved into the performance of the play (around 1 hour 10 minutes), which had three scenes. The play was stopped after each scene to explore what had happened. The tasks varied depending on the response of the children, while sustaining a focus on the centre (fear, isolation, reality and imagination): asking young people to be the imaginary friends at the table, articulating the Father's thoughts and responses to the Girl, examining the objects such as the broken bowl to explore what had been shattered. The actors worked to respond to what the children offered by taking the social understandings into performance, perhaps changing the way something was said or done to deepen it. The aim was to make the play useful to the participants; the changes were nuanced and subtle but helped to aggregate new meaning, 'perfect the sphere'. At the end of the play the actor-teachers explored moments from the play with the children, inviting them to step into the shoes of the Father, the Girl or the Mother, in the understanding that it's not just what is done but how it is done that reveals understanding; the process of exploration continued in groups before sharing in order to learn from each other about the site.

In the enactment of a play, then, the actor is a mediator through which the play needs to speak and through which the audience speaks to the play. It's not a question of finding the inner motivations of the character but playing the character on the site of the play, playing the play. Bond consistently advises actors to stop acting. 'He means start enacting: start to lay bare the processes which enable, or deprive us of, our humanity' (Davis 2009: 1). Acting closes down meaning, enactment opens meaning up and the world becomes an open question.

How do we keep the world open? To return to *The Broken Bowl*, the Girl uses a bowl to feed her imaginary friend, which is a source of immense conflict with the Father; it disturbs and confounds his grip on reality. In the second scene he smashes the bowl with a hammer to end her play. In an act of courageous defiance the Girl, determined to feed her friend, brings a tin bowl back into the room. The Father comes in and the Girl tries to hide the tin bowl from him but he doesn't notice it:

> *Father*: We've got to chop the furniture up.
>
> *Mother*: Chop the – ? Why?

*Father*: The whole street's doing it.

*Mother*: Why?

*Father*: To burn for firewood. There's no electricity – there won't be anymore.

*Mother*: Good heavens! But burn the –

*Father*: If you don't you lose it. There's looters. Going in gangs. They're taking all the furniture they can find!

*Mother*: But burn the – !

*Father*: Help me! If we don't we'll lose all of it! *(Gives the tin bowl to Girl)* Take it. … That's how we have to live from now on – on the floor!

The Mother and Father take the table and three chairs. The fourth chair (the one at which she seats her imaginary friend) remains in the Girl's protection. She sits on it, pleading with her absent friend to return to help her. The father re-enters:

*Father*: I want it.

*Girl*: It's his.

*Father*: What's in the bowl?

*Girl*: *(She twines her legs round the chair legs)* His meal.

The Father threatens to chop the seat from under the Girl when he returns for the chair. She leaves the house in search of her friend in the street. Father returns with a hatchet.

*Father*: Damn. *(Under his breath)* Run off. *(Goes towards the kitchen. Stops)* How do I tell her mother? Be a row. Be my fault. *(Sucks his thumb)* Hurts. *(Shakes his hand)* Blood tastes of nails and hammers. *(Turns back to the chair. Stares at the food. Hooks a finger in it. Licks it from his finger. Slowly moves it around in his mouth. Suddenly drops the hatchet, grabs the bowl and eats all the food. Licks the bowl.)* Waste food on a zombie when the world's starving.

What are the options available to the actor in the site? The actor must find all the possibilities, but they can only be found in the moment, in the situation. It is important *not* to determine how the actors respond to each other in advance, but to let the logic of situation dictate this. There is no blocking, the actors need to find the topography of the situation. We used the sites and the centre as a guide to break the situation down precisely to avoid generalisation. In rehearsal it is very important not to make decisions on what is 'right' too soon and fix things, only to eliminate what is not reflecting the centre. There are virtually limitless possibilities for exploration that, if properly centred and sited, can continue to be unearthed in performance.

In the rehearsal we worked with the central concepts of isolation and fear – what feeds them? The Girl and her Father occupy two different realities, as if in two different worlds – his is existential, hers is ontological. The Father is driven by the fear of what is happening outside. The Girl is driven by the imperative to feed her friend. It's her intuitive connection, through imagination, to understanding what is happening outside in the street; she has 'cathected' the bowl, investing it with a different value to the Father's.[2]

To return to the text quoted above, the Father re-enters the room in a panic about what is happening outside and no longer registers the significance of the tin bowl; he simply tells the Girl to take it so he can move the table because they must now eat from the floor. He has a bigger (more extreme) problem, embodied in the furniture, to deal with. Yet the bowl retains a different value for the Girl; she is driven by the imperative to feed her friend and the bowl has to go on the table. The clash of values is of critical importance if we are to access the sites for the audience and specifically engage Site D – not simply tell the story but open it up for the audience's analysis.

This is achieved by creating the two coexisting realities on the site. For example, looking at the sequence from 'The Girl tries to hide the tin bowl from him but he doesn't notice it' to where the Father 'Gives the tin bowl to the Girl', the text is silent on how it gets on the table. But it has to be put on the table at some point in order that the Father can hand it to the Girl. It would be easy to miss this detail or simply step over the problem by making it a technical problem: 'I could put it down when he's looking the other way'. But it is *not* a technical question. It's a question of the site and centre. It is perhaps far more useful that the Father sees her put the bowl down on the table before giving it back to her to create more of a gap for Site D.

The actors began to define their territory in the site, focused their energy on the centre through the objects in the situation: the Mother clinging on to the furniture (her family), the Father (blinded by fear) insisting that reality demands living and eating off the floor, the Girl clinging to the tin bowl for autonomy, seeking to feed another rather than herself. This is an extraordinary collision between reason (the Father), accepting their fate, which becomes socially mad, and the imagination (the Girl), which is seeking another way of dealing with the crisis – two different but interconnected realities coexisting in the movement of the bowl. The Girl becomes absorbed in the bowl; she cradles it like a vulnerable baby, yet because she is at the same time acutely aware of the threat of the Father, the cradling is also a shielding. It creates a gap for the audience to fill with meaning. In the playing of it, though, the actor has to remain in the logic of the situation. The cradling of the bowl is practical, not symbolically abstract. To play it this way (symbolically) would be to close down the meaning. The Girl has to protect the bowl from her Father. The Father has to destroy the table and a bowl is in the way.

The journey of the bowl is not yet completed, though, because the tin bowl is re-cathected once the Father returns from the kitchen and realises that it is a replacement for the one he has smashed. His hunger for control is reasserted when confronted once again by her determination to feed her imagination. The Father's decision to eat the food through existential self-pity also opens up ontological meaning for the audience, who have access to all the values invested in it in the site: the Girl sees future life in the bowl; the Father sees zombies, the living dead.

The way the actor playing the Father enacts eating the food is also a Drama Event; it is achieved without comment from the en-actor and in doing so he reconfigures the world as a question for the audience. Why are they doing what they are doing? Could I be him? What would I do now in his situation? The actor leaves the answers to the audience/participant. We are forced to decide because the reason for what is happening has not been interpreted for us. 'We don't experience second hand in the Drama Event but first hand, we don't echo the characters' emotions, as in realist drama, but, imaginatively seeking reasons, we have to generate our own emotional response' (Davis 2005: 210). For the audience/participant to take this on is an act of self-creation; it means taking responsibility for ourselves and therefore contains the potential for being *socially* responsible: how can we take responsibility for others if we cannot take responsibility for ourselves?

Finally, it is perhaps worth making a brief note on character. Focusing on the site and the centre does not make character and characterisation redundant in Bondian drama, far from it. But characterisation is not our starting point; it can only be created through exploring the centre of the play and understanding the situation.

Through this the actor comes to know the characters in a much more profound way because playing the situation isn't just about grasping the social but also the particular psycho-social dimension, the human dimension. The actor has to react or respond creatively to the situation the character is presented with. Then the humanness of the Mother and Father and Girl in *The Broken Bowl* will emerge and embody all the humour, fallibility and inconsistencies that make for 'character' in conventional drama but in a particular and not generalised way: fallibility, irony, anger or laughter are particularised. The emotion that characters express in the site is not cathartic or manipulative but precise and appropriate. Through enactment, the actor experiences the play and creates the means by which the audience come to recognise themselves in each character in each particular situation.

I hope I have provided enough of an insight for the reader to want to look further into Bond's work in books such as *Edward Bond and the Dramatic Child* (Davis 2005), the student edition of *Saved* (Davis 2009) and not least through his plays and theoretical writings like *The Hidden Plot* (Bond 2000), as a development of the struggle to 'perfect the sphere' as Williams put it. Whatever the long-term future for TIE in the UK, tools like the site and centre, and the enactment of them, can be applied to making theatre in any context where the play allows such freedom – using the skill of the actor to engage the audience's creativity and facilitating meaning-making through a world of open questions.

## Notes

1 See chapter 2 (pp. 56–7) for further discussion of this play.

2 Cathexis occurs when an object is imbued with energy and emotional value or meaning greater than the object itself, while still retaining the original use value. For the Girl the bowl is invested with new value. When the father devours the food in the bowl he is destroying what she imagines: stealing his daughter's food is like an act of cannibalism. The object can be de-cathected and re-cathected. One of the strategies for creating the Drama Event (DE) is the use of objects in action. To create a DE, it is necessary to focus on the object at an extreme moment (not necessarily violent) and to show it in such a way that it can be examined both in its own right and in relation to the rest of the drama. It ruptures, but does not interrupt, the story enough to surprise us and create a gap for reflection and analysis.

## Works cited

Bas, Georges and Hankins, Jérôme (2005), 'A Glossary of terms', trans. from French by Alison Douthwaite, in Davis, ed. (2005), pp. 201–20.

Bond, Edward (2000), *The Hidden Plot*. London: Methuen.
——(2012), *The Broken Bowl*. Unpublished.
Davis, David (2009), 'Introduction' to Edward Bond, *Saved* (students' edition), London: Methuen.
——, ed. (2005), *Edward Bond and the Dramatic Child*. Stoke on Trent: Trentham Books.
Williams, Cora (1993), 'The Theatre in Education Actor', in Jackson, ed., *Learning Through Theatre*, 2nd edn. London: Routledge, pp. 91–108.

# 8

# CHALLENGING FACILITATION

## Training facilitators for Theatre for Dialogue programmes

*Lynn Hoare*

Let's talk about sex, baby (sing it)
Let's talk about you and me (sing it, sing it)
Let's talk about all the good things
And the bad things that may be
Let's talk about sex (come on)

Salt-N-Pepa, 1991

Sex. How do college students talk about it, especially with partners, without 'spoiling the mood' and in a way that isn't awkward and embarrassing? Facilitating honest conversations with college audiences about sex, boundaries, safety and consent is the focus of *Get Sexy, Get Consent*,[1] a Theatre for Dialogue programme at the University of Texas at Austin (UT). In this essay I examine the complex responsibilities inherent in facilitating interactive theatre programmes, especially when dealing with sensitive personal and interpersonal issues. I propose that training effective facilitators requires an understanding of three key constructs: programme content, interactive intent and facilitator function. Through a case study of *Get Sexy, Get Consent*, I examine the skills and responsibilities of effective facilitators and argue that when training includes preparation for dealing with content, intent and facilitator function, novice facilitators will be more prepared to respond authentically to a group, going 'off-script' as necessary.

### Theatre for Dialogue: the programme

Flashback, Spring 2011: Four college-aged actor-facilitators have engaged their peers for the past fifty minutes through a carefully structured programme that alternates theatrical/performative moments (music – such as the song that opens this essay, frozen images, monologues and scenes) with interactive activities (debating pick-up lines, enacting 'consent conversations' about sexual boundaries, discussing ways to check for consent with a partner).[2] Throughout the programme, the audience has evolved from observers in a traditional theatrical relationship to participants engaged in discussion about what they have just seen, reflection on what they think it means and debate about what they think should happen differently. We now arrive at the final conversation. An actor-facilitator steps out of her character role and asks for responses to the theatrical moment they have witnessed: 'Is this realistic? What stops people from talking about sex with a partner before it happens? How can asking for consent be sexy?' Hands slowly move into the air and the discussion begins. Referencing the theatrical moments they have all witnessed, audience-participants deliberate these questions with the facilitator and each other. The careful placing of interactive activities, woven through a dramatic framework, builds an environment of permission to talk about sex within the drama and because of the drama, in a way that rarely happens in a room of fifty strangers.

The Theatre for Dialogue programme serves the UT campus through various styles of collaboratively devised, interactive and facilitated theatre pieces. Theatre for Dialogue is part of the Voices Against Violence programme, which addresses sexual assault, relationship violence and stalking, through a variety of services including individual and group counselling, public events and prevention workshops. I direct the Theatre for Dialogue programme which includes a year-long academic course and multiple performance ensembles that devise and tour interactive programmes on a range of issues including dating violence, building healthy relationships, sexual assault and consent.

Theatre for Dialogue shares the same theories, techniques and objectives as Theatre in Education (TIE). Both fit under the larger umbrella of Applied Theatre: theatre that happens in alternative, non-theatrical settings and works with a group or audience to confront an event, a relevant question, or a pressing issue (Taylor 2003). I could call this work TIE; however, the label 'Theatre for Dialogue' offers an instant reference for what will happen in the room. Theatre for Dialogue creates opportunities for difficult discussions that help participants confront assumptions, gather information and make meaning around a topic or question – through the theatrical frame. The tools of theatre allow investigation of and reflection on an issue through the safety of this frame, such as when participants debate the choice a character must make, or a character asks for advice, or the audience is invited to enter a dramatic moment and rehearse change.

Theatre for Dialogue programmes do not invite sharing of specific personal experiences, though there are points at which reflection is encouraged outside of the story: 'Why might someone make this choice? What stops people from talking about these issues?' These questions require participants to connect the content to their own lives, though at a distance. If a personal example or story is shared by a participant (which happens infrequently), the comment is acknowledged and the conversation is redirected to the entire group. The content of Theatre for Dialogue programmes often hits home for members of the audience, so it is essential that the action of the programme keeps participants moving forward without focusing exclusively on, or inviting analysis of, one participant's experience.[3]

By the end of *Get Sexy*, the audience participants will typically talk openly and honestly about sex, typically a challenge for a group of 18- to 21-year-olds unfamiliar with each other. They are drawn in by the energy and relevance of the theatre, but kept at a distance by the frame (*this is not my life, but the issues are relevant and realistic enough for me to respond as if this could be my life*). The performance elements are dynamic enough to motivate audience members to become involved when the opportunity arises for participation. To move intentionally towards moments of open and often risky dialogue, the programme must be carefully structured to support participants as they delve into a topic, unpack complicated moments of a story, and interact in various ways with characters, actor-facilitators and each other. Managing this journey for participants falls on the shoulders of a facilitator. In her book, *Understanding Facilitation: Theory and Principle*, Christine Hogan captures the challenge of defining the facilitator: 'As with many evolving phenomena, there is no one agreed definition of facilitation' (Hogan 2002: 10). In TIE and applied theatre we have standard expectations of what a facilitator should do, but few common definitions, possibly because this role changes depending on programme goals and expectations. Hogan offers her own definition: 'Facilitation is concerned with encouraging open dialogue among individuals with different perspectives so that diverse assumptions and options may be explored' (ibid.). Though not the only goal in a Theatre for Dialogue programme, encouraging open dialogue is an essential task for a facilitator.

## The facilitator

A Theatre for Dialogue piece combines elements of theatre with educational purpose to investigate, reflect, provoke dialogue and rehearse action. These tasks require a facilitator who guides the experience. In Theatre for Dialogue, as in TIE, I call this person an actor-facilitator.[4] The actor-facilitator may be in role with students or audience participants, or out of role and external to the performative moments, such as the Joker in a forum theatre performance.[5] Facilitation is the most challenging component for novice actor-facilitators to learn because of continually shifting responsibilities and skills. The facilitator is a guide for the group experience: he or she invites participation, encourages diverse viewpoints and solicits problem-solving techniques. A facilitator is aware of who is in the room and understands that people are present for different reasons and often arrive with varied levels of information related to the topic. Moreover, a facilitator helps a group uncover knowledge – information already in the group and/or useful to the group – and provides an opportunity for individuals to develop understanding and make new meanings through the combination of theatrical event, programme content and individual participation.

A unique combination of skills and responsibilities is required of the actor-facilitator in a Theatre for Dialogue piece, different from those needed to facilitate a group workshop or classroom lesson, primarily because of the negotiation of theatrical and participatory frames. It is the actor-facilitator's responsibility to help the audience understand when they are in role as audience-observers, audience-participants, or characters in the drama themselves, and exactly what is expected of them in each frame: to brainstorm ideas, offer advice, join a conversation with characters, make a decision, reflect on the situation, or stop the action in a scene, for example.[6] The facilitator is also responsible for understanding the context in which the programme takes place,[7] as this can reveal potential barriers to audience involvement. In the *Get Sexy* programme, facilitators must understand the particular context of a Texas college campus: the majority of UT students come from Texas public schools that use an 'abstinence only' curriculum for sex education. It can be assumed that the majority of the *Get Sexy, Get Consent* target population has limited experience of open discussion about sexual decision-making and consent. This affects how the programme employs theatrical framing and how actor-facilitators build toward an open, honest conversation. For example, in the first 'consent conversation' a couple *in a relationship* (played by an actor-facilitator and an audience volunteer) discuss sex – one character is ready for sex and the other is not. This conversation happens within a relationship to make it more accessible to a population that has been taught 'abstinence until marriage' and may attach sexual decision-making to relationships rather than casual sex. Following this first conversation, the *Get Sexy* programme progresses – building content, deepening participation and pushing risk level – to the second 'consent conversation' about safe sex between new sexual partners, and, finally, to a scenario that addresses the challenges of honest conversation during a one-night stand. Theatrical moments in combination with interactive activities offer participants a variety of ways to explore attitudes and perceptions, and reflect on and experiment with (possibly) unfamiliar behaviours.

The facilitator is also responsible for developing rapport with audience-participants – a trusting relationship that invites honest participation and dialogue. Rapport is developed through eye contact, tone, inflection, an authentic but mostly neutral presence, an appropriate use of humour at specific moments to break tension or create connection, a degree of confidence (over-confidence can be just as problematic as under-confidence in creating rapport) and body language, among other qualities. Rapport is often connected to personal style, and both develop over time and with practice. Taking time intentionally to develop the nuanced characteristics of rapport with novice facilitators is sometimes considered secondary to delivering content or rehearsing performative moments, particularly in a short rehearsal and training period. However, strong rapport enables the actor-facilitators to question and challenge participant assumptions and to invite differing viewpoints. Ultimately, it is because of the relationship between facilitator and participants that honest dialogue about sex happens in the *Get Sexy* programme.

Beyond the responsibilities of clarifying participant roles, understanding context and developing rapport, a facilitator must master a variety of skills required to negotiate the different frames of theatrical event and participant involvement. 'The artists' teaching skills are just as important, if not more so, than theatrical presentation for it is in the teaching ability of the artists that the … nature of the work will be realized' (Taylor 2003: 54). These skills include active listening, awareness of non-verbal cues, a thorough understanding of the programme goals and objectives, knowledge of various tools for engagement including questioning strategies and dramatic techniques, a sense of timing, a capacity to improvise and gauge the next appropriate question, and the aptitude to read the dynamics of a group and guide the audience. Facilitation may be embedded within an acting role and thus also require acting proficiency in translating the character, context and frame of the theatrical event. In *Get Sexy, Get Consent*, the facilitator role is shared among all actors and happens both within and outside character roles, thus requiring clear transitions between actor and character, between facilitators, and in and out of theatrical frames.

Of absolute necessity for effective facilitation is an understanding of the role of questions and questioning.[8] Though an essential skill, facilitation is more sophisticated than merely having the right question at one's fingertips. The choice of question at every moment relies on a variety of factors such as the goal of the programme and how it intersects with participant response and engagement. How can we prepare novice facilitators for such a layered and complex task?

## Training the actor-facilitator

In addition to considering responsibilities, skills and questioning techniques, analysing three key concepts will help a novice actor-facilitator prepare for and respond to participants throughout an interactive event. I identify these three concepts as programme content, interactive intent and facilitator function. Though I will include examples of each key construct, it is impossible to be comprehensive as the specific content, intent, and function will change from programme to programme.

### *Programme content*

An essential component of training actor-facilitators is to help them learn the content upon which theatrical and interactive moments are built. Which pieces of information absolutely must be communicated to audience-participants in order to meet the goals of the programme? When actor-facilitators are part of a devising process, understanding of content and decisions about what to include may happen organically through the research, development and piloting phases of a programme. The original *Get Sexy, Get Consent* ensemble helped to shape elements of the core content through their questions and experiences in the first tour. *Get Sexy, Get Consent* is now an ongoing programme at UT Austin, requiring the annual training of new actor-facilitator teams. Though the core content of the programme is set and must be mastered by each new ensemble, new actor-facilitators continue to analyse content based on changes in slang/language, the law and cultural or campus trends, leading to minor updates as necessary.

In *Get Sexy, Get Consent*, preparing facilitators to accomplish programme goals includes making sure they understand content and feel confident sharing it. Some information will be delivered at a predetermined point in the programme, while other pieces will be shared through audience interaction and dialogue as the need arises. Content includes:

- the definition of sexual assault;
- statistics about sexual assault for this age group (18–24);
- a definition of consent;
- a definition of safer sex, including physical and emotional safety as well as protection from pregnancy and infection;
- common myths and assumptions around sexual assault;
- the difference between regretted sex and sexual assault; and
- campus and community resources for survivors of sexual assault.

Near the end of the *Get Sexy* programme, the actor-facilitators make the transition to a higher-stakes interactive moment that is based on the content learned earlier. The group has already identified a definition of consent, discussed why consent is necessary (sex without consent is sexual assault), explored negotiating safe sex and setting boundaries and listened to statistics about the rates of sexual assault in college populations. A quick series of frozen images sets the stage for the next moment: 'Let's say you are at a bar. You see someone you are interested in. You meet them. You decide to go home together. You end up in bed with them.' While two actors freeze in a tableau of this moment, a third actor-facilitator steps out of role to talk to the audience. 'Let's pause here. There isn't usually a lot of conversation at this point. But there is a lot that gets negotiated in the heat of the moment. How does each person make sure the other wants the same thing?' From here, the facilitator gives the group its task. 'Your job is to watch this scene and to freeze the action anytime you see or hear something that doesn't seem consensual. Let's review how you defined consent earlier in the programme. What were the words you used?' After recalling the group definition, the 'One-Night Stand' begins, with the audience in active observer mode. The content previously explored in the programme has prepared participants to understand the stakes at this dramatic moment. It is clear by this point that proceeding to have sex with someone without consent would equate to sexual assault.

Looking beyond this programme, content can also include understanding historical context, factual information (definitions or statistics), social and cultural norms related to the issue, and dramatised references to actual events. The nature of this work demands that facilitators be flexible and responsive to an audience, which requires balancing when and how programme content is shared. Not only must they be attuned to programme objectives and understand how to deliver content through the theatrical framework, but facilitators often need a deeper understanding and analysis of content beyond the specific goals of the programme in order to handle confidently open-ended conversations and questions.

### *Interactive intent*

Interactive intent requires the facilitator to acknowledge the goal behind each moment of participation. Ideally, opportunities to interact become increasingly complex as we move through a programme, relying on previous moments of participation to advance investment in the story, to develop knowledge of the topic or issue, and to promote action within the context of the dramatic event, or in one's own life. The intent of the 'One-Night Stand' scene is for participants to:

- identify verbal and non-verbal signals of non-consent;
- practise intervening (if only verbally) in non-consensual situations;
- brainstorm ways to check for consent and offer advice to a character;
- witness a character enacting participant suggestions and observe potential responses; and
- learn ways to ask explicitly for consent rather than rely on assumptions.

Widening the lens, interactive intent can also include opportunities to practise participation through low-risk moments, build towards deeper involvement, share and listen to varied perspectives and opinions, reflect on the past experiences and discuss future choices of a character, identify potential consequences of a decision, rehearse options through simultaneous dramaturgy[9] or by volunteering to replace a character in a dramatic moment, draw connections to current events, and to problem-solve, individually or as a group.

This is only a sampling of the possible interactive intent for each moment of participation. Specifying why and how we want participants to be involved means interrogating programme objectives. We can build engagement early in a programme by asking participants to discuss what they saw; later in a programme we may need a more

*Figure 8.1* '*Get Sexy, Get Consent* ...' (Theatre for Dialogue, UT Austin, 2012). An actor-facilitator invites participants to respond to a role-play between actor and audience volunteer. Photo: Andrew Mendoza.

challenging mode of interaction that requires creative problem-solving. If we are not specific about the intent of each moment, we risk alienating an audience because we ask them to risk too much, too early or too late.

## Facilitator function

If *intent* refers to what we want the audience members to explore and experience through their active participation in the programme, *function* describes the role of the facilitator in helping realise this intent. Facilitator function is the most nuanced and interpretive component of the three constructs. Moment to moment, the actor-facilitator must determine how to balance serving the participants, the process and the programme. Identifying the facilitator function allows actor-facilitators to understand how to help meet the intent of interactive moments, although it does not lessen the necessity of improvisation in responding to what comes up in the room.

During the 'One-Night Stand' sequence, the facilitator has multiple, often overlapping functions she must employ. At any point, her function may be to:

- encourage participants to identify and verbalise non-consensual behaviours they have observed;
- gather creative suggestions for asking for consent;
- assess whether the audience believes suggested choices are realistic;
- normalise conversations about negotiating sex and consent; and,
- keep it real – if audience members suggest ideas that aren't believable, it is essential that the facilitator challenge the group to find realistic options that don't 'spoil the mood', often through further questioning of the entire group: 'Is this realistic? Why or why not? What other suggestions do you have?'

These varied functions constantly overlap throughout the 'One-Night Stand' scene. Typically, participants freeze the scene when they witness 'Tina's' non-consensual reaction to 'Martin' taking off her shirt. Through discussion, participants offer ideas about how Martin can check in with Tina about consent, including a few lines of dialogue. The actors replay the moment using audience suggestions. Another participant calls freeze, saying, 'I don't think that's realistic, that someone says, "May I take off your shirt?" It doesn't happen like that.' The facilitator encourages further dialogue to find out what could be realistic in terms of verbalising consent. Participants debate various options. Some argue that it's awkward to talk about sex while it is happening, while others advocate openly asking for consent: 'It's totally realistic … you can be sexy about asking someone to take off their shirt.' The facilitator moderates, making sure that varied perspectives are heard, but also encouraging specific behaviours for the actors to implement in replaying the scene. New suggestions for the actors include the original line about asking to take off Tina's shirt but also incorporate pace (how fast do you move things forward?), tone (how can it be sexy?) and non-verbal signals (what tells you they are into it?). The actors rewind and replay the moment using these suggestions, and this time the audience decides that what they just saw is realistic.

A facilitator must always be ready to employ a variety of functions in any interactive theatre programme. She must:

- create a space safe enough for participation and opinions;
- question why characters or participants make a specific choice;
- establish clear boundaries and give direction;
- monitor programme goals;
- include all participants (whether they participate verbally or not); and

- challenge assumptions, myths and stereotypes in a way that is responsible, consistent with programme goals, but also keeps participants engaged and learning.

It is important for the director of an interactive programme to help a novice facilitator identify how to balance the needs of the programme and the audience, and which function might take priority at any given moment.

## In closing

Facilitating honest conversations about negotiating sex and consent requires that facilitators walk a delicate line, particularly when working with a group of peers. Helping actor-facilitators identify the necessary programme content and effective delivery of that content, the intent of each interactive moment, and the (often changing) function of the facilitator throughout a programme is one way to support the growth of novice facilitators without sacrificing the audience-participant experience. This model is applicable in any context that asks participants to engage with dramatic moments in an active way. No matter what the specific goal, content or target age may be, when involvement of the audience participants is central to the programme, it is essential to offer facilitators in-depth training and skill-building in group management, questioning skills, development of rapport, guiding participant roles, assessing the particular needs of context or population, and negotiating audience expectations and programme objectives. Additionally, in a programme that provides the opportunity to learn through theatre, it is necessary to consider these questions:

- What content underpins the programme? How will it be shared and discussed?
- Why and how will individuals be invited to engage? How do we create opportunities for meaningful participation?
- How do interactive intent and programme content shape the facilitator's function in each moment of a programme?

Acknowledging programme content, identifying interactive intent, and clarifying facilitator function is good practice. It requires that we approach each moment of a participation-based programme thoughtfully and deliberately and with respect for audience-participants. When we are conscientious about how we train our actor-facilitators to guide challenging conversations, we support complex facilitation of interactive programmes, and offer truly meaningful opportunities to explore, experience, rehearse and learn through theatre.

## Notes

1 The original title for the *Get Sexy, Get Consent* programme was *The Sexy Sex Kind of Sex*, which piloted at UT Austin as part of the David Cohen New Works Festival in 2011 and was co-devised with Ben Snyder.

2 *Get Sexy, Get Consent* was created to promote conversations and decision-making around sex and consent. It opens with an 'image montage' of brief silent scenes that end with frozen pictures and cover a variety of interactions around sex and consent. After a conversation with the audience, the actor-facilitators present monologues in character about experiences of sexual assault. These are followed by statistics that reference the reality of sexual assault on college campuses. The audience is then invited to help practise, or role-play, conversations around sexual boundaries and safe sex. In the final scene of a one-night stand, the audience is challenged to stop the action whenever they perceive non-consent from either character. This prompts the final conversation about what stops us from talking about sex and consent with a sexual partner, and how a conversation about consent can be sexy. *Get Sexy, Get Consent* runs for one hour and is performed on the UT Austin campus for classes, student groups, student organisations (both social and academic) and departmental programmes.

3 The Theatre for Dialogue programme is housed in the UT Counseling and Mental Health Center (CMHC), but operates as prevention-focused programming rather than counselling or drama therapy. At the beginning and ending of every performance, an actor-facilitator acknowledges that these issues can be difficult to discuss and can bring up personal experiences. Students are encouraged to seek support, if needed, through CMHC and/or the crisis hotline available to all UT students.

4 This terminology has changed over time, and various terms are now used across the field of applied theatre and TIE. I prefer 'actor-facilitator' to 'actor-teacher' because it references the specific and entwined roles expected of the facilitators in Theatre for Dialogue programmes. See Introduction, p. 13, and Taylor (2003) for further discussion of the terminology.

5 See Boal (1985 and 1992) for discussion of the role of the 'joker' – one who problematises and challenges responses in an effort to produce a realistic outcome, thereby creating a 'rehearsal for reality.'

6 See Jackson for a thorough discussion of participation frames in educational theatre work, including narrative, investigative, representational and involvement frames (Jackson 2007: 166).

7 Prendergast and Saxton (2009: 17) argue that the facilitator must be one who is 'familiar with the social structures and community contexts'; and knows 'how to do something … why it is appropriate, when it needs to be done and how to do it in the most effective way'.

8 *Asking Better Questions,* by Morgan and Saxton (2006), is an excellent resource in helping facilitators understand the role of questions in an interactive programme.

9 Simultaneous dramaturgy is one technique for involving audience members in a forum theatre production. Boal (1985: 132) describes this as a situation in which the audience stops a scene in order to give the actors suggestions and ideas for how to play it out differently in an attempt to solve the problem or crisis.

## Works cited

Boal, A. (1985), *Theatre of the Oppressed*, trans. Charles and Maria-Odilia McBride. New York: Theatre Communications Group, Inc.

——(1992, 2nd edn, 2003), *Games for Actors and Non-Actors*, trans. Adrian Jackson. London: Routledge.

*Get Sexy, Get Consent* (2011), Austin, TX: unpublished.

Hogan, C. (2002), *Understanding Facilitation: Theory and Principle*. London: Kogan Page Ltd.

Jackson, A. (2007), *Theatre, Education and the Making of Meanings: art or instrument?* Manchester: Manchester University Press.

Morgan, N. and Saxton, J. (2006), *Asking Better Questions*, 2nd edn. Markham, Ontario: Pembroke Publishers.

Prendergast, M. and Saxton, J., eds. (2009), *Applied Theatre: International Case Studies and Challenges for Practice*. Chicago: Intellect.

Salt-N-Pepa. (1991), *Let's Talk About Sex*. Blacks' Magic Album. London: London Records.

Taylor, P. (2003), *Applied Theatre: Creating Transformative Encounters in the Community*. Portsmouth, NH: Heinemann.

# 9

# REGIONAL THEATRES AS LEARNING RESOURCES

*Steve Ball*

This chapter will explore the evolving relationship between regional theatres in England and education. Some theatres, fearing that the term 'education' is often regarded as being solely concerned with the experience of children in schools, use a number of other terms including learning and participation, creative learning and creative projects to describe their work. Funding has also been an influential factor. Regional theatres in the UK have long relied on subsidy from local authorities and Arts Councils to enable them to experiment and to innovate as well as providing affordable seats for audiences. For some time there has been an expectation that this subsidy will not just support the artistic process but will also enable theatres to provide learning opportunities particularly for children and young people.[1]

In the 1960s and 1970s when regional theatres began to develop education or outreach programmes they concentrated almost exclusively on two main strands of participatory engagement with children and young people: youth theatre and theatre in education. Whilst most regional producing theatres still run youth theatres there have been no TIE companies attached to regional theatres since the Belgrade Theatre in Coventry disbanded its TIE team in 1996.[2] Those TIE companies that have survived the political and funding challenges, such as M6 and Big Brum, have done so as independent companies diversifying their remit and forging close partnerships with local schools. They often showcase their work in regional building-based theatres but operate independently of them.

Theatre in Education has – at least in its 'classic' sense as practised through the 1970s, 1980s and 1990s – largely been replaced by a broader, more holistic approach to Theatre Education. The dropping of the 'in' is a direct reflection of the ways in which theatres have diversified their practice and of their focus upon the core activity of the theatre – audience development and the main stage repertoire. Whilst much of this activity continues to take place in schools and community settings, there has been a shift in emphasis from 'outreach' programmes and projects to 'in-reach' activities which provide opportunities to engage with the whole theatre. This approach considers the theatre – including its stages, resources, productions and staff – as a learning resource for schools, colleges, individuals and communities. Recent policy developments in schools in England, including the introduction of a slimmed-down National Curriculum which excludes Drama as well as most other arts subjects, have resulted in a significant decline in the number of specialist drama teachers in schools and in some cases the marginalisation of arts subjects to extra-curricular activities. Within this context it can be argued that regional theatres have an increasingly important part to play in providing drama and theatre opportunities to schools, many of which will look upon their local theatres as principal providers of drama and theatre education.

A central aim of regional theatres' learning and participation programmes is to animate the theatre's repertoire. Some of these activities seek to enrich the theatre-going experience by providing pre- and post-show events for ticket holders including post-show discussions with members of the cast and creative teams, meet the director/writer/designer events, as well as longer enrichment experiences in which groups, usually schools, are introduced to the play they are about to see. This typically involves a combination of question-and-answer events in which students are given the opportunity to ask questions and discuss the production with the director and members of the creative team, an introduction to the technical aspects of the show and opportunities for participants to take on the role of director in a simulation of the rehearsal process.

Similarly, many theatres recognise that few children and young people are independent theatregoers, so they offer 'Family Day' activities for children and their parents in an attempt to engage the whole family. These participatory activities are usually drama- and theatre-related, but often involve other art forms including storytelling and the visual arts.

This shift in emphasis from outreach provision, which often took little account of the theatre's main repertoire, towards one which focuses on the theatre and its productions, utilises the unique contribution that a producing theatre can make to the learning process. It recognises that theatres are in the business of making and presenting plays. But however ambitious and extensive their learning and participation programmes are and however much their work is underpinned by a commitment to personal development and social justice, theatres are not education organisations or social services departments of local authorities. It is their role as producing theatres that separates them from other drama and theatre provision.

For many years there existed an inherent tension between two key objectives of theatres: audience development and theatre education. This often manifested itself in strained relationships between theatres' marketing and education departments, too often characterised by mutual suspicion with theatre educators opposed to the crude notion of getting 'bums on seats' and marketing teams bemused by the lack of connectivity between education programmes and the plays they sought to promote. Fortunately many regional theatres now enjoy much more harmonious inter-departmental relationships, with marketing and learning teams by and large working together to develop audiences and promote learning and participatory activities.

Most regional theatres share the key principles of lifelong learning, social inclusion, and a commitment to partnership working in their approach to learning and participation. Many have to varying degrees integrated their learning and participation work into the mainstream provision of the theatre. Whilst some theatres still locate their education teams in offices at the end of corridors, this physical and philosophical isolation is now the exception rather than the rule. It's now common for the post holder responsible for learning to sit on the senior management team, to inform the artistic programme and to play a central role in the theatre's operations. In some theatres, such as the Birmingham Repertory Theatre, all theatre staff have a learning brief and some learning initiatives are managed by other departments in the theatre.

Similarly most regional theatres make efforts to reflect the cultural diversity of their region in the programme, staffing and learning and participation activities they produce, and all recognise that working in partnership with other arts and non-arts organisations provides additional value to the work.

Many regional theatres, often incentivised by Arts Council and other funding agencies (see ACE 2012), share a commitment to social inclusion, using consultation and positive action to involve different sections of the community and recognising and addressing the invisible barriers which prevent many people from accessing theatre.

Breaking down barriers to access and engaging communities is central to the work of many theatres. A colleague once likened the invisible barriers surrounding many cultural organisations to her own attitude to betting shops. Every year when the Grand National[3] takes place she intends to place a bet on a horse in order to enter the spirit of this national sporting event. But she has never set foot in a betting shop; such 'shops' appear to be full of people not like her and, even were she to cross the threshold into the alien world of the bookmaker, she doesn't understand the terminology of 'odds on' and 'each way'. Consequently, in order to avoid embarrassment and a sense of alienation, she never places a bet. For many people, theatres represent the same degree of challenge and alienation. We need to recognise and address this dilemma if we are to make our theatres truly accessible to all sections of the community.

In order to illustrate ways in which theatres seek to provide learning opportunities and engage communities I will provide three short case studies of projects at the Birmingham Repertory Theatre, the New Vic, Newcastle under Lyme, and the Royal Exchange Theatre, Manchester.

## Early years theatre: the Birmingham Repertory Theatre ('The REP')

The REP is the leading producing theatre for the West Midlands, located in the city centre adjacent to the new Library of Birmingham (Birmingham Rep. 2012). The theatre has an extensive learning and participation programme, including participatory work with adults, partnership work with schools, a network of thirteen youth theatres and early years provision.

The REP's early years work began with a simple offer: every baby born at Birmingham's City and Sandwell hospitals in October 2004 was promised a free theatre experience every year for the first ten years of his or her life. The impact on the theatre was twofold. First, it engaged families from the REP's local neighbourhoods in the life of the theatre, and second, it compelled the theatre to produce theatre for babies and very young children, something which, despite some notable exceptions, rarely happens in the UK.

The project was overseen by a steering group which included members from the hospital trust, Surestart,[4] the primary care trust,[5] Birmingham City Council Family Learning Service, the School of Health Sciences at the University of Birmingham, who evaluated the project, and *REP's Children* parents. The recruitment of parents to the project was undertaken by community midwives who registered 230 families. Some of the parents took part in backstage tours before their babies were born and others attended the theatre with their newborn babies.

The first dedicated production for the *REP's Children* babies took place in the front of house spaces at the REP in 2005 when the babies were six months old. *Open House* was a multi-sensory installation featuring a bedroom, kitchen, bathroom and garden with three actors who performed and interacted with the babies and their parents. The production toured to Surestart and early years settings and was followed by further bespoke work for this specific group: *Dreams Come Out to Play* (2006), *Princess and Ginger* (2007) and *Lick* (2008). By 2009 the children were five years old and able to access the REP's main stage production *The Snowman* and have since attended the theatre's main stage family shows.

The *REP's Children* project has been enhanced by the appointment of an Early Years Officer who works in partnership with the REP and Birmingham City Council's Family Learning Service to provide year-round drama and arts provision for 0–3-year-olds and their parents. One of the early years projects led by Early Years Officer Peter Wynne-Willson was *Playmakers* which involved very young children in the creation of a professional theatre production.

The project began with a series of activities including a mixture of play, discussion, exploration, role-play, art-work and story making. The 'plot' to the project was that Peter's storybook was empty, and he needed the children's help to find a new story. Their carers became the 'ideas-catchers', charged with capturing any ideas that came from their children. A website was set up, so that parents could feed ideas back to Peter between the weekly sessions. By the end of the first half of the project, the groups had created a single story from which Peter created a draft script, his brief being to stay as faithful as possible to the desires and ideas of the young playmakers in putting their story on stage. The story centred around Princess, a little girl who likes to make a lot of noise, and Ginger, an angry woman who hates noise. When Princess loses her kite, she embarks upon a complicated adventure in order to find it with Special K the flying elephant, the tortoise-monkey, a dinosaur with chicken-pox, One-Stop the snake and the bouncing 'Bannagans'. By the end, Ginger and Princess are flying their new kite together.

The second half of the project involved the children, now aged three, working with the actors and the designer and attending rehearsals. They worked with the actors and contributed to the design process suggesting colours and concepts to the designer who incorporated them into the set and costumes. Finally the groups came together to watch the REP's production of their story, *Princess and Ginger*, in the REP's studio. The result was a play with a structure, style and logic that reflected the creative play of the children from which it grew.

The *REP's Children* project was the subject of a three-year evaluation conducted by the University of Birmingham which indicated that the project had been successful in breaking down preconceived ideas about theatre and the arts. Parents identified many expected benefits, which included the project improving their children's personal, cognitive, motor, speech and language, social, educational and creative development skills. The barriers to access they identified included initial recruitment and misunderstanding of early information-giving, other life pressures taking priority (such as family, having time), cultural, socio-economic and language barriers, and feelings of 'being out of place' (Coad 2005: 4).

The project proved very successful, not just by engaging local families in the life of the theatre but in capturing the imagination of the press and media thereby raising the profile of the REP not just as a producing theatre but as a venue making a unique cultural offer. The REP is planning to repeat the project with a new cohort in 2013 to coincide with the theatre's centenary.

## Engaging hard to reach communities: the New Vic, Newcastle under Lyme

Whilst the Birmingham Repertory Theatre has developed community engagement initiatives which target local communities and families, other theatres have established a reputation for engaging hard-to-reach communities. One such theatre is the New Vic in Newcastle under Lyme in Staffordshire (www.newvictheatre.org.uk), the first professional company in Britain to perform permanently in the round. The company's first home opened in 1962 in a converted cinema and moved to a new, purpose-built theatre, The New Vic, in Newcastle under Lyme in 1986. Under the leadership of founding director, Peter Cheeseman, the company became known for documentary drama with productions such as *The Fight for Shelton Bar* and *The Jolly Potters*, reflecting the preoccupations of and the issues affecting the communities of North Staffordshire, with its economy based on ceramics, coal and steel.

In 1998, Peter Cheeseman was succeeded as Artistic Director by Gwenda Hughes, who adopted an increasingly outward-looking and collaborative approach to the communities the theatre serves, seeking to redefine the ways a theatre can contribute to the cultural, educational, social, recreational and economic lives of local communities.

She established the New Vic Education Department to work within formal education, and in 1999 the company's outreach department launched *New Vic Borderlines*, which concentrates on work that encourages, enables and promotes social inclusion, community cohesion and neighbourhood renewal. Hughes believes that despite the theatre's reputation for community theatre and taking theatre to communities it had missed opportunities to work closely with those communities and tap into the new breed of theatre specialists working in applied theatre contexts. She drew upon her experience as a board member of Geese Theatre (a company dedicated to working in the criminal justice system), her professional experience as an actor and director in young people's theatre, her knowledge of how to secure funding and the expressed local need to pioneer this new strand of work. The whole process involved, in Hughes's words (interview 2011), 'changing the narrative' of what a local producing theatre is about. Central to the company's ethos is the belief that each aspect of its work is of equal value. The language of 'audiences' has given way to one of 'engagement'.

The name Borderlines reflects people existing on the margins of society and the factors which lead people to become marginalised. The project is central to the artistic policy of the theatre and epitomises the New Vic's belief that the building and its activities are a resource for everyone. Hughes believes that it is important that the whole theatre – the stage, the green room, the rehearsal rooms – are a shared space for everyone. By placing this community-based work in a theatre it raises the profile of the activities and attracts senior policymakers and politicians who may be less likely to visit a youth or community centre.

The young people engaged in the Borderlines project are often described as 'hard to reach' or disadvantaged, and many have first-hand experience of the criminal justice system. Some have been 'sentenced' to working with the theatre as part of a community service order. Many of the young people benefit from the 'backstage experience', working alongside professionals, having other adults engaging in their lives and working together in an *industrial* space. This term, not usually associated with the arts, epitomises Hughes's belief that the theatre is a working space in which professional theatre makers establish a sense of purpose and work together to produce specific outcomes. For some parents, watching their sons and daughters performing in a Borderlines production is often the first time they are engaging in their children's lives outside a courtroom.

The work is not therapy, but the therapeutic benefits are apparent. When a young person performs on a stage, reveals something about

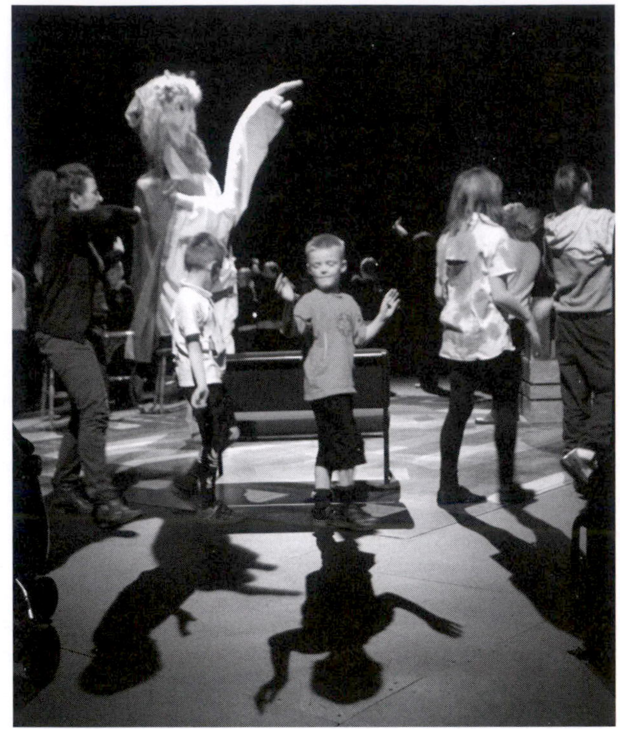

*Figure 9.1* *Knutton's bothering us* (The New Vic Theatre, Newcastle-under-Lyme, 2012). A New Vic Borderlines inter-generational community project. Children and young people from Project House Youth Club and Knutton St Mary's C of E (VC) Primary School in a performance at the theatre about their community – 'bringing light to dark places'. Photo: Julianna Skarżyńska.

his or her own life and receives applause from an audience, they stop being an outsider. 'The New Vic is neutral,' states Sue Moffat, Borderlines Director: 'we are not governed by the same legislation that social workers and youth workers have to abide by so we can ask awkward questions and demand that local agencies do their jobs properly' (Moffat 2011). Most of the work with young offenders is done in partnership with other agencies – social workers, probation officers, youth offending and family intervention teams.

At first glance the development of the Borderlines programme may appear to be a radical departure from the early days of the Victoria Theatre. But in many ways it pays homage to Cheeseman's vision of community theatre with people themselves telling their own stories in their own words. And it exploits the architecture of the theatre by using the theatre in the round to democratise and transform the acting experience.

## Working with adults: the Royal Exchange Theatre, Manchester

Virtually all regional theatres state their commitment to lifelong learning, providing education opportunities for very young children, school pupils, students and older people. However, whilst many theatres regard lifelong learning as a key principle of their work, in practice most focus almost exclusively on engaging children and young people in their learning and participation programmes. The Royal Exchange Theatre in Manchester (www.royalexchange.co.uk) is, however, an exception. Founded in 1976 in the old Cotton Exchange in Manchester the seven-sided steel and glass module seats 700 and is the largest theatre in the round in Britain.

The theatre provides a number of opportunities for adults to engage with the theatre. This includes *Acting for Scared People*, a six-week practical course; *Between the Lines*, a play-reading group which reads and discusses a wide variety of classic and contemporary plays which connect in some way with current productions; as well as drop-in events in the theatre's Education Lounge with directors, designers, writers, actors and members of the creative teams.

One project in particular seeks to engage hard to reach adults. *WWW* (*World Wide Workshop*) targets adults with little or no experience of the performing arts and focuses on practical drama and the creation of pieces of theatre from scratch. It was initially set up in 2005 to provide opportunities for refugees and asylum seekers but is now open to all individuals over the age of 18 from Black, Asian and Minority Ethnic communities, those for whom English is not their first language, and people whose circumstances mean they feel displaced. This multigenerational group creates and performs all its own work, taking inspiration from varied starting points. They created *Scared*, inspired by the Refugee Action Campaign on Destitution and performed in the theatre's studio and at neighbouring theatres, and have delivered workshops for other refugee organisations.

*Scared* was the third play from the company and was put together over ten two-hour sessions. The participants were encouraged to share their thoughts and discuss their experiences of 'destitution' as refugees who were afraid or unable to return to their country of origin. The key objectives of the project were to provide a platform for expression for the participants and to develop their theatre skills. For some it was the first time that they had ever engaged in a theatrical form, let alone performed on a stage. The combination of the performers recounting their own stories and direct address to the audience was appropriate for the performers involved and, whilst there was no direct audience participation on this occasion, the attendees, many of whom were friends and peers of the cast, were deeply engaged with the material.

The resulting performance provided a unique opportunity for the adult participants to express themselves. The challenging and relevant themes chimed with the audiences, thus generating further interest in the group and the potential for increasing membership.

The benefits of the project are clearly characterised by feedback from one of the participants:

> *WWW* offers me the opportunity to do what I love most, acting, and affords me the chance to meet with people who have different backgrounds and come from different countries, culture, religions and languages, and even people of different ages. We learn to work with each other to create a performance which includes many diverse views in harmony.[6]

The theatre's programme of work for refugees and asylum seekers also includes tours, workshops and tickets for a number of groups including students from the Windrush Centre (Manchester College), Stockport Refugee Support Group and the Zimbabwe Association. Three members of *WWW* were also cast members in a main house professional production of *A View from the Bridge* in May/June 2011. The engagement with these adults is such that this group has become, in the words of Chris Wright, the Royal Exchange's Education Producer, 'part of the fabric of the organisation' (Wright 2012).

All publicly subsidised regional theatres in England have learning and participation programmes of some kind or other and some theatres have gained national recognition for specific areas of work. Chichester Festival Theatre has a large and well-respected youth theatre for example and the West Yorkshire Playhouse (Leeds) *Heydays* programme provides participatory arts activities for 350 older adults in the spacious theatre foyer every week.

## Conclusion

Cuts in local government funding, the introduction of the National Curriculum in schools in England and the desire by artistic directors of regional theatres to align their outreach programmes to their main stage repertoire has resulted in the virtual elimination of TIE teams from regional theatres. However, the culture of these regional theatres has been directly influenced by the TIE movement. This is in part because TIE companies provided an important training ground for actors, directors, writers and administrators, many of whom have gone on to occupy senior positions in regional theatres. Likewise many of the practitioners from these companies have gone on to lead specialist courses in TIE and Theatre for Young Audiences in colleges and universities. But in the current economic and political climate, with increased tuition fees affecting the likelihood of young people being able to go to university and the threatened closure of some higher education arts courses, there are questions about how this training will be provided in the future. In many cases regional theatres are already beginning to fill this gap through internships and informal and formal training.

Education practitioners in regional theatres do, like the actor-teachers they have largely replaced, possess a hybrid of teaching and performance skills. Many theatres invest in developing close and sustainable relationships with teachers in schools and colleges. But the influence of TIE has extended beyond the education function of many of these theatres to the philosophy of the organisation as a whole. Many such regional theatres now regard a commitment to social inclusion, engaging disadvantaged communities and providing meaningful ways for audiences of all ages to engage practically with productions as central to their mission.

Within the theatre ecology in England, in which large- and small-scale commercial and subsidised theatres coexist, learning and participation are central to the identity of regional subsidised theatres. Whilst some audiences still regard theatres as places where people go to see plays, increasing numbers of children, young people, teachers and parents are looking to regional theatres to provide them with learning and participation opportunities.

## Notes

1 Arts Council England is the lead body charged with developing the arts in England. In 2010 it launched a ten-year strategic framework for the arts with five long-term goals including ‘Every child and young person has the opportunity to experience the richness of the arts’ (www.artscouncil.org.uk).

2 Although not a TIE company, West Yorkshire Playhouse in Leeds still has a Touring Company that performs at the Playhouse and tours to schools.

3 The Grand National is a world-famous National Hunt horse race, held annually at Aintree Racecourse, near Liverpool, England.

4 Sure Start is a government programme which provides services for pre-school children and their families in England. It works to bring together early education, childcare, health and family support. Services provided include advice on health care and child development, play schemes, parenting classes, family outreach support, and adult education and advice.

5 Primary Care Trusts (PCTs) were part of the National Health Service in England until abolished in March 2013. PCTs commissioned primary, community and secondary care from providers.

6 From an evaluation form completed by a participant (name withheld) after the performance of *Scared* on 21 May 2008.

## Works cited

Arts Council England: www.artscouncil.org.uk/funding (last accessed 30 June 2012).

The Birmingham Repertory Theatre: www.birmingham-rep.co.uk (accessed 28 February 2012).

Coad, J. (2005), An Evaluation of 'REP's Children': An Early Years Arts project. Unpublished.

Hughes, Gwenda (2011), Personal interview. New Vic Theatre, 24 October 2011.

Moffat, Sue (2011), Personal interview. New Vic Theatre, 24 October 2011.

The New Vic Theatre: www.newvictheatre.org.uk (accessed 28 February 2012).

The Royal Exchange Theatre: www.royalexchange.co.uk (accessed 28 February 2012).

Wright, Chris (2012), Personal interview. Royal Exchange Theatre, 28 March 2012.

# Part III

# GLOBAL PERSPECTIVES

## Introduction

The chapters in this section represent just some of the developments and current practices in TIE and TIE-related work across the world. This is not a comprehensive coverage nor remotely a directory of international practice, nor does it represent all the main types of work to be seen. Rather it is an attempt to illustrate the *range* of that work and some of the ways it has emerged from and been influenced by the particular circumstances in which it takes place. The international section of the previous edition focused on work in Australia, Canada, USA and Scandinavia. This time we have felt it imperative not just to update but to acknowledge the wider and more disparate evolution and application of TIE (or TIE-type) methods and approaches across the globe. Four of the chapters offer quite detailed accounts and critiques of work – in Australia, Southern Africa, India (Delhi) and the USA (New York). In other sections of the book there are of course accounts of practice elsewhere – including New Zealand, Zambia, the UK and the USA – but we are also conscious that there is a range of interesting, and interestingly different, practice across the globe that gets overlooked or all too rarely mentioned in 'mainstream' accounts of contemporary theatre. A further chapter therefore attempts to catch a wider glimpse of that practice – in the form of selective 'snapshots' of work in Ireland (Cork and Dublin), in Norway and the Nordic countries, in India (in and beyond Delhi), and in Jordan.

Some countries (such as Australia and New Zealand) at an early stage took the British TIE model as their main starting point, with several British personnel having played pioneering roles; some have evolved similar models influenced at least as much by other developments in education and theatre. In all these countries, however, the work has evolved in its own way, and we have allowed contributors a fairly wide brief in how they describe it. While some offer a broad overview of TIE work in their country, others have been more selective and attempt to illustrate approaches through 'case studies' of recently presented programmes or have focused solely on the work of one company. Others again have chosen to highlight particular problems or challenges, practical and/or theoretical, which are currently being faced. Thus the style, approach and emphases vary from chapter to chapter and country to country.

Given the size of the USA and its long and impressive history of children's theatre, it is important to stress that the chapter on New York City's Creative Arts Team does not represent educational theatre across the country. CAT is indeed one of the largest and most progressive TIE companies in the USA, but there is a variety of other American companies too. Chapters by Lynn Hoare and Wendy Lement elsewhere in this volume look at aspects of TIE beyond New York. But mention should also be made of other prominent companies, all of which display characteristics of classic TIE practice, even if the scope of their work has widened or changed over the years.

The award-winning CLIMB Theatre, based in Minneapolis–St Paul, Minnesota, founded in 1975 to work with disabled populations, now employs 'actor-educators' to work with thousands of students annually across the entire school age range dealing with issues such as bullying, friendship and the environment. In New York City, ENACT, founded in 1987 by Diana Feldman, a former CAT employee, shares approaches in common with other educational theatre companies, but emphasises the work as a means for students to explore and communicate their feelings. It now incorporates drama therapy strategies and uses trained drama therapists and clinical social workers to mentor and support its actors. Graduate students at the University of Texas at Austin founded Creative Action, formerly Theatre Action Project (TAP), in 1997 after exposure to TIE methodology at conferences and with CAT. At first, TAP described itself as a TIE company but latterly has expanded its work beyond the classroom to include youth theatre, youth arts camps, community-based projects and a range of art forms, and now refers to its creative staff as 'teaching artists'. Looking for Lilith was founded in 2002 in Louisville, Kentucky, with a focus on examining and celebrating women's histories but also has a broader commitment to education, offering a variety of participatory programmes for young people. The founders are graduates of the New York University Program in Educational Theatre, where they were also exposed to CAT's influence. It does not call its work TIE, but the connections with both TIE and Theatre of the Oppressed are clearly evident.

TIE is not confined to the countries represented by chapters in the book. It has spread far and wide and companies continue to operate explicitly under its banner. For example, in Eastern Europe the Kava Drama/Theatre-in-Education Association in Budapest and CEDEUM (Centre for Drama in Education and Art) in Belgrade both explicitly acknowledge the influence of TIE. We could go on. The key points we are making are that the coverage we offer is far from exhaustive; and reports of TIE's demise have been greatly exaggerated.

What is clear from these essays, despite the local difficulties that may be faced in terms of funding, educational demands, and social and cultural biases, is the strength and vitality of the projects described and the sense of collaborative exploration that characterises them. Even where conditions do not allow for participatory programmes with class-sized groups, all the companies described here share a broad understanding of the need to reach young audiences in ways that go beyond the straight performance of a play, and have between them explored a variety of strategies to encourage the active engagement of young people in their own learning.

# 10

# ALTERNATIVE POLITICS OF LEARNING

## The legacy of TIE in Australia

*Mary Ann Hunter*

Mention the term TIE in Australia these days and you are likely to face bemusement. Once the vanguard of socially critical teacher-actor praxis seeking to emancipate young people's learning, TIE has for some time been co-opted by small and highly successful operators in Australia delivering pre-packaged plays to school audiences. The drive to empower young people with new knowledge may remain, but mostly the trend has solidified in our cultural imaginary: precisely clocked shows with minimum set-up and pack-up; perky adults playing children characters; and relevant didacticism based on bullying, Australian history or adaptations of short-listed Children's Book Council award texts. In recent years, the occasional Science Spectacular has lent some extra pizzazz to this caravan kind of TIE.

In an environment of Web 2.0-inspired creativity and multi-modal literacy, it is easy to be cynical about TIE as something of an educational theatre cliché. Indeed, discourse on TIE in the latter half of its forty-year history in Australia is replete with metaphors of decline, disappearance and even death (Milne 1998; O'Toole and Bundy 1993; Ryan 1990). But the legacy of what was once, all too briefly, a progressivist partnership between the institutions of theatre and education is far more wide-reaching. For in Australia, it is not the original *form* of Coventry-style TIE that has survived, but its *intent*. And this intent – which has as much to do with politics and agency as it does with aesthetics and curriculum – survives in arts education initiatives and partnerships that are unlike those of our caravanning players working under the name of TIE today.

In an essay of this length, it would be foolhardy to attempt a comprehensive overview of what has been a 'considerably complicated'

(O'Toole and Bundy 1993: 136) history of TIE in Australia. This chapter therefore owes considerable scholarly debt to those who have synthesized the field before, particularly John O'Toole and Penny Bundy (1993) and Geoffrey Milne (1998). By expanding on their foundational work and drawing on my own observations in the field, I offer, by any measure, an idiosyncratic account. Having myself worked with the drivers of many educational theatre initiatives since the early 1990s, it is apparent that theatre and education gains in Australia have rarely followed distinct *nation-wide* pathways of consequence or categorization (that is, until the very recent journey towards a national curriculum). My modest contribution to this timely review, therefore, is not to chronicle a path but to suggest that 'Coventry-style TIE' has had far-reaching impacts over time in Australia, despite its mixed fortunes as a form. TIE provided a focus for early attempts to dissolve school/community boundaries and its lineage can be seen in stand-out arts and education innovations of today. My understanding – as a former TIE practitioner turned educator, researcher, policymaker, parent – is that the contemporary nexus of theatre and education in Australia is resilient and very much alive because there continue to be artists and educators striving – as their TIE 'teacher-actor' predecessors did – for an alternative politics of learning within the school environment.

Thus, this chapter lends its focus to continuities of intention rather than an investigation of form. I do this by discussing TIE and its legacy with reference to the regulatory practices and values of the 'institutions'[1] of theatre and education in Australia. How have intersections of theatre and learning related to a wider politics of Australian theatre? What has been the connection to the institution of compulsory education? And where have young people, teachers and the earliest progenitors of arts education in this country been positioned in all that? Following a revision of TIE's early history using this lens, I draw attention to a number of recent key initiatives: some which may echo TIE in practice and others which distinctly and deliberately do not. My aim is to provide snapshots that capture the ways in which Australian theatre practitioners have participated in a refocusing of the capacities of artists in schools while, at the same time, keeping the ideals of early TIE alive.

## Of positioning and politics

It could be said that the Belgrade Theatre (Coventry) style of TIE[2] was fated in Australia from the start. While TIE's championing role in schools and communities in the UK was enabled by a concomitant growth in participatory drama education as well as an openness of localized educational and arts authorities to theatre's benefits, in Australia a very different story emerged. As has been argued elsewhere, geographic challenges, educational conservatism and tensions over the value (and therefore funding) of TIE in a fledgling professional theatre industry saw the progressivist approaches of early TIE morph into a performance-only typology in Australia (O'Toole and Bundy 1993; Milne 1998). Yet, for all the benefits that the national distinctiveness of TIE as a writers' theatre yielded, any hopes for a TIE *movement* ultimately suffered from an internalized *in*distinction about its place in the nation's education and cultural sectors.

As various accounts of the beginnings of TIE in the UK explain (Vallins 1980; O'Toole 1976; Jackson 1993), TIE teams in Coventry and other regions during the 1960s and early 1970s aimed to be educationally progressive, participatory and political by forging new understandings between schools and their local communities. In Australia in the early 1970s, there was no equivalent locally focused arts or education infrastructure to enable a copycat TIE to flourish. But the challenge was not solely to do with the lack of local resources nor the difficulty of reaching audiences across vast distances. There was a more fundamental question of the role and purpose of TIE itself in this 'new land'. Roger Chapman, a British practitioner who led the education programme of the South Australian Theatre Company at the time (later to become the highly successful Magpie Theatre in Education), echoed others in identifying the inappropriateness of a full-scale adoption of British TIE methods. He suggested instead a vision unique to Australia:

> How nationally does TIE form itself into a movement with an energy and identity of its own? How can we raise the prestige, standard and consciousness of our work so that theatres will regard the work outside their buildings as of equal importance as the work done in the main house?
>
> (Chapman 1976: 47)

Chapman's ideal was to marry Coventry-style TIE's political intent with a strategy to position Australian TIE as the driver for community outreach of the mainstage theatre. As Chapman was based in a youth programme of a larger company, this made good sense. However, in the context of Australia's fledgling professional theatre industry – one that was only beginning to come to terms with a new era of government support following the recent establishment of the Australia

Council (in 1973) – and with process drama yet to gain traction within school curricula, this approach may have both exacerbated and driven underground a fundamental tension around how the institutions of education and theatre should choose to marry. If TIE was to aspire to become a movement with its own 'energy and identity' in Australia, what was going to unify it internally while defining its relationship to other movements and sectors?

Unlike the British variety, early TIE in Australia did not originate from spirited independent theatre companies agitating for change and coalescing into a movement challenging the very basis of theatre's role in school and community, although some practitioners voiced that aspiration. Rather, antipodean TIE grew from stimulating ideas shared by 'expat' artists mostly employed in offshoot programmes of theatre companies whose core business was something else entirely. TIE practice grew not from the fire of opposition or from a pact of committed alliance. It had trouble from the start in asserting its value from a place that was already marginalized within a struggling and ambitious Australian mainstage industry. Its continuity of political intent with the British practice was evident. Outspoken practitioners foregrounded their desire to emancipate young people from the constrictions of conventional school curricula (Bakaitus 1979a and 1979b; Bray 1979; Brown 1979; Chapman 1976; Hardy and Hayes 1976; Lonie 1979; Westwood 1979), but rarely did quality practice get recognized beyond the circle of players that constituted TIE in Australia in the 1970s.

There was certainly quality work going on and there were certainly beacon organizations that struck important alliances across education and professional theatre sectors. For instance, Salamanca Theatre Company in Hobart emerged out of the youth activities arm of a mainstage theatre, the Tasmanian Theatre Company. Under the direction of Barbara Manning, Salamanca's TIE work became widely respected for its merging of goals in school/community engagement and quality theatrical experience. Theatre company members were frequently embedded in a school's life for up to five days, mostly leading in-class drama activities to support the creation of a theatre piece they in turn used as a pre-text for further process drama. Espousing a politics congruent with the early progenitors of TIE, Manning believed that

> theatre presented to young people should be excellent, accessible and at all times relevant; that young people should be encouraged to be involved in matters of social concern such

> as housing, pollution, care of the aged, war, unemployment and poverty and they should always be treated as an intelligent, responsible and participatory audience – in fact … as a community.
>
> (Manning 1987: 42)

Salamanca enjoyed a relatively stable financial base by developing, in Manning's words, 'an excellent working relationship' with the State Education Department of the time with 'censorship-free financial backing' in addition to baseline support from the Theatre Board of the Australia Council and project funding from the Literature, Community Arts and Aboriginal Arts Boards. This enabled the company to provide integrated TIE programmes that maintained something of the political framework of Coventry-style TIE – an emancipatory approach to learning that dissolved the borders between school and community – while demonstrating a certain cultural capital in the Australian theatre industry with funding recognition from the various boards of the flagship national arts agency. By merging education and artistic values in this way Salamanca's approach evolved into one where 'theatre may be used as a catalyst for a dynamic … generative situation in which students, teachers and actors share in the shaping of their own thinking. … It is about young people and older people together shaping their common reality' (Salamanca Theatre in Education 1982: 8).

But such teacher-actor TIE teams as Salamanca, so strongly embedded in classroom work with young people, were the exception rather than the rule of the emerging signature Australian TIE. While State and Territory education departments played a leading role in a number of key companies' formation – including Salamanca, Jigsaw in Canberra and La Boite's Early Childhood Drama Project, later to become Kite, in Queensland – for the most part, Australian TIE initiatives were underfunded and undervalued. Practitioner and Australia Council Theatre Board member of the time, Margaret Wallace, recounts that in 1974 the field of young people's theatre – of which TIE was a part – was 'depressed and depressing':

> Desperately underfunded, the companies were caught in a vicious circle … With a few shining exceptions, my memories are of exhausted, underpaid and inexperienced young actors performing dull scripts on battered and ill-designed sets, to classrooms full of fidgeting children.
>
> (Wallace 1987: 26)

Few artists or educators got to experience or understand exemplary participatory and community-integrated TIE in the style of the British form (O'Toole and Bundy 1993). Therefore, without a critical mass of Salamanca-style approaches across the country, neither the arts industry nor the education sector confidently claimed TIE or its benefits. As a result the work was often lowly valued by both sides and, perhaps consequently, the vision of it as a community-engaged practice was piecemeal. But a kind of revolutionary zeal remained among quality TIE practitioners committed to the form's potential as an educational alternative within the curriculum limitations and institutionalized settings of Australian school life. As such, TIE survived in the margins of the mainstage theatre industry by evolving, as O'Toole and Bundy have explained, into a writers' theatre.

## From movement to genre

What Geoffrey Milne describes as the 1980s heyday of the TIE form was in no small part due to TIE companies taking a more conventional approach to writing theatre, as befitting of their mainstage parent counterparts. This period saw companies such as Magpie in South Australia (grown from Chapman's initiative) enjoy the benefits of a full-time staff of eleven (including writers), and the physical resources and cultural clout of a mainstage State Theatre Company (Milne 1998: 160). By Milne's careful reckoning, there were almost three dozen professional TIE companies in Australia receiving government funding at this time.

But arguably, through this boom, TIE became less a *movement* than a *genre* of school-appropriate plays in Australia. Some of its early progressivist energy appeared to wane under a divisive funding politics: was it 'real theatre' or 'educational service'? In the oft-quoted words of one of Australia's eminent theatre artists of the time, Alex Buzo: 'The TIE people do a great job educating children, but it's not art and it's not education' (1988: 44). Conversely, while TIE was disparaged as work that robbed from the 'real theatre' industry, it was clearly being used as a desperately needed stepping-stone for artists wanting to land those 'real theatre' jobs. The tensions and ambiguities around the form weren't helped by the gradual reduction in education and arts funding over time that saw struggling TIE operatives look to other sources such as health and community development to remain viable.

We arrive then at a contentious point in TIE's history in Australia. On the one hand, it could be argued that this necessity to turn to other funding freed practitioners to explore their previously thwarted emancipatory intents – thereby fuelling the beginning of dynamic new understandings and practices of applied theatre. On the other hand, there is the lament that during TIE's short and dramatic demise, the spirit of TIE as a progressivist *educational* intervention was lost. At its best, post-boom TIE delivered extraordinary dialogic plays for school audiences; but, at its worst, it short-cutted to thinly veiled didacticism promoting everything from safe cycling to safe sex.

Either way, a consequence was that those Australian schools that were fortunate enough to receive visits from TIE companies were provided with a packaged commodity. Difficulties of distance and limitations on resources meant that in an effort to remain financially viable, companies needed to perform to as many people as possible in each working day. Time-consuming complementary workshops with students and teachers quietly disappeared and audiences of 300 students were not unusual. Travelling players were rarely afforded the opportunity to integrate their work within regional communities because of the fiscal necessities of performing 'on the run'.

Unsurprisingly, by the late 1980s, the future of Australian TIE was seen to be in crisis. In the *Lowdown* magazine article, 'Zen and the art of bookmaking', John Emery (1988) surveyed a number of TIE companies around the country, suggesting that TIE practitioners had translated 'creative crises' into 'marketing problems' in an effort to find scapegoats for their own lack of inventiveness. The next edition of the magazine carried a flurry of objections to Emery's 'snotty critique', seeking to reaffirm the political intention and integrity of TIE in Australia. Signed 'Minty Lombardo McGwythwrall, A.O.', a lead letter read,

> It is common knowledge that Theatre in Education represents one of the only means of palliating the infrastructural moral and supra-moral damage inflicted daily on our young people by means of the officially sanctioned subcurricular hand of latter day pseudofascist piggery – I refer of course to education systems and their extensions in the community.
>
> ('McGwythwrall' 1988: 59)

The debate – if comically interposed in this quote – invested a sense of urgency into the task of recuperating TIE's original intent to provide an alternative politics of education in school sites. According to playwright and director, Peter Charlton, the political framework for TIE had been diluted and neutralized in Australia by this point, resulting in a 'deadening homogeneity of both form and style which eschewed real political analysis for a soft-line "issue-based" approach to political social education' (Charlton 1987: 13). His concern was that a formulaic provision of isolated fragments of issue-based TIE in schools served to reinforce rather than challenge the school as a hierarchical place that limited student choice, viewing students as passive consumers of theatre.

Charlton's alternative framework – influenced by his understanding of Gramsci – went beyond the community engagement rhetoric of earlier days to one based on a necessary acknowledgement that young people constitute a community in themselves, needing to establish a sense of internal hegemony. In his work as a playwright, Charlton therefore engaged with cultural forms familiar to young children – citing fairytales and traditional children's theatre as potent theatrical forms because they combined highly visual staging with observable and understandable social structures. Charlton took to reframing these forms in an attempt to infuse the best of traditional storytelling with an explicit politics of community empowerment. Charlton's approach was most evident in his TIE script, *Wolf Boy*, first performed by Arena Theatre Company in Melbourne in 1982. The play deals with philosophies and methodologies of education through the historical story of Victor, a 'wild child' captured in France in 1800 to be educated in the ways of civilization. What *Wolf Boy* portrays in script and performance style is the complex interrelationships which serve to influence Victor's (and by extension, young people's) awareness of self and society.

Charlton both directed and wrote *Wolf Boy* as a TIE piece that intentionally challenged the formula that had developed in Australia. Neither naturalistic nor agit-prop, *Wolf Boy* was narrated by a chorus of three performers dressed in top hat and tails. This reflected something of Charlton's ideal fusion of old and new form: he saw the value of a political edge in TIE work, but not in the sense of toeing a party line or lapsing into didacticism. Instead, he grounded a work about the issues of power in education and society in the conventions of 'once upon a time' children's story. *Wolf Boy* therefore tapped into a familiar stylistic vernacular (with costumes and seemingly fairytale morals) to enable students to see through the familiar authoritarian structures of family and school life. But the morals – and the ending of the play – are ambiguous. The 'victory' for the teacher (in testing whether Victor knows right from wrong through a process of wrongfully punishing him and inviting a violent reaction) is not necessarily a victory for Victor, although he has been 'civilized' into leaping with joy at the V for victory hand sign:

> CHORUS: Happily ever after
> Is what the stories say.
> But is that true?
> And what do you do
> When the stories just don't end that way?
>
> (Charlton 1985: 33)

Employing the best of Brechtian integration of learning and entertainment, its dialogic retelling of the story of Victor raises the wider, more troubling political implications of his situation:

> Many people feel that Victor's life was tragic, but if that is so, then so must all our lives be, for what was done to him, is still done to us all. … Victor was being patterned according to certain held beliefs which were 'unchallengeable', and that is the true tragedy, not only for Victor, but for all children in all schools.
>
> (Charlton 1985: 46)

While Charlton's commitment to restoring a political framework for Australian TIE was evident in his practice as a writer and director with Arena Theatre, it is difficult to ascertain the impact of this politicized approach on teachers of the time. For all the anti-schooling sentiments of Australian TIE practitioners, the historical record rarely mentions perspectives of, or partnerships with, teachers. Practitioners and industry leaders such as Anne Godfrey-Smith frequently acted to raise awareness of the value of TIE in educators' minds (1980) but there seemed to be not so much a critical tussle between teachers and artists, but a growing ambivalence. Milne cites former Arena Theatre director Barbara Ciszewska, in saying 'teachers teach and actors act. Why should we pretend to take over the teachers' role in the classroom?' (Milne 1998: 163); an attitude similarly reflected in classrooms and halls around the country as many teachers looked to visiting TIE shows as a welcome respite to catch up on other things.

Of course, this chapter suffers, as any narration may, from selective perspective. There would be evidence, no doubt, of committed and passionate teachers supporting integrated inclusion of artists in schools during the period of TIE's rise and demise. But, when it comes to the 'institution' of education, O'Toole and Bundy convincingly argue how an attitude of moral guardianship over the provision of outside programmes in schools overshadowed the work of committed individuals seeking more collaborative arts and education partnerships. Quality assurance measures by gatekeeper organizations such as the Queensland Arts Council meant that artists self-regulated their work on the basis of what had worked before to gain accreditation to perform in schools. The audition and approval process, which continued through the 1990s – and which I personally experienced as a performer and director of a number of TIE programmes – was a multi-stage process of script submission, audition, critique and resubmission, when necessary. The power dynamics were opaque as artists were separated from teachers, who were separated from young people, in the process of 'assessment'. The stock-in-trade question of TIE practitioners, 'will it pass?', had little to do with aesthetic integrity, giving some indication of the politics at play, in states such as Queensland at least.[3] This is not to suggest all TIE deserved to be performed – possibly quite the contrary. But battle-scarred by certification processes that did little to reflect the desired participatory processes of early TIE, Australian practitioners found themselves losing what little agency they may have felt they had (or warranted) to act as alternative educator-artists in sites of institutionalized learning.

By the 1990s, therefore, many working at the interface of arts and education at a policy and programming level were trapped in very *un*dialogical framings of their work: product-driven theatre versus process-oriented education; actors do acting while teachers do teaching; students as observers versus students as agents. There were, of course, pre-eminent drama educators, such as Gavin Bolton, engaging with similar issues in terms of pedagogy and curriculum (Bolton 1993); the point here being that these same tensions were impacting upon the wider institutional naming and framing of theatre artists choosing to work in schools. So, Australian TIE died off – despite some extraordinary individual examples of the genre[4] – as young people's positioning in school-based arts education, and the wider field of Australian cultural production, changed.

## Of 'grounded aesthetics' and anxious futures

Naysayers will argue that TIE was already beyond its use-by date by the time Paul Willis's influential ideas about young people's 'grounded aesthetic' (Willis 1990: 14) became popularized by youth arts practitioners in the 1990s. Willis's central concept – that young people engage in their own 'symbolic creativity' through everyday cultural practices – gained particular currency with those concerned about the relevance of theatre to young people's lives, both from a class-based perspective and in an age of such rapid technological change. Here I discuss the impact of some of the wider changes in young people's relationship to the institution of theatre in Australia at this time, and how a reconstituted view of young people's agency emerged in initiatives that resonated with the politics of an earlier TIE age.

Against a background anxiety about the future viability of the theatre industry, it is interesting to note the ways in which young people were rebadged as participants and co-creators of theatre in the 1990s. As I have argued elsewhere (1999 and 2001), the reasons for this were numerous, but one piece of 'institutional' thinking was central: that it was critical to the success of securing future audiences and a more sustainable future that young people be embraced by the theatre industry in a different way than they had been before. This was reflected in national youth arts strategies and a range of State-based cultural policies of the time and was a key underlying feature of significant changes in youth-specific programmes of mainstage companies across the decade. These changes included experimental diversions away from educational imperatives (such as Magpie2, a 'new generation' theatre for young adults, which replaced the former Magpie TIE) and more focused attention on youth audience development as distinct from solely curriculum-aligned education programming. Potently partnered with a 'grounded aesthetics' politics, these changes contributed to a re-evaluation and reorientation of the whole classificatory system that had defined youth-specific theatre in Australia to that point: i.e. that it had to be TIE *or* community-based youth theatre *or* professional theatre for young audiences. Instead, multi-modal approaches to performance and new ideas about what constituted participation ruptured these categories and created a fresher, messier nexus of theatre and education. Community-engaged companies such as Canberra Youth Theatre, Contact Youth Theatre, Street Arts, and Urban Theatre Projects were embedding digital art, martial arts and skateboarding in their work with young people. Changes in existing theatre festivals for young people (such as the longstanding Come Out in Adelaide) and a rash of new festivals including Next Wave, Stage X and, later, Newcastle's This is Not Art indicated the new energy around the idea that young people were fundamental to a thriving arts ecology: they were not just consumers but creators of culture. With more accessible means to the tools of cultural production – including early internet shareware and self-publishing applications – young people's education was no longer as confined to institutionalized settings as before and the learning needs of aspiring 'emerging artists' gained new attention. Young people were, therefore, no longer in need of exposure to the kinds of participatory, politically engaged, awareness-raising opportunities proffered by TIE. By the mid-1990s, it is evident that many TIE companies had realized this and had either disbanded or morphed into youth theatres to reflect the changing times (Milne 1998).

Around the same time, there were major new developments in arts education policy and curriculum in Australian schools (Australian Government 1994 and 1997). While it is beyond this chapter's scope to assess whether these were as similarly 'democratizing' for young people, it is worthwhile noting that a growing public profile of the benefits of arts education was occurring simultaneously with this new attention to young people's role in Australia's cultural and creative industries. Evidence of the impact of this can be found in innovative partnerships that emerged at this time. A key example is the *Shortcuts/ XL-D* initiative led by Drama Queensland,[5] a professional association of drama educators, and the flagship Queensland Performing Arts Centre. This partnership grew in the mid-1990s, from 'the desire of drama teachers to see students' creative work valued by receiving the same level of resources as other professional performance groups' (Hogan and Readman 2006: 49). In this model of 'school-initiated youth performance' (48), professional artists worked collaboratively with teachers and students in the creative development of an original theatre piece for performance in a professional venue. It is interesting to note the way in which later projects began to reflect the kind of integrated participatory work of earlier Coventry-style TIE models. In the 2003 *XL-D Express*, for example, members of physical theatre company Zen Zen Zo worked over an extended period of time with students from six schools to devise a work for public performance. This process began with students being given the one pre-text (the story of the prominent Mayne family) and the one performance style (that of physical theatre[6]) with which to engage aesthetically with the City of Brisbane's early settler history. The multi-generational Mayne family's story included compelling themes of 'ambition … loss, insanity and redemption' (Hogan and Readman 2006: 51); thereby providing a rich launching pad for students to discover and explore new meaning about their city. With aesthetic scaffolding provided by the participating artists and teaching artists, the students then developed and transformed these new meanings into symbolic action that resonated with Zen Zen Zo's characteristic physical theatre form. Each school's work was further refined and brought to a level of public performance such that the Mayne family legacy and the stylized physical theatre approach served as focal points for the curation of the multi-school event.

Key teaching-artist participants Sharon Hogan and Kylie Readman describe the *XL-D* process as dialogic – drawing on McLean's work on co-artistry (1996) – and supportive of students' agency. Yet a politics of agency different from early TIE was at play here, for the project was explicitly about *creative agency*: young people negotiating the tools of creative production in a process of learning not just about themselves and the world around them, but about the very machinery of professional theatre performance. Initiatives like *XL-D* therefore represented a new politics of learning that astutely rode the waves of change at the time.

Ironically, around this time, TIE was being repopularized in the classroom; not, however, in the spirit of Chapman and Manning – as an intervention – but as a topic in and of itself in school curricula. A recipe-ready TIE had now been authorized as a *topic* of learning by the very institution of education it had previously been seeking to challenge. What was a politicized and committed TIE practitioner to do?

## Playing partners

Strategic players did a number of things: they stuck it out with touring to schools; they kept sight of how to write quality scripts for young audiences; they kept abreast of young people's changing everyday aesthetics; and they were rewarded by a committed following and, in some cases, mutually beneficial partnerships with larger producing organizations.

Zeal Theatre is a critical case in point. Founded in 1989 by actor, writer and director, Stefo Nantsou, Zeal Theatre has produced forty-three original plays for school and community audiences. Based in Newcastle, New South Wales, it currently defines itself as a 'touring theatre' (Zeal Theatre 2011) although its roots were firmly within an Australian writers' TIE. Zeal's first production, *The Scam* (1989), for example, dealt with the effects of government cuts to funding for schools on students and their families. The company's early repertoire had its fair share of historical dramas and history of science shows, but some of their edgier work, such as *Joyride* (1992) and *The Stones* (1996), was researched closely with young people and was particularly effective in communicating the diverse lives and vernacular of, and tough choices faced by, young people in the outer suburbs and regional areas of Australia. In 2005, Zeal was commissioned by Sydney

Theatre Company (STC), a major mainstage company, to write *Gronks*, a play engaging with the Macquarie Fields and Redfern riots that occurred the year earlier among young people in Sydney. Making critical links between the related causes of domestic and community violence, the play toured schools and professional theatre venues across Australia. Three commissions from STC later and, in 2009, Zeal became an associate company to the larger organization. The partnership – based on the commissioning of new work, but encompassing shared use of resources – has clear benefits for both partners: it expands their respective audience bases, in particular, widening the mainstage company's educational, regional and community reach; and it further contributes to Zeal's already significant national and international profile (Nantsou 2010). Apart from the economic benefits, this successful partnership validates the early vision of TIE practitioners in Australia to have TIE provide a focus for community initiatives and engagement – although it is crucial to note that one is hard-pressed to find the moniker 'TIE' anywhere in Zeal's history or publicity.

Unlike earlier Australian TIE initiatives struggling in marginalized youth and education programmes, however, Zeal's work is embedded in a multi-layered youth and education programme at STC that offers multiple entry points for young people into the experience of theatre. Zeal's visits to schools are thus complemented by actor and teacher collaborations in other components of the STC programme. In the Drama in Schools project, for example, STC actors and school teachers work as co-mentors in classrooms to improve drama pedagogy skills and enhance student literacy (Ewing et al. 2011). This approach brings together the participatory elements of process drama with the discipline-specific skills of quality theatre performance in contemporary ways of which early TIE pioneers in Australia would have approved.

Attention could be drawn to a growing batch of similarly multi-layered and responsive initiatives to support young people's engagement in theatre companies in Australia. Furthermore, a number of State and Territory government programmes in arts and education are fostering frameworks that support young people's 'creative agency'. For example, longstanding intra-governmental partnerships have been sustained in Victoria (State Government of Victoria 2012) and in Western Australia (Government of Western Australia 2012) that have further resulted in quality 'on the ground' arts and education collaborations.

At a national level, the *National Statement on Education and the Arts*, co-signed by all Australian State and Territory Ministers of Arts and of Education in 2007, asserted that:

> Community-based arts and education partnerships build social cohesion, respect, community spirit and active local citizenship … increase community awareness of educational issues and can help mobilise and draw on communities' local arts and cultural resources.
>
> (MCEETYA and CMC 2007)

The Australian Government operationalized this statement in 2008, with the launch of a four-year $5.2m Artist in Residence (AIR) Initiative. Reflective of similar schemes in the UK and Canada, it places artists in education settings for a minimum of one month and is based on fostering school/community partnerships. The AIR programme was founded on principles of collaboration at every level: from its individually negotiated Commonwealth/State funding agreements[7] to its goal to provide for mutual professional learning among teachers and artists. Early-stage evaluation suggests that, for the most part, the collaborative aims of the programme are being realized (Hunter, in press).

Whereas, in the past, drama education and TIE may have been on related but distinct tracks of development in Australia, currently teacher–artist partnerships in programmes like Drama in Schools and the AIR initiative are being recognized as critical to the sustainability of theatre and education in the face of ongoing challenges to the arts in education. In response to broader socio-cultural shifts, participatory projects such as these foreground young people's central role as co-agents of meaning-making in the arts. But they also encourage teachers – particularly those not specifically trained as arts educators – to become skilled enough to continue to be catalysts for further arts-rich learning in school environments.

## Forward thinking?

But are these institutional partnerships really signalling change? Does the current nexus of theatre and education in Australia still bear the legacy of early TIE practitioners' attempts to collapse school and community barriers, frustrate institutional dichotomies, and emancipate young people from schooling? In concluding this chapter, I offer two observations that give pause for thought.

The first is the way in which the current development of Australia's first national curriculum in The Arts is providing a new locus for old tensions. Judging from current debate on the matter it is evident that, while nationalizing the curriculum has brought increased attention to the benefits of arts education generally,[8] regimes of value are still colliding. Public response to the pre-curriculum Draft Shape Paper, for instance, indicates that stakeholders are still divided on whether the priority purpose of the arts in schools should be for students to master arts disciplines or to encounter the arts as a tool for cross-curricular learning (ACARA 2011a). To put it bluntly, in terms of drama education, should it teach skills or teach ideas? The debate is a far cry from the declarations of the *National Statement on Education and the Arts*, where partnering among artists, teachers and students in more community-engaged ways were prioritized.[9] In a recent compendium of arts education research, Robyn Ewing discusses the uneasy relationship between the arts and education in Australia, citing O'Toole in saying the institutions 'have often regarded each other with suspicion' (Ewing 2010: 5). This suspicion continues to haunt the present and may serve to limit the opportunities and capacities for a more fluid engagement with theatre, drama and performance in schools.

The second is an observation that potentially disrupts the very foundation of this analysis and alerts us to continuing gaps in research at the nexus of theatre and education in Australia. It is based on an acknowledgement that the origins of arts education in this country lie in the ancestral and intergenerational cultural practices of Aboriginal and Torres Strait Islander communities. This has been overlooked in discussions of Australian TIE – understandably, though, given that this *form* of work was introduced by British expats, circulated in institutions cultivated by British settlers, and aligned with British systems of cultural value. This is not to diminish TIE's history in Australia, nor to discount the fact that there has been a substantial body of TIE-style work devised by Indigenous and non-Indigenous artists about the stories and experiences of Aboriginal and Torres Strait Islander young people and communities.[10] But a number of questions deserve further inquiry. How is the very concept of 'a nexus of theatre and education' changed by referencing Indigenous world-views: in particular, Australian Aboriginal and Torres Strait Islander ways of knowing that value creative practice and performance differently from Australia's settler communities? In the present context, what could be understood about the potential of visiting theatre artists and curriculum-aligned drama education to support 'common-ground pedagogies of multiple worldviews' (Kaawoppa Yunkaporta 2009: xv)?

Recent institutional initiatives in arts and education reflect the legacy of early TIE practitioners' political intent and have embraced changes in the ways young people are positioned and valued in the wider social and cultural sphere. There has been much gained from the innovations and the struggles of those who worked to establish TIE and to maintain a place for theatre artists in school settings. Yet, while young people's creative agency is foregrounded in much contemporary practice and writing in the field, conditions continue to exist in the institution of Australian education that can still make the contribution of an artist in school a sometimes highly charged political act.

## Notes

1 This work is based on an understanding of 'institution' as a collection of regulatory practices, attitudes and authorizing agents that evolve structures of power over time. I draw on the work of political scientist B. Guy Peters (2000) in acknowledging that institutional structures are amenable to processes of change, design and manipulation.

2 As the form has been amply described elsewhere in this collection, the characteristics of this 'style' may be summarized as: driven by educational objectives and a desire for student participation; small or local audiences; multi-part or extended programmes; delivered by actor-teachers.

3 See O'Toole and Bundy (1993) and Gattenhof (1998) for further discussion of the differences between State and Territory practices of certification at this time.

4 Notable examples are: Nick Enright's *A Property of the Clan* (1994), Sancia Robinson and Wendy Harmer's *What's the Matter with Mary Jane* (1996), Tom Lycos and Stefo Nantsou's *The Stones* (1996), David Milroy's *Windmill Baby* (2007), and Angela Betzien's *Children of the Black Skirt* (2005) and *Hoods* (2007).

5 Drama Queensland was then known as Queensland Association of Drama in Education.

6 The definition of 'physical theatre' is a contested one. Therefore the 'form' referred to here is that of Zen Zen Zo's work, which, at the time, was inspired by Japanese Butoh and the predominance of physical and visual elements of aesthetic communication over verbal elements.

7 Funding for the programme is devolved by the Australia Government to State and Territory jurisdictions based on individual negotiated agreements.

8 Also evident in recent arts participation research commissioned by the Australia Council (2010).

9 Of course, the institutional frames and purposes of these two documents (one, a curriculum discussion paper and the other, an intergovernmental position statement) are vastly different. Nonetheless, industry and community connection only rates a small mention in the pre-curriculum Shape Paper – diminished substantially in the second draft of the Paper following public consultation (ACARA 2011b).

10 For instance, Yirra Yaakin in Perth has produced and toured extensively in schools, with plays such as *Head Space* by Maude Sketchley, a 1997 coproduction with theatre company, Barking Gecko, and the acclaimed *Windmill Baby* (Milroy 2007). Ilbijerri, the longest running Indigenous Theatre Company in Australia, toured *Chopped Liver* by Kamarra Bell-Wykes (on the impact of Hepatitis C on the lives of two young Aboriginal

young people) for almost four years in schools, communities and prisons. Kooemba Jdarra in Brisbane partnered with Kite Theatre for Early Childhood to produce *Binnie's Backyard* (2000), an interactive theatre piece for young children and their families based on Torres Strait Islander stories and culture.

## Works cited

Australia Council (2010), *More than Bums on Seats: Australian Participation in the Arts*. Sydney: Australia Council for the Arts.

Australian Curriculum, Assessment and Reporting Authority (ACARA) (2011a), *Consultation Feedback Report on the DRAFT Shape of the Australian Curriculum: The Arts*, August. Online at www.acara.edu.au/verve/_resources/ Consultation_Feedback_Report–The_Arts.pdf (accessed 13 October 2011).

——(2011b), *Shape of the Australian Curriculum: The Arts*, August. Online at www.acara.edu.au/verve/_resources/Shape_of_the_Australian_Curriculum_The_Arts – Compressed.pdf (accessed 13 October 2011).

Australian Government (1994), *A Statement on the Arts for Australian Schools*, Canberra: Curriculum Corporation.

——(1997), *Profiling the Arts*. Canberra: Curriculum Corporation.

Bakaitus, H. (1979a), 'Interview', *Theatre Australia* 3.7, pp. 35–36.

——(1979b), 'The politics of children's marketing', *Theatre Australia* 3.7, p. 37.

Betzien, A. (2005), *Children of the Black Skirt*. Strawberry Hills: Currency.

——(2007), *Hoods*. Strawberry Hills: Currency.

Bolton, G. (1993), 'Drama in education and TIE', in Jackson, (ed.) *Learning through Theatre*, 2nd edn. London and New York: Routledge.

Bray, E. (1979), 'Process and product', *Theatre Australia* 3.11, pp. 45–46.

Brown, G. (1979), 'Youth performing arts: forcefeeding the innocent?' *Theatre Australia* 4.4, pp. 44–45.

Buzo, A. (1988), *The Young Person's Guide to the Theatre and Almost Everything Else*. Melbourne: Penguin.

Chapman, R. (1976), 'Relevant theatre for children', *Theatre Australia* 1.2, pp. 46–47.

Charlton, P. (1985), 'Wolf Boy', in J. Lonie, (ed.) *Learning from Life: Five Plays for Young People*. Sydney: Currency, pp. 43–71.

——(1987), 'Everything changes, everything stays the same', in *Theatre Childhood and Youth*. Paris: ASSITEJ (International Association of Theatre for Children and Young People), pp. 12–19.

Emery, J. (1988), 'Zen and the art of bookmaking', *Lowdown* 10.4, pp. 12–22.

Enright, N. (1994), *A Property of the Clan*. Sydney: Currency.

Ewing, R. (2010), *The Arts and Australian Education*, Australian Education Review 58, Camberwell: Australian Council for Educational Research.

Ewing, R., Hristofski, H., Gibson, R., Campbell, V. and Robertson, A. (2011), 'Using drama to enhance literacy: the "School Drama" initiative', *Literacy Learning: The Middle Years* 19.3, pp. 33–39.

Gattenhof, S. (1998), 'Providing for the Arts: a comparative critique of performing arts school touring programmes in Australian states and territories', *Lowdown* 20.4, pp. 5–7.

Godfrey-Smith, A. (1980), 'People not Shadows', *Education News*, pp. 8–13.

Government of Western Australia (2012), *On the cutting edge of learning: arts edge*. Perth: Department of Culture and the Arts and Department of Education. Online at www.artsedge.dca.wa.gov.au (accessed 10 January 2012).

Hardy, J. and Hayes, J. (1976), 'Programme and protest', *Theatre Australia* 1.3, pp. 52–53.

Hogan, S. and Readman, K. (2006), 'Oscillations: proposing a new model for school-initiated youth performance', *NJ: The Journal of Drama Australia* 30.1, pp. 47–56.

Hunter, M. (in press), *Artist in Residence Program Evaluation*, report to Australian Government, Sydney: Australia Council.

Jackson, T. (1993), 'Education or theatre? The development of TIE in Britain', in Jackson (ed.) *Learning through Theatre*, 2nd edn. London and New York: Routledge, pp. 17–37.

Kaawoppa Yunkaporta, T. (2009), *Aboriginal Pedagogies at the Cultural Interface*, unpublished thesis. Townsville: James Cook University.

Lonie, J. (1979), 'TIE: Education and community', *Theatre Australia* 3.10, pp. 45–46.

Lycos, T. and Nantsou, S. (1996), 'The Stones', in T. Lycos and S. Nantsou (2011) *The Zeal Collection*. Strawberry Hills: Currency, pp. 1–33.

'McGwythwrall, M.L.' (1988), 'Letters', *Lowdown* 10.5, p. 59.

McLean, J. (1996), *An Aesthetic Framework in Drama: Issues and Implications*. NADIE Research Monograph Series. Brisbane: National Association for Drama in Education.

Manning, B. (1987), 'Two boards and a heart', in R. Fotheringham (ed.) *Community Theatre in Australia*. North Ryde: Methuen, pp. 40–6.

Milne, G. (1998), 'Theatre in education: dead or alive?', in V. Kelly (ed.) *Our Australian Theatre in the 1990s*. Amsterdam: Rodopi, pp. 152–67.

Milroy, D. (2007), 'Windmill Baby', in V. Cleven, W. Enoch, D. Milroy, G. Narkle, J. Harrison, *Contemporary Indigenous Plays*. Strawberry Hills: Currency, pp. 201–28.

Ministerial Council for Education, Employment, Training and Youth Affairs (MCEETYA) and Cultural Ministers Council (CMD) (2007), *National Statement on Education and the Arts*. Canberra: Department of Communication, Information Technology and the Arts.

Nantsou, S. (2010), Personal communication, 15 October.

O'Toole, J. (1976), *Theatre in Education: New Objectives for Theatre – New Techniques in Education*. London: Hodder and Stoughton.

O'Toole, J. and Bundy, P. (1993), 'Kites and magpies: TIE in Australia', in Jackson (ed.) *Learning through Theatre*, 2nd edn. London and New York: Routledge.

Peters, B. G. (2000), *Institutional Theory: Problems and Prospects.* Vienna: Institute for Advanced Studies.

Robinson, S. and Harmer, W. (1996), *What is the Matter with Mary Jane?* Sydney: Currency.

Ryan, T. (1990), 'Grim Pickings', *Lowdown* 12.3, pp. 18–20.

Salamanca Theatre in Education (1982), *Annie's Coming Out: A Study of a Residency Program.* Hobart: Tasmania Education Department.

State Government of Victoria (2012), *Arts in Education.* Melbourne: Arts Victoria. Online at www.arts.vic.gov.au/Arts_in_Victoria/Arts_in_Education (accessed 10 January 2012).

Vallins, G. (1980), 'The beginnings of theatre in education', in Jackson (ed.) *Learning through Theatre*, 1st edn. Manchester: Manchester University Press, pp. 2–15.

Wallace, M. (1987), 'Coming of age: young people's theatre in the 1970s and 1980s', in *Theatre Childhood and Youth.* Paris: ASSITEJ, pp. 26–30.

Westwood, C. (1979), 'Women, theatre and education', *Theatre Australia* 3.8, pp. 39–40.

Willis, P. (1990), *Moving Culture: An Enquiry into the Cultural Activities of Young People.* London: Calouste Gulbenkian Foundation.

Zeal Theatre (2011), *Company History.* Online at www.zealtheatre.com.au/htm/company_Zeal_history.html (accessed 10 November 2011).

# 11

# *PANDITA RAMABAI*

## The making of a participatory theatre programme around a character from Indian history

*Maya Krishna Rao*

### Introduction

This essay discusses the making of a participatory theatre programme in India, and considers its significance in expanding the concept of drama as a participatory form of learning, both for teachers and for students – especially in a country where, within the school system, such a concept is barely known. The subject of the programme is the extraordinary life and work of a woman social reformer of nineteenth-century India, a subject that resonates with themes that are still relevant today.

*Pandita Ramabai* was devised with thirteen actor-teachers of the Theatre in Education Company of the National School of Drama (NSD), New Delhi. It was completed in September 2010 after two and a half months of research, a ten-day preparatory workshop, and then the production of the play itself. Although originally intended for students of class IX (14-year-olds), once the show began to tour schools we realised that, with a little adjustment by the actors, older students could also be involved. Thus the show now goes out to students of classes X and XI (15- and 16-year-olds) as well. It has had seventy performances to date, involving more than 5,000 participants. Although we initially thought we should play to gatherings of no more than forty-five students, given the size of a class in schools in the Delhi area, we were obliged to push this to around seventy. We were, of course, conscious that the quality of participation can suffer when, at a given session, the participants are so many.

*Pandita Ramabai* has also toured teacher education colleges, with the aim of introducing the role of drama in primary school classroom teaching. In fact, a positive (and unplanned) spin-off of the programme has been the interest it has generated in teacher workshops. On account of the impact it has wherever it goes, it is deemed to be one of the NSD TIE Company's most important productions.

## The life and times of Ramabai

The extraordinary life of Ramabai spanned the latter half of the nineteenth century and the first decade of the twentieth. A large part of it was spent in poverty, and was marked by both personal tragedy and social upheaval. Great and ceaseless conflict with the restraints imposed by traditional mores was the hallmark of Ramabai's life and work. She made it her mission to travel to the interior of western India, in the hinterland of the city of Bombay, to gather hundreds of child widows who had been deserted by their families following custom, and to give them food, shelter, basic education and occupational training so that they might lead a life of dignity. Although her life's work would be capped by public recognition in her own lifetime, at first grudgingly and then more readily, Pandita[1] Ramabai remains a minor character in the history textbooks of today's India and is not widely known.

The reason for this is probably that the cause she served was not part of the primarily anti-colonial agenda of the mainstream national movement, which was fundamentally political and today forms the main thrust of history in school textbooks. There are also other reasons. Born into a Brahmin (the highest caste in the Hindu hierarchy) home, Ramabai chose to renounce the faith of her ancestors and embraced Christianity as she progressed in her work. Unlike her male peers among the social reformers, who campaigned for widow remarriage and education, Ramabai sought to provide these young widows with opportunities for betterment without bringing to bear any pressure to remarry. Hers may not have been a consciously feminist choice, but it was certainly a deeply individual one and intrinsically different from the causes espoused by other social reformers of the time.

Much of what we know about Ramabai is from her own writings, books and letters. There are also a few researched accounts of her life and work. She was born in 1858, south of Bombay. Her mother was only nine years old and her father about forty when they were married, an instance of child marriage among girls that was common in those times. However, her father was a man of unusual temperament, and he walked out of his paternal home when refused permission by his family to educate his child bride. He then tried to make ends meet by doing the traditional work of educated men of the Brahmin caste: reciting the scriptures and helping perform religious rituals at Hindu temples. But theirs was an enforced peripatetic life. He and his family had to keep moving from one village to another, and sometimes lived in the forest. They could not be a part of their own community because he had defied a hallowed custom. So, the family had no regular home, neighbourhood, school or friends. Four children were born to the couple, the last child being Ramabai. Her teachers were her parents, particularly her young mother, who had been taught by her husband. Ramabai learned and committed to memory Sanskrit verses from the Hindu scriptures.

The latter part of the nineteenth century saw many famines in India as a consequence of the British colonial policy towards agriculture, which favoured cultivation of non-food crops. Thousands died. Ramabai lost all members of her family, save a brother. In search of food and livelihood, the two, who were by then in their late teens, walked all the way to Kashmir in the north-west and then to Bengal in the east of the country, covering more than 2,000 miles on foot. For Ramabai, two life-changing events took place in Bengal. She lost her brother, and she got married, not to a Brahmin but to a *Shudra*, the lowest in the hierarchical Hindu caste system. They had a daughter, Manorama, but when the child was only two years old, Ramabai lost her husband. At that point, Ramabai packed her bags, returned to south India, and decided to devote her life to the cause of child widows, who were considered outcastes and a bad omen. She converted to Christianity. She wrote and sold pamphlets on the subject of child widows to make enough money to set sail for England with her little girl, to train as a nurse. Her plan was to come back and train child widows so that they might stand on their own feet.

Not long after commencing her nursing course in England, Ramabai began to lose her sense of hearing. She abandoned her study, left little Manorama in the care of missionary nuns, and sailed for America with the intention of raising funds to set up a home for child widows back in India. She travelled the length and breadth of America giving lectures and collecting funds before returning home with her daughter, having spent six years overseas.

On her return she set up 'Mukti Sadan' (literally, 'Home for Deliverance') at Pune, near Bombay, with a governing body consisting of local social reform leaders and scholars. Vocational training units for child widows – in dairy farming, printing, textile weaving and picklemaking – and even Braille units, were set up alongside large dormitories. In times of famine, which were still frequent, Ramabai would travel in disguise to the remote interiors and bring back malnourished child widows to Mukti Sadan. The disguise was necessary because it was against colonial law to pick up abandoned children. At its peak, Mukti Sadan housed 1,500 child widows and famine-affected children. Contrary to what the critics said, spreading the gospel was not part of the programme in Pune, although some of the young women did follow Ramabai's personal example and became Christians.

From time to time Ramabai found herself at loggerheads with the British authorities in India, the Church, Hindu parents of the girls at the Pune centre, and even some of her own colleagues, each finding fault with her activities from different perspectives. Rumour was rife about the life the young girls led. There were also whispers about forced conversions to Christianity. Soon a campaign began to take shape against Ramabai; the governing body of Mukti Sadan, unable any longer to refute questions raised by parents of the widows and the general public, resigned *en masse*.

Life was now not easy. Ramabai packed her bags again and this time went to Australia in order to replenish the depleted funds of her institution. When she returned home she reconstituted the governing body of Mukti Sadan, which survives in some form to this day. Ramabai died in 1911. Tragically, her daughter Manorama, who had worked with her at Mukti Sadan, had died a few years earlier.

## The choice of theme

As can be seen from the above narrative, the life of Pandita Ramabai offers rich material from the perspective of TIE. However, before we chose to present it as a project of the TIE Company, we debated different aspects of it. Her life and work raised issues of both universal and contemporary relevance: questions relating to personal agency and freedoms, as well as social, religious and political themes and the cross-connections between them. What should we focus upon?

Interestingly, there was a dilemma as well, articulated by the company at the start. How could such a rich tapestry, with so many exciting twists and turns woven into the story, be made into a worthwhile participatory programme, giving the students enough room to explore the issues for themselves, and all in the space of an hour and a half? Should we focus on a theme or an issue from the story rather than Ramabai's life? The decision was made to focus on Ramabai herself. For many in the TIE Company, the reason for this choice was simple – they wanted to learn more about her, and also answer the question, 'Why did she convert to Christianity?'

Apart from one Muslim, the rest of the company were from a Hindu background. While all were broadly secular in temperament, the Ramabai story appeared to stir some unspoken discomfort in them. Why would a person of the highest Hindu caste convert to another religion when there was no force or incentive? Were we disappointed that she did not fight the crusty Brahmin authorities from within, as a Brahmin? Why choose Christianity – the religion of the colonial rulers, the British? Would the question of conversion hijack the programme and become an unintended focus in the participatory sections? Was the company intellectually and artistically equipped to deal with such tricky questions in role, if these came from the students?

There is nothing like the devising process in theatre to churn up your own devils and make you face them! Let me share a significant revelation that was made to me long after the initial run of shows had ended. The actor who had played one of the leading parts (no longer with the TIE Company) wrote back in response to some questions I had posed. She said that as an unmarried young woman from a conservative, middle-class Delhi home, she had faced considerable resistance for choosing to work in theatre and for not entering into a marriage arranged by the family – the two were linked in their minds. But, she said, her mind was made up once she had internalised the *Pandita Ramabai* material, with its emphasis on adversity and the need to make choices. It gave her 'solace'. She has subsequently gone to another city for more theatre training and work, and has found a husband of her choice. She continues to be in theatre!

## The workshop process

Before introducing the Ramabai story to the company, I ran a ten-day workshop on participatory theatre for them. Only four of the thirteen members were familiar with the concept, although they were all part of a functioning TIE group. The closest the members of the NSD TIE Company had come to participatory theatre was 'interactive' theatre, in which the character simply elicits responses from the audience to prearranged – and rarely significant – questions.

In designing the workshop, I drew on my short but intensive stint with the Leeds Playhouse TIE Company in the mid-1980s, and on readings of Dorothy Heathcote and Gavin Bolton, two pioneers of the drama in education (DIE) movement. In India we need to build our own practices of drama and TIE, in which our histories, cultures, dance, music, languages, rhythms and folk art traditions will influence the form, content and approach to the work. This is the search that engages me currently. However, at the time of making *Pandita Ramabai* it seemed 'safer' to fall back on what I had gained during my time at Leeds, and my subsequent reading of the literature on the 'classic' British TIE concept and its practice.

In the training workshop, company members divided into groups and chose events with a universal resonance – often taken from newspapers – that could be used for TIE treatment. Starting with 'freeze frame' and 'thought-tracking', we moved to more complex devices such as 'dressing a room', 'conscience alley', 'empty chair' and 'forum theatre' to reveal and explore possible hidden meanings.[2] Once the members became familiar with the approach, they were encouraged to create variations on these techniques. We worked with a selection of props, images and text as exciting starting points for creating drama with students. Dorothy Heathcote's concepts of 'dropping to the universal', 'brotherhood of ideas' and 'protection from emotion' formed the spine of our approach.[3] There was a particular focus on the role of the facilitator. Each company member was encouraged to plan and try facilitation with an emphasis on the use of attractive yet accessible language that could trigger responses in the students. 'Hot-seating'[4] was tried and retried by the actors. How to give information in such a way that it opens up new worlds, and takes curiosity and investigation to another plane; how to use silences and let the body express a deeply felt moment; how to use props in the hot seating so they might become, as symbols, a focus for the relationships between their own characters and other people in the story – these were some of the elements we concentrated on in the workshop.

However, once we began work on the production, hot-seating was the device the company resisted the most. Nothing else in the process seemed to make them more vulnerable. To have to sit so close to the student-participants as a completely believable character from the nineteenth century, ready to respond authentically to unpredictable questions, was daunting. The thought of introducing themselves to the audience as contemporary actors who are about to go into role seemed to be even more demanding. Today, however, after the experience, the company is ready to take on more complex artistic forms.

## Improvisation process

The work on the Ramabai project involved a combination of study of the biographical material, with the guidance of a noted scholar who has written an authoritative biography of Ramabai (Chakravarti 1998), and long improvisations that I designed. In these, the actors took on different roles and went in and out of the improvisation in real, rather than dramatic, time.

An exploration of Ramabai's childhood years was challenging. What was life like, growing up as a nomad? What food did the family eat? What games did she play with her siblings? The actors would spend some quiet time in the mornings, dressing up and sourcing and making appropriate props. In my experience, finding the right prop can sometimes open a door, be a metaphor for the content of a programme, or a clue to building a character from another time. In our case, we discovered the potency of a handful of seeds of berries treasured by Ramabai from her starvation days in the forests, the same seeds that her father had used to teach her mathematics.

From early on, unprompted, the male actors would often wear saris and play female characters, probably because those were the more challenging and interesting roles – those of the child widows and Ramabai herself. They created some moving improvisations. The men brought a certain poignancy to the role that was unmatched by the female actors. They would get their white saris tied by the women in the company and quietly walk around, sitting in corners and muttering to themselves to get into role. This was a first for all of them.

The wide range of the research – from larger social processes at one end, to personal stories from biographies and diaries at the other – helped to pack the improvisations with details of actual, lived life. This rescued the actors from the trap of sentimentality, which is so easy to slip into with this kind of material. Ramabai's letters are full of heart-rending accounts of child widows that could, if not handled carefully, arouse both horror and distance in urban children who are approximately the same age as those widows. To avoid this, we were careful to make our main focus Ramabai herself, not so much the child widows she rescued. We placed circumstances centre stage – her event-filled life, actions, dilemmas and decisions – rather than the emotions experienced within them.

Another advantage of making Ramabai the centre of attention – and this was confirmed during the tours of the show – was that boys in the student body were engaged with the material from the very start. They didn't see *Pandita Ramabai* as a 'girl's play' for the simple reason that the girls of Mukti Sadan were not the focus – Ramabai was. To take an example, a question that the child Ramabai asks as she is growing up, 'What's the point having all these hundreds of Sanskrit *shlokas* (verses) stuffed in my head when my family can't afford one square meal?' had reverberations for society as a whole – boys and girls, men and women. Keeping the appeal wide enough to engage with 12–13-year-old boys and girls was a particularly difficult part of the process.

To induce excitement in the actors about hot seating, I gave them the large volume of Ramabai's correspondence which has, sprinkled through it, fine details of the condition of child widows, various social and political events, and portrayals of people connected with the Church and the government – in short, a flavour of the times. In the course of a day's schedule, the actors would create a character (real or imagined), choose details from the letters and then create a 'solo situation'. They were encouraged to choose an object and create some tension-filled circumstance or action around it, as a way to draw the participants into engagement.

## Themes that emerged

From these long improvisations emerged the key themes for the programme. I decided not to work the other way round, that is, to identify themes first and then make improvisations around them, for I was convinced that our chosen method would throw up a layered complexity which 'theme-generated' improvisations often do not – particularly when the actors are relatively inexperienced devisers.

Some of the themes, and consequent debates, generated by our long improvisations were as follows: (i) The nature of 'home': is it always located where your family is? For many child widows it was Mukti Sadan and not their own families that gave them a home with the promise of a better life. (ii) Different kinds of 'education': the formal institution (school) that the student-participants attend, and non-formal kinds of learning, such as Ramabai's, acquired from her parents and the world at large. Is one more legitimate than the other? (iii) Notions of 'freedom', 'conformity', 'identity', 'status', 'values', which have different connotations, depending on the times and the context. Can the new-found freedom of a child widow in Mukti Sadan be equated with the release of a child from bonded labour in India today? Freedom to be and to do, what? (iv) In different eras, individuals have opted out of the prescribed norms of society and furrowed a different path. Where are those possible 'spaces' in contemporary urban life in India? Does social class (and education) play an important role in affording this option? Did it, in the case of Ramabai? (v) How can we project those times without making simplistic comparisons with life today? Were parents and families of those days 'bad' because they abandoned their young, widowed daughters?

Having decided that Ramabai's life should be the focus, a further question arose. What did this mean for our participation? How much historical detail would we need to give? How open-ended could it be? We decided to leave those difficult answers for later. We hoped that the improvisations would give us a clue to the possible nature of participation.

At the end of the exploratory process, the company was divided into three groups to work on possible scenarios. They voted that I should prepare the final script and dialogues, including the interventions by the facilitator. This was a challenging task: holding on to the theme; weaving it into select, rich improvisations (of which there were many!) created by the company; choosing a range of devices – some that the actors were comfortable with and others, like hot seating, that would stretch them; allowing for humour; allowing for some important personal moments to resonate with universal dimensions; allowing for boys and girls to 'enter' the context, making it visually exciting … It was hard!

## Acting style

The style of playing that the NSD TIE Company seems to have adopted over the years is broadly a type of realism or naturalism. The engagement is with plot, scene, dialogue, blocking, and so on. This places limits on style and imagination. My first effort was to set up improvisations that would pull them out of this mode. Fortunately, just before the work on *Pandita Ramabai* began, the actors had been through a rigorous 'physical theatre' workshop conducted by a visiting Polish theatre company. I saw this as an opportunity and asked them to incorporate their exercises in the daily warm-up. So, although it did not impact on their overall style of acting, in 'the jungle sequence', for instance, we were able to use rolls and tumbles to express the 'home-schooling' aspect of the Ramabai family. The company, though initially hesitant, was happy to rediscover acting through these new modes.

## The programme

The performance space consists of a long rectangular strip as playing area with participants flanking it along the two long sides. At the shorter ends sit the characters, awaiting their entrances. Behind one row of actors, a black cloth is hung up for slide projection. (We incorporated Ramabai's rich archive into slides and projected them as if the facilitator were looking through and sharing an album.) A three-foot-high canopy-enclosure was erected that included the audience-participants, made of strips of hand-embroidered cloth, to suggest Mukti Sadan, so that the student-participants have a sense of sharing the atmosphere with Ramabai. The floor is covered with cloth: patchwork embroidery with broad running stitches suggestive of a river, rough earth and a 'forgotten world'. The costumes, like the production itself, were meticulously researched by a designer. So, to have thirteen authentically dressed characters sitting formally in two rows, facing one another, with music (specially designed for the piece, contemporary in tone) playing as the student-participants walk in at the start, was an instant draw. Without giving details of the entire production, I outline below some of the sequences that seemed to have the most impact on the students.

The opening sequence is a still image that comes to life, of a child widow being chased by a barber in order to shave her head. She runs to her sister who pushes her away. A toy falls out of the girl's hand. Ramabai, as she often did, observes the goings-on, in disguise. The barber 'shaves' the girl's head (male actors actually shaved their heads to play the roles of child widows). At this point, the facilitator freezes the action and, as if thinking aloud, asks, 'So, how old is she?' And further, 'Do you think she goes to school? Does this kind of thing happen today?'

The 'jungle sequence', mentioned earlier, was a high point for many students. Ramabai and her brother get their lesson in astronomy by actually gazing at the stars and in maths by counting the seeds collected after eating fruits; they learn Sanskrit verses by reciting them to time with rolls and tumbles; and finally, we see their parents die of starvation and they are left all alone, with just their father's umbrella, to fend for themselves.

Then comes a comic sequence in which a health department employee chases the caretaker of Mukti Sadan and the child widows with his 'phoos phoos' machine (an anti-plague fumigation device). The scene ends with one of the widows being 'struck dumb' by a visitor, Mr Karve (the facilitator rushes off to get dressed to play this love scene!). This was based on a true story: the two were later married and set up a primary school.

There was poignancy in watching male actors playing child widows, complete with white sari and covered, shaved heads, and sitting very close to the students, both boys and girls, in the simultaneous hot seating sequence – moments which, interestingly, had filled the actors with dread to start with. Not once did the students giggle or give evidence of any 'break in the belief' while the widows (clearly played by males) were engaged in deep conversation with them. The company took courage from this and even the Ramabai role was sometimes taken over by a male actor. The students accepted her for who she was.

The facilitator was everyone's favourite, though his role was a difficult one to play. How do you ask, 'So, what's going on here?' in a

*Figure 11.1* *Pandita Ramabai.* Father imparts a lesson to the young Ramabai in the forest. Photographs: S. Thyagarajan. Courtesy, National School of Drama, New Delhi.

*Figure 11.2* *Pandita Ramabai* (National School of Drama TIE Company, Delhi). Students hot seat a child widow of Mukti Sadan.

thoughtful, reflective way (and not in the manner of 'I actually know the answer, but I'm pretending I don't … '); how do you get more than seventy students in the audience to concentrate on a small detail like an embroidered bag that a widow presents to Ramabai; how do you open up a thematic area gradually, through questions, keeping in mind the particular social composition of the class of students? It is difficult but the students warmed to his approach – that of a fellow-participant to begin with, rushing around, trying to make sense of what is going on, along with them, and finally jumping into the fray to take on a role himself, that of the visitor smitten by one of the widows.

The most difficult sequence for the actors was the 'meeting' at the end of the play. When the Trust members announce their *en masse* resignation and some of the widows share with the facilitator their worry of losing their home if Mukti Sadan shuts down, the student-participants opt (when asked) to 'go into Mukti Sadan to find out what's happening'. They meet, in groups, with some of the inmates (simultaneous hot seating), and finally in a larger meeting with the members of the Trust. The struggle for us was how to frame the meeting. Here are the members of the Trust, well-known social reformers of their time who had supported Ramabai all along in her effort to give young widows a new life. They are friends, not enemies, and yet they are all resigning from their posts because they cannot cope with mounting questions from the public and parents of the child widows: 'Why are girls in Mukti not following prevailing norms?' 'Why is Pandita not getting them remarried?' 'Is she forcibly converting them to Christianity?' In short, the Trust members are caught in a dilemma. To stay on is proving difficult, but to quit means to betray a cause that they had championed and an institution they had helped set up. At this point in the play, the widows sit more or less silently among the students. Only once do we hear their thoughts – their questions, their fears – spoken aloud. For the rest, they let the students negotiate on their behalf with the Trust.

To start with, we thought of setting up the meeting as a 'forum' where the students, through the facilitator, could stop it at any point and argue on behalf of the widows, or, if they felt compelled to, take on the role of a Trust member. However, we soon realised that keeping them as themselves, i.e. as students, was actually more challenging for them. By being themselves they could better appreciate, from a distance, the dilemma of the Trust – how, even while holding sympathetic, liberal views, they were compelled to let down the widows in the face of public outrage. After all, the intention was not to get the students to take sides but to help them come to an understanding of how, *given* the times they lived in, the two sets of people – the Trust and the widows – could find ways to address the problem,

So the forum idea changed to a 'meeting' (with students in role as the 'general public' outside Mukti Sadan). But the question still remained: what exactly did we expect the students to do in the meeting? What was the frame? Giving advice to the governing body members that would help them retract their resignation? Yes, up to a point the students did try to advise the Trust: 'Give frequent press conferences so that the public are made aware of the good that Mukti Sadan is doing for the widows'. 'Don't listen to the public.' 'Be steadfast in your support of the widows, for they will be homeless if you resign and Mukti Sadan shuts down.' But we felt this was not enough.

After a few shows we shifted the focus to drawing a comparison between 'then' and 'now'. At critical points in the play the facilitator gets the students to think of and analyse a parallel situation today, where the march of ideas, generally speaking, is ahead of social practice – and one not necessarily to do with widows or even the gender question. When the meeting gets into a spirited discussion, he 'freezes' the Trust members and asks the students: 'What's going on here?' 'Are we helping them solve their dilemma?' Sometimes he switches the time-scale and asks, 'Does this kind of thing happen today? Is this notion of "freedom" far ahead of what the majority are ready for? What radical ideas do we have today that are not yet generally accepted?' The students usually point to the family system and then the facilitator asks, 'So what is considered to be "stepping beyond the line" within the family today?' A vibrant discussion follows with the facilitator steering it in the direction of: 'What will help change relations within the family? … What is already in the process of change? … What are the repercussions of this process of change?'

Finally, at a high point of the debate (and before it drops its momentum), Ramabai, who has been sitting pensively and quietly all this time, voices the students' innermost concern (usually expressed to her and the other inmates of Mukti Sadan earlier on): 'If some of us have to part ways, so be it; but we need a home and we will find a way to keep it.' The facilitator freezes the action again and tells the students:

> A meeting as heated as this must have taken place at the time when the Trust did resign and Mukti Sadan got itself a new Trust. Ramabai journeyed far once again to collect funds for Mukti Sadan. Here is Mukti today and here is a stamp

> [*slides are projected*] commemorating Ramabai's 150th birth anniversary.

## The response

Considering that the form of the programme was new to the participants, the response to *Pandita Ramabai* has typically been one of high appreciation. Even after two long hours of 'being with Ramabai', the students usually do not depart in a hurry but linger to talk to the actors, particularly the facilitator.

The company has played to a range of schools – from privileged, well-off 'public schools' at one end, to under-equipped, under-privileged, over-populated government schools at the other. In India, this can be a very wide range. Interestingly, as the actors often observed during their tours, the latter schools were more engaged and attentive to the facilitator's navigating questions than the former. While government schools in India are much less exposed to theatre, not to speak of the complex devices of participatory theatre, than the private schools, their students 'jumped in' more willingly than their more privileged peers. Perhaps this was because they were less self-conscious.

## An evaluation

Here is an excerpt from an email (dated 30 March, 2012), sent by our biographical guide, Uma Chakravarti, a retired history teacher at Delhi University, who has done extensive research and written a book on Ramabai (Chakravarti 1998):

> I had written about Pandita Ramabai as part of the rewriting of history that feminists have explored, but when I was called in as a sort of subject specialist to talk to the performers I had to unravel the range of issues hidden under my own writing because the performers had numerous questions that carried my account of Pandita Ramabai much further. Confronted by 'why this?' or 'why that?' my own ideas on Ramabai required further fine tuning. For example, a query that I myself had when I began my explorations of Ramabai ('Why did she feel the need to convert to Christianity?') was the dominant 'resisting' question for the performers too. It remained one of the issues that was taken up in the interactive sessions with school students as well, and perhaps at the end of

> the process all of us had moved forward in our understanding of the issue.

Interestingly, our apprehensions on this score were, to a large extent, misplaced. Either due to unfamiliarity with the form of participatory theatre or simply because it is not an issue as central to children as it is to adults, the question of Ramabai's conversion was never too hard to handle for the actors. In fact, to a certain extent it can be read as one of the problems of the show: fairly early in the programme, the students were won over by Ramabai and so the question of why she converted did not become an issue of primary concern for them. The facilitator's questions, though designed to encourage reflection, unfortunately did not provoke enough debate among the students, or between the students and the characters. This is probably because we had opted to prioritise telling the story rather than opening out the many themes for exploration.

In the final analysis, I think the value of the project is that it offers students a 'live history lesson' where they can enter the 'picture' through the facilitator, who can 'start and stop' the action at will for questions to be asked and issues to be aired. It works as a microscope of the life and times of Ramabai. The conventions of TIE were used to engage the students with Ramabai's story and the hidden but still relevant themes – but not in order for the students to actually take charge of the play.

I think one important impact of the programme has been on the TIE Company itself. Creatively using methods and devices like hot seating, facilitation and forum over so many shows (and facing some really sticky moments, in the process) has not only changed their view of theatre, but also changed them as artists, as people. They have said so themselves, as in the example of the actor cited above. The response from students and teachers in schools has been overwhelming for them. It has whetted their appetite for devising more such programmes. At the same time, they realise that *Pandita Ramabai* is only the tip of the iceberg. To get into real participation, they will perhaps have to leave the story they want to tell and be ready to play the story the students want to make. And that is where I think the real challenge lies – to take a couple of actors and get them to design explorations in drama where the reins of the production can be shared with the participants. In other words, a cross between a full-fledged TIE company production and teacher-initiated drama in the classroom – but with the advantages of both. This will serve the purpose of both extending skills and opening up job opportunities for freelance drama teachers/actors (of whom there are many seeking work). Also, this same pool of drama-skilled individuals can fan out into teacher education colleges to train future schoolteachers, a process that has made a small beginning in Delhi.

## The teacher, the future

The journey has led me to the realisation that we in India need to find our own approach, in terms of shaping both content, and artistic forms and conventions. Our folk forms – in song, dance, theatre, art – are rich with devices of 'distancing', storytelling, play-making and participation. For me, the most exciting part of the journey begins now: to rediscover some of these forms, distil them and take them into workshops for teachers, so that they can be equipped to use them for promoting learning with students. However valuable, the TIE company is ultimately a luxury in India – setting up and running theatre companies in our country is expensive. As mentioned above, sending actors into schools with material that can be explored through drama by the students, or empowering a teacher with an approach, some skills and artistic forms, is considerably cheaper and goes much further.

In India, only a very small number of schools in the cities offer a once-a-week drama class, and that is usually only up to class VIII (12-year-olds). These are, predictably, privately funded institutions. Government schools have next to no drama on their timetable, apart from the dreaded 'Annual Day' play, which is usually an exercise in dressing up children and getting them to imitate adult behaviour or an adult's notion of child behaviour. Such plays are usually directed by a language teacher with little or no theatre background. In recent years, a trend has started among the privileged private schools to invite theatre directors and choreographers to produce their annual extravaganzas, but these are more for the benefit of the parents than the children.

The way ahead, therefore, is through the class teacher (in primary school), even more than the drama teacher. Probably in recognition of this, alongside the traditional BEd (Bachelor's in Education) and MEd (Master's in Education) courses, in 1994, Delhi University introduced a unique four-year BElEd (Bachelor's in Elementary Education) course, aimed at training teachers for classes I–VIII (ages 4 to 12). The course is currently offered in eight colleges in Delhi, with an average of thirty-five trainees in each cohort. I have designed the drama syllabus for the course and taught in some of the colleges for a time; and was recently commissioned by the National School of Drama to write a drama manual for elementary (class I–VIII) school teachers to be completed by 2013. It is a beginning.

A further boost to drama in the school curriculum came when in 2006 the National Council for Educational Research and Training (NCERT, the research and textbook-making wing of the central government) endorsed the role of arts in education, and drew up syllabi for dance, drama, craft and music for classes I–XII. The task now is to get these syllabi off the shelf, and translate them into teacher education.

The latest challenge and massive opportunity for drama and theatre in education has come with our parliament having recently passed momentous legislation that makes education compulsory for children up to the age of 14, giving it the status of a fundamental right. With this, the school classroom, in the near future, will become more heterogeneous in terms of social class, income, caste, religion, community and language. And along with it will come the potential for tension and conflict. It is the teacher who has to get the child to recognise and empathise with 'the other' in its class – and a very wide range of 'the other' at that. Here lies the potential and challenge of using drama: to appreciate what it is to be human in all its varied manifestations.

## Notes

1 The honorific *Pandita* is the feminine form of *Pandit*, the Sanskrit expression that denotes a high master of scriptural learning, reserved for those born into the Hindu priestly caste of the Brahmin. Though the feminine form exists in the language, it was rare for women to be honoured with it as education of women – even within the confines of the home – went against traditional cultural norms. Ramabai continued to be referred to by the title *Pandita*, which pointed to her deep and widely acknowledged scholarship of Hindu religious texts, even after she embraced Christianity.

2 These and subsequent terms used in this section of the chapter are drama devices and can be briefly summarised as follows: *freeze frame* – participants create a static moment using their own bodies to represent a moment in life, idea or a theme; *thought-tracking* – participants in role speak aloud their thoughts at a specific moment of the action; *dressing a room* – participants imagine and place appropriate personal effects, belongings and objects in the personal room of a character; *conscience alley* – participants as a whole group become and speak aloud the 'conscience' of one participant in role; *empty chair* – an empty chair, representing a role, is placed before the participants and participants become the 'voice' of the role, speaking aloud the role's thoughts/statements; *forum theatre* – while a situation is being enacted, others observe. Both actors and observers may stop the action at any point to advise the actors if they need help or the

situation is losing authenticity. Observers may take over and replace actors and continue the enactment in role. (See also chapter 3, p. 65.)

3 Dorothy Heathcote's terms can be summarised thus: *dropping to the universal* – a process of reflection within the drama when a particular moment in a situation is identified as having universal significance, a moment that has been experienced by human kind over the ages, in one form or another; *brotherhood of ideas* – a cluster of ideas/situations that have similar characteristics: a process of identifying ideas with similarities, e.g. if you wear a necklace, you are in the company of all those who adorn themselves; *protection from emotion* – a concept in drama whereby the participant's personal emotions are not exposed, and are separated from the emotions of the role they are playing in the drama; *protection into emotion* – a process, in an age-appropriate manner, of allowing children access to the experience of significant yet controversial emotions and life situations, e.g. death, prostitution, etc. (See Heathcote 1990.)

4 *Hot-seating* – a device much used in drama and TIE: participants interview an actor 'in character' in order to gain more information about that character.

## Works cited

Chakravarti, Uma (1998), *Rewriting History: The Life and Times of Pandita Ramabai*. New Delhi: Kali for Women.

Heathcote, Dorothy (1990), *Collected Writings on Education and Drama*, ed. L. Johnson and C. O'Neill. Cheltenham: Stanley Thornes Ltd.

# 12

# *SENZENI NA* (WHAT HAVE WE DONE?)

## Educational theatre in southern Africa[1]

*Veronica Baxter*

In the film version of John Le Carré's *The Constant Gardener* (2005), a scene set in the slum of Kibera in Kenya dwells over a piece of educational theatre about HIV. Performed in the open air on a raised platform with a painted backdrop, the short extract from the play *Huruma* is framed by the crowds waiting for the train to pass, the detritus of human settlement amidst livestock and open sewers, and the shacks. On stage, the vividly dressed but very thin women sweep the floor, demonstrating their housekeeping skills to well-dressed men of marriageable age. The actors speak in unison, as it is announced that the well-dressed men have tested positive for 'AIDS', and the sweepers back off rapidly. They react to a collective sneeze by the well-dressed men, no longer marriageable, telling them to keep 'it' to themselves.

The scene turns to show the sweeping women, embarrassed by their lack of humanity, pleading with the HIV positive men to stay, asking that they should 'continue as we once were' in the community. The scene is met with laughter from the audience as stereotypes are recognised and ironies revealed. The theatrical style is large and loud, unison choral work carries the words across the open space. The play is instructive of the need to be compassionate to HIV positive members of the community.

This scene from the film is what most people worldwide envisage as educational theatre in Africa, perhaps even typical of all African theatre. This may be with good reason since educational theatre has a long history in Africa, deriving from oral performance traditions, the theatre for development movement, anti-apartheid and anti-colonial theatre, as well as models from elsewhere in the world. At the time of writing, health education through theatre is probably the most widely known manifestation, but for this chapter to focus exclusively on health education through theatre would do a disservice to the theatre makers and educators who do this and more on the continent.

This chapter will therefore introduce some of the ways in which theatre companies seek to develop critical thinking and social commentary on identity, history, governance and heritage in sub-Saharan Africa, using examples from Malawi, Zimbabwe and South Africa. Several TIE initiatives at universities will be briefly considered, as well as the dilemma of funding educational theatre, before a more extended discussion of health education through theatre. Limitations of space and the sheer breadth of the continent's practices mean that the majority of the study will focus on South Africa, but a few examples from elsewhere in southern Africa will also be discussed.[2] The chapter will try to assess what has been done recently in the field of educational theatre, especially in South Africa since the end of apartheid.

Inevitably, considering South Africa post-1994 raises the question of what innovation may have been produced in the climate of freedom from apartheid. This chapter will suggest that, while many programmes have been developed in southern Africa, education through theatre has been deeply compromised by intractable attitudes, on the part of governments and funders, to the arts in education. The sector is beset with poor infrastructure and organisation, and lack of sustained funding. There is a tension between the role of the arts as education and social commentary, and their perceived position as part of a 'knowledge and creative economy'. African governments and funders are increasingly requiring that the arts become self-funded and sustainable, treating them as a consumer item. This leaves little room for theatre committed to education and development that arose in opposition to systematic underdevelopment and inequity.

## Theatre's role as social commentator

In keeping with the ethos of theatre's social role in Africa, Nanzikambe Arts Collective has staged and toured a number of plays on themes of governance and democracy in Lilongwe, Malawi (Nanzikambe Arts 2011). Nanzikambe perform these productions in their own theatre space to paying audiences, as well as in theatres further afield in neighbouring countries. The company was originally set up to reinterpret western classics for Africa, but recent productions like *Tariro* (2008–10) and *Makwacha Hipopera* (2010), show that the company extends its role to that of social commentator and educator. *Tariro* (in collaboration with Zimbabwe's Timbuku Dance Company) was based on extensive research into violence in Zimbabwe and South Africa. Tariro ('hope' in Shona) returns to Zimbabwe after the death of her father, to find her brothers set against each other over politics and their inherited land, echoing the Robert Mugabe and Morgan Tsvangirai conflict. *Makwacha Hipopera* (Schafer 2010) was adapted from the story of Brecht's *The Threepenny Opera*, with original musical collaborators from Malawi providing a satirical soundtrack. The production focused on the underworld of greed and corruption in Malawi, asking 'what is morality in a country plagued by poverty?'

In late 2011 Nanzikambe revived a production of *The Frogs*,[3] a political satire showing the food, fuel and foreign exchange shortages, and a government that fails to learn from history, repeating the same mistakes. According to Nanzikambe's production manager Mphundu Mjumile (2011), the 'grassroots' people of Malawi are the frogs, who will not keep quiet in the face of misery.

The emphasis of Nanzikambe's community work is on developing cultural expression in the arts and fostering opportunity for Malawians to work as professionals. A large component of its funding brief (from the Norwegian Embassy Consolidated Arts Programme: NECAP 2008) is focused on development goals set by the Malawian government and the country's Millennium Development Goals (MDG), and Nanzikambe is promoted as a model for other Malawian companies. Nanzikambe employs 150 'activators' of their methods in Malawi, involving a community-based, problem-solving interaction between a locally based activator and a community group. The work involves addressing questions that each community raises, and finding solutions to local problems through dialogical means that they call the *Tiyeni* ('let's go' in Chechewa) Interactive Methodology; that is, storytelling, theatre, community mobilisation and education. However, Nanzikambe organisers argue that training community activators in their methods of education and development is not an expense that many funders will consider, instead preferring the large-scale, urban performances of professional theatre that should set a benchmark for a theatre industry in the region. In this case it seems that the emphasis on high-profile performance outcomes privileges the concept of a 'creative economy', but without providing the requisite resources to equip a broader base of practitioners. At the same time, Nanzikambe's work continues to be critical of governance in Malawi and the region, *The President's Prerogative* (2012) being a recent example.

Cont Mhlanga and Amakhosi Theatre Productions continue to attract controversy in Zimbabwe, revealing the contradictions in that society through theatre. Cont Mhlanga has been making theatre since the early 1980s despite harassment and imprisonment. In 2008 he was awarded the *Freedom to Create* Prize by ArtVenture,[4] for his consistent and artistic critique of Zimbabwe's leaders. Several of his plays, including the ironically titled *The Good President*, have been closed by police (Karimakwenda 2007). In addition to this social commentary, various other projects by Amakhosi address community concerns of health education and development, and Cont Mhlanga writes and directs for television. In 1997 the Amakhosi Cultural Centre opened; it acts as a performing arts academy that trains young people for future work in theatre and television. In 2012, Amakhosi worked on a collaborative project with Sabelo Ngema, called *Inyelane*, which explored the history of the region at the time of Cecil John Rhodes. The production was rehearsed publicly, which, along with a barbecue (Dube 2012), attracted crowds of eager theatregoers and was seemingly reminiscent of the public rehearsals of *I Will Marry When I Want* and *Mother Sing For Me* in Kenya (Byam 1999: 90).

## Interpreting history

UBOM! in the Eastern Cape, South Africa, also excavates the history of its region as a lens through which to interpret the present, using the historical frame to interpret contemporary politics. The company's style is strongly influenced by physical theatre,[5] mime and clowning, and it serves artistic development by training local actors and hosting an annual development festival for township-based theatre groups,[6] including disaffected youths in the 'Art of the Street' project (Ubom! website). Community engagement was evident in their 2009 collaboration with Barefeet Theatre (Zambia) on *Float*, about water usage and community development. Ubom! has also worked extensively with the South African National Science Festival (SciFest), an annual event for school pupils. In *The Square Root of Dreaming* (2009), school pupils 'PJ' and 'Natasha' have to decide on their future careers, reconciling their dreams with the realities of subject choices at school, especially questioning why there is little science education in schools. *Muti Inc*. (Medicine Incorporated), a narrative about biotechnology, specifically scientific research into indigenous plants used as medicine by African traditional healers, was also redeveloped for the national Sci-Fest in 2011. Framed as participatory theatre, the piece used Xhosa-speaking community actors, part of Ubom!'s training programme, to perform to delegates. The production interrogates the ownership of traditional, indigenous knowledge, and the rights to use and profit from it.

*Figure 12.1* *Float* (UBOM! Eastern Cape Drama Company, South Africa, and Barefeet Theatre, Lusaka, Zambia). Performance at National Arts Festival, Grahamstown, 2009. Photo: Lindsay Callaghan, courtesy of *CuePix*.

Ubom! will often provide analysis of the history and contemporary politics of the region. Several of their productions have, like Nanzikambe's, spoken about issues of governance and corruption. One of their earliest touring productions in South Africa, called *Scorpion* (2005), was loosely based on Gogol's *The Government Inspector*. The production was comically analytic of the corruption in government departments that led to poor service delivery and lack of money for developing infrastructure. Most recently Ubom! has revived *The Dogs Must be Crazy*, a social satire from the point of view of dogs.

The company also creates shows specifically for the school curriculum, for example adapting *Romeo and Juliet* in 2011. During apartheid, English texts, and Shakespeare in particular, were privileged in the curriculum; at the same time, the assumption was that black learners (and teachers) would find the material inaccessible. The production of *Romeo and Juliet Censored* therefore had a great deal of significance, demonstrating the competence of local Xhosa actors, the accessibility and relevance of themes in the text, and the significance of theatre as a learning medium.

In 2008, Ubom! developed a production called *Hush*,[7] which is still performed annually at the start of the academic year in schools and universities and at local festivals. The production, which is followed by a participatory workshop, questions audience attitudes to sexual behaviour and values. It has been revived in several iterations, popular for its satirical analysis of stigmas and taboos, and successful in combating 'HIV fatigue'[8] and the formulaic approach to teaching about HIV through theatre.

Like other companies in South Africa, From the hip: Khulumakahle (FTH:K) is in constant touch with its immediate social context, working in both schools and community education. Its mandate is to integrate the deaf and hearing communities through non-verbal and visual theatre, making full use of clowning, mask work and physical theatre. Clowns without Borders (South Africa) tours extensively in schools, especially in rural communities, presenting stories and clowning. With the tagline 'no child without a smile', the group collaborates with children and adults across the southern Africa region, to develop resilience through humour and the creative arts.

## University drama departments

Most of the companies and productions mentioned above would not have emerged without the institutional support provided by universities and the work done in various drama departments in the region. Several South African university drama departments have taught educational theatre since at least the 1980s, providing field placement opportunities for their students in schools or other community settings. Many of these students have gone on to be productive in educational contexts. The University of KwaZulu-Natal, Pietermaritzburg, has placed students in schools and communities as part of its curriculum since the 1980s, and toured TIE pieces related to the school curriculum (for example, *Things Fall Apart* 1988, *Crocodiles* 1998). Productions of Shakespeare texts were produced annually at the Durban campus of the same university, as was significant work for prisons in the region.

Since 2004, Pretoria University (Coetzee 2011) has conducted TIE programmes with the South African Police Services on issues like bullying, crime, substance abuse and sexual misconduct. On tour they perform to audiences of between 30 and 800 pupils, and the extent to which interactive work is possible is determined by the size of audience. The University of Cape Town's Drama Department has conducted theatre in education programmes in local schools since 1990, reaching between 1,500 and 3,500 learners each year. The University of the Witwatersrand continues to have a vibrant community of applied theatre practitioners, recently invigorated by the establishment of the Drama for Life programme in 2008 (www.dramaforlife.co.za). Having begun with the explicit aim of improving education through theatre, this programme is an exciting venture in training new generations of practitioners and academics in applied theatre in the southern African region, and is already emerging as a major influence in the region.[9]

However, the extent to which TIE work reaches school audiences in the region is limited, and little of it is designed to augment the curriculum. TIE is not understood by the educational establishment, and therefore not supported financially.

## Funding

Many companies in South Africa have difficulties in getting sustained funding. There is an historic tension involved in funding the arts, between the pressure to provide artistic products for national stages (as evidence of the creative economy), and the need to provide development opportunities for future artists. The arts sector has been notoriously underfunded, and suffers from neglect, delays and a great deal of maladministration – in part because of the lack of arts management education at higher education institutions. As a result, many theatre companies reflect these patterns of instability in the ways they seek to respond to funders' criteria – for example, by trying to present professional productions for the national stage and at the same time running local theatre-making and performance programmes to educate out-of-school and unemployed youths. Many companies also provide educational theatre productions for schools, the majority of which cannot pay. Arts organisations who wish to make theatre accessible to schools and community audiences are therefore left to raise external funds through the National Arts Council, the Lottery or donor funding, with no contribution from the national or provincial government departments of education. Theatre is generally perceived to be primarily entertainment and 'culture', and as such the responsibility of the National Department of Arts and Culture. The ever-changing policy demands of the main government and non-government funding bodies also means that theatre companies are inevitably in constant flux.

The one area for which funding has been consistent across most of sub-Saharan Africa has been health education, in particular related to the HIV/AIDS pandemic. In South Africa this was nearly undermined by the scandal around Mbongeni Ngema's *Sarafina 2*. When the rampant HIV and AIDS epidemic was acknowledged as the enemy for the newly democratic South Africa, the freshly elected government of National Unity, led by the African National Congress, was quick to harness struggle-era theatre to the cause of HIV education. In 1995, it controversially awarded a tender to Mbongeni Ngema to produce a large-scale musical theatre production intended for this purpose. *Sarafina 2* tried to capitalise on the success of *Sarafina!* (1986), but the production was a public relations fiasco for everyone concerned. Critics panned the production and objected to its high cost, the tender procedures and lack of accountability for the vast amount of money involved. But, most pertinent to this discussion, it was pedagogically flawed as a vehicle for HIV education. There was a mismatch between the overt message (safe sex, abstinence, living positively) and the style of Ngema's theatre, involving much hip gyration and over-sexualised gesture; and an implication that death was an inevitable result of being HIV positive (Lindfors 1999: 184). *Sarafina 2* did much damage to the reputation of theatre as an educational medium. A few initiatives using theatre in health education did, however, manage to carve out a niche in the 1990s, and of these, DramAidE (in South Africa) became best known.

## DramAidE and HIV/AIDS education

Initiated by Lynn Dalrymple in Zululand in 1992, DramAidE (Drama Approach to AIDS Education) worked in the region's schools on preventative education at first. Dalrymple piloted a three-phase intervention at local high schools, using drama students as facilitators and actor-teachers. The early practices were based on a mixture of DIE and TIE, strongly influenced by the participatory methodologies of Paulo Freire (Singhal 2004: 377). The first phase required a play to be performed to high school pupils as a catalyst to their education about HIV. These plays were devised by the actor-teachers in collaboration with nurses who were seconded from the Department of Health to DramAidE. The performance demonstrated scenarios where high risk behaviours could be identified and discussed in a plenary session. The nurses worked with the actor-teachers to field questions, and to lend credibility to the educational process. In return the nurses were able to develop their knowledge and understanding of the disease, as well as the skills of presentation and public discussion of otherwise taboo subject matter.

The second phase included teacher training workshops on HIV, with sessions on where and how this information could be integrated into school subjects, such as Biology or English. Educational drama methods were used in classrooms in the senior years, and with teachers, using participatory techniques to explore the social context in which risky behaviours could be challenged.

The last phase of the intervention was a return to the school for the community Open Day, where pupils would perform their own plays, songs and dances, as well as display posters on the theme of HIV prevention. In this way the community's cultural forms were used to re-present information to a wider audience beyond the school.

DramAidE's work evolved to introduce different approaches, phases of intervention and models of evaluating impact. Lynn Dalrymple (2006b: 209) outlines some of these developments which moved on from purely rational-cognitive models used in earlier phases, and from the preventative approach, to working on how best to deal with infection, living 'positively' and peer education. She argues that earlier work in DramAidE (as with other health education initiatives) was based on an assumption that people will respond or behave reasonably so long as they have the correct information. Since decisions about sex are seldom based on reason, and because power relations in a gendered, hierarchical society skew behaviours, the rational-cognitive models were inadequate to halt the spread of HIV. The socio-cultural context has led DramAidE to develop other programmes that can intervene more effectively, based on social or community mobilisation (for example peer education through clubs at schools), collaboration with health promoters at universities and colleges, and the hosting of multi-media events.

The complexity of cultural problems that DramAidE facilitators face is best illustrated by a dramatic example, in a scene enacted by actor-teachers, between sexually active boyfriend Sipho and girlfriend Thandi, negotiating the use of a condom. In the early days of DramAidE's work, this was controversial because many organisations faced accusations of promoting sex (where there supposedly had been none) through encouraging condom use. As the prevalence of HIV infections has grown, promoting condom use has become considerably less naïve an option than abstinence; but often it seemed that education became pitted against African customs. The Sipho–Thandi scenario brought these contradictions into the open and allowed for a dialogue to develop between the participants.

Foremost amongst the contradictions was that the female character Thandi was the character who asked her boyfriend, Sipho, if they could use a condom in their future liaisons. This demonstrated more assertiveness on the part of a woman than was expected amongst

Black rural pupils. Many participants in these workshops would argue vigorously that this was because she, Thandi, was being unfaithful to Sipho with another man, because only promiscuous women would want to use condoms. The participants would say that Thandi didn't trust Sipho, and therefore the basis of their relationship was flawed anyway.

Many male participants argued that condom use was against their culture, that it was a sexual turn-off, that 'skin on skin' gave sexual pleasure, which was reduced by wearing a condom. Less frequently, the custom of 'dry' sex was justified as a cultural preference, which condom use also eliminated. Some young men claimed that condoms were too small for them or that they came off during sexual intercourse. Much debate was centred on the condom's efficacy, and where this was presented as 98 per cent *if used correctly*, it inevitably led to requests for demonstrations in an attempt to disrupt the session. When Thandi became insistent that either Sipho wore a condom or she would withhold sex, the male participants argued that men were *biologically compelled* (for reasons of sanity) to have sex on demand, urging the actor-teacher playing Sipho to assert his control, on several occasions advocating that he hit Thandi, because it was his right. Many argued that having sex was the way to demonstrate that you loved the other person.

Amongst the female participants there was some discomfort about being asked to assert themselves by even asking for a condom to be used, as well as incredulity at the idea of refusing to 'give sex'. The fear of being hit was raised frequently as the reason not to ask for safe sex. Many debated that under traditional or customary law women had no right to refusal, and a married woman was her husband's possession because she had been '*labola'd*' (the bride price had been paid).

In the workshops on sex education, the reluctance of females to assert their rights over their bodies, in face of male opposition, became obvious. Female participants found it difficult to suggest lines of dialogue for Thandi to argue for condom use, and said that if a male 'proposed love' to them, they would have to have sex. The males dominated the situation, and the words 'in my culture' seemed impossible to counter in the early days of South Africa's freedom from apartheid. In school performances, Sipho's character was often perceived as blameless by the young men whose arguments supported traditional practices that placed them and particularly their female partners at risk. This allowed the young women to take the attitude that they were victims, 'more done to, than doing'. It is arguable that denial of the AIDS pandemic is partly rooted in an unwillingness to place responsibility at the door of traditional attitudes to, and norms of, Black masculinities (Posel 2005). The invective aimed at Black male sexuality by colonial and apartheid legislation makes this understandable.

The dialogic element of participatory theatre also provided an opportunity to examine the beliefs and attitudes of young students in high schools and, more recently in DramAidE's work, in universities. Amongst the aspects studied was that of 'locus of control'. Hester Steyn et al. (2005) argue that developing an internal 'locus of control' is an important psychological skill for high school pupils to acquire, especially if they are to develop the ability to make decisions about their own lives, based on what is beneficial to them.[10] As the Sipho–Thandi scene demonstrates, gender inequality and issues around 'locus of control' have a profound impact on the ability of young people to engage with each other on equal terms, and this has contributed to the rapid spread of HIV in South Africa (Dalrymple 2006a). As Kennedy Chinyowa (2009: 51) suggests, until patriarchy and the subjugation of women and girls can be significantly altered in southern African society, the spread of HIV will continue.

In her discussion of DramAidE's work, Emma Durden (2010: 254) problematises participation, asserting that ideally, for empowerment to take place, theatrical participation needs to begin as problem-posing rather than problem-solving. She argues persuasively that participatory work is most effective when rooted (as in the case of DramAidE) in the performance aesthetics of Zulu and African culture combined with interactive techniques borrowed from Augusto Boal. She further suggests that peer education through drama clubs at schools, set up by DramAidE more than ten years previously, is evidence of the company's sustainable model – indeed that the success of a theatre for development project depends upon a strong organisational infrastructure, clarity of purpose that is informed by local context and ongoing research, and a network of organisations engaged with the same objectives (Durden 2010: 67). All of these elements have contributed to the survival – and continuity – of DramAidE for more than twenty years.

## Keeping it light and playful

An organisation that has consistently stayed in schools' education is arepp: Theatre for Life (www.arepp.org.za), based in Johannesburg and Cape Town, and touring programmes to schools across most of the provinces of South Africa. The organisation has steadily grown since its formation in 1987, offering human-rights based approaches to education about health and well-being. The programmes are tailored to different ages using puppets for primary school audiences up to age 9, and actors in programmes for ages 10 and above.

The organisation is meticulous in training its actor-facilitators in performance methods. Actors are trained in a quasi-Brechtian acting style, presenting the social *gestus* and 'selective realism' through physical and verbal characterisation, and costuming. Generally using younger actors close to their prospective audience's ages, the productions are tailor-made for specific geographic regions of southern Africa. For example, in primary schools, the teams use the mother-tongue of the pupils, since this best facilitates learning.

Most South African actors speak more than one language fluently, and since there are eleven official languages in the country most urban people switch between languages frequently. This is used to great advantage in the productions for older pupils, in which actors, for example, might switch between English, Xhosa, Afrikaans, Sotho and Zulu. It allows teams of actors to represent a multilingual society, thereby also suggesting that specific social problems are not the exclusive preserve of one language group.

The company presents touring plays that have been fine-tuned over many years of development and in response to extensive evaluation processes. For example, the Grades 8–12 (14–19 years) are presented with plays from the repertoire of *Look before you Leap*, which deal with adolescent sexuality, abstinence, gender roles and identity, and homosexuality. The artistic directors are determined not to provide overtly didactic and formulaic HIV messages, but to present ordinary young people navigating their way through the dilemmas of growing up. The style of performance includes dialogue between characters, as well as monologues delivered to the audience. Extensive use of humour in the plays allows for collective recognition of the awkwardness of adolescence – the boy wonders if he should confess to his girlfriend that he is a virgin, the girl wonders how she can practise kissing. Several key issues facing young people are raised in the dramatic action, such as homosexuality, sexual abuse, alcohol and drug abuse, and suicide. However, none of these points is laboured – they are raised as part of the narrative as life decisions that the young person is processing. The central theme of the performance is the fact that young people have choices to make, and the narrative suggests that a healthy self-esteem is the best guide. This is the essence of arepp: Theatre for Life's approach, in keeping with the idea of 'modelling', drawn from social cognitive learning theory (Singhal 2004).

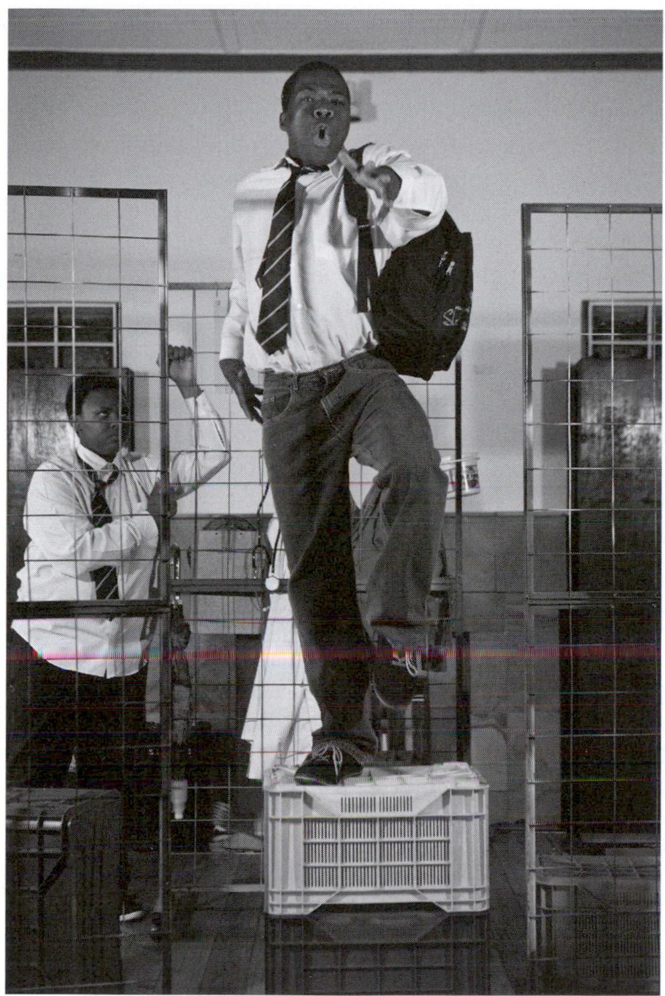

*Figure 12.2 About Us: Stepping Up* (arepp: Theatre for Life, 2011). A project for Grade 4–7 students. © Andrew Aitchison Photography. Courtesy of STARS Foundation.

Some of arepp: Theatre for Life's critics suggest that their work should present more overt messages, and are confused by the openness that the narrative presents. The only didactic messages, complete with wagging fingers, are delivered by authority figures, such as parents and teachers. These are intended as gentle spoofs of the well-intended but ineffectual lessons often given by adults. In one scene, a boy is getting ready for his first big date, and his parents embarrass him by giving him a pack of condoms. His father tries to be up-beat and knowing, subtly pressurising him to be 'a man'. His mother calls him her child, and even while handing over the condoms, makes her high moral standpoint clear. Together the parents warn him that if he 'gets the girl pregnant' he is in trouble. The boy, who would have been happy to have had a first kiss on his date, is even more stressed after all these contradictory expectations are identified. The audiences recognise this situation, even though the actors are each speaking from a different cultural vantage point. In one performance (13 January 2012), the three actors were from different racial or cultural groups, speaking three different languages in the scene. In a multicultural society like urban South Africa, these stereotypes are understood, as is the convention of playing 'colour blind' so that a 'coloured' boy can have a Black Zulu mother and a 'Cape Malay' father, each speaking different languages.

Performances for high school pupils last approximately 35 minutes, with a facilitated discussion afterwards. The teachers are encouraged to leave the venue for the duration of the performance to enable the pupils to ask questions freely. The actors are trained to facilitate these sessions in order to achieve a deeper engagement with the subjects raised in the performance, and to encourage critical thinking with the aim of developing self-efficacy (Singhal 2004).

Like other theatre companies, arepp: Theatre for Life faces challenges in securing adequate funding even though it has conducted extensive evaluation over time and has ample evidence of its ongoing success (www.arepp.org.za/evaluations.html). In 2011 the company received a Stars Foundation Education Impact award, but still faces an uncertain future, reliant as it is on funding from external sources.

## Industrial Theatre

It would be difficult to discuss educational theatre in southern Africa without taking into consideration that much of this work is devised with adults in mind. A *quasi* educational theatre emerged in the early 1990s under the title of Industrial Theatre, a communication medium for adults in the workplace, to promote their 'transformation' into the workforce of manufacturing, industrial and corporate companies.

South African theatre companies working in the field variously refer to Industrial Theatre as 'behaviour change consultancy' (Wrottesley 1999), transformation theatre (van Eeden 2000) and 'internal communication and marketing process' (Blue Moon Company

2000: 3). Theatre companies are hired to communicate messages through Industrial Theatre, and the theatre piece is pre-scripted by a writer in consultation with the hiring company. The script does not usually provide any open-ended opportunity for discussion, allowing for message-giving only.

Regular topics include HIV/AIDS education, Health and Safety regulations, downsizing and retrenchments, and transformation of the workplace. Michelle Caldeira (2000) managing director of Blue Moon, argued that the methods used in Industrial Theatre are effective in educating their audiences, because the style of theatre used is familiar to the target groups, and the actors are professionals who can adapt to the specific contexts of the performance. Many of the Blue Moon productions were styled after *Woza Albert!* (Caldeira 2000), a seminal South African work (devised in 1981 by Percy Mtwa, Mbongeni Ngema and Barney Simon) that was centred on issues of apartheid, and inspired in form by the 'poor theatre' of Jerzy Grotowski (Mtwa et al. 1983).[11]

The Learning Theatre Organisation (LTO) explains that Industrial Theatre

> provides for little or no feedback from the audience and can be used effectively during launches and for the dissemination of information policies, Employment Equity, Safety, Customer Service, etc.
>
> (LTO 2005)

The LTO was initiated by three directors, Henk du Plessis, Theo Potgieter and Ben Kruger, in 1996, and still claims to combine 'the disciplines of drama, psychology and organisational development … dramatic solutions for the clients' needs' (www.learningtheatre.co.za/index.htm). The LTO distinguishes between Industrial Theatre and Interactive Theatre (where more involvement and questioning with the audience takes place), Facilitated Theatre (with facilitators who 'extract' learning from the group or individual) and Participative Experiential Theatre (where a workshop is facilitated in order for participants to learn at a deeper level). Its approach is explicitly different from that of other companies by virtue of including the interactive or experiential workshop in their 'corporate' repertoire. While the LTO still does Industrial Theatre, the company makes it clear that the model is for information-giving only. It does not equate information-giving with education or transformation. The company's approach to theatre and learning is outlined in an online publication, *The Business Stage*, where it is argued that emotions are neglected in the business place, but are crucial to manage:

> No other communication, training or development tool such as presentations, workshops, lectures, video conferencing and training courses can provide learning on an emotive level (and influence mental models) to the extent that drama or a theatre production achieves.
>
> (LTO 1999: 2)

In a subsequent article (LTO 2000), the LTO provides a case study of the use of its 'theatre or drama methodology'. Over a day and a half, thirty participants were taken through an experiential and participatory process that involved rethinking their roles in the workplace. Two theatre pieces were performed to the participants – stories that were carefully chosen to provide opportunity for analysis. The participants were then asked to relate the themes of the stories to their work situation. In this way 'theatre … allows employees to discharge pent up emotions by watching and experiencing the theatre performance' (LTO 1999: 2). The emphasis of the LTO's work, however, is on creating effective means by which to improve productivity and efficient service, with drama and theatre methods used to manage emotions that may get in the way of 'good business practice' (LTO 1999: 3).

## Who pays the piper?

The rapid growth of Industrial Theatre in South Africa demonstrates that there is some acknowledgement that theatre is an effective medium for education. However, as Christopher Odhiambo (2005) points out, many ethical problems also emerge as dubious theatrical practices masquerade as education. During the 1990s and early 2000s, donor-funded theatre dealing with HIV and AIDS, female genital mutilation, conflict resolution and many other social problems attracted facilitators who would pocket the money and conduct workshops that achieved very little. Odhiambo's research into facilitators suggested that 60 per cent had had no training in theatre or facilitation, did not know the principles that underpin the practices, and were mostly motivated by personal enrichment. The terrain in southern Africa has become de-politicised, and to some extent this has opened the way for what Peter Abbs (2003: 20) has called 'the rapacious, the thug and the quack'. The facilitation of development and education using theatre may well have become a growth industry for opportunists with an eye on international development aid funding.

Funding for educational theatre across southern Africa remains a contested issue, open to exploitation by opportunistic and unethical practices, and the attitude to arts funding and sustainability in current South Africa is nothing short of baffling. The funding crises of 2012 have created insecurity and many threats of closure for arts companies. Government and quasi-government funding strategies for the National Arts Council and lottery funds have changed recently, and many arts and heritage organisations face closure or cutbacks.

Recognition of the value of educational theatre by key government departments has been crucial, but the current lack of transparent and responsive funding of educational work is a major obstacle. Educational theatre endeavours cannot become self-sustaining in the southern African region, since poor but needy schools and communities are unable to pay. Most companies raise funds through a variety of strategies, including 'crowd-sourcing' through social media and pay-what-you-can-afford offers. Even for those companies that have a strong health education focus (such as arepp: Theatre for Life), the current recession, the euro zone crisis and perhaps some compassion fatigue have adversely affected international donor agencies. At a regional level, theatre groups are under pressure to mount large-scale productions that fulfil the government's mandate for supporting and developing arts and cultural heritage (the creative economy), even while the grassroots development of new artists lacks support. There is no funding from national or provincial education departments for learning through the arts, and precious little for teaching the arts in schools.

In mid-2012 the future for educational theatre organisations looks fairly grim. While blockbuster musicals like *Phantom of the Opera* are imported at enormous cost for elite audiences in Johannesburg or Cape Town, the tour of a modest educational theatre piece appears to be unaffordable and perhaps even politically undesirable, especially in areas that theatre does not normally reach. The social chasm remains between urban and rural, rich and poor, educated and uneducated. Where once there was the political will to work through the arts for social change, now the focus is on entrepreneurship and a business plan. Even the benefits of being associated with a university (as is the case with DramAidE, Drama for Life, Ubom! and the LTO) do not wholly shield companies and practitioners from the vagaries of the market.

There is much to commend the innovation and development of educational theatre in the southern Africa region, and the resilience of the theatremakers who make work under these difficult conditions, but the work is generally unsustainable without substantial funding and structural support. As the cultural policies of southern African countries fall in line with international trends towards creative economies, so the theatre risks becoming the preserve of the elite who can afford it, and its educational value moves towards commodification.

It is evident that producing innovative educational theatre is in part an act of political will and dogged determination on the part of many arts practitioners. Companies like those discussed above sustain the dream of a theatre practice that serves its audiences, and develops ideas of democracy, participatory citizenship and liberatory education. While it is disheartening to see that educational theatre still has to prove itself to some influential policymakers and funders, it is clear that there is a great deal of ingenuity and imagination at the forefront in arts education.

## Notes

1 The author dedicates her chapter to the memory of Lynn Dalrymple (1941–2012), founder of DramAidE, South Africa.

2 The work of several companies, such as Magnet Theatre Company, Themba Interactive, Maratholi, is discussed in such journals as *South African Theatre Journal*, *Research in Drama Education* and *Research in African Literatures*. The history of educational theatre in Africa is described in Mda (1993), Byam (1999), and Boon and Plastow (1998 and 2004). Discussions of HIV/AIDS education through theatre include Bourgault (2003) and Marion Frank (1995).

3 Aristophanes' original tale is adapted to tell the story of a respected warrior on a journey across south-eastern Africa, meeting many challenges en route to Malawi, where he has to judge the value of traditional versus contemporary life by its artistic outputs.

4 Freedom to Create was set up in 2006, and ArtVenture awarded prizes in several categories until 2011. See www.freedomtocreate.com/ (accessed 30 June 2012).

5 For more information on physical theatre in southern Africa see inter alia, the *South African Theatre Journal*, 24 (2010).

6 Many companies and theatres offer the same opportunities, including the Market Theatre Laboratory in Johannesburg, the Baxter and Artscape Theatres in Cape Town, Maitisong in Gaborone, Amakhosi Theatre Company in Bulawayo.

7 Originally devised and presented as *Risky Business*, by Alex Sutherland.

8 By the time most students reach college or university they will have been saturated with HIV/AIDS messages.

9 Drama For Life hosts an annual research conference in applied theatre, an annual festival, and has an ongoing academic programme for postgraduate students in applied theatre.

10 In their study of male adolescents, Hester Steyn et al. (2005) found that the locus of control was still predominantly located externally.

11 The Serpent Players and Athol Fugard (*The Island* and *Sizwe Bansi is Dead*), Matsemela Manaka and Rob Amato (*Egoli*) and others acknowledge their experimentation with 'poor' theatre.

## Works cited

Abbs, Peter (2003), *Against the Flow: Education, the Arts and Postmodern Culture*. London: Routledge Falmer.

Arepp: Theatre for Life (2011), 'Look before you leap'. www.arepp.org.za/repertoire.html (accessed 18 November 2011).

Blue Moon Company (2000), *An Introduction to The Blue Moon Company: Marketing and Internal Communication Company*. Johannesburg: Unpublished company document.

Boal, Augusto (1979), *Theatre of the Oppressed*. London: Pluto Press.

Boon, Richard and Plastow, Jane (2004), *Theatre and Empowerment – Community Drama on the World Stage*. Cambridge: Cambridge University Press.

——(1998), *Theatre Matters: Performance and Culture on the World Stage*. Cambridge: Cambridge University Press.

Bourgault, Louise M. (2003), *Playing for Life: Performance in Africa in the time of AIDS*. Durham, NC: Carolina Academic Press.

Byam, L. Dale (1999), *Community in Motion – Theatre for Development in Africa*. Westpoint: Bergin and Garvey.

Caldeira, Michelle, personal communication (4 November 2000).

Chinyowa, K. (2009), 'Theatrical performance as technology: the case of Drama in AIDS Education (DramAidE) in South Africa', *Studies in Theatre and Performance*, 29.1, pp. 33–52.

Coetzee, Marie-Heleen, personal communication (12 November 2011).

*Constant Gardener, The* [Motion Picture]. (2005), Produced by Simon Channing-Williams and Gail Egan, directed by Fernando Mereilles. United Kingdom: Focus Features.

Dalrymple, Lynn (2006a), 'DramAidE: An evaluation of interaction drama and theatre for HIV/AIDS education in South Africa'. In Balfour, Michael and Somers, John, eds., *Drama as Social Intervention*. Toronto: Captus Press, pp. 195–206.

——(2006b), 'Has it made a difference? Understanding and measuring the impact of applied theatre with young people in South Africa', *Research in Drama Education*, 11.2, pp. 201–18.

——(forthcoming 2013), 'Applied Art is still art, and by any other name would smell as sweet'. In Barnes, Hazel, ed., *Applied Drama and Theatre volume 2. Arts Activism, Education and Therapies: Transforming Communities across Africa*. Amsterdam: Rodopi, pp. 181–94.

Dube, Innocent (2012), 'Inyelane – The Musical is on the cards!' IYASA. http://iyasa.net/ (accessed 25 June 2012).

Durden, Emma (2010), *Staging Empowerment: An Investigation into Participation and Development in HIV and AIDS Theatre Projects*. Unpublished PhD, University of KwaZulu-Natal, Durban, South Africa.

Frank, Marion (1995), *AIDS Education through Theatre*. Bayreuth: Bayreuth University Press.

Karimakwenda, Tererai (2007), 'Police Ban Amakhosi Theatre Play in Bulawayo'. http://allafrica.com/stories/200706141062.html (accessed 10 November 2011).

Learning Theatre Organisation (1999), 'A Terrific Trio: Emotion, Business and Drama'. *The Business Stage*, vol. 1: 2 September 1999. Online at www.learningtheatre.co.za/news9909.htm (accessed 22 May 2001).

——(2000), 'Case study: Dramatic solutions for Strategic Planning (The Rhino)'. *The Business Stage*: December 2000, vol. 2 no. 2. Online at www.learningtheatre.co.za (accessed 22 May 2001).

——(2005), *Types of Theatre*. www.learningtheatre.co.za/types.htm (accessed 12 August 2005).

Lindfors, Bernth (1999), 'The Rise and Fall of Mbongeni Ngema: The AIDS play'. In Blumberg, M. and Walder, D., eds., South *African Theatre as/and Intervention.* Amsterdam: Rodopi.

Mda, Zakes (1993), *When People Play People: Development Communication through Theatre*. Johannesburg: Wits University Press.

Mjumile, Mphundu (2011), cited in Nkawihe, Maurice, 'Nanzikambe Arts speaks out in Frogs', *Nyasa Times*, 7 November.

Mtwa, Percy, Ngema, Mbongeni and Simon, Barney (1983), *Woza Albert!* Methuen.

Nanzikambe Arts. www.nanzikambearts.org (accessed 9 November 2011).

Norwegian Embassy Consolidated Arts Programme (NECAP) (2008), NGO draft agreement, dated 23 July 2008, with Nanzikambe Arts Collective. Online at www.norway.mw/PageFiles/335524/Nanzikambe.doc (accessed 9 November 2011).

Odhiambo, Christopher (2005), 'Theatre for development in Kenya: interrogating the ethics of practice'. *Research in Drama Education*, 10.2, pp. 189–99.

Posel, Deborah (2005), 'Sex, Death and the Fate of the Nation: Reflections on the Politicization of Sexuality in Post-Apartheid South Africa'. *Africa*. Vol 75: 2. Edinburgh University Press, pp. 125–53.

Schafer, Nicole. Makwacha Hipopera. Youtube clip. Online at www.youtube.com/watch?v=5tOxlFIzeIo (accessed 9 November 2010).

Singhal, Arvind (2004), 'Entertainment-Education through Participatory theater: Freirean Strategies for Empowering the Oppressed'. In Arvind Singhal, Michael J. Cody, Everett M. Rogers and Miguel Sabido, *Entertainment-Education and Social Change: History, Research, and Practice.* Mahwah NJ: Lawrence Erlbaum Associates, pp. 377–97.

Steyn, Hester, Myburgh, Chris P. H. and Poggenpoel, Marie (2005), 'Male Adolescents' View on Sexual Activity as Basis for the Development of Aids-Prevention Programmes'. *Education*, vol. 125: 4. Alabama: Project Innovation, pp. 584–601.

Van Eeden, Johanna (2000), 'Drama help mense om die lewe te hanteer' (Drama helps people to cope with life). *Rapport*, 1 October 2000, p. 2.

Wrottesley, R. (1999), 'Sandra's view'. *Cape Argus*, 23 July 1999, p. 11.

# 13

# WALKING THE TIGHTROPE

## The complex demands of funded partnerships

### The Creative Arts Team, New York City

*Helen Wheelock*

As it approaches its fortieth anniversary in 2014, the Creative Arts Team (CAT), a professional educational theatre company in New York City, can reflect with satisfaction on how it has survived and thrived over a long and, at times, bumpy road.[1] An educational outreach initiative of The City University of New York (CUNY),[2] CAT currently employs nearly fifty full-time professionals, including actor-teachers, programme directors and arts administrators, serving approximately 11,000 people annually. Working with populations from pre-kindergarten to adults in the City and beyond, the Company offers interactive theatre and drama experiences that examine curricular themes and social issues including race relations, HIV/AIDS, bullying, literacy, college readiness, parenting and life skills. CAT's mission is to use the power of theatre to encourage participants to engage critically in the world around them and actively participate in their own learning. For many years now, the work has been process- rather than product-focused, having shifted away from the play with an accompanying workshop to a more integrated mixture of performance and participation. It is typically developed through a combination of topic research, target population assessment and devising.

The projects described in this chapter exemplify how funded partnerships have impacted this work, highlighting specific challenges that a TIE company faces in the present political, financial and increasingly outcome-driven educational climate as it tries to balance its own priorities with those of its funders. How does a company decide what it is willing to do to meet financial needs, how does it satisfy its partners, and what does it need to do to maintain its artistic and educational integrity?

CAT's work currently consists of six programmes, each managed by a director, who is responsible for training the artistic staff, planning and creating the work, and sustaining its quality and integrity. The programmes consist of a citywide CAT Youth Theatre with two groups for 10- to 13-year-olds and 14 years and upwards, and five TIE-based programmes: the College/Adult Program, the High School, Middle School, Special Projects and Early Learning (EL)[3] Programs. (I am the EL Program Director.) In this chapter, three of the programmes will be discussed in detail: the Early Learning, Middle School and High School Programs.

CAT's philosophy and methodologies are rooted in the concepts and practices of the British TIE movement of the 1970s and 1980s. Translating those unique approaches to learning into the American educational system was an early and frequent challenge for the Company. In the late 1980s, as the scope of CAT's work expanded, it also began to incorporate the Theatre of the Oppressed techniques of Augusto Boal. Then, beginning in 1993, with the arrival of Chris Vine as the new Artistic and Education Director, there was a review of pedagogical principles and a conscious effort to integrate Paulo Freire's educational theories into its practice, with a particular emphasis on developing problem-posing theatre and strengthening the student-centred facilitation skills of its actor-teachers.

Many factors have contributed to the Company's continued existence: the creativity of its administration and artists; rigorous self-reflection; and the long service of its senior staff – many of whom have been with the Company for a decade or more. CAT has also benefited from many long-term partnerships with state and city agencies. These relationships have informed, and frequently determined, the content of the work, pushing CAT to experiment with form, implementation structures and evaluation methods. At times, the collaborations have also challenged the Company to negotiate the very real tension between its stated artistic and educational mission and the contractual bottom line.

'We have never had the luxury of saying "no",' says founder and Executive Director Lynda Zimmerman. 'Although at times,' she adds, 'I know some people here would like for us to do that' (Zimmerman 2011: interview). This is an ongoing challenge for anyone charged with keeping a publicly funded organisation afloat, relevant and responsive. It can create strained relationships within an organisation as well as between the organisation and its funding partners.

There is no doubt that CAT has benefited from many dynamic partnerships with federal, state and city agencies. 'These partnerships have allowed CAT to experiment, reflect, consider outcomes, reconfigure, and reapply,' says Zimmerman (ibid.). There have been times when project requirements have conflicted with what the Company has seen as its 'on the ground assessment' of the population being served or its own pedagogical principles. The most rewarding partnerships have been those in which CAT has been able to bring all parties involved to the table – funders, CAT staff, and community representatives – to share different, yet often complementary, perspectives on how best to meet the needs of its audience. The best of these collaborations have led to a deep trust between CAT and its partners, often allowing CAT to negotiate and modify partners' expectations while exploring ways of using drama effectively in innovative ways.

## The Early Learning Program: developing age-appropriate drama work and sharing those skills with classroom teachers

An ongoing collaboration with classroom teachers has been a vital part of the ELTA Program's growth and evolution. Created in 1993 to take CAT's drama work into the early childhood classroom, ELTA initially worked with a few Department of Education (DOE) schools and then partnered with New York City's Administration for Children's Services (ACS) to offer five-day residencies with citywide Head Start programmes.[4] Under the guidance of then Director Karina Naumer, and drawing on the child development theories of Piaget[5] and subsequent critiques by authors such as Margaret Donaldson (1978), a core group of actor-teachers used feedback from teachers and education directors, as well as their own hands-on experience, to create a successful drama structure. Typically, guided by two actor-teachers playing engaging characters within the drama, the children would be put into role as members of a community with important responsibilities. The stories would unfold over four or five days; at some point something would put that community at risk. Then the children would be challenged, in role, often pulled in opposing directions by character conflicts and their own emotions, to decide how to address the problem. The drama's resolution would reflect their choices and decisions.

The developing language skills of the early childhood population pushed actor-teachers to explore how characters could communicate physically through gesture and demeanour, not just words. Committed to working in a student-centred manner, they used open and closed, challenging and agreement-forming questions, carefully scaffolded to be developmentally appropriate and to support the emotional investment

*Figure 13.1* *Alphabet Keepers.* CAT Early Learning Program 2003. The Fixing Elf, Snip (actor-teacher Max Ryan), and the new Fixing Elves, practise using the imaginary tools needed to fix broken books, letters and signs. Later they will create 'literacy spells' to protect the Book of Letters, containing the world's alphabets, from a word-stealing Wicked Wizard. Photo: Krista Fogle.

and intellectual comprehension of the children. As the dramatic tension escalated over the arc of the drama, actor-teachers could pose higher-order questions and present rich dilemmas for the young people to address.

For instance, in *The Magic Drum*, a drama exploring inclusion and exclusion, the students become the new villagers who must help the leader, Oba (an actor-teacher), take care of a drum that magically produces food. Life is good, until Oba makes a mistake that puts the drum in the hands of Ijapa (a second actor-teacher), a tortoise who has always coveted the drum. When drought hits, everyone must come to Ijapa for food. Thrilled with her new-found power, she starts to exclude some of the children – now in role as flamingos, zebras and elephants to add a second layer of distance and protection for those being excluded – from the feasts. Ijapa's actions would always prompt a variety of responses, for example: 'Call Ijapa's mother!' 'Let's move to Ghana. Or Florida!' One particularly memorable reaction occurred in a kindergarten class when a child, in role as a flamingo who had been invited to dinner, stalked up to Ijapa and said:

> You know what you need? *She points a finger up into Ijapa's face.* You need to go to school and get some sharing lessons! *She turns and walks back to the other animals.*
>
> (Kindergarten student 1998: ELTA residency)

Because Head Start teachers had such strong, positive reactions to how CAT's student-centred strategies were impacting their students on a cognitive and emotional level, ACS asked CAT to lengthen the residencies and include a professional development component. In the beginning, the training objectives – to have the teachers create and lead a two-day issue-based drama in two 45-minute planning sessions – were decidedly overambitious. Even when additional professional development days were added to the residencies, teachers struggled to master the skills needed to create their own TIE work in their classrooms.

The challenges of the teacher-training process led ELTA to develop and draft an 'early childhood actor-teacher' rubric that included the following assessment areas: role-play, transitions/segues, spatial arrangement, creating an imaginary world, classroom management, questioning, pantomiming and narration/storytelling. Acknowledging the complexity of the work helped the programme come to an important realisation: it should stop trying to transform classroom teachers into actor-teachers! Few teachers had any theatre background, much less experience with educational drama. The goal should not be to replace ourselves, but to find a way to make connections between our work as artists and the potential for teachers to infuse drama strategies into their existing classroom practices.

Conversations with educators began to generate questions: Where might a classroom teacher's skills connect with those of an actor-teacher? What drama strategies could the classroom teachers learn that they could realistically lead *on their own*? What was the best residency structure for training teachers? What drama form could CAT use that would capture the artistry of its two-person work and yet be led by just one actor-teacher, mirroring the solo role of the classroom teacher? Finally, considering the pressures teachers were under to 'teach to the test', how could we support curricular goals such as literacy, yet maintain our aesthetic integrity?

ELTA began to reshape its professional development and employ a new drama strategy, one that could indeed be led by a solo actor-teacher – and by extension, a solo teacher – yet still highlight the drama techniques and artistic skills of ELTA's earlier work: interactive storytelling.

Interactive storytelling involves taking the text of a picture book, turning it into a storytelling, and then adding specific call and repeat points of participation that invite listeners to participate physically and verbally. The points of participation serve a threefold purpose: they actively engage the audience, essential for the early childhood student; they support emergent literacy skills such as fluency, vocabulary acquisition, recall and sequencing; and finally, the actor-teacher and, by association, the young people, embody multiple roles throughout the storytelling that allow the students to explore different points of view and emotional dimensions. The actor-teacher uses questions to add details and engage participants in creative problem-solving. For instance, in Kevin Henkes's book, *Kitten's First Full Moon*, a kitten thinks the moon is a bowl of milk:

> The actor-teacher is seated on a chair; the students are clumped around his feet.
>
> *AT:* … and still the kitten couldn't reach the milk. *In a loud, reedy voice.* 'I won't give up!' Let's all say that. *All repeat.* He was so frustrated! So again he said, *Finger pointing to the sky.* 'I want that bowl of creamy, white milk!' Let's all say that. *All repeat, fingers pointing to the sky.*
>
> *AT:* So, how else could he get up into the sky and get that bowl of milk?
>
> *Child 1:* Use a rocket!
>
> *AT:* That's an idea. Would it be a big one or a little one?
>
> *Child 1:* BIG!
>
> *AT:* So that's one great way. Are there any other ways?
>
> *Child 2:* Wings.
>
> *AT:* Where would he get the wings?
>
> *Child 3:* From a bird.

*Child 2:* Or he could take some big leaves.

*AT:* How would they stay on?

*Child 2:* Glue!

*At this point the actor-teacher negotiates with the children as to which of the 'good ideas' – there are often many – they want to incorporate in the story. Sometimes it might be possible to use more than one.* (Here, 'wings' were the clear favourite, but it was important that the children heard that the other ideas were not wrong.) *The story then continues.*

*AT:* So the kitten said, 'You know what I need?' Let's all say that. *All repeat, 'You know what I need?'* 'Some wings!'
(CAT actor-teacher with student 2009: ELTA residency)

A simple exchange such as this captures what we want to do, and what we want to encourage teachers to do: access the imagination of young people, ask open-ended questions, incorporate as many creative suggestions as possible, but negotiate the choices that have to be made to move the story forward. After a storytelling, the actor-teacher will often 'picture walk' through the original storybook, inviting students to compare and contrast the book with the story they co-created. This reinforces literacy skills such as prediction and recall, but it also underscores the concept that story is changeable, and the power to change it is in the children's hands.

### *A new model*

Since 2009, ELTA has partnered with the NYC DOE's Office of Early Childhood Education to support emergent literacy goals through an intensive professional development model. Teachers are introduced to interactive storytelling during a five-hour professional development day. Throughout the session teachers are asked to consider how certain classroom practices – either their own or those imposed by their administrators – might inhibit a child's acquisition of emergent literacy skills and how oral storytelling might offer students another way in. They listen to a storytelling based on a book, and then critique the experience. Frequently they observe that it is more engaging than a reading, noting that without the book in hand, a storyteller is free to use specific dramatic skills – vocal pitch and volume, sound effects, characterisation, gestures and emotional embodiment linked to dramatic tension, and strong eye contact. These skills form the rubric teachers use for strengthening each other's storytelling skills as they collaborate to create their own interactive storytelling. In doing so, they are stepping into a realm of artistry that resembles that of the actor-teacher: performing drama work with an educational intent. For the teachers, storytelling may seem somewhat less complex than drama work, and therefore more achievable, but its purpose in this context is similar – to use story not simply to develop imagination or build language skills, but to understand that even a child's storybook has the potential to be complex, profound and engaging, on many levels.

Teachers can then participate in five-day follow-up 'mentoring' residencies at their schools during which an actor-teacher models four interactive storytelling sessions and on the fifth day, with the actor-teacher side coaching, the teachers lead a solo session themselves. Teachers come together for a final professional development reflection day to share what they have observed and learned. They often highlight the social-emotional impact of the storytelling. 'Children who were unable to express themselves, whether it was through voice or through actions, were able to participate, to be part of a group', said one teacher. 'To contribute in a positive way without being pointed out in a negative way. It was an awesome experience for them' (Teacher 1 2010: interview).

Though it is a work session, the gathering often feels like a celebration of the teacher's own creativity. Said one teacher afterward:

> So many teachers have one way of thinking and teaching. Storytelling takes you outside the box. It is not only where teachers need to go, but where administrators need to go. That's where we want our kids to go – to think outside the box. So we have to model it.
>
> (Teacher 2 2010)

In many ways, the comment reflects what has become the Program's mission: to bring interactive, student-centred drama work into the early childhood classroom, through the work either of actor-teachers or of the classroom teacher. Our teacher-training model continues to evolve with the interests of our participating teachers and the goals of our partners.

The move from working with two actors in a drama to solo work is also a pragmatic one, allowing the programme to negotiate the changing economic realities imposed by restricted school budgets and a shrinking demand for expensive residencies, while also responding to the increasing emphasis on teacher training and sustainability. As a direct consequence of these trends, the EL Program has contracted from a staff of thirteen in 2000 to only three today.

Solo work is more cost-effective, but it has raised some challenges: how do we train new actor-teachers to lead work with students *and* negotiate the partner-building processes needed to make our work with teachers successful? How do we keep the work satisfying, both personally and professionally? What needs to be done to create continued and increased opportunities for the TIE work that originally fostered this current model? Is that possible or is that model a permanent victim of today's economic climate? What does the shift of roles from creative artists (actor-teachers) to teacher-trainers mean to the EL Program, and CAT as a whole? Is this where we, as artists, want to go? At what point do financial imperatives negate the very essence of what we do?

## The Middle School Program: the struggle for artistry in the face of instructional-based work

The NYC Department of Youth and Community Development (DYCD) is tasked with providing New York City youth and their families with a range of high-quality programmes that offer academic, social, emotional, recreational, vocational and civic learning opportunities during the day and after school. CAT has been funded by DYCD since 1978 through a variety of educational outreach contracts, and in 2007 it partnered with the agency to address the needs of adolescent students with low scores in New York State's English Language Arts (ELA) tests – exams that assess reading and writing skills.

There are multiple stakeholders within the Middle School Program's Adolescent Literacy Project:[6] DYCD, CAT, the schools' administrations, the classroom teachers, and the students themselves. Balancing all the competing needs, many of which are instructional, while maintaining CAT's commitment to use theatre as a stimulus for discovery and creative critical thinking, has been an extremely demanding enterprise.

The plan for this three-year project was for teams of two actor-teachers to visit pre-selected classes at specific schools twice a week throughout the entirety of each school year, and to work with classroom teachers to support their pursuit of curricular goals. The primary objective of the contract was to raise the ELA scores of specific students by two to three points, and to track their improvement during the academic year using report cards, actor-teacher observation notes and an assessment tool called Dynamic Indicators of Basic Early Literacy Skills.

CAT believed that drama was an appropriate medium through which to address the challenges these students faced but it also had some serious misgivings about participating in such a test-orientated, outcome-specific project. Several factors contributed to the decision to move forward: the proposal offered the Company some long-term financial stability; the Company believed it could help DYCD negotiate its move into the classroom; and CAT staff were intrigued by the possibilities of multi-year, long-term collaborations with teachers and students.

Over the course of the project the very specific outcomes sought by DYCD, and the manner by which data has to be collected, documented and evaluated, have profoundly impacted CAT's processes, its internal structures and administration, and the skill sets and duties of its actor-teachers.

Unlike other CAT projects, ADL has no set programmatic design or performance that actors can prepare and rehearse before residencies begin. Instead, on a weekly basis, actor-teachers meet with classroom teachers to review the challenges and progress of the class, identify the goals of the teacher, and then devise the next session to support those goals. 'There are times when a teacher has a really great idea and we work with that idea,' says Erika Ewing, the Junior High School Program Director. 'There are also times when we have the great idea and they work with ours' (Ewing 2011). The challenge for the actor-teachers is to maintain an ongoing dialogue with the teacher, to get them to identify what is or is not working. 'We need the teacher to be comfortable enough to discuss with us how best to use our skills in the classroom. … We created a "devising menu" by which the teachers could tick off what literacy skills they wanted to work on,' says Ewing. 'That was useful because we were sharing the same language' (ibid.). The teacher identified a skill, and then the actor-teachers devised and implemented a literacy-based lesson plan to bring it alive for the students.

The bigger challenge lay in implementing a result-based assessment. For example, if the focus is on a particular kind of vocabulary, 'the actor-teachers need to show how they used the words in their drama', explains Ewing. 'The effectiveness of the drama work might be measured by how successfully the students identify or re-use them (the words) in a subsequent quiz' (ibid.). The danger of these kinds of outcomes-driven expectations from a funder is that

CAT runs the risk of merely providing a teaching-aid, lacking in artistic quality or emotional resonance.

### *Redefining the actor-teacher job description*

The extensive administrative requirements of the project have made Ewing revisit her criteria for hiring. 'In the beginning, we were looking for the actor who had a sensitivity and passion for working with adolescent students. Someone who knew that learning could be difficult and understood that, through drama, students could be engaged and participate in their own learning. We're still looking for that – but also for someone with the writing and analytical skills to complete the required monthly student progress notes,' says Ewing. It is also essential that the actor-teachers and the classroom teacher develop and maintain a good working relationship. 'You've got to be an actor with an educator's eye. We look for people who have had classroom experience because they not only understand the craft of teaching, but they also know the pressures teachers are under. You have to work with the classroom teachers in the same co-intentional way you do with the students' (ibid.).

Additionally, the initiative's focus on specific literacy standards targeted by the English Language Arts (ELA) test has influenced how the actor-teachers prepare. 'People talk about "issue-based work." Here, literacy is the issue,' explains Ewing. 'We had to research, ask questions, and attend trainings to learn about current literacy trends and curricular targets.' The training process centred on making the Common Core Learning Standards (New York State Education Department Office of Curriculum and Instruction 2012)[7] meaningful and engaging. 'For example, we looked at the five key elements of text structure: sequence, cause and effect, description, comparisons and contrasts, and conflict. Then I said to my staff, "Talk to me about the theatrical potential of taking all this information and turning it into a dramatic moment"' (ibid.). The challenge is not to become some kind of animated grammar and vocabulary book, but to create drama work that both supports the literacy goals *and* gives the students opportunities to make emotional and personal connections to the process of learning.

The focus of the Standards has changed the actor-teachers' facilitation vocabulary. In past middle-school workshops, after performing a scene the actor-teachers might take the students through a sequence of questions such as: Who were the characters? What was the setting and what was the conflict? What would you do in their place? Now, for example, when asking questions about an historical character, the task is not just to speculate, but to help students see through the eyes of that character in that time period. 'We're asking students, "What do you know about this world? What questions does it raise for you?"' says Ewing (ibid.). In one instance, a class was reading *The Boy in the Striped Pajamas*, by John Boyne. The main character, Bruno, is a naïve young German boy whose father is the commandant of a Second World War concentration camp. When Bruno stumbles upon Shmuel, a young Jewish boy in the camp, he seems unable to accept the reality of the conditions within the camp as compared to how his father portrays them. To explore the many conflicting messages Bruno is getting, the actor-teachers introduced the concept of propaganda in a parallel contemporary drama.

In the session, the actor-teachers took on the roles of Gerald and Sarah, students running for president of the 'All Kids Get Ahead' programme. The students became the two opposing campaign teams. Each group was asked to create smear-ad campaigns against their opponents using words and images that illustrated various school stereotypes: Party Girl, Clown, Nerd and Ditz. The students then watched as both 'Sarah' and 'Gerald' came across the posters and were visibly upset by their content. The students were then taken out of role and asked to write an inner monologue from either Sarah's or Gerald's viewpoint, revealing what they thought and felt upon seeing the posters.

The actor-teachers acknowledged the smear campaign concept was a risk. Might it simply reinforce stereotypes? Would creating the posters be more fun than writing the characters' monologues? But the students were clearly moved by the characters' reactions, and produced some thoughtful writing. One student changed the assignment and wrote a letter of apology to the character Sarah. 'He expressed remorse for his behaviour', recalls the actor-teacher. 'To him, the things he and his group had made up about Sarah had become real. He had truly come to believe the statements he fabricated about her. He said, "Because I didn't know anything about her, I could believe anything I made up. I got caught up and didn't question the bigger impact of what I was doing"' (CAT actor-teacher quoting student at Hostos Academy 2010–11: ADL residency).

At the heart of it all, ADL has reminded Ewing and her team that education is a political process. 'It is a place for activism, activation and motivation', says Ewing. 'Sometimes I feel that education can become a form of bullying. Drama allows us to level the playing field because it's not based on a hierarchy of who has the right answers and who has the wrong answers. It's not "us against them". It's about empowering students to activate their own learning styles so they can impact their own educational experience. We've got to get young people involved, engaged and accountable, not just taking the steady diet of information and accepting it without question. We need to give students the power to stop and ask *us* questions, because this is their education and it should be co-intentional' (Ewing 2011).

For Ewing and her staff, this is where artistry is effective in the larger scope of learning. It helps students understand their world in a different way beyond simply defining an adjective or a verb. The ongoing challenges of the partnerships are not simply instructional but artistic, in trying to create fictional experiences that resonate at a deeper personal level within the students' real lives. This also entails ongoing advocacy, working to persuade the stakeholders that in order to be fully *effective* the work should also be *affective* including, but reaching beyond, the limited goals of standardised, measurable outcomes.

## The High School Program: meeting funder expectations while addressing the changing needs of HIV/AIDS prevention

Public funding through specific contracts has been a mainstay of CAT's survival strategy and success since its very early days. One of the longest, largest and most rewarding partnerships has not been with an arts or education funding source, but with the New York State Department of Health (DOH), implementing an HIV/AIDS prevention programme. Gwendolen Hardwick, once an actor-teacher with the High School Program but now CAT's Artistic and Education Director since 2009, remembers working on the first HIV/AIDS initiative in the late 1980s. The mission was simple: to combat the scourge of AIDS in NYC by communicating accurate information to every high-risk community, including the City's high school students. Hyper-aware of the volatile nature of the issue and how different communities might react to this outreach, the workshop content was prescribed, reviewed and approved by a cautious DOH. 'We were afraid to cough in a classroom without getting prior approval,' recalls Hardwick (2011).

As a result, at the beginning of the partnership, workshops were theatrical, though not particularly student-centred. A team of three actor-teachers would enter a classroom, spouting rumours and fantastical speculation about AIDS and its transmission. Once they had the students' attention, they would present several scenes addressing these myths and misconceptions. 'It was a way to correct the misinformation,' says Hardwick (ibid.). However, as young people began to share their stories, this presence in the classroom brought CAT's actor-teachers face-to-face with the human toll the disease was taking and the need to create forums that allowed open discussion about the virus.

CAT shared the stories it was encountering with its DOH partners. In a display of trust, the DOH began to relax its hold on the content of the workshops. The curriculum began to evolve, reflecting the changing manifestation of the virus, the ways it was affecting different populations *and* the need for dialogue. 'At first it was this distant thing', remembers Hardwick. 'When we asked, "How many people know someone with HIV?" there might be one hand raised. But over the years, there would be more and more hands. Those hands forced us to say, "Okay, let's start to bring the issue home"' (ibid.). Bit by bit, CAT negotiated a balance between art and instrumentality, offering accurate information while also creating space for young people to talk about their own choices – without the Company either moralising or resorting to didacticism.

As the impact of the epidemic became clearer, the DOH began to emphasise testing as a prevention component, in the belief that knowing one's status might encourage more responsible behaviour towards self and others. As a consequence, the DOH began requiring that CAT track the young people from its workshops to see how many were motivated to be screened. Also, by the mid-1990s, the NYC Department of Correction had joined the partnership with CAT and the DOH to bring HIV/AIDs prevention to the incarcerated teen population at Rikers Island, the City's main detention facility. This new partnership soon highlighted a conflict between CAT's pedagogical principle of acknowledging its audience's reality, and the funders' expectation that CAT would follow its agenda.

If collecting the required data was challenging in the City's public schools, it was almost impossible at Rikers Island, where even expressing an interest in being tested put an inmate at risk of physical retribution. CAT tried a variety of strategies to obtain information, but all proved unsuccessful. Finally, it was decided to attempt to renegotiate the DOH objectives, even though such a step might put the entire contract at risk. Fortunately, after discussion, the DOH agreed to drop the testing requirement while allowing the team to continue to implement work with interactive content. 'If this had happened in the first year of our contract, they probably wouldn't have listened,' recalls Keith Johnston, who piloted the Rikers Island work and now directs CAT's College and Adult Program, 'but we had a strong track record. When we finally said "We can't test this population," they believed us' (2011: interview).

In 2010, the DOH contract requirements changed again. The shift was from a TIE model led by professional actor-teachers to a peer education model. This change gave CAT reason to pause. A new five-year contract required that young people take significant leadership roles in every aspect of the project. This was to include defining needs, creating and implementing a plan of action, devising and performing original scenarios, building community education networks and evaluating the outcomes of the work. It was a youth development agenda. Amongst other things, CAT would have to train and mentor a cohort of college-aged students in interactive theatre strategies, build its leadership skills, and develop its outreach capacity to reach other young people in various communities with high infection rates. CAT hesitated. It had seen how in many peer education theatre models elsewhere, the student facilitators frequently lacked the ability to probe beneath the surface of an issue.

'We consider the facilitation of interactive drama to be a real skill – both an art and a science,' explains Hardwick (2011). The CAT actor-teacher is expected to set the tone and atmosphere through the theatrical work as well as have the ability to dialogue with an audience through questions that raise contradictions and offer challenges, not simply deliver information. 'You have to be trained to handle audience responses and then take them deeper into the topic,' continues Hardwick. 'You need a certain level of experience and maturity to do that' (ibid.), especially with a topic many still consider taboo.

Ultimately, several factors contributed, as Hardwick acknowledges, to 'CAT saying "yes" to trying something we said we'd never do' (ibid.). The artistic personnel had years of experience with HIV/AIDS prevention and had a professional and personal investment in seeing the programme continue. They also knew other colleagues could support them. The project could draw upon CAT Youth Theatre Director Helen White's fifteen years of expertise in building youth ensembles and developing devising and performance skills. CAT also had years of experience training actor-teachers; in addition, its professional development work with teachers gave it an understanding of how to introduce non-actors to the use of interactive drama strategies. Finally, says Hardwick, CAT agreed to commit to the project because it was what young people needed. 'All the surveys that we did asked, "Who do you talk to when you have a problem?" Overwhelmingly, the responses said, "My friends." Because the infection rate is so high among teens, it became obvious we had to respond, to keep looking at new ways to educate and influence young people to change their behaviours' (ibid.). If they would listen to their peers, we had to raise those voices.

### *The model shifts: facilitators, mentors and trainers*

Project CHANGE (Community Health Action for Growth and Empowerment) began its pilot under the direction of Carmen Kelly, CAT's Director of Special Projects. Twenty students from two CUNY colleges, York and Medgar Evers, were selected through an audition and interview process. These 'CHANGE Agents' received a small stipend and were expected to attend trainings twice a week throughout the academic year – one on their campus, one at CAT's mid-Manhattan premises. The goal was for the students to create and implement an interactive TIE piece. It was targeted to the needs of young people in two specific communities with high infection rates. The CHANGE Agents' initial training included: basic theatre improvisation and devising skills; an introduction to specific games and interactive drama techniques; *in situ* and internet research of the two communities; guided discussion around adolescent sexual health, and the development of facilitation skills.

With the support of CAT actor-teachers, the peer actor-teachers devised four scenarios focused on key issues and made their first presentations. The learning curve was steep. Each time they presented their TIE pieces, they were amazed by the power of the work to engage an audience emotionally, and challenged by the task of managing that engagement into a deeper understanding. Although the learning was of different kinds, it is debatable as to who learned most: the audience or actors. That question seems to be inherent to all peer educator models.

While there are already signs that the work is having a positive effect on both the targeted communities and the CHANGE Agents themselves, this young project has highlighted many challenges. Veteran actor-teachers were asked to mentor the CHANGE Agents. They willingly brought all their experience to the training process, but this was not the role to which they were accustomed or necessarily suited. The shift from actor-teacher to supervising mentor caused them unexpected professional frustration: ultimately they wanted to do the work *themselves*, not train non-professionals to do it in their stead. Both actor-teachers have since resigned.

Another challenge has been the sustainability of the CHANGE Agent cohort. The initial concept envisioned an ensemble composed

*Figure 13.2* CHANGE Agents, from the CAT *Project CHANGE*, perform for young adults at the 'More Than Just Sex' Youth Conference (2012). The scene highlights tensions within a family when someone tries to discuss sexual health issues. Photo: Krista Fogle.

primarily of second- and third-year college students willing to make a multi-year commitment to the project. Class schedules, family commitments and financial needs have made that goal unrealistic.

Addressing the evolving expectations of the DOH has also proved taxing. The insistence that the CHANGE Agents implement a pre-determined, DOH approved, evidenced-based curriculum[8] has created considerable tension. Curricula of this nature are not theatre-based and therefore, by implication, relegate the Company's primary expertise to a secondary role. Although many aspects of CAT's CHANGE Agent training have been successful – both as measured by the personal development of the CHANGE Agents themselves and from community feedback – CAT now has to prioritise the contractual demands and overarching goals of the DOH. Its primary goal is to develop and build a network of young people as effective health advocates: whether or not theatre is used as a medium is of secondary interest. Even after many years of successful collaboration, CAT's partnership with the DOH is still a work in progress, ultimately subject to the Department's priorities. A refocused and reorganised project team is entering a new year of the contract with some unresolved questions.

## Conclusion

When CAT was founded in 1974, the field of TIE was only nine years old. In a typical CAT programme, actor-teachers conducted a five-day TIE classroom residency. Upon completion, participants or teachers filled in an evaluation form. Results were generally positive. But, as CAT developed and began to absorb the internal shifts in its pedagogical and artistic approach inspired by Boal and Freire, outside funding agencies also began their own shift, requiring more precisely defined and rigorously assessed goals and outcomes. 'In the '70s and into the '80s, all of CAT's programs were funded to address student deficits,' reflects Executive Director Zimmerman (2011). 'This wasn't just CAT; our society used negative labels. In the early '90s, research started happening both in education and social service spheres looking at positive attributes of young people. Agencies began to focus on the assets of a group or community. "Start from where they are and what they can do, build those dreams and it will lower the deficit."' The concomitant implication was that the results could and should be measured.

CAT believed it could contribute more to this enterprise. With the support of its partners, the work expanded and changed. This has had both positive and negative effects. It has shifted the balance of the work from the broad, humanistic goals of changing perspectives and deepening understanding, through the aesthetic experience, to a more instrumentalist approach to building specific capacities, improving skills and changing targeted behaviours. Along with this has come the demand that CAT implement ever more challenging assessment structures, based upon individual student progress towards specific curriculum goals or health education goals. In so doing, it has shifted the original desired balance between 'actor' and 'teacher' functions in the 'actor-teacher' role, firmly towards the side of the 'teacher', or 'mentor', with the consequence that it has become harder to find actor-teachers with the right skills, experience – or desire – to move in this direction. In turn, this has led CAT to alter its employment profiles and the nature of its training, emphasising the importance of teacher conferences and professional development, literacy skills, curriculum planning, evaluation methods, youth and community development strategies, youth–adult partnerships, evidence-based curricula, and more, rather than focusing on the core actor-teachers' skills of devising, interactive drama strategies and performance styles, and facilitation.

Arguably this is what good partnerships do. They push you, individually and collectively, to grow. It may not always be a comfortable experience, and there certainly will be instances when a partnership will be a bad match, but the long-term benefits can sometimes trump the short-term risks and painful learning curve. Certainly CAT has persevered, and many company members have risen to the challenge. For example, Ewing has become something of a literacy expert. 'It's been fascinating work,' reflects Hardwick. 'It certainly has kept us on the cutting edge of how creatively to keep our audiences engaged and ourselves updated on the information and research being produced' (2011: interview).

CAT remains committed to exploring ways to use interactive theatre to prepare students and adults to engage with each other and the world around them in a proactive, responsible and progressive manner. To do so demands an honest, ongoing process of self-examination and internal evaluation of the work in relation to its core values; but of course that is only part of the story. Those who fund the work are increasingly focused on narrow outcomes, susceptible, in their view, to finite measurement. They want proof that their money is being well spent, and their priorities and criteria are frequently at odds with those of the Company. This raises another spectre. The more pressure that is applied from the outside to meet these apparently divergent needs, the more likely it is that the differences within the Company will become magnified. Financial priorities can, understandably, change the nature of the work by default. This, in turn, can cause artistic and educational dissonance, rapidly undermining the previously consensual nature of the mission. These dilemmas are not new or peculiar to CAT. However, the current financial climate, and the related priorities in social policy, including those affecting education, have conspired to sharpen them.

As CAT moves toward its fifth decade, it must be prepared to answer some new, yet familiar, questions. How can it meet its student-centred, progressive educational goals in an increasingly antithetical educational environment? Can it respond to current educational priorities without compromising either its pedagogical or aesthetic values? How can it meet its financial obligations – including job preservation – and stay true to its mission? What will it take to find new financial partnerships, or maintain the old ones – so long the lifeblood of the Company? What does CAT want to become, what should it become, and what can it become? As a Company that has proudly described its role as being a 'catalyst for change', it is now challenged to engineer its own transformation. The next chapter in its history will determine what kind of force CAT becomes and may, as so often before, prefigure the further development of TIE-related, applied theatre practices in the USA.

## Notes

1 Sections of the introductory paragraphs originally appeared in the 1993 edition: Chapter 11 ('The Creative Arts Team').
2 When CAT began in 1974, it was housed at New York University. In 2004, it became part of CUNY.
3 The Early Learning Program is a regional site of the Wolf Trap Institute, the educational branch of the Wolf Trap Foundation for the Performing Arts in Vienna, VA, USA. As such, its official title is the Early Learning Through the Arts Program: NYC Wolf Trap and is also often referred to as ELTA.
4 Head Starts are federally funded, state-managed sites that promote school readiness by enhancing the social and cognitive development of children 2.9–4 years; 2.9 is the earliest age a child can attend Head Start classes.
5 See for example, Ginsberg and Opper (1988).
6 The Program's work falls under two DYCD contracts: Adolescent Literacy (ADL) and Neighborhood Development Area (NDA).
7 The Common Core State Standards were adopted by New York State in 2010 for grades K–12. The standards emerged as part of the Common Core State Standards Initiative, a state-led effort coordinated by the National Governors Association Center for Best Practices and the Council of Chief State School Officers. They are designed to reflect the knowledge and skills that young people need for success in college and careers.
8 Evidence-based curricula are curricula, developed for social interventions, that have been endorsed as effective, and widely accepted, often by government agencies, as a result of scientifically rigorous studies.

## Works cited

Actor-teacher and kindergarten student participating in a CAT ELTA residency at Public School 211, the Bronx, NYC, winter 2009. (CAT archives).

Actor-teacher quoting a student participating in a CAT Adolescent Literacy residency at the Hostos-Lincoln Academy, the Bronx, NYC, academic year 2010–11. (CAT archives).

Donaldson, M. (1978), *Children's Minds*. New York: W. W. Norton & Company.

Ewing, E. (2011), Interview with the author. New York, 30 September.

Ginsberg, H. and Opper, S. (1988), *Piaget's Theory of Intellectual Development*, 3rd edn. New Jersey: Prentice Hall.

Hardwick, G. (2011), Interview with the author. New York, 30 September.

Johnston, K. (2011), Interview with the author. New York, 30 September.

Kindergarten student participating in a CAT ELTA residency at St. Rita's Catholic School, Brooklyn, NYC, academic year 1998–99.

New York State Education Department Office of Curriculum and Instruction, *NYS P-12 Common Core Learning Standards*. Available online at www.p12.nysed.gov/ciai/common_core_standards/ (accessed 20 August 2012).

Teacher 1 interviewed by author after participating in a CAT ELTA mentoring residency, multi-site professional development session, spring 2010.
Teacher 2 speaking during in a CAT ELTA mentoring residency, multi-site professional development session, spring 2010.
Zimmerman, L. (2011), Interview with the author. New York, 27 September.

# 14

# SELECTIVE SNAPSHOTS OF TIE PRACTICE ACROSS THE GLOBE

To complement the more detailed accounts in the earlier chapters, the following section consists of brief personal overviews by professional directors, practitioners and teachers of TIE in their own countries, identifying the specific aims and characteristics of their work, and outlining the challenges they face. Allowing for individual approaches and emphases, we have organised their inputs under three broad headings:

- Context: the ways in which TIE (or TIE-related practice) in that country has developed and adapted to a changing world over the past 5–10 years;
- Practice: a discussion of one or more recent productions that exemplify particularly well that company's current achievements, together with a note on methods and models used or developed, and how those have changed in recent years;
- Vision: aspirations and challenges faced in the forthcoming years.

In alphabetical order, the countries represented here are: India (in and beyond Delhi, complementing the practice discussed in chapter 11), Ireland (companies in Cork and Dublin), Jordan, and Norway and the Nordic countries.

## India: TIE in and beyond Delhi – a personal journey

***Subhash Rawat***

Subhash Rawat is founder and director of Purvabhyas Theatre Group in New Delhi, and is on the committee formed by India's National Council of Educational Research and Training (NCERT) to develop training material on theatre for teachers of upper primary classes (years VI, VII and VIII).

### *Context*

TIE in India – since the early 1990s when the National School of Drama in New Delhi (NSD) established its TIE Company[1] – has come to mean two very different kinds of practices: presenting plays for specific age groups of children; and conducting non-performance theatre or drama workshops for children and young people focused mainly on aspects of their personal development. For me, TIE in India means the use of drama and theatre for children to create a space where they can share their experience, think critically and express themselves.

In 1987, I was one of the founder members of the theatre group 'Kalaa Darpan' in Uttarkashi, a small town on the banks of the holy river Ganga, in the foothills of the Himalayas. After staging several plays we realised the need to connect with the children of our town. In 1990, Kalaa Darpan supported my initiative of running a theatre workshop with local children. We were immensely surprised by the response of the children in the workshop and extended it from fifteen days to thirty. A vibrant closing ceremony included a play in Hindi, *Girgit* (based on the story 'Chameleon' by Anton Chekhov), with more than thirty children acting in it. I was inspired to continue the same venture in subsequent years. Some ten years later, I joined the NSD's TIE Company in New Delhi, and, for six years, enjoyed the opportunity to plan and execute theatre workshops with children and teachers in many states across India. I acted in many plays too, although they were more like children's theatre than TIE. During this period I made a point of returning to my home town Uttarkashi every year to run a theatre workshop for children and, when I could, to run workshops in all thirteen districts of Uttarakhand. Almost everywhere people wanted such workshops at least once a year, but neither I nor anybody else could ever fulfil this demand.

### *Practice*

I went on to set up a new theatre organisation, Purvabhyas, in Dehradun (the capital of Uttarakhand), but there was little scope there for a professional TIE company and in the summer of 2007 Purvabhyas organised its first theatre workshop for children in New Delhi. As we were unknown and had to charge, it was an uphill struggle to establish ourselves. But persistence pays. The principal of the Mira Model Public School extended enthusiastic support for our programmes and today her school has become the centre of our activities in New Delhi. The majority of our plays are for children of 12 years and above. We also run drama workshops for children at this venue, the main objectives of which are to promote creativity, creative thinking, confidence building and teamwork.

Is Purvabhyas Theatre of New Delhi a TIE group? Yes and no. It is not TIE in the conventional sense. Any theatre group can call itself a TIE Company if it devises plays with and for children and runs theatre workshops for them as well. In practice, the TIE work that is done in India tends to be carried out by individuals rather than by theatre groups – and undertaken mostly for other non-theatre organisations. For example, one of our engagements was a theatre project for the 'Gandhi Smriti and Darshan Samiti' organisation[2] in New Delhi, the aim of which was to devise a play on the childhood of Mahatma Gandhi with a group of underprivileged children. I researched the subject and worked with children for five months. The plan was to engage the children in an exploration of the life of Gandhi, and to encourage them to reflect on their own lives in comparison with the life of Gandhi as a child. Almost all of them were doing theatre for the first time so we used plenty of theatre games and improvisations before working on the final script. *Moniya, the Child that Mahatma Gandhi was*, the first ever play on Gandhi's childhood, was a great success. The audiences, young and old, whose image of Gandhi was mostly of an old man, found the story of his childhood very relevant and thought-provoking. However, only two performances could be given – it could not be taken to public auditoria or any other school. That is the flip side of working with other organisations – they generally see a play as a one-off special event.

### *Vision*

Purvabhyas, which literally means 'rehearsal', suggests our emphasis on the 'process' and 'preparation' in our work with children (see www.purvabhyas.org). We are practitioners of both TYA and TIE. That is the best possible combination for a theatre group that wants to work with and for children in India. We value our plays for children for the way they can generate a collective experience of joy and understanding of life. We try to do justice to every word, every action and every minute that we share with children. Children are not numbers for us. They have unique identities and they deserve to get maximum space to grow with the opportunity of more and more freedom of self-expression. Isn't it their right?

In theatre workshops outside the schools with children of different backgrounds in many states of India, from Uttarakhand to the Andman and Nicobar Islands, I have felt the joy, the awareness and the confidence added to their lives. For example, in 2003, Anmol, a teenage boy who had been coerced by his parents to join the workshop, wrote, 'After joining … I got some changes in my life. … now I have started studying independently. After coming here I can write better … have increased my creativity' (from my collection of reflections written by the children after the workshops). Unfortunately, the more I see them enjoy their creativity in these workshops the more it underlines how much is lacking in their schools. Most children in India do not get any chance to watch professional theatre performance during their school career. Schools may however be more willing to welcome TIE teams if we focus our work in certain areas of the curriculum.

In order to progress, we need to have a common forum or network of TIE-related practitioners; to document every kind of TIE work, however small it is, and to disseminate it; to have a resource centre; and to convince theatre institutes like NSD to do more to develop study courses in TIE. There are some efforts to include TIE within theatre courses but they focus more on how to create theatre with children: mask-making and puppetry for example. Fortunately, there are organisations across India that are seriously engaged in TIE-related work. Notably, Nandikar, India's premier theatre group in Kolkata, has been developing TIE projects for over twenty years (www.nandikar.net); Yellow Cat Company and Khilona Theatre in Delhi and Imago Theatre-in-Education Company (part of Imago Media Co.) in Mumbai, are engaged in TIE or TIE-related work, though they are little known outside their cities (see Yellow Cat and Imago websites). The NCERT (see NCERT website) has also taken an initiative to bring the arts from an 'extra-curricular' and 'co-curricular' position into the forefront in the formal curriculum, to ensure that theatre and other arts become as integral a part of the elementary school system as any other subject. So theatre is expected to come closer to children in the schools of India in the near future.[3]

The sooner that we can find ways of enabling the individual-driven TIE practices to become group-driven, and the more we can encourage the existing groups to become more professional in their delivery, the faster we will see a brighter picture. The demand may at present be limited, but the supply is even more so. It is heartening to see government and the education system (through the NCERT) beginning to play a greater role.

## Ireland: Graffiti, Cork

### *Emelie Fitzgibbon*

Emelie Fitzgibbon is Artistic Director of Graffiti Theatre Company, Cork, which she founded in 1984.

### *Context*

Since the turn of the new century, Graffiti Theatre Company has extended and developed its practice to create a complex and diverse model of practice, which approaches learning through drama and theatre in a holistic way, in which performative and participatory practice engages children and young people through a variety of models, in formal and informal contexts, allowing learning to occur in both structured and, seemingly, unstructured ways.[4] Our values, philosophy and method hark back to 'classic' TIE, but we now approach our practice through a model which uses the elements but rarely the form. The deconstructed elements of excellent TIE seem to me to be: the stimulus and questioning potential of strong dynamic performance; the interactive workshop and moments when the participants are vitally engaged in addressing the stimulus and investigating the questions arising from their own immediate response and reality; the teacher's involvement in further addressing and unpicking the stimulus; and the social, personal and curriculum links of specific relevance to the students at that time. Our practice has led us to explore the many different forms of engagement through drama and theatre that this deconstruction suggests. We develop these elements with a wide age range of audiences and participants, critiquing our work in relation to the aesthetics of our practice, our model of reflective practice and analysis, and international trends, developments and initiatives in the field.

### *Practice*

At the core of our practice is the theatre event and the artistic quality we try to attain. We seek to place at the heart of each programme of work a piece that is aesthetically rich, redolent with complexities in its themes, structures and presentation. The performance should always have the capacity to stand alone outside the education system but, within it, will enrich and stimulate students and teachers alike. We aim for a rich and dense educational experience, rooted in the sensory experiences of the theatre event.

The Company has commissioned work from both first-time and well-established writers in Ireland and abroad including Ray Scannell, Enda Walsh, Angela Betzien (Australia), Laurie Brooks (USA) and Mike Kenny (UK). The length of time we allow for play and programme development (typically two and a half to three years), underlines the value we place on writers.

Our workshops use practices related to DIE (for example, sustained and complex working with teacher and students in role on the topic of the Kindertransport[5]) and youth theatre. Several workshop programmes in disadvantaged area schools combine the active techniques associated with youth theatre with an underlying agenda of personal development and educational aspiration. One particular research project with students in 'last-chance' education now utilises a writer and a facilitator engaging the participants as both writers and actors. The experience we have in developing our own youth theatres, and our long engagement with the development of youth theatre practice in Ireland, gives us knowledge of the different models of engagement and keeps us aware of up-to-date practice and the changing interests, rhythms and lives of young people. This, in turn, informs our performances, workshops and resource materials. Our Early Years Arts Team now blends performance and participatory activities across three theatre-related arts forms. The variety of experience, the knowledge of forms and the confidence to move into new areas of practice greatly assists the development of a comprehensive range of work.

Until recently, a grant from the Department of Education and Science has enabled us to develop intensive programmes in schools, engaging teachers and pupils in in-depth explorations, frequently in-role, in order to enhance the educational development of a performance. One such programme was a sequence of nine different creative and educational encounters with each class participating in an installation-style production of Laurie Brooks's *The Lost Ones* (2006). The action of the play took place in a specially created 'den', made of detritus that feral children could have found on a battlefield. Audience and players were enclosed in this 'dangerous' place, surrounded by the sound of a steadily advancing conflict and anticipating the arrival of the enemy: grown-ups. The follow-up workshop involved the students creating their own version of the den in their classroom and, in-role, having to convince sceptical grown-ups that children were entitled to their rights.

### *Vision*

The Company learns through its own integrated experiences and its analysis of the effectiveness of its practice. This practice is rooted in reception theory; we are consistently reflective practitioners documenting, questioning and developing the validity of every element of the work we do.

The economic and social climate in Ireland over the last ten years has been extremely volatile. During the 'Celtic Tiger' phase, we experienced net immigration and new populations enriched our schools. Because we work bilingually we are very aware of linguistic difficulties experienced by some young people in receiving performance and participating in workshops and are able to adjust our assumptions and practice to accommodate this. Recently, cuts to the education budget have impacted heavily on our sector, with all funding withdrawn from theatre providers to disadvantaged area schools.

Sustained programmes such as *The Lost Ones* are no longer financially possible at present but we keep our skills honed by retaining workshops such as the *Kindertransport* in our workshop repertoire. On the positive side, there is now in Ireland a Minister for Children and the cultural rights and entitlements of young people are acknowledged and enshrined in various arts plans. Nearly one third of the Irish population is under 18 and the TYA sector is determined to keep what we have all achieved alive, active, positive and looking to international developments in order to be able to serve that cohort into the future.

## Ireland: TEAM, Dublin

### *John Breen*

TEAM was founded in 1975 following the closure of Young Abbey, the Abbey Theatre's company specialising in work for young people. John Breen took over as Artistic Director in 2009 and has continued the move in recent years to reimagine the model for educational theatre.

### *Context*

Our audiences are school children but our clients are principals and deputy principals in primary and secondary schools. By and large the clients have been very happy with the traditional TEAM model of play, workshop and resource materials. This fitted well with their schedules and we were not under any pressure from them to change the model, although there were some exceptions to the model, particularly working at primary level (see Gurden 1999). However, the company found that the rigid structures applied by secondary school schedules was constraining what it could offer. My predecessor, Thomas de Mallet Burgess, and I moreover felt that the model was failing to ignite audiences in the way it once had and that we as a company needed to reimagine the kind of work we offered.

De Mallett Burgess made a short film about cyber bullying and produced a play by Leo Butler, *Devotion*, which was more abstract than a traditional TEAM play and the content of which was very challenging to our audience. We subsequently toured this play to townships in South Africa in 2009 where it received a great response.

### *Practice*

One of my priorities in 2009 was to improve the theatrical experience for our audience. I had seen TEAM shows and, although the acting and writing were always first rate, they were staged on sets that sat in the school hall or large classroom. I felt that this sold the company and the audience short. I purchased a large dome which fits inside most school gymnasia and allows us complete control of the environment in which the work is presented. This means that we can bring a great deal more technology to bear on our work with lighting, sound and video projection now standard in our productions.

Another change in the way the company works has been to acknowledge other forms of theatre and performance and to incorporate ideas of 'postdramatic theatre' (Lehmann 2006) into our canon of work. We will be generating learning and discovery in new ways using forms other than narrative-based theatre to achieve our objectives. This is an internally driven decision. Our schools would be happy if we just produced 'well made plays' but as a company TEAM is keen to expand the boundaries of what TIE could be. The response from our audiences has been very positive. Our follow-up workshops are the next area which we need to look at to see if there are ways in which we can change the form and encourage a deeper engagement with the work.

Our next production, *Knots into numbers*, represents a new watermark in TEAM's long history. It will I think shift our audiences' perception of what educational theatre can and should be. I expect it to generate much heat and light in terms both of critical discourse around the forms we have chosen and of its suitability for our audience. Scheduled for production in October 2012, it will be a collaboration between two choreographers, a composer, a digital artist, a sound designer, and two writer/directors to create a show around some of the ideas at the fringes of mathematical thinking. The objective will be to plant an impulse of wonder and excitement in the heart of 14-year-old students about mathematics. As one of the writer/directors, I have deliberately sought out someone with a conflicting set of beliefs about what theatre is and can be to collaborate with, in the hope that this conflict will create an interesting piece of work. Other recent productions, *Devotion* by Leo Butler, *Skin and Blisters* by Audrey O'Reilly and *Doughnuts* by Eoin Byrne, were extraordinarily well received by our audiences, stimulating wide, varied and heated responses in follow-up workshops with the actors; they were models of how theatre can facilitate discussion and learning about challenging subjects.

### *Vision*

The way our work has developed is a reflection of how the country itself has changed. Ireland has arguably changed more in the last ten years than in the previous fifty. This is reflected in the outlook of our subject matter and in the expectations of our audience. We no longer inhabit a monocultural island: inward immigration during our boom has made us a multicultural society. All our institutions have failed us: the church, the government and the banks have been found to have bad moral hygiene. Our nation is in the process of rebuilding and reimagining itself. TEAM's work must reflect this and will.

I would argue that TEAM is art led rather than education led. We seek out material that excites or provokes us and we try to find a way of making that impulse relevant to our audience in an educational context. Any well-written piece of theatre is educational in some way and therefore TEAM will start with a broad theme and calibrate the educational aspects in follow-up workshops or in the support material we provide to teachers after the students have seen the show. In fairness to our client schools, there has never been a heavy expectation or demand for us to link directly into the curriculum. Our motto of 'TEAM goes where teachers can't' means that we deal with issues that teachers shy away from, we reach beyond students' cognitive barriers and engage them where only art can. For example, I am currently discussing with a number of writers the creation of a work that examines the effect pornography is having on teen sexuality and body image.

TEAM faces similar challenges to the rest of the arts community and Ireland at large. Given our recent experience of austerity and the constant shrinking of discretionary funding provided to schools we had to trim our cost base, investing more in our production values and diversifying our sources of revenue. I want the company to do work which confounds expectations about form and (in the words of Shelley Winters) hits our audiences 'where they live' (*Routledge Dictionary of Quotations*: 264). I would like to continue to raise our production standards, to enhance the reputation of educational theatre in the arts sector and to increase the company's international profile. I would also like to be able to have more than one production on the road at a time, as at present we have more demand for our productions than we can service.

## Jordan

### *Lina Attel*

Lina Attel is director of Jordan's National Center for Culture and Arts. She encountered and was impressed by TIE while undertaking postgraduate studies in theatre and in education in Wales in the 1980s and returned to Jordan determined to introduce it to Jordan's schools.

### *Context: the beginnings of TIE in Jordan*

In 1987, I was hired to start a TIE programme at the Noor Al Hussein Foundation, whose work was mainly in socio-economic development at the grassroots level to create a better quality of life for Jordanians. My first production was in 1989 in collaboration with Dr Waleed Saif, a well-known playwright in the Middle East. The play, *Time Impressions*, produced in collaboration with the Ministry of Education, was performed in high schools for students aged 16 and 17 across the Kingdom over a period of twelve months. The form of audience participation included 'depictions' (still images moving into dialogue): the students were divided into groups, each of whom worked with an historic (thirteenth-century) character from the play discussing the key conflict situation during that period, after which each group created a depiction representing their own views of similar situations in the present.

In 1990, the Noor Al Hussein Foundation established the first National Theatre in Education Troupe in Jordan with five actors. In cooperation with the Ministry of Education, it went on to produce TIE programmes for public primary and secondary schools in the Kingdom, all of which used theatre and participatory drama methodology to teach areas of the curriculum, social issues, and life themes and ideas. It also conducted several DIE training courses for school teachers throughout the kingdom which later culminated in the production of a guidebook for elementary school teachers on how to use drama as a teaching method.

Formative in our work was the unique relationship between the National Center for Culture and Arts (NCCA) and the International Centre for Theatre in Education (ICTIE), formed in 1992 and supported by the British Council in Amman.[6] It was an inspiring example of sustainable cross-cultural cooperation and we were grateful to Geoff Gillham, founder of ICTIE, for his valuable contributions that assisted our TIE programme to flourish in Jordan. ICTIE held its second international conference in Jordan in 2000, entitled 'People in Movement', under the patronage of Her Majesty Queen Noor Al Hussein. The conference hosted TIE practitioners from 23 countries and included keynotes, performances and practical workshop sessions on TIE methodology led by members of the Standing Conference of Young People's Theatre (SCYPT). We devised a special TIE play for the conference entitled *Humanity.go* which we subsequently performed at several theatre festivals locally and internationally. *Humanity.go* was a black comedy that portrayed the decline of human values within a fast-changing world. It took you on a thought-provoking journey through the minds of the metaphoric characters of 'cats' and human beings, each having conflicting views and ambitions, all aspiring to live in dignity. But then what happens when they are confronted with an abandoned baby?

### *Practice: developments and changes in our method, 2001–2011*

Because of the positive impact of our TIE plays and the high visibility they enjoyed in the media, we were commissioned by civil society organisations working on socio-economic development programmes in Jordan to take part in their national awareness campaigns by producing interactive plays for adults on issues such as reproductive health, honour crimes, domestic violence, unemployment and the culture of shame, democracy and human rights, and women's empowerment.

We produced several plays using a variety of audience participation methods led by a facilitator, including depictions, simulation, role playing and adaptations of Augusto Boal's forum theatre. They were performed for a wide spectrum of Jordanians from various socio-economic backgrounds including villages and remote areas. The impact was magical: people were intrigued by the method and felt empowered and free to express their opinion about the content of the drama.

As we were performing for adults, we discovered that the word 'education' led to a misconception about the nature of our plays. Many thought they must be boring and didactic. To avoid such misconceptions, we renamed ourselves the National Interactive Theater Troupe. This proved more attractive: we now offered a new artistic dynamic to audience members, who became active participants in the play rather than remaining passive observers.

Our work was considered to be a valuable artistic tool for social change and the promotion of a better quality of life and thus we became an integral part of national initiatives in Jordan. We have furthermore received sponsorship from international organisations, such as the European Commission in Jordan, USAID, United Nations Population Fund, UNICEF, the American, Norwegian, Dutch and Australian Embassies, and the British Council, to produce interactive plays on specific social issues. The NCCA has, with this assistance, gained international recognition and successfully implemented projects that use the performing arts as a creative and effective tool for change. Important interactive plays, produced by NCCA, and regularly performed in Jordan, regionally and internationally, include the following:

*Memoirs of a Woman* (2004 and still touring in 2012) tackles the issue of gender inequality and the physical and emotional violence inflicted upon women; through its engagement of the audience in the drama, it highlights the importance of developing communication skills to tackle and solve problems instead of resorting to mental and physical abuse.

*Paintings on the Wall* (2009, produced in cooperation with The International Organization for Migration and with the support of the Australian Government) was part of a project that addressed the psycho-social needs of migrants. The play promotes cooperation, respect for cultural diversity and creative peaceful conflict resolution skills. It has toured schools and cultural centres across the kingdom.

A *Community Theatre Project* was implemented in cooperation with the Jordanian National Forum for Women with the support of Care International. A diverse group of men and women from an underprivileged area in Amman, including housewives, teachers, university students and unemployed graduates, attended a three-month training course conducted by our troupe on how to form an interactive theatre group and produce a play that addresses gender-based violence. At the end of the project (2012), the participants, despite their lack of experience in theatre, were able to create and perform a play, called *Cries*, so full of passion and conviction that its impact on the audience was overwhelming. Participants told us this experience made them consciously aware of the adversities and negative impact of violence on the well-being of their families and society; it helped many of them transform from being passive, afraid and lacking self-confidence into powerful advocates for human rights in their community. Under our supervision, this group will also perform *Cries* in other cities in Jordan.

### *Vision – and impact in the region*

We have participated in theatre festivals in our region, which has created an interest among several institutions and theatre groups in adopting the interactive theatre methodology. The NCCA has run a number of training workshops on the use of drama as a creative effective teaching method in the classroom and on the methodology and practice of Theatre in Education in Saudi Arabia (2005, 2006), Syria and Lebanon (2004), Palestine (2000) as well as in Jordan. More recently, a Memorandum of Understanding was signed in 2011 between NCCA and the Sharjah Theatres Group (UAE) to establish an interactive theatre troupe in Sharjah, conduct DIE workshops for teachers, and present interactive plays from the NCCA repertoire in Sharjah schools.

We are currently witnessing an increasing willingness of non-governmental organisations and international donors to fund projects that utilise theatre as an effective tool to promote issues that deal with social justice, cross-cultural understanding and peaceful conflict resolution. Hence, we aspire to form more interactive theatre companies in Jordan to perform in educational and community centres in addition to assisting our interested counterparts in the wider region to develop their theatre movement through networking, cooperation and co-productions.

## Norway and the Nordic countries

### *Kari Mjaaland Heggstad*

Kari Heggstad is Associate Professor in Drama at Bergen University College (BUC) in Norway. Here she offers an overview of developments and initiatives in, and international influences on, TIE practice in the Nordic countries (Denmark, Finland, Norway, Sweden and Iceland), seen from a West Norwegian perspective.

### *Context: Norway*

The first Norwegian TIE programme (*The Judge's Day*) was produced in Bergen in 1986 (Heggstad 2010: 55). Shortly afterwards, Oslo

University College started the first undergraduate course in TIE in Norway in 1988, and continues to offer a module in TIE every year. As a result of this programme, the first full-time professional TIE company in Norway called TIU-teatret was established in 1989, following which the company toured schools for the next ten years. In 1992 Bergen University College developed its own TIE module, as part of which some twenty-five TIE programmes have been produced for local schools. The module at BUC is now open to exchange students and conducted in English. For five years Volda University College also offered a TIE module. Both in Oslo and Bergen the student teams tour to school classrooms prior to their examinations. The more enthusiastic groups polish and refine their exam-production and continue touring after the college term has ended. Some go on to create companies that survive for years (eg. Eventus TIE in Bergen). However, at the time of writing there are no *full time* TIE companies in Norway. Companies come together for specific one-off projects and apply for funding from a variety of government-funded cultural programmes.

### *Context: other Nordic countries*

In 1997 the Nordic drama conference Drama Boreale, held in Jyväskylä, **Finland**, put TIE on the agenda and staged one performance and one lecture. Aabo Academy in Vasa and the University of Applied Sciences, Novia, give courses in TIE, and the universities in Jyväskylä and Helsinki are important institutions for the development of the genre through specific projects. Groups like Taivaltajat, TOP-TIE and DOT TIE have resulted from this work. The last one is a Swedish-speaking company based in Helsinki which tours all parts of Finland with their TIE programmes. Essays, articles and theses on TIE have been published in both languages. In 2009, at the Drama Boreale conference in Vasa, TIE was prioritised through a keynote speech, TIE presentations, workshops, and a special-interest group (Heggstad 2010). At the same conference representatives from **Iceland** showed an interest in both TIE productions and research. TIE is not widely practised in Iceland, although forum theatre productions tour to schools.

In **Sweden** children's theatre has been very strong – as has forum theatre as an interactive form. Now there is a growing interest in TIE in the Umeå district, both through an introductory course at Umeå University, optional student projects and theses – but even more through productions by the Umeå Art Centre for Young People. The national cultural programme *Creative School* promotes professional theatre performance in schools. Even if they do not label themselves as TIE, quite a few companies make use of the same principles in the ways that they create theatre that is engaging, provocative and important, and include participatory sessions within the performance or follow-up workshops, along with preparatory and follow-up materials. Examples of such companies are: Tage Granit, Teater De Vill and UngHästen (The Young Horse).

**Denmark** was the first Nordic country to present a TIE programme as early as in 1976 (Illsaas and Kjølner 1993: 195). There are interesting examples of productions and debates about the genre in the 1980s and 1990s, during which time some universities and university colleges initiated and supported TIE work. But in the last decade forum theatre has become a more frequent form, both as part of study courses at universities and as a participatory form used by companies visiting schools. Some theatre companies define their visiting theatre as TIE, but offer plain performances with no participation. A recent example of TIE is a programme (made by The Old City Museum in Aarhus) called *Crime, justice and punishment*. Its success will now result in a new TIE production. Danish children's theatre has achieved international recognition, both for its artistic quality and because it takes children seriously. Indeed recent statistics reveal that one third of all theatre audiences in Denmark are children (online newspaper *Søndag Aften*, Jan. 2011).

### *Practice*

The inspiration for BUC has been British TIE practice through companies like the Belgrade, The Dukes, Lancaster and Big Brum; and guest teachers such as Chris Cooper, David Davis, Geoff Gillham, Tony Goode, Ian Yeoman and Jane Rash (from Denmark). In recent years Edward Bond's articles and TIE plays have provided new inspiration (Bond 2000; Davis 2005). Bond's concepts such as *centre* and *site* have become especially important in the devising and rehearsal stages of productions (see also chapter 7). The poetics of facilitation is also a major focus in our work.

One example from 2011 is *Milk and Murder*, devised by six drama students at BUC for 14–15-year-old students. The focus of the programme was 'What is evil?' It shows the unfolding of a violent domestic tragedy, resulting in a murder, between three people: two sisters and the boyfriend of one of them. Guided by a facilitator, the participants explore the relationships, examining their feelings, attitudes and actions through interviews and improvisations. A final discussion allows them to reflect on how this tragedy could happen, on communication, and on more philosophical questions like 'what is evil?' and 'what does it mean to be human?'

### *Vision*

There is a rich source of themes, pre-texts, forms, levels of interaction, structures, dramatic frames and facilitating methods to be found in programmes created both by drama students and by professional companies. In 2000 BUC arranged a Nordic conference, 'TIE in Focus', which presented TIE programmes by eight companies,[7] was attended by about 110 participants and provided great optimism at the time. Our plans for the future are for more cooperation between the five Nordic countries in three areas: creating a space for exchange between companies; initiating and developing TIE modules at Nordic universities; and developing common research projects – especially to map the terrain thoroughly and to develop a better understanding of the TIE genre, and its impact, in the Nordic topology. A common effort has begun.

## Notes

1 For a more detailed account of the work of the Theatre in Education Company of the National School of Drama, New Delhi, see chapter 11.

2 A body of the government of India. The basic aim and objective of the Samiti is to propagate the life, mission and thought of Mahatma Gandhi through various socio-educational and cultural programmes. The Prime Minister of India is its Chairperson and it has a nominated body of senior Gandhians and representatives of various government departments to guide it in its activities.

3 NCERT, in its National Curriculum Framework (NCF) 2005, strongly recommended that the arts form an important part of the school curriculum, up to Class X (14–15-year-olds). This provides for the Arts the status of one of the Curricular Areas. NCF 2005 also recommends the integration of the arts with other subjects in the interests of better learning. NCERT is in the process of preparing and publishing a training module on theatre for the teachers of upper primary classes.

4 See www.graffiti.ie which contains examples of Teacher Resource material and trailers of current shows; also has summary and full report of our Early Years Research Project (the team is called BEAG – the Irish word for 'small'). See also www.nayd.ie: The National Association for Youth Drama offers an excellent model of practice; www.tya-ireland.org provides links to other companies working in Ireland; and the TYA Newsletter at www.tya-ireland.org/2012.

5 The rescue programme for refugee Jewish children at the start of the Second World War.

6 ICTIE was an international initiative of the Standing Conference of Young People's Theatre (SCYPT), created in response to the increasing demand from practitioners and trainers outside the UK for training in the theory and practice of TIE. ICTIE also served as meeting point for theatre practitioners from across the world to share experience and methodology in using theatre for educational purposes with young people or adult communities.

7 Thespis TIU (Finland), Stop Theatre (Iceland), Teater TR3 (Sweden), Aarhus Drama Centre (Denmark) and Eventus TIE, Voba-teatret, Kateterkompaniet and Vestlandske Teatersenter (Norway).

## Works cited

Bond, Edward (2000), *The Hidden Plot*. London: Methuen.

Brooks, Laurie (2006), *The Lost Ones*. Cork: Graffiti Theatre Company.

Davis, David, ed. (2005), *Edward Bond and the Dramatic Child: Edward Bond's plays for young people*. Stoke on Trent: Trentham Books.

Gurden, Kristen (1999), 'With opened eyes: a critical analysis of TEAM educational theatre company'. M. Litt thesis (unpublished), Trinity College Dublin.

Heggstad, Kari Mjaaland (2010), 'TIE – in winds and calm – an attempt at reframing "framing"' in A.-L. Østern et al., eds., *Drama in Three Movements – An Ulyssean Encounter*. Åbo Akademi University: Report no. 29/2010, pp. 55–66.

Illsaas, Tove and Kjølner, Torunn (1993), 'TIE in Scandinavia', in Jackson, ed., *Learning through theatre: New perspectives on theatre in education*, 2nd edn. London: Routledge.

Lehmann, Hans-Thies (2006), *Postdramatic Theatre*, trans. Karen Jürs-Munby. London: Routledge.

*Routledge Dictionary of Quotations* (2004). London: Routledge.

## Websites

Graffiti Theatre Company, Cork. www.graffiti.ie (last accessed 15/08/12).

Imago Theatre-in-Education Company, Mumbai. www.imagoindia.com (last accessed 09/09/12).

Nandikar theatre group, Kolkata. www.nandikar.net (last accessed 09/09/12).

NCERT. www.ncert.nic.in (last accessed 12/12/12).

Purvabhyas Theatre Company, Delhi. www.purvabhyas.org (last accessed 09/09/12).

*Søndag Aften*. www.cultur.com/2011/0106.html (last accessed 14/09/12).

TEAM Theatre, Dublin. www.teamtheatre.ie (last accessed 15/08/12).

Yellow Cat Company, Delhi. www.yellowcat.in (last accessed 09/09/12).

# Part IV

# TIE IN THE TWENTY-FIRST CENTURY – ISSUES AND CHALLENGES

## Introduction

Almost all the chapters in this book could have justified a place in this section, for most look to relate practice in particular contexts to larger concepts and contemporary challenges; and most look forward as well as back. The chapters that follow, however, have a particular claim to be about the future directions that TIE may, or may need to, take.

Wendy Lement considers the particular appropriateness of TIE techniques and forms to the generation of 'civic dialogue' – the promotion of a genuinely critical, participatory notion of citizenship which, in the unstable, fraught and uncertain world we inhabit in the second decade of the century, Lement considers to be more vital than ever.

Charles Adams takes a more theoretical standpoint but pushes the argument for critical pedagogy further still, echoing in some respects Pammenter's essay in chapter 4 and offering a critical perspective from which to view the dilemmas highlighted by Wheelock in chapter 13. He is concerned to look for ways in which TIE (alongside other forms of educational theatre and drama) might contribute, perhaps uniquely, to the progressive education of young people both within and outside conventional school contexts. Participation, dialogue, the use of metaphor and the stimulus to think again about aspects of the world we too readily take for granted have been recurring themes throughout the book; Adams offers a theoretical perspective which challenges us to reaffirm the originally radical nature of TIE's artistic and educational practices, and helps us to see more clearly the threads that connect them.

Finally, Peter O'Connor provides a very different though wholly complementary – and inspirational – insight into the power of TIE as a learning medium, drawing on his own personal experience of using drama to help children traumatised by earthquake. This was drama, in a number of transitional phases, from DIE to TIE, that was for many therapeutic in its impact but not in its intent. It also offers a compelling, concrete example of the relationship between DIE and TIE that Cooper explores in chapter 2. O'Connor's essay effectively articulates some of the ways in which TIE practice at its best works – not as a direct, head-on confrontation with personal issues, but, more subtly and indirectly, through appropriately chosen metaphor, through aesthetic distance, through an art form that can engage, transport – and perhaps transform – its audience on many different levels at the same time.

# 15

# TIE AS A CATALYST FOR CIVIC DIALOGUE

*Wendy Lement*

## A rationale for promoting civic dialogue through TIE

In 2006 the *American Sociological Review* published an article about the decline of social discourse in America (McPherson et al. 2006). The authors studied network groups and discovered that our population is less likely to be involved in discussions about important matters, especially with people who hold differing opinions, than they were in the previous two decades. Of particular concern was that people have become more insular, avoiding public discussions on topics that affect their community, the nation and the world. The proliferation of blogs and other social media continue to change the ways we communicate. In the U.S., National Public Radio's call-in shows may offer the best source of public debate. But radio consists of disembodied voices; callers are not engaged in face-to-face dialogue with people with whom they disagree.

TIE offers an effective means of promoting civic dialogue in our schools and community. Through TIE, we can create dynamic forums for civic dialogue that encourage collective reasoning, foster critical thinking skills and help people articulate their thoughts. In so doing, we should be mindful of both the possibilities and potential limitations we may face. What are the benefits and theoretical dimensions of using TIE as a tool for encouraging civic discourse? What methodologies and techniques can be used to motivate participation? How can we evaluate our success? What are the pitfalls and challenges inherent in this endeavour? What separates dialogue from didacticism when drawing upon historical content that is susceptible to one-sided or simplistic interpretation? How can a TIE company avoid endorsing its own values? This chapter will examine these questions using examples from Theatre Espresso's twenty-year history as a TIE company to illustrate the topics discussed.

## About Theatre Espresso

In 1992 I co-founded Theatre Espresso influenced both by my use of process drama in the classroom and by my desire to explore issues of social justice through theatre. Through process drama I discovered that, given a compelling situation, young people in role were surprisingly articulate in expressing their views. I helped devise interactive plays with a 'gut feeling' that the power of what I had witnessed in the classroom would be amplified with actors creating situations of conflict that needed to be solved. Through subsequent training with experienced TIE practitioners Chris Vine (The City University of New York), Lynne Clark[1] (Queen Margaret University in Scotland) and Emelie Fitzgibbon (Graffiti Theatre Company in Ireland), the company became more methodical in its devising process.

Theatre Espresso did not start out with a mission to produce historical dramas. One of our earliest pieces dealt with problems faced by homeless children who attended public schools. We interviewed homeless families, social workers and school administrators. We spent a year developing a piece that was never performed. As one teacher informed us, 'Homelessness is not in the curriculum.' We were advised that schools would not book plays that scrutinised their own policies. Also, schools became increasingly tied to mandated curriculum frameworks, and teachers had to justify out-of-classroom activities. The need to 'connect the dots' between our dramas and what was being studied in the classroom became essential. These factors forced us to look for less direct ways to help students explore societal problems. Since we couldn't address current events head on, we found times in history when people faced similar dilemmas. Schools might be hesitant to book a play about the Iraq War, but have no trouble exploring the responsibilities of an occupying force during the Boston Massacre of 1770. Treatment of U.S. citizens of Middle Eastern descent following September 11, 2001 isn't in the curriculum, but the use of internment camps for Japanese Americans during the Second World War is. Boston public schools aren't ready to deal with the bussing crisis of the 1970s.[2] But every student in Boston learns about the 1957 school desegregation in Little Rock, Arkansas.

Today Theatre Espresso uses its own version of established TIE methodology to devise and perform plays that bring history to life. Our dramas place students in important decision-making roles such as

Supreme Court justices, state legislators or jury members. We challenge students to question historical figures – both famous and lesser known – debate vital topics, and make judgements on significant events in history. Through TIE, students explore social relationships, reflect on the role of law in society and examine accepted truths about American history. While our plays are based on historical events, our post-drama discussions and study guides help students draw parallels between the past and contemporary issues.

In 2006 we launched the Boston Youth Initiative for Theatre and Civic Dialogue, engaging students in complex debates on history and social justice through grant-funded performances at the John Adams Courthouse in Boston. In 2010 we replicated the programme with a residency of *American Tapestry: Immigrant Children of the Bread and Roses Strike* at the Lawrence Heritage State Park; and in 2012 we received a National Endowment for the Arts award to expand the Lawrence programme during the centennial of the strike. Our diverse company of actors serves over 15,000 students per year in grades 3–12 (ages 8–18).

## Theoretical foundations

Early DIE theorists laid the foundations for Theatre Espresso's work. The concept of placing students in roles of authority is rooted in Dorothy Heathcote's 'mantle of the expert' approach to education, which Cecily O'Neill describes as 'purposeful, dialogic, emancipatory and metaphoric' (foreword to Bolton and Heathcote 1995: vii). Mantle of the expert was conceived as an intricate process for classroom learning. Students are trained as 'experts' in a specified field and then presented with a series of increasingly complex tasks. Heathcote's approach challenges students' assumptions and builds on what they already know in order to make meaning of the world around them. Her premise, that placing students in role encourages empathy, analytical thinking and moral judgement, lays the underpinnings of Theatre Espresso's work.

Heathcote's 'teacher in role' method, as explained by O'Neill, provides a TIE facilitator (Theatre Espresso's term for the person who liaises with the audience, equivalent to Augusto Boal's 'Joker') with sound advice for meaningful interaction with students. O'Neill advocates creating an environment of trust, accepting all contributions and pursuing 'fruitful areas of exploration' (O'Neill et al. 1976: 65). By following these ideals, TIE can provide a non-judgemental forum for discussion. All questions and comments are taken seriously and all viewpoints respected. Placed in decision-making roles charged with deciding the fate of others, students often struggle with their thoughts and feelings. With the help of an effective facilitator, students are compelled to ask questions, convince their peers of their opinions, and take a stand for what they believe. Through open dialogue in the drama, students participate in a process of negotiation. A good facilitator pushes for deeper responses so that a variety of ideas can emerge and grow. This is all done in public, much like a town meeting, a trial or a legislative hearing. Practice in critical thinking through questioning characters and debating important issues in public helps students realise their potential to become active citizens.

Years of observing the above principles in action have convinced me that TIE presents an ideal training ground for civic dialogue. TIE is particularly effective in encouraging honest debates about vital issues that transcend both time and place. Together students witness, in real time, historical figures in conflict. If the drama is complex, students listen to and are influenced by diverse opinions. In role as authority figures, students often change their minds several times before making a decision. When students take ownership of what they say, they have a personal investment in the outcome and are generally empowered by the process. Participating in TIE helps students realise that what they say matters and can have an impact on those around them.

From examining the theoretical foundations of TIE as a catalyst for civic dialogue, and based on my observations of the practice, I have made the following working assumptions. Face-to-face communication about issues of conflict is fundamentally different from that generated through social and other media. While interacting electronically, we can choose to be anonymous, easily attacking a person or idea without taking direct ownership of what we say. We can choose to communicate only with those with whom we agree. In a public forum, by contrast, we lose our anonymity and are more inclined to think about what we want to say before we speak. While peer pressure and insecurities cause some students to avoid speaking in public, TIE has the power to help them overcome their hesitations. In the context of a high-stakes drama they become emotionally invested in the plight of the characters. Their need to speak and be heard often compels them to take a stand for what they believe.

Free and open debates increase the likelihood that we will listen to opposing views and consider various ways of dealing with problems. Ideally, some sort of compromise can be reached. Of course this is not always the case; many public forums end in discord. Any meeting that gives the illusion that people have a say in the outcome when decisions have already been reached inevitably propagates ill will. Similarly, a TIE piece that provides the 'correct answer' rather than provoking an open-ended dialogue will likely fail to elicit honest responses.

*True* civic dialogue provides a forum for people to express their views, even when they are unpopular, to listen to a variety of opinions and to try to reach a resolution. The process allows us to rethink our beliefs. We sharpen our thoughts in order to express them clearly. While not everyone may be content with the results, each person has been given an opportunity to make a difference. If nothing else participants gain a deeper understanding of the central conflict and opposing views. TIE provides a training ground for real-world problem solving. Through open dialogue students make meaning of the confusing and divisive world in which we live. This process requires careful planning, a well-trained company of actor-educators, follow-up and evaluation to ensure that insightful connections made during the drama are not lost.

## Methodology

Theatre Espresso's devising method is closely modelled on one created by Chris Vine and Lynne Clark. Through a detailed process of brainstorming and analysing the needs of the students, we determine central questions for our dramas. These questions aim to help students connect history to current events and generate honest debates about issues that affect their lives. As we perform primarily for school students, we select historical topics that intrigue us, relate to contemporary issues and coincide with what is being taught in local schools.

Devising our dramas involves a process of negotiation between a small team of researcher-writers. We immerse ourselves in primary and secondary sources and sift through the materials to decide what should be included. We debate options for the central question, select characters, and develop a sequence of scenes. Sometimes we write scenes together. More often team members volunteer to write specific segments. I compile and edit the scenes to ensure that the play is cohesive, then share each draft with the team for suggestions. We hold readings with our company members and invite teachers and scholarly advisors who offer feedback.

Although each play has its own content and style, we have developed a basic format. Most of our dramas start with a brief prologue, something evocative and visual – often with sound – that catches students' interest and brings them into the time period. Then the facilitator introduces him/herself in role and places students in their role. The facilitator outlines the central conflict and the students' task. This introduction segues into a play that explores the complexity of the dispute and brings the students up to the point of the crisis that they need to resolve. After viewing the scripted portion of the play, students question the actors in character, debate their points of view and vote on the issue at hand.

At the conclusion of the programme we hold a further discussion, during which students ask questions of the actors (out of role) about what happened in history and about the drama. Students often ask the actors how they would have voted. We never answer that question. Instead, we suggest that students continue discussing these issues, as they have the power to help shape the future. These discussions and our study guides help students make connections between past and present. For example, after *Justice at War*, about the Japanese internment camps, students are asked to consider other times in history when groups have been singled out because of race or ethnicity. Follow-up questions encourage students to think critically about issues raised in the play and how they affect us today. After *The Nine Who Dared: Crisis in Little Rock* students are urged to reflect upon how much progress has been made in desegregating our schools since *Brown v. Board of Education* in 1954. A glance around the room often reveals that de-facto segregation is still prevalent in Massachusetts; with few exceptions urban audiences tend to be primarily Black, Hispanic and Asian, while suburban audiences tend to be primarily white.

While the realities of touring to schools prevent us from exploring current events directly, history provides powerful metaphors for our times. Playwrights from Euripides to Shakespeare to Brecht have used history as a means to educate and inspire the public about the political issues of their day. Historians, such as the late Howard Zinn, widened our view of history to include everyday people caught in extraordinary situations (see Zinn 2005). Uncovering personal stories in letters, journals, biographies, depositions and testimony help us bring characters from the past alive. These documents contain surprising and multifaceted portraits of people who have been overlooked. Students relate to real people facing genuine dilemmas.

Dramas based on primary source documents and personal narratives can affect students in profound ways. Reading about the contributions of the labour movement in the early twentieth century may seem remote and abstract to a ten-year-old. But during *American Tapestry*, students gasp when a young Carmela Teoli[3] describes how her scalp was torn from her head while working at a machine in the Lawrence mills. Students discover why Carmela joined the strike and witness the hardships she and her family endured as a result. They are transfixed as Carmela and another child striker testify at the congressional hearing; the children's testimony helped change the course of history and eventually led to the enactment of child labour laws.

Congressional transcripts of the hearings provide rich details of life in the mills from a variety of perspectives. Countering the children's testimony, students hear from a paymaster at the Ayer Mill, who argues that workers are paid fairly and that if strikers obtain a 15 per cent pay increase, the mills will be forced to close. Given our current economic climate, students take the paymaster's warning to heart, making their choice more difficult. Students in Lawrence are primarily from immigrant families. They connect with the characters more closely than we had anticipated. Their questions and comments indicate a genuine concern for the health and well-being of the strikers and their families. They understand the sacrifices being made and weigh the consequences of a protracted strike more carefully than our suburban audiences.

Students' active participation in the drama is the key to intellectual engagement, not only with history but also with concepts of social justice, human rights and the evolutionary nature of the law.

*Figure 15.1 American Tapestry: immigrant children of the Bread and Roses Strike* (Theatre Espresso 2012). The audience are in role as members of a Congressional committee charged with determining the causes of the strike and recommending steps to end the conflict. This performance was given in Everett Mill, Lawrence, Massachusetts, where the strike began 100 years earlier. Photo courtesy of Theatre Espresso.

*Figure 15.2 Uprising on King Street: The Boston Massacre* (Theatre Espresso 2006). Confrontation between Captain Preston and citizens of Boston in 1770. Students are placed in role as members of the jury in the trial of Captain Preston. Photo by Sandy Kim.

Following our dramas, students ask about specific laws examined in the plays. In *Uprising on King Street: The Boston Massacre*, students play jurors in the trial of Captain Preston. Preston was in command that infamous night when soldiers fired on civilians. During our post-drama discussions students are genuinely intrigued by details of British laws in 1770. They want to know why Preston didn't testify on his own behalf during the trial; British law prohibited defendants from testifying, assuming they would be compelled to commit perjury. They ask why Preston was tried separately from his men and how the soldiers' cases were handled.

Acting as jurors in a pre-American Revolution trial stimulates students' curiosity about the evolution of our justice system. Most importantly, students are compelled to examine the central question of the drama: who should be held responsible for the death of civilians under military rule? The drama serves as a springboard for discussions about civilian casualties in occupied countries today. The question of who should be held accountable for such tragedies is a complex one. Our study guide contains follow-up questions and activities for students to explore this dilemma further.

## Techniques for fostering civic dialogue

In promoting honest civic dialogue the role of the facilitator is a difficult one, requiring training and practice. There is an art to eliciting insightful questions, encouraging deeper responses and challenging students to think critically. For many students, there's an emotional risk associated with speaking in front of classmates, especially if they disagree with the majority. When students believe that their contributions are valued, they are more likely to articulate their views and try to sway their peers.

To encourage participation, it is important to present high-stakes situations. If students care about the fate of the characters, they tend to take their role seriously and have a stake in the outcome. TIE has the power to encourage students – even those who are normally quiet in class – to speak out. When a shy student asks an insightful question or argues a point articulately, that student can be perceived in a new light. After performances, teachers often tell us that they were surprised to learn that a particular student was capable of contributing to the discussion in such a thoughtful way. One teacher reported to me that a student who had been routinely teased at school was now treated with greater respect as a direct result of his brave participation in the drama.

In order for students to 'suspend their disbelief', TIE companies should aim high in terms of the complexity of issues addressed and the language used. Students often reference seemingly small, but important, details from the drama when they ask questions and offer opinions. Even when students miss specific words or phrases, they grasp the basic concepts and arguments well enough to participate in the drama. The heightened language and complexity of the subject matter lets students know that the actors believe they're capable of dealing with complicated material. Generally, students receive that message and rise to the challenge.

The artistic integrity of the performance also affects the quality of student engagement in TIE. While our touring set has to be minimal, well-designed costumes and carefully chosen props help transport students to a specific time and place. A high-quality performance hooks students and increases the chances that they will participate. Over the years I have hired performers with varying levels of training and experience. Students are significantly more engrossed in the drama when watching professional actors. Strong actors instinctively raise the stakes, reveal internal conflicts, and transform what could be a dry re-enactment into a riveting play.

During *The Trial of Anthony Burns* students play Massachusetts State legislators deciding whether Judge Loring should be impeached for returning a fugitive slave, Anthony Burns, to his master, Charles Suttle. Prior to the trial of Burns, Leonard Grimes, an African American minister, tries to buy Burns as a means of securing his freedom. To avoid a contentious trial, Loring initially supports the sale. In an awkward scene that requires nuanced performances, Grimes and Suttle negotiate an agreement to sell Burns on Sunday, the following day. Students witness Grimes frantically raise $1,200. Meanwhile Suttle learns that selling a slave in Massachusetts is illegal. On Sunday evening at Loring's home Suttle demands to know whether he could be arrested for selling Burns. Loring replies, 'Technically, yes, but I can't imagine that happening.' Suttle then stalls, stating that he 'never signs anything on the Lord's Day'. Grimes protests at the delay, but Loring assures him that they can complete the sale in his chamber on Monday morning. Grimes arrives at the chamber as planned, but Loring and Suttle are nowhere to be found; by now both men want to distance themselves from an illegal sale. After a desperate search Grimes finds Suttle and hands him the agreement. Suttle reminds Grimes that his offer was only good for Sunday, calmly adding, 'Does this look like Sunday to you?' Suttle tears up the agreement and hands it to Grimes, who stares at the ripped paper. A groan of disgust is frequently heard from the audience. Seasoned performers make this scene memorable. When students question Loring, they demand to know why he didn't meet Grimes as promised. In the subsequent debate, students who argue for Loring's impeachment often cite his betrayal of Grimes, and his vacillation over the legal issue as key factors in their decision.

While high artistic standards help pull students into the world of the drama, there are no guarantees. Students occasionally try to 'trip up' the actors. On those rare occasions, we take all questions and comments seriously. The facilitator may misread the motivation behind a student's question or comment; what seems like a joke could be a sincere contribution. Even if a student is obviously attempting to be funny, an actor can, by taking what has been said seriously, redirect the tone of the discussion.

In our drama *Nine Who Dared*, students are placed in role as members of the community in 1958, midway through the first year of integration at Central High School. Acts of violence against the nine black students have increased and one student, Minnijean Brown, has been recently suspended for dropping a bowl of chili on a white student and expelled for a subsequent altercation. After viewing what has occurred thus far, students are charged with offering advice to two of the remaining students about how to move forward. Ernest Green is in his senior year and wants to graduate, but Melba Pattillo is traumatised and hesitant to go back. A student inevitably suggests to Melba and Ernest something along the lines of, 'You should just punch them in the face.' This type of comment is usually followed by laughter from the other students.

Rather than admonishing the student for making an inappropriate remark, our facilitator, in role as Reverend Crenshaw, Head of the local chapter of the NAACP, takes the comment seriously. He asks Melba and Ernest why they don't use violence to protect themselves. The question of retaliation opens the door for Melba and Ernest to share some of the horrific challenges they face that were not shown in the play. These new revelations strengthen the interactive portion of the drama.

- There are over 2,000 white students and only eight black students in the school.
- There's a good chance they'd be killed if they attempted such an action.
- Melba has had acid thrown in her eyes and was almost blinded.
- White students throw broken glass into the showers of the black students in the gym.
- Black students have sticks of dynamite thrown at them in the stairwells.
- The students' families face bomb threats and other risks to their safety.
- The black students were warned that if they retaliated, they would be expelled.

While explaining the potential consequences of such an action, the actor playing Melba becomes highly emotional at the thought of using violence against a white student. Once the stakes are clarified, the tone of the discussion changes and students are more thoughtful in their suggestions. The serious nature of the actors' responses also encourages students to consider the level of harassment the eight black students will face when they return to school. From students' subsequent suggestions, it is clear that Melba's fears prompt students to reflect on whether they would have the courage to go back. This interaction deepens the central question: should the students go back to school immediately or wait until September when better policies can be put in place and hopefully tempers have cooled? It is interesting to note that urban audiences tend to be more mixed in their opinions, while suburban students vote overwhelmingly for the eight remaining students to return immediately.

## Evaluation

Proving that TIE programmes actually meet their intended outcomes is not an easy task. Theatre Espresso's evaluation process is ongoing and takes many forms. Within the drama actors continually monitor student engagement and make changes accordingly. If students' questions or comments are simplistic the facilitator delves deeper with follow-up questions. If a debate seems one-sided, an actor plays devil's advocate. Post-show discussions, out of role, offer us opportunities to assess students' comprehension of core issues. We hold debriefing sessions, particularly when the students' interaction was not particularly productive. We constantly ask ourselves, 'Are we really doing what we say we do? If not, what can we do differently?' We learn from each other, from our audiences, and from teachers and scholars who view our programmes. But a more systematic approach is also needed. Therefore, we ask teachers to complete evaluation forms. Teacher assessment provides feedback that helps us improve our work. In general teachers' comments are positive and confirm that we are meeting our objectives.[4] Criticism that rings true (for instance, that actors speak too quickly and important information is lost) prompts us to make needed changes to our programmes. Teacher evaluation forms also serve as an essential component of our grant reports. Foundations want to know whether our programmes are successful in meeting their goals.

## Challenges and pitfalls

Promoting civic dialogue is difficult to achieve. Given constraints of time (our programmes range from one hour to an hour and a quarter), it is difficult to know if participation in the TIE experience has a long-term effect on students. Dramatising history in an educational setting presents a variety of dilemmas. It is important to make what could easily become a one-sided view of an historic event, a complicated drama for students. Balancing the goals of a TIE company with those of schools and scholarly advisers can be problematic. I will discuss some of the most frequent challenges that Theatre Espresso faces and how we approach them.

Given adequate funding, we would visit classes prior to and following each performance to prepare the students and extend the learning.

Rarely is that possible. Parent volunteers generally arrange school bookings, and our first contact with teachers is often just prior to performances. So we provide study guides for preparation and follow-up. When teachers use the guides, our interaction with students tends to be more detailed and complex. But we also perform for students who have little or no prior knowledge of the play's topic. We therefore work from the assumption that students may know nothing about the historical event to be explored. The drama needs to hook students quickly and provide essential facts in a dramatic way that doesn't feel like a history lesson. Similarly, we have no control over what happens when the students leave the performance space. Post-performance discussions ensure some reflection. Reminding teachers about the study guide can also help. Ultimately, we must make our time with the students as meaningful as possible, as we cannot guarantee what happens before and after the performance.

Dramatising history is fraught with challenges. Teachers may have strong opinions about how an historical event should be depicted. There are disagreements among scholars regarding what actually occurred. TIE companies need to wade through this minefield carefully. For the purposes of creating a dynamic drama, the devising team may need to imagine conversations, create fictional or composite characters, and/or change the timeline of events. But an angry response from a teacher who claims that you've got 'the facts' wrong can have a ripple effect and undermine your credibility. One of the best strategies we have used is to bring the contradictions between historical documents to the forefront of the drama. In *The Trial of Anthony Burns* conflicting testimonies of what occurred during the case are juxtaposed, enhancing the tension in the drama.

Scholarly advisers provide us with resources that embellish our work. They aid us in striking a balance between artistic integrity and historical accuracy, helping us decide when dramatic licence can be taken. When a book has been particularly helpful, we ask the author where possible to read our script and offer feedback. If a teacher raises an objection following a show, it's beneficial to explain why and how that choice was made. If we view the teacher's point as valid, we rethink our decision. Listening to teachers' comments and sharing our rationale demonstrates that we are thoughtful in our approach to the material and diffuses potentially damaging situations.

There can be a discrepancy between your goals and the advice you receive from scholarly advisors, but once you explain your rationale their fears usually subside. For example, unless the topic of the drama specifically focuses on race or gender, we practise non-traditional casting. In addition to giving actors equal access to roles, the practice empowers our diverse student audiences to be vocal participants. Occasionally, historians raise concerns about specific casting choices. In *Uprising on King Street* an African American female plays the judge. When she walks on stage in her period wig there is a moment of surprise. But once she introduces herself as Judge Trowbridge and instructs the audience as to their responsibility as jurors, students accept her as the judge. Moreover, young African American females in the audience watch her in awe. While I can't assume to know what audience members are thinking, I sense the role model identification process is at work, and that female students are imagining themselves as the judge. Students know that Trowbridge was a Caucasian male, but the casting choice helps bridge the gap between the past and present for our diverse audiences.

## Dialogue versus didacticism

Facilitators need to remain neutral within the drama. Students pick up on the smallest suggestions that one side is being favoured over the other. But it would be disingenuous to claim that members of TIE companies hold no biases. The very act of selecting an historical topic for a drama is often influenced by ideology. Acknowledging one's biases is essential in transforming what could easily become a one-sided drama into a complex exploration for students.

One way to deal with this dilemma is to portray characters with popular views as disagreeable and those with unpopular views as sympathetic. In the 1990s we performed *Lincoln's Final Hope*. Students played members of a post-Civil War Congress deciding whether Confederate soldiers captured during the war should continue to be imprisoned or released.[5] We observed that Boston students held a simplistic view of the war, perceiving the North as good and the South as evil. Therefore, Secretary of War Stanton, a staunch abolitionist, was portrayed as a gruff, dislikable character. He insisted that if Confederate soldiers were released, they would take up arms and slavery would return. His argument was compelling but, when questioned by students, he was rude and dismissive. Students then questioned Confederate prisoner Jeffrey Rhodes, a likeable young man. Jeffrey defended the institution of slavery, but promised he would follow the law. He described the horrific conditions in which he was being held and begged 'Congress' to release him so he could help his family who had been left destitute from the war. When students were led in debate about the implications of imprisoning men indefinitely in order to ensure that slavery would not return, the personalities of the characters complicated their moral quandary. It is possible to overcompensate for unpopular views by making a character too likeable in the pursuit of fairness. Ultimately, dramas should focus on issues rather than personalities.

One of the most effective ways to avoid a one-sided drama is to identify a central question that has valid points on either side. The best questions are those that company members honestly agree have no clear answers. Finding a complex central question is easier said than done, and we have had varying degrees of success. Two of our most successful dramas in this regard are *The Confession of Ann Putnam* and *The Trial of Anthony Burns.* Both topics, the Salem witch trials and the fugitive slave case, could easily become history lessons with simplistic decisions for the students to make: Should an accused witch be hanged? Should an escaped slave be sent back into slavery? In both cases we decided to make the trials a backdrop for deeper questions. When we performed *Ann Putnam*, Reverend Green served as the facilitator. Addressing students as the congregation of Salem Village fourteen years after the trials, he presented the decision before them: should they forgive Ann Putnam for accusing innocent people of witchcraft and accept her into the congregation, or should she remain an outcast? The drama explored questions of responsibility, repentance and forgiveness. For students to draw connections between the witch trials of 1692 and their world, it was important for them to relate to Ann and not dismiss her as merely evil. Students witnessed the pressures placed on Ann by her parents and peers, and her actions against the accused. Though she made false accusations, Ann was manipulated by her parents in their quest for revenge for past disputes and their desire to acquire land owned by the accused. Led by Reverend Green, students questioned Ann about her motivations. The often-heated debate that followed and varied outcome of the vote reflected the complexity of their task. Students were torn between their compassion for Ann and for the victims.

In *The Trial of Anthony Burns* students play state legislators deciding on the fate of Edward Loring four years after the trial. At the start of the drama, the facilitator urges students to pay close attention to Loring's actions during the recreation of the trial, as they will decide whether or not he should be impeached. It is made clear that Loring was following an established law – *The Fugitive Slave Law* of 1850. Prior to the vote, abolitionists argue that immoral laws should not be followed. But Loring and Burns' attorney Richard Henry Dana caution that impeaching a judge who follows the law because you disagree with his decision sets a dangerous precedent. Students struggle between defending a strong moral principle and upholding the law.

We had more difficulty finding a complex central question for *Justice at War: The Story of the Japanese Internment.* But we have learned that current events and interaction with the audience can add depth to what could be a one-sided drama. In *Justice at War*, students, in role as Supreme Court Justices, examine the case of *Mitsuye Endo v. the United States.* We knew from the outset that the government would have a difficult time convincing students that the Internment Camps should remain open. We decided to focus on the constitutional aspects of the case, and to challenge students not to let their personal feelings interfere with their judgement. For many years the vote was lopsided towards Miss Endo. We consoled ourselves knowing that the students left with a better understanding of the Constitutional arguments underlining the case. Personally, we were heartened by the vote for Miss Endo. But as a TIE company, we were concerned that the central question was too simplistic.

We searched for ways to strengthen the government's case. For example, the actor who currently plays Solicitor General Fahey – the attorney for the government – is African American. For years students grilled Fahey and his client General DeWitt (commander of the Western Defense) about singling out Japanese Americans based on race. During one performance the actor playing Fahey pointed out that it's perfectly legal to discriminate based on race, and that our government does it all the time. He reminded 'the justices' that in parts of the country, laws determine where people can live, go to school and sit on buses. His response sent a chill through the room. It brought students back to the time period of the drama and made them think more deeply about the question before them. We now include that response in each performance.

September 11, 2001 changed the interactive portions of *Justice at War.* Audiences have become increasingly mixed in their opinions on the case. What seemed like a simplistic question suddenly became more complicated. It has been one of those 'be careful what you wish for' moments. The drama is now timelier than we could have imagined. A debate about whether the government has the authority to hold American citizens without trial is real and immediate. The drama creates a forum for students to express their honest opinions on what has become a controversial topic. We maintain a non-judgemental atmosphere to allow students to talk freely. While it challenges us to observe students voting in larger numbers to keep the internment camps open, we adhere to our mission – to provide an open forum for discussion, keeping our personal beliefs to ourselves. By challenging all views, we deepen students' understanding of complex issues. To help students move beyond simplistic assumptions we reveal contradictions and bring ambiguities to light. Students hold a variety of opinions, and we must refrain from imposing our own in order to foster true civic dialogue.

## Conclusion

TIE is democratic by nature. It encourages students to listen to opposing sides, decide what they think and take a stand. There is also an emotional component, as students empathise with characters whose fates are on the line. Sometimes students struggle between their emotional response and what they think is right. In real time, in one room, people are free to speak their minds on intellectual, ethical, moral and legal issues. For many students this is a new and empowering experience. We live in a world of emails, text messages and blogs that connect us in cyberspace, but isolate us in terms of having face-to-face conversations about how to solve vital problems. In that context, something profound happens when – in a public venue – students ask challenging questions, make heartfelt comments and collectively reach a decision about a complex issue. There is also a sense of pride that is palpable in the room at the end of each performance when students have successfully met the challenge.

## Notes

1 Lynne Clark was known as Lynne Suffolk when she and Vine worked together at the Greenwich Young People's Theatre.

2 In the 1970s federal courts ordered Boston to integrate its schools by bussing students across the city. This action prompted violent riots. Photos of white parents throwing stones and bottles at buses carrying black children were published in newspapers across the nation.

3 In Congressional transcripts of the hearings on the Lawrence strike of 1912, Carmela Teoli's first name is misspelled as Camella. Historians have used this spelling in books and other publications about the Bread and Roses Strike. In *Through Carmela's Eyes* (2012), Teoli's grandson Frank Palumbo corrects this error.

4 From September 2010 to December 2011, eighty-six teachers completed evaluation forms. We asked teachers to gauge the level at which they thought participation in our dramas helped students more fully comprehend the complexities of historical events; develop an interest in learning about historical figures; and articulate questions and opinions about issues of justice. Eighty-six per cent of respondents 'strongly agreed'

and 14 per cent 'agreed' that these core objectives had been met. We also elicited comments about the artistic quality of the performance.

5 *Lincoln's Final Hope* was part of our repertoire prior to the detention centre at Guantanamo Bay, which may have influenced students' responses to the drama.

## Works cited

Bolton, G. and Heathcote, D. (1995), *Drama for Learning: Dorothy Heathcote's Mantle of the Expert Approach to Education*. Portsmouth, NH: Heinemann.

McPherson, M., Smith-Lovin, L, and Brashears, M. (2006), 'Social Isolation in America: changes in Core Discussion Networks over two decades', *American Sociological Review* 71, pp. 353–75.

O'Neill, C., Lambert, A., Linnell, R., and Warr-wood, J. (1976), *Drama Guidelines.* London: Heinemann.

Palumbo, Frank (2012), *Through Carmela's Eyes.* Bloomington: AuthorHouse.

Zinn, Howard (2005), *A People's History of the United States.* New York: Harper Perennial Modern Classics (reprint).

# 16

# TIE AND CRITICAL PEDAGOGY

*Charles N. Adams Jr*

I want TIE to be radical.[1] I see a need for practitioners to think of TIE as a radical performance methodology of teaching and learning and to devise programmes with a radical intentionality. With roots in Bertolt Brecht's *lehrstücke* and Workers' Theatre as well as progressive education movements such as John Dewey's ideas of participatory, democratic and arts-based education, one could argue that TIE is already radical simply because of its history and traditions. Yet I am not convinced this is always the case.

The various origin narratives for TIE often state that TIE is simply participatory theatre in the service of education or in support of a specific curriculum. For example, in Gordon Vallins's report from 23 June 1965, the first report documenting the emergence of TIE, Vallins describes TIE as 'an animated visual aid to both teachers and children acting as a stimulus to the creative work in the school' (Vallins 1965: 1). That does not seem radical. Of course Vallins's thinking here is very early in the process of imagining what TIE might be, but such statements begin a historical trajectory of descriptions and definitions of TIE that mark it as a project which supports the needs of the (state-mandated) curriculum.[2]

Rather than criticising how people have talked about TIE in the past, I want to confront the fact that such definitions do not describe the potential of TIE or even what actually happens in many TIE programmes, and that such descriptions leave TIE open to co-option and redeployment as a medium of schooling rather than an opportunity for education (I'll come back to this distinction between schooling and education shortly). I think of TIE in terms similar to those of practitioner Romy Baskerville who, in her 1973 position paper, articulates her radical purpose for TIE: to engage working class children by producing socially conscious theatre that resists the domination of the working class by the middle class (Baskerville 1984: 8). She argues that working class children cannot relate to the forms and content of middle class theatre, and that the middle class own and control 'all means of production and media' (ibid.). Therefore TIE must create new forms that young people can comprehend and that allow them to name and challenge forms of domination that work to constrain and control them. Baskerville also calls for TIE to resist the propaganda of the 1944 Education Act – equal opportunity for all, which for Baskerville was really a liberal 'cover-up' for the task that state-controlled education actually performs, dominating the working class (ibid.: 9). For Baskerville, most theatre works to 'mystify and cloud over real issues', making the priority for TIE the handling of real issues by taking up historical perspectives to help young people understand their own histories:

> And this, of course, is where some TIE companies are getting their (justified) left wing reputation from. We want to show kids what their own history has been, not that of their 'superiors', but the bits that are always left out. We want them to have some understanding of the real nature of racialism, of a woman's role in society, of trade unionism, of pollution, of old age. It is necessary to understand that politics is not a dirty word; it involves, expresses, and influences every emotional and material condition of our lives.
>
> (ibid.: 9–10)

It is important to note that Baskerville's ideas of a radical practice are rooted within a specific historical moment and within a specific understanding of Marxism that posited class domination as the chief, or perhaps even sole, force of oppression that must be overcome through radical activity. Some forty years later, and with a more common understanding that oppression unfolds not only along lines of class but also those of race, sex, gender identification, sexual orientation, ethnicity, language, ability, age, religion, and other potential differences, it is easy to dismiss Baskerville's ideas as mere Marxist propaganda with little relevance today. However, her statement still opens up the possibility of a radical vision. When she calls for the sort of TIE that explores the 'bits [of history] that are always left out', in her charge for TIE to explore racism, sexism, and questions of the environment, ageing, and class, she is invoking a nimble, acrobatic practice that can unmask and work against the many forms of oppression that materialise in different historical, cultural, and economic circumstances. What is particularly useful about Baskerville's statement is the challenge to explore questions of power and oppression, and to relocate this political power from the realm of the oppressors to the realm of the everyday and everyone (particularly young people) through TIE. When TIE manages to resist multiple forms of oppression and brings the everyday political reality into focus, then something much more radical is happening than theatre working in the service of the curriculum. It is this radical 'something more' that I want practitioners to engage with as the critical education that can happen in TIE.

TIE works as a way of knowing – by participating in TIE young people can understand not only the world as-it-is but also their relationships to, with, and in that world. Education, as a process of learning, might be imagined as the processes by which young people come to these sorts of critical understandings, of conscientisation.[3] However, formal education most often happens in schools presenting a state-mandated curriculum and means of assessment, and schooling as a function of the state is an altogether different process from education.

Michael Apple has explored how schooling works to allow certain groups to assert power and control through economic and cultural distribution. That is, schools work as machines that reproduce hegemonic and ideological relations through knowledge selection and transmission (and in some cases the withholding of knowledge), ultimately positioning people in society so that cultural control and economic relations, the status quo, are maintained (Apple 2004: 30). Viewed in this way, schools often function as places and spaces of domination that acculturate young people into world-views that see the dominant classes (which in Western cultures are often male, white, middle/upper class, able-bodied, heterosexual, and adult but not elderly) as the proper ruling classes (ideology) and the historical, philosophical and material conditions which establish them as the ruling classes as natural and inevitable (hegemony). The instruments of schooling include state-mandated curricula, standardised testing, textbook selections, school architecture, the arrangement of furniture and objects in classrooms, and the mechanisation of students to assume certain postures, positions and gestures in order to move successfully through the schooling environment.

Education, on the other hand, might be imagined differently. In many cases these two terms are used synonymously, thought of as deeply intertwined so that education is what one receives as a process of schooling. I suggest that there are useful distinctions in thinking of education as a process of critical learning, and schooling as the state-directed processes and practices which shape and position young people to maintain the status quo. Genevieve Lloyd presents etymological ideas of 'education' as a term by interpreting *educare* as a process of drawing out of the student's mind aspects that were already there (Lloyd 2006: 98). Lloyd also looks to *educere* as a root of education, noting that this root refers to leading forth (ibid.: 97).

These two ideas, drawing out and leading forth, suggest two different strands of thought on education. Education as drawing out might manifest itself as situations that enhance students' capacities to learn by engaging (drawing out) innate capacities of young people such as desire, imagination, curiosity and passion. According to Lloyd, the other strand, leading forth, has become the dominant strand of education as a practice and incorporates the idea of learning as the completion of processes that prepare learners for 'the privileges and responsibilities of adult life' (Lloyd 2005: 98–99). Young people are led forth into the predetermined responsibilities of citizenship by acquiring the official knowledge authorised by those in power.

It may be useful to imagine 'education' as a manifestation of the first strand, drawing out, and 'schooling' as a manifestation of the second strand, leading forth. The realm of education, then, is where the best TIE programmes dwell, while many traditional academic programmes exist in the realm of schooling – socialising and distributing young people into pre-existing cultural, social and economic power structures. Not all schooling has this aim but this is frequently the effect of many dominant schooling structures. I am not making this distinction as a polemical argument that one strand is wrong and bad and the other is correct and good, that one strand has always been malicious in intent, or even that the strands are completely separate (certainly part of drawing out in education is to prepare young people for active participation in society), but rather to foreground education and schooling as complex, sometimes contradictory endeavours requiring differing projects, modes of thought, and methodologies for teaching and learning to achieve their goals.[4]

If TIE is to develop as the potentially radical project that Baskerville's comments invoke and for which practitioners like myself and educators struggling within certain systems of schooling yearn, it needs to focus more on drawing out and less on leading forth. This might best be realised by an intentional engagement with critical pedagogies – philosophies of teaching and learning that pursue education as a practice of freedom and a process of coming to a critical understanding of the world and the relations that order the world. The purpose of this chapter is to articulate some of the foundational concepts of such a pedagogy and explore ways in which TIE might engage these ideas.

## Critical pedagogy

Critical pedagogy is a bricolage of approaches and philosophies of teaching and learning that view education as the practice of freedom and work in opposition to forms of schooling that, as bell hooks states, serve to reinforce domination (hooks 1994: 4). Critical pedagogy posits that education is never a neutral act, but is deeply embedded in power relations. A claim of neutrality in education ignores the choices that are made in determining which knowledges are worthy of note and preservation, who chooses, and how those choices work to privilege limited, selected knowledge over and above the many possibilities available (Apple 2004: 7). Critical pedagogy labours to unmask the hidden curriculum that naturalises domination and the power structures inherent in schooling and education. It also works to resist oppressive power relations by creating spaces of equality in which students can engage in a participatory democracy and co-create knowledge in ethical encounters with others and self.

Critical pedagogy is grounded in the notion that education can be a means of working toward justice and equality, and works towards this by questioning and critiquing the privileged role that positivism plays in shaping knowledge selection and production. Positivism, as Joe L. Kincheloe notes, is rooted in a belief that all knowledge is objective and scientific, free from emotional and other biases, and therefore that all knowledge is empirically verifiable by the scientific method (Kincheloe 2008: 28). In a positivist epistemology the scientific method becomes the sole means of determining the facts that comprise knowledge, regardless of the discipline.[5] Because knowledge exists outside of social constructions and can be viewed as objective, it can be transmitted effectively from one human to another, and teaching becomes the process of transmitting knowledge while learning becomes the process of receiving that knowledge.

Positivism also implies that there are correct ways of teaching and learning and that education can be standardised and measured uniformly for all students. This is the logic that underscores reforms such as the No Child Left Behind Act of 2001 in the United States and supports systems that rely on high-stakes standardised testing as the chief means of measuring academic success, such as the National Curriculum of England, Wales, and Northern Ireland.[6] Critical pedagogy, in contrast, maintains that knowledge is situated and socially constructed in specific historical, philosophical and material conditions that impact the ways students learn, and therefore there are no universal methods of teaching and learning. Teaching should be responsive to student need and rooted in the curiosity and passion of both students and teachers.

These ideas underpin pedagogies that prioritise the development of critical consciousness.[7] They are central to my belief that TIE can engage critical pedagogy effectively. TIE materialises as art. It provides ways of teaching and learning that engage the entire human being cognitively, affectively and kinaesthetically. Through theatre, TIE brings together thought, emotion, and embodiment as ways of coming to new understandings and means of experiencing and knowing the world. By working through metaphor, image, symbol, story, and by constructing new ways to experience time and space, by engaging heteroglossia and polyphony,[8] by embodying complexity and contradiction in action, theatre has the potential to forge new and different connections, linking to theories of constructivist and experiential learning proposed by progressive thinkers such as Lev Vygotsky, Dewey, Paulo Freire and others.[9] Theatre questions the notion of 'objectivity' and the privileging of empirical knowledge and also resists positivism's idea that the scientific method is the only valid means of producing knowledge.

TIE can support critical pedagogy effectively by emphasising the social construction of knowledge as participants and practitioners work together to make their own meanings from the material. This intention separates progressive TIE from other practices that attempt to use performance to transmit predetermined answers to students: what I call instructive or instrumental theatre. Constructivist TIE is the opposite. It allows participants to engage in what Kincheloe calls 'world-making', to construct knowledge of hidden reality, revealing how it came into being, how it is structured and maintained and how it oppresses many peoples; and it encourages participants to ask what alternatives, that value social justice, liberation, and human interconnection, might be imagined instead (Kincheloe 2005: 11).

Another link between TIE and constructivist learning is the notion of play. TIE as radical theatrical performance is playful in at least two senses. First, it plays with the assumption that the dominant power structures are inevitable, allowing participants to imagine other potential ways of acting and being. Theatre teases out conflicting ideas and allows participants to form, test, and practice new configurations. Because theatre participants engage in a certain set of conventions, playing with power structures is simultaneously real, within the fictive world of the performance, and unreal, given that the fictive world evaporates with the conclusion of the performance. It is this nature of being simultaneously real and unreal that may make TIE a safe space for playing with ideas, notions and structures.

The second sense of play is connected to TIE's legacy of audience participation. Rather than being assigned the roles of traditional, passive spectators, TIE audience members become participants: taking actions, making choices, and influencing the outcomes of both the programme and the knowledge being constructed. Participants may, for example, engage in activities such as questioning and challenging the characters (hot-seating), constructing images by using their bodies (image theatre), and role-playing new situations and possibilities. Participants engage ideas by playing. This links to the educational development theories of Vygotsky, who saw play as essential and complex social development for young people (Vygotsky 1933/2002; 1978: 92–104).

These two ideas, that TIE is play-full and that TIE resists positivism by engaging cognition, affect, and physicality in order to construct knowledge socially, make TIE a strong ally of critical pedagogy. In the next section I pose three foundational tenets of critical pedagogy that can enhance TIE and move it even closer to being a radical practice and explore ways these tenets have manifested in two sample TIE programmes: *The Giant's Embrace*, a literacy programme toured by Theatr Powys in Wales in 2005, and *Jus' Once*, an HIV/AIDS intervention programme first toured by Arts-in-Action in Trinidad and Tobago in 1998. The tenets are that: (1) critical pedagogy employs a problem-posing model; (2) critical pedagogy works through tactics of dialogic participation; and (3) education should be a transformative process of liberation grounded in social justice.

### *Critical pedagogy employs a problem-posing model*

Paulo Freire, arguably at the heart of critical pedagogy, proposes that traditional models of schooling engage an oppressive model of teaching that he calls the banking model (Freire 2003: 70–73). In the banking model, all-knowing teachers deposit knowledge into students, who are imagined as empty vessels waiting to be filled. Students then memorise and store, or bank, information until such time as they need to withdraw it, for example in standardised tests. The banking model anaesthetises students and inhibits their creative power because the world is presented as something-that-is as opposed to something constantly changing; students are transformed into spectators rather than co-creators of the world and as a result must adapt and submit themselves to the world-that-is (ibid.: 75). In contrast, Freire offers a model for liberatory education through problem-posing (ibid.: 79).

Problem-posing models replace teachers as sole authority and students as empty objects with collaborative relationships in which teachers and students become co-investigators co-constructing knowledge. Education moves from the transmission of ready-made facts about the world-that-is to a process in which students become co-creators in a world that can be changed by constructing knowledge in order to solve problems. Because the world can be co-created, oppression can be replaced with social justice.

For an example of how this relates to TIE, let us turn to *Jus' Once*. Devised originally for secondary schools, this programme was also performed, in 2001–3, in schools and 'liming spots', public spaces where people gather informally in Trinidad and Tobago to socialise, and continues to be a part of Arts-in-Action's repertoire. It attempts to explore cultural questions around HIV/AIDS transmission and prevention, including what might be imagined as a positivist fight against dangerous social myths about HIV/AIDS. However, and perhaps more importantly, *Jus' Once* also attempts to question socially constructed cultural practices that allow HIV/AIDS to spread, such as male sexual initiation rituals in which many males have forced sexual relations with one woman, as well as the culturally embedded attitudes that support such sexual abuse of women. The programme does this by presenting participants with the stories of several people through image work, monologues, scenes, music, and games. Each character embodies an aspect of culture or a specific attitude towards HIV/AIDS that the Arts-in-Action team discovered in their research for the programme. Spectators took opportunities to hot-seat characters as well as give them advice and engage in role-plays, allowing them to critique and challenge cultural practices and social myths that have led to the HIV/AIDS epidemic in Trinidad and Tobago.

*Jus' Once* utilises several characters to embody and explore problems such as why sexual violence against women is acceptable; and what we can do to change our culture so that sexual violence is no longer acceptable. For example, one character, Johnny, has participated in the male sexual initiation ritual. Even though one of his friends, who also participated in such rituals with him, has died from AIDS-related complications, Johnny delivers a monologue in which he denies that HIV/AIDS might be transmitted through such a ritual and states that he is immune because he always 'goes first'. The participants have the opportunity to hot-seat Johnny and to challenge his naïve beliefs. They also have (and often took) the opportunity to challenge the ritual as a cultural practice, which Johnny defends, and engage in dialogue not only with Johnny and the facilitator, but also directly with each other. Instead of being lectured on dangerous sexual practices, through careful problem-posing participants challenge complex cultural structures that encourage such practices.

A potent moment happened in a public performance I witnessed in a liming spot in 2007. Another character, Sheldon, has just tested positive for HIV, yet continues to have unprotected sex with women and not tell them he is positive. In a hot-seating session, one of the female participants asked Sheldon why he was sleeping with women without using a condom, and he replied, 'They [women in general] gave it to me; I'm just sharing it back.' This allowed the facilitator to pose the problem: how are women seen here (in our culture), and how might that support violence and sexual abuse? This question activated many responses in participants, from anger with Sheldon, to mocking women in society, to actual dialogue between men and women observing the programme, and resulted in a role-play in which a male participant gave Sheldon advice, imploring him to face the realities of HIV/AIDS and his attitudes toward women. It was an electric moment, and everything else stopped while this scene was playing. Until this point much of the dialogue had really been banter as men mocked the less-powerful positions women held in their society and women responded in turn. This was the first statement by a male outside the TIE team that imagined another possibility and opened a forum for more serious reflection and discussion in the programme. While I cannot prove that the male participant came to this realisation during and because of this iteration of the programme, it seems to be potent anecdotal evidence of possibility. Something powerful happened in this performance as a result of problem-posing; this was critical pedagogy working well.

While evaluations funded by the Canada Fund in 2001, 2002 and 2003 indicated that *Jus' Once* was highly effective in increasing personal knowledge of HIV/AIDS transmission, debunking cultural myths about HIV/AIDS, and forming links with community resources for information on and treatment of HIV/AIDS, the difficulty in measuring cultural attitudes towards women and sexual violence has left no 'hard evidence' of necessary and important cultural shifts (UNAIDS 2004: 43–45). However, in 2004 the *Jus' Once* project was named by the UNAIDS/United Nations Institute for Training and Research AIDS Competence Program as one of the top ten techniques and practices for local responses to HIV/AIDS, including a note that *Jus' Once* worked effectively to shift cultural and social perceptions (George 2005).[10] Perhaps this also serves as evidence of possibility.

By posing these problems, the actor-teachers are able to engage in dialogue with participants and build relations in which participants can teach each other rather than positioning themselves as the authority on HIV/AIDS and telling the participants what to do; they draw out rather than lead forth. And although there are aspects of *Jus' Once* that may seem more instrumental and transmissional and therefore of the banking model, ultimately the emphasis on shifting cultural practices through problem-posing and engaging the entire human being through play helps align *Jus' Once* usefully with critical pedagogy.

### *Critical pedagogy works through tactics of dialogic participation*

Critical pedagogy works to develop conscientisation through dialogic participation. Freire notes that dialogue is an ethical encounter taking place in the world between humans who meet as equals in order to name the world (Freire 2003: 88). This means that people evacuate their normal positions in power relations to come together on a similar footing with as little domination as possible – not teacher and student, but teacher-student and student-teacher. Dialogic encounters take place in the 'real' world with all its complexities, power struggles, and oppressions, and allow participants to engage in world-making.

Dialogue, rather than monologue, allows participants to engage in praxis, that is, action and reflection that are inexorably linked, so that participants work through active reflection and reflective action. Critical education working towards praxis must therefore be participatory – if student-teachers cannot participate in dialogue, then the model of education is a banking model relying on the monologue of the teacher. While banking models may employ superficial forms of participation to help deliver messages, such as role-plays that require participants to rehearse ways of performing roles 'correctly', such participation does not allow for genuine dialogic encounters and still can be seen as a form of monologue.[11]

TIE engages this foundational tenet. Participation in the action of the programme is a key component of TIE, and participants have opportunities to engage in discussions with each other and with actor-teachers or the characters they are playing. Discussion is not the same as dialogue, and even active decision-making may not be dialogic if participants remain in a subordinate position to the actor-teachers. Power inequalities disrupt genuine dialogue so it may not always be possible for actor-teachers and participants to be on completely equal terms, but it is possible to work to equalise relationships as much as possible.

This coming together as 'equals' for dialogic participation happens in *The Giant's Embrace*, a half-day TIE programme for young people aged five to seven originally devised by Big Brum TIE and then adapted and toured by Theatr Powys in Wales in 2006 in both English and Welsh. (See also chapter 2.) I will be looking at the Theatr Powys version. In *The Giant's Embrace*, students contract to become 'storymakers' and to help Mrs S, a storyteller, find an ending to a story she does not know how to complete. Mrs S shares the story of Tom, a boy living with his mother and infant brother in a land dying because a Giant has consumed everything. Two actor-teachers perform the story as Mrs S tells it, using their bodies, puppets, and artefacts on a set representing a destroyed forest. There is no more food, and even the rivers and lakes have gone dry because of the Giant's never-ending consumption. Tom ventures into the forest in search of food for his family and finds leftover crumbs in the sleeping Giant's spoon. Tom enters the forest a second time to find water and discovers a drop left behind in the Giant's spoon. Hunger and thirst force Tom to make a third journey into the forest. As he approaches the Giant this time, the Giant awakens, grabs Tom, represented by a puppet, and begins to swallow him whole. In order to save his life, Tom promises to bring his own mother and brother for the Giant to eat. The Giant lets Tom go, and Tom heads home, miserable because he cannot think of any way out of his promise. This is the part of the story that Mrs S knows, and the participants must work together, using only the elements already introduced in the story, to find and write an ending.

This programme allows participants to engage in dialogue in numerous ways. In trying to create an ending to the story, the participants must engage in dialogue with the Giant, with Mrs S, and with each other. Participants dialogue with the Giant metaphorically by creating his memories and images of how he views the world using image theatre, the construction of tableaux using their bodies. The Giant has a magic mirror that will show anything, and participants become the images within the mirror. This helps them understand why the Giant might be consuming everything at hand and what his relationship with society might be, and may give them ideas on how to end the story. This is also an excellent example both of the social construction of reality (the participants collectively create the reality of the story rather than being given a completely predetermined world) and of critical pedagogy as the drawing out of education. By forming images and then interpreting these images collectively, participants draw out not only their own curiosity and imagination but also their own ideas of how individuals and societies exist in relation with each other as they construct meanings together.

Dialogue with Mrs S becomes possible when she contracts with the participants to endow them with the authority necessary to write the end of the story with her – this move repositions the participants as co-investigators and collaborators with Mrs S, an attempt towards equalisation which allows them to engage in genuine dialogue. It is also through the contracting that the programme becomes an ethical encounter, as the nature and purpose of the programme become visible to participants. At the moment of contracting, Mrs S transforms from teacher to teacher-student, and the participants transform from students to students-teachers. Contracting, the explicit agreement and coming-together for the purposes of problem-posing and world-making through theatrical performance, may be an absolutely necessary precondition for TIE to operate as a critical pedagogy and as a dialogical encounter.

Finally, participants must engage in dialogue with each other, as they collectively write an ending to the story. Once the story comes to its climax and can go no further, students are invited to enter the performance space in order to manipulate the puppets and objects that have been used in the performance of the story so far. Participants rehearse actions and scenes and try and retry ideas as they make propositions for ending the story and negotiate these propositions through mutual dialogue. Once an ending has been agreed, students work with actor-teachers first to perform the ending within the theatre set and then to record it through writing, practising their reading and writing skills, as individually they commit to paper their visions of the collective ending of the story.

Participants activate praxis to create the end of the story. They practise action and reflection to understand the situation, the background to the situation, and potential solutions. In these moments of proposition and negotiation, participants are engaging in a critical pedagogy that not only helps develop literacy skills but also helps participants form coalitions with each other to name the world, understand relationships within the world, and change those relationships into a vision of the world-as-it-could-be.

### *Education should be a transformative process of liberation grounded in social justice*

This is the third foundational tenet of critical pedagogy. Education can resist forms of domination that are inherent in some kinds of schooling, particularly processes that work to homogenise students into specific ways of thinking and behaving. Critical pedagogy transforms learners into active subjects working for liberation and social justice by exploring subjugated knowledges alongside official knowledges.

Subjugated knowledges are, according to Michel Foucault, ones 'that have been disqualified as nonconceptual knowledges, as insufficiently elaborated knowledges: naïve knowledges, hierarchically inferior knowledges, knowledges that are below the required levels of erudition or scientificity' (Foucault 2003: 7). Subjugated knowledges might include the cosmologies of specific indigenous peoples, the values and survival skills of people living in poverty, or cultural beliefs and practices that are not dominant in a given society. The histories Baskerville notes as left out of the history books might be thought of as subjugated knowledges. Subjugated knowledges offer ways to resist homogenising meta-narratives and normalising ideologies by acting as counter-sources of truth and alternative ways of knowing and being.

One way in which critical pedagogy works for liberation grounded in social justice, then, is through exploring subjugated knowledges, and this exploration, in turn, has the possibility of de-socialising learners, that is, of allowing learners to question, resist, and potentially rewrite the ways that social behaviours and the experiences of schooling shape them into citizens.[12] Ira Shor notes that desocialisation occurs through the critical questioning of received values, traditional narratives, and existing knowledge and power relations (Shor 1992: 114). The ultimate goal of desocialisation is to allow learners opportunities to develop a critical consciousness and to free them to shape their lives as citizens along lines of social justice. Desocialisation allows people the opportunity to become the authors of their own lives.

It is in exploring subjugated knowledges alongside official knowledges and in the potential for desocialisation that TIE is most radical. As we have seen, *Jus' Once* questions dominant cultural knowledge that positions women as inferior and so works to desocialise participants. The Theatr Powys production of *The Giant's Embrace* resists the colonising properties of the English language as a homogenising force by touring in Welsh as well as in English. Participants explore the subjugated knowledges of Welsh language and culture and desocialise from the idea that English is the only appropriate way of communicating (in Great Britain). It also challenges the notion that 'people other than me' decide how our stories are written. This is critical pedagogy at work in TIE.

## The radicalisation of TIE

*Jus' Once* and *The Giant's Embrace* offer potent examples of how TIE might be radicalised by an intentional, thoughtful engagement with critical pedagogy. TIE can work not as just a play-full way of delivering the official curriculum, but also as a radical way of calling into question the 'truths' of dominant culture and power and imagining other ways of thinking and being. In our current historical moment in which students, teachers, and schools work non-stop, albeit not always uncritically, to be seen as succeeding in education by achieving high scores on standardised tests, it is necessary for TIE practitioners to highlight the ways in which their programming meets certain standards just to be able to reach students. However, I contend that TIE that only works to meet such standards without providing opportunities for genuine dialogic encounters rooted in problem-posing and social justice may be culpable in the oppression and domination of young people.

Rather like progressive classroom teachers and certain liberatory schools, TIE has the awkward need to work both inside schooling systems (by being seen to support the official curriculum) and outside schooling systems (by working for social justice) at the same time. Intentional and thoughtful engagement with critical pedagogy may help TIE negotiate such tensions while also operating as a radical mode of theatre and education. On the surface *The Giant's Embrace* is a programme for enhancing literacy and so supports the schooling curriculum.[13] However, *The Giant's Embrace* also works for education and social justice by attempting to equalise relationships between actor-teachers and participants, exploring environmental consumption, engaging subjugated knowledges, and enhancing praxis through dialogic participation and problem-posing. Intentional engagement with critical pedagogy helps *The Giant's Embrace* negotiate tensions between schooling and education to enhance multiple types of learning. A similar thoughtful engagement may help TIE programmes find those modes of schooling that support education. Critical pedagogies do not have to ignore the content of traditional modes of teaching and learning but can look at the same materials in a different way.

I keep emphasising the notion of intentional and thoughtful engagement because critical pedagogy, as any human construction, is not without flaws and dangers. Critical pedagogy has been criticised for being a thinly veiled attempt to force students into political alignment with their teachers. While this is possible, working for ethical encounters that activate learning through problem-posing and dialogic participation helps avoid such problems. Encounters with subjugated knowledges and attempts at desocialisation must not be forced on participants, but rather should be genuine offers that can be accepted or rejected without penalty. Forcing students to agree that certain cultural practices are violent is just as oppressive as models of teaching that do not allow students to question cultural practices at all. An intentional, thoughtful engagement with critical pedagogy has self-reflexivity as a precondition; practitioners must continually reflect not only on the subject matter to be presented but also on the means by which the subject matter is to be encountered and explored. Drama conventions such as hot-seating, image theatre, and even forum theatre interventions can be oppressive or liberating, depending on how they are used and structured within TIE programmes. Constant reflection is necessary to identify potentially oppressive modes of domination in TIE and to transform them into modes of liberation allied to social justice.

I started this chapter by stating that I want TIE to be radical. Thinking of TIE as radical performance helps us as practitioners make direct links to notions of freedom and liberation, goals TIE has historically worked towards. When TIE works as radical education, it can act as an ally of progressive forces that are often to be found in even the most conservative educational settings. When TIE works as both radical education and radical performance, it can do even more. Baz Kershaw claims that radical performance has the potential to create various forms of freedoms, not only freedom from oppression, repression, and exploitation, but also the freedom 'to reach beyond existing systems of formalized power, freedom to create currently unimaginable forms of association and action' (Kershaw 1999: 18). The power of such radical performance is that it does not just represent such freedom; it actually creates freedom for both performers and audience members. This is the sort of radical performance I want TIE to embrace. TIE has the potential to produce freedom for its participants, practitioners, school and community-based allies in multiple ways. Thoughtful engagement with critical pedagogy is essential to create radical performance. By working with critical pedagogy, TIE can become a radical practice of freedom.

## Notes

1 I mobilise the term 'radical' not in the pejorative sense often used by conservative thinkers to dismiss any social change as an extreme, militant overthrow of order, but rather in line with Richard Johnson's idea of

'radical' as a political term that emphasises exploring questions of knowledge and power through lenses provided by social and critical theory (feminist, queer, anti-racist and neo-Marxist especially) (Johnson 2005: 296–97).

2 For examples of work that discuss such a trajectory, see Prendergast and Saxton (2009), Jackson (2007), Redington (1983), and Nicholson (2007, 2011).

3 *Conscientização* (anglicised as *conscientisation*), or developing a critical consciousness, is a key concept of Paulo Freire's work as a critical educator. Freire's goal was for students to see themselves as active agents capable of changing the world, and this agency required *conscientização*. For more details, see Freire (2000, 2002 and 2003).

4 While my sympathies lie with education, schooling has certain important aspects, particularly in helping young people acquire the codes and cultural capital necessary to survive and perhaps even thrive. As Lisa Delpit reminds us in *Other People's Children* (2006), schooling children who do not come from a background of privilege is especially important so that they may participate in and even change the dominant culture.

5 For more information on and critiques of positivism, particularly in respect to theatre, see McConachie (1995) and Nellhaus (1993).

6 The *No Child Left Behind Act of 2001* calls for all children to 'reach, at a minimum, proficiency on challenging State academic achievement standards and State academic assessments' (NCLB 2001: 115 Stat. 1439). The National Curriculum of England, Wales, and Northern Ireland, introduced in 1989 following the passage of the *Education Reform Act* of 1988, requires standardised testing at Key Stages 2 and 4 (Children, Schools and Families Committee 2009).

7 For more detailed groundings in critical pedagogy, see Kincheloe (2008), Darder et al. (2003), Giroux (2003), McLaren (2003) and Freire (2003).

8 'Heteroglossia' is Mikhail Bakhtin's notion marking the presence of two or more embodied voices or discourses offering conflicting perspectives and therefore opening the possibility of debate and genuine dialogue. 'Polyphony' is a similar concept that refers to the presence of multiple distinct voices that engage in a sort of play with each other but which remain distinct and are never silenced.

9 Constructivism is an epistemology that claims that knowledge is socially constructed and disseminated and is influenced by both cognition and affect, and has foundations in thinking by Dewey, Vygotsky, Freire, and many others. See Vygotsky (1978) and Dewey (1938 and 1958). See also Freire's discussion of affect in relation to teaching and learning (Freire 2003). Kolb (1984) builds on Dewey's work and incorporates aspects of Freire's notions of praxis as action and reflection.

10 I am not claiming that *Jus' Once* single-handedly reduced the rates of HIV/AIDS in Trinidad and Tobago, but, as one part of a multi-pronged approach, this programme may have had great impact. David Soomarie, director of the NGO Community Action Resource in Trinidad, notes that a combination of programming brought about significant positive change in the battle against HIV/AIDS in Trinidad and Tobago (Warwood 2011: 4). While he does not cite *Jus' Once* specifically, he does mention theatrical actions that began making an impact on the public imaginary.

11 I am thinking here of the sort of anti-violence work that teaches correct ways to respond to potential violence and then asks participants to practise these responses correctly through role-plays.

12 'Desocialisation' is the term Ira Shor (1992: 114) uses to indicate the capacity to question the social behaviours and experiences of daily life, including schooling, that shape us into the people we are.

13 Literacy programming is often an example of developing essential knowledge and skills as well as the cultural capital necessary to survive and succeed in dominant society, and therefore can be imagined as the sort of schooling that is in one sense empowering. However, it can also be a means of colonising and acculturating people into one dominant culture and language, and therefore potentially oppressive. The context is vital. An official (state) curriculum may encourage questioning and exploration, but those activities I would describe more as education and less as schooling. Schools are rarely only all one thing and not anything else.

## Works cited


Apple, Michael (2004), *Ideology and Curriculum*, 3rd edn. New York: Routledge.

Baskerville, Romy (1984), 'Theatre in Education', *SCYPT Journal*, 13: 7–12.

Children, Schools and Families Committee (2009), *Fourth Report: National Curriculum*. Online at: www.publications.parliament.uk/pa/cm200809/cmselect/cmchilsch/344/34402.htm (accessed 16 July 2012).

Darder, Antonia, Baltodano, Marta and Torres, Rodolfo, D., eds (2003), 'Critical Pedagogy: An Introduction', in Darder et al., *The Critical Pedagogy Reader*. New York: Routledge, pp. 1–21.

Delpit, Lisa (2006), *Other People's Children: Cultural Conflict in the Classroom*, 2nd edn. New York: New Press.

Dewey, John (1938), *Experience and Education*. New York: Touchstone.

——(1958), *Art as Experience*. New York: Capricorn.

Foucault, Michel (2003), *Society Must Be Defended: Lectures at the Collège de France*, 1975–76, trans. David Macey. New York: Picador.

Freire, Paulo (2000), *Pedagogy of Freedom: Ethics, Democracy, and Civic Courage*. New York: Rowan and Littlefield.

——(2002), *Education for Critical Consciousness*. New York: Continuum.

——(2003), *Pedagogy of the Oppressed*, 30th anniversary edn, trans. Myra Bergman Ramos. New York: Continuum.

George, Marvin (2005), 'Cultural Industries as a Motor for Development: Arts-in-Action as Testimony', panel discussion hosted by the Inter-American Development Bank, Culture Center.

Giroux, Henry (2003), 'Critical Theory and Educational Practice', in Darder et al. (eds), *The Critical Pedagogy Reader*. New York: Routledge, pp. 27–56.

hooks, bell (1994), *Teaching to Transgress: Education as the Practice of Freedom*. New York: Routledge.

Jackson, Anthony (2007), *Theatre, Education and the Making of Meanings: art or instrument?* Manchester: Manchester University Press.

Johnson, Richard (2005), 'Radical', in Tony Bennett et al. (eds), *New Keywords: A Revised Vocabulary of Culture and Society.* Malden, MA: Blackwell, pp. 296–97.

Kershaw, Baz (1999), *The Radical in Performance: Between Brecht and Baudrillard*. New York: Routledge.

Kincheloe, Joe L. (2005), *Critical Constructivism*. New York: Peter Lang.

——(2008), *Critical Pedagogy.* New York: Peter Lang.

Kolb, David A. (1984), *Experiential Learning: Experience as the Source of Learning and Development*. Englewood Cliffs, NJ: Prentice Hall.

Lloyd, Genevieve (2006), 'Education', in Tony Bennett et al. (eds), *New Keywords: A Revised Vocabulary of Culture and Society.* Malden, MA: Blackwell, pp. 97–99.

McConachie, Bruce (1995), 'Toward a Positivist Theatre History', *Theatre Journal* 34.4, pp. 465–86.

McLaren, Peter (2003), 'Critical Pedagogy: A Look at the Major Concepts', in Darder et al. (2003), pp. 69–96.

Nellhaus, Tobin (1993), 'Science, History, Theatre: Theorizing in Two Alternatives to Positivism', *Theatre Journal* 45.4, pp. 505–27.

Nicholson, Helen (2007), *Theatre & Education*. New York: Palgrave Macmillan.

——(2011), *Theatre, Education & Performance.* New York: Palgrave Macmillan.

*No Child Left Behind Act of 2001* (NCLB) (2002), Pub. L. 107–10, 115 Stat. 1425–2094.

Prendergast, Monica and Saxton, Juliana, eds (2009), *Applied Theatre: International Case Studies and Challenges for Practice.* Bristol: Intellect.

Redington, Christine (1983), *Can Theatre Teach? An Historical and Evaluative Analysis of Theatre in Education*. Oxford: Pergamon.

Shor, Ira (1992), *Empowering Education: Critical Teaching for Social Change.* Chicago: University of Chicago Press.

United Nations Programme on HIV/AIDS [UNAIDS] (2004), *Techniques and Practices for Local Responses to HIV/AIDS: Part 2: Practices*, Amsterdam: KIT Developmental Policy and Practice.

Vallins, Gordon (1965), 'Theatre in Education: General Notes July 1965', Belgrade Theatre, Coventry. Unpublished.

Vygotsky, Lev (1933/2002), 'Play and Its Role in the Mental Development of the Child.' *Psychology and Marxism Internet Archive.* trans. Catherine Mulholland. Online at: www.marxists.org/archive/vygotsky/works/1933/play.htm (accessed 10 May 2008).

——(1978), *Mind in Society: The Development of Higher Psychological Processes.* Cambridge, MA: Harvard University Press.

Warwood, Joshua Ramirez (2011), 'David: Acting on HIV/AIDS.' *Outlish.* June. Online at: www.outlish.com/david-acting-on-hivaids/ (accessed 30 June 2011).

# 17

# TIE: THE PEDAGOGIC AS THE AESTHETIC IN A CRUMBLING WORLD

*Peter O'Connor*

Theatre in education, prison theatre, reminiscence theatre and Theatre of the Oppressed are some of the more popular theatre practices included under the umbrella term, applied theatre. Ackroyd (2000) has argued that these practices share an intentionality to provoke or shape social change. Although only recently named within the academy, the origins of applied theatre can be traced to the 'soil of progressive, radical people's movements in various places around the world' (Prentki and Preston 2009: 13). The pedagogic and aesthetic intents of applied theatre practice have in large measure been shaped by the left-wing, progressive politics of these movements. This chapter starts with a brief examination of the major influences on the pedagogy and aesthetics of theatre in education. Several case studies of TIE projects in earthquake zones then explore how relationships that exist between the pedagogical and aesthetic intents have shaped and formed each project.

## The pedagogic in TIE

The pedagogic intents of TIE can be usefully traced to the democratic notions of active civil engagement signalled by John Dewey. For Dewey

> education is a regulation of the process of coming to share in the social consciousness; and … the adjustment of individual activity on the basis of this social consciousness is the only sure method of social reconstruction.
>
> (Dewey 1916: 16)

Dewey recognised that

> The teacher is not in the school to impose certain ideas or to form certain habits in the child, but is there as a member of the community to select the influences which shall affect the child and to assist him in properly responding to these influences.
>
> (ibid.)

The emancipatory writings of Paulo Freire have also deeply influenced the pedagogical imperatives both of applied theatre in general and of TIE in particular. Applied theatre and critical pedagogy share a common philosophy in that both are primarily concerned with the ability to name and remake the world. For Freire the aim of critical pedagogy is to enable

> peoples' control over their lives and their capacity for dealing rationally with decisions by enabling them to identify, understand and act to transform …
>
> (Lankshear and Lawler 1987: 74)

Freire argues that

> the educator, rather than deposit 'superior knowledge' to be passively digested, memorized, and repeated, must engage in a 'genuine dialogue' or 'creative exchange' with the participants.
>
> (Freire, quoted in Blackburn 2000: 8)

These educational thinkers (among many others) deeply influenced the development of TIE alongside the development of drama in education (DIE). John O'Toole (2009: 482) suggests 'a volatile mix of progressive and constructivist educational philosophies, and Marxist and liberatory ones underpinned the TIE team's work (and the whole Drama in Education movement)'.

These imperatives created revolutionary pedagogic practices including mantle of the expert and teacher-in-role, both central approaches to TIE and drama in education. These approaches can be understood in Heathcote's demand that what is needed in schools is 'to move from holding the information and doling it out like charity, to creating the circumstances where it is imperative to inquire, search out and interrogate the information we locate' (Heathcote 2006: xiii).

## The aesthetic in TIE

The essential aesthetic in TIE is the integral participation of children in the construction and resolution of the theatrical narrative alongside visiting actor-teachers in classrooms. Teacher-in-role, hot-seating and other theatrical devices were developed 'in parallel and jointly by theatre in education and drama in education practitioners' (O'Toole 2009: 482). Increasingly TIE and DIE have incorporated aesthetic conventions from

> Moreno's psychodrama techniques, agit prop and other forms of political theatre and the rehearsal techniques of Brecht, Meyerhold, MacColl, Littlewood and other socially committed theatre practitioners.
>
> (Neelands, cited in O'Connor 2010: xviii)

There has been a growing appreciation of the tensions that exist between the political, pedagogic and aesthetic imperatives of TIE. O'Toole (2009: 482) suggests: 'The joint history of drama (and/or theatre) and education is full of battlefields between the two, and the unmourned bones equally of dull and worthy instrumentalism, and of stimulating but vapid magic.' Yet what is clear is that TIE's aesthetic and pedagogic dimensions are inextricably linked. Theatre that deliberately engages in democratic and participatory forms collapses not only the old dichotomy of actor and spectator, but also that of teacher and student. Exciting theatre and powerful learning are the true potential of TIE when the aesthetic truly acts as the pedagogic.

In the following case studies, theatre work in two areas connected by the common experience of earthquakes is explored to investigate further the relationship between the aesthetic and pedagogic in TIE.

## TIE in earthquake zones

In 2008 I was invited to Beijing to work with theatre companies who had been working in Szechuan following the series of deadly earthquakes in the region. One company had worked in the immediate aftermath of the quake and had struggled as it worked directly with the stories young children shared of their quake experience. The companies wanted to use theatre as a process for the young quake victims to make sense of the ongoing trauma, but had found that working directly with personal stories was re-traumatising. Over a period of several days I worked with several companies who were heading to the quake zones. Together we focused on finding and using Brechtian theatre techniques to disrupt the flow of naturalistic role-play that they felt had hindered the initial work. This led to one theatre company using traditional acrobatic dance forms, another group using dream sequencing as the basis of community devising, and yet another company using forum theatre.

Although the Chinese government had permitted artists to enter into the quake zones, once the communities started to use in their dramas the stories of the poorly constructed schools which had been responsible for so many child deaths, the various theatre groups were banned. The open-ended nature of the art forms, and the principles of democratic education that underpin them, were not to be tolerated in the quake zones. Theatre companies could work in the zones if they moved away from participatory forms and instead provided information about government rebuilding efforts. The Chinese government required theatre companies to tell the story of the state's role in managing the quake, not to use drama as a process for telling the stories of those damaged by the state in the lead-up to the disaster. None of the companies I worked with went back into the quake zone after this change in government policy. The companies made a choice that it was better to make no art rather than bad art, art that would be compromised by a pedagogy rooted in propaganda. The Chinese government recognised that the democratic nature of the aesthetic forms used by the theatre companies was potentially politically dangerous for the regime. They clearly recognised the potency of the theatrical forms to create disquiet about government policy.

In 2011 my work in earthquake zones became more intense following a series of quakes in Christchurch, New Zealand. On 22 February 2011, 185 people were killed and many others injured in a series of devastating quakes. New Zealand is a small, highly interconnected society and over those next days many of us held our breaths as we waited to know the fate of family and friends. Schools were shut; the quake had literally ripped some of them apart. The water, electricity and sewerage in some parts of the city would remain marginal for months. Media talk of what would happen when schools reopened focused on teachers being the healers, those who would return life to some sort of normality for thousands of children, even if their own lives were shattered. It was a role for which teachers hadn't been trained and for which, because of their own personal predicaments, they were unprepared.

Two days after the quake I contacted Ginny Thorner, who runs a charitable trust in Christchurch called Learning Through the Arts.[1] Ginny's home had been badly damaged in the quake and she was living with her children and husband in someone else's home. Together we planned a two-day workshop for teachers and children to be held on the first days that schools reopened.

A colleague, Juliet Cottrell, had told me about a classroom-based drama she was working on with children that involved repairing a torn cloth of dreams. The metaphor resonated deeply and I found that other colleagues in Australia had written a drama resource about dream makers (Dunn and Stinson 2000). They sent me the plans. Maybe because I was spending so much time in planning the logistics of our visit to Christchurch I only read the first line of the story that sat at the heart of the resource:

> A girl wakes up in the morning and when she gets up, she trips and tears her cloth of dreams.

I could envisage using this short pretext to engage the children in looking at what they might need to do to hope and dream again. The pretext helped to form a range of possibilities for structuring the work in Christchurch. However, by the time we were ready to go to Christchurch the workshop plans remained vague and sketchy at best. The plan involved getting the children to work in role to repair the cloth and return the dreams to the little girl. It involved a teacher in role as a dream maker, looking for experts in repairing damaged dream cloths. There would be a recipe we could write down that listed what needed to be done to mend broken dreams. There was only time to plan a few questions to attempt to provide a rich aesthetic experience for the children. To complicate things further the plan was to model a process to teachers that they could then use in their own classrooms. I needed to create a process that was simple and easily reproducible. The only resources I had to begin the work in Christchurch were two lines of a story, three or four questions, some blank cloth and a box of crayons.

I caught a flight to Christchurch from Auckland twelve days after the initial quake with Molly Mullen, a PhD student in applied theatre at the University of Auckland. The plan was for a full day working with children, with teachers watching, and then a second day of workshops with seventy teachers from around the city whose schools were still closed. As we took our seats on the plane we became very aware that we were amongst only a handful of people not in uniform. The men and women who had been involved in the search and recovery efforts immediately after the quake were returning for their second spell with a steely-eyed resolve for the heart-rending job of recovering bodies from the rubble. I sat on the plane wondering what I had to offer, intensely aware of critiques of the limitations of the arts and what they might do at such times – the arts don't literally save lives.

The day before a colleague had given me a book to read and I reached for it from my cabin bag. Almost as an answer to my doubts about the task ahead, these words of Freire leapt from the page:

> The privileged routinely look for solutions in the wrong places and then when they cannot find the solutions they feel despair, and become convinced that broader change isn't possible and therefore not worth aspiring to or acting towards.
>
> (Denborough 2008: x)

The next fourteen hours passed in a whirl of emotions and activity. We headed into the school past scenes of destruction shown daily on television, struggling to replace what we saw with what we remembered from earlier visits to the city.

That night, back in the motel room I sent the following email to my Dean, and to friends and colleagues around the world:

> We've just got in from our first day having just had dinner with our local support team here (and got a good 5.1 aftershock to stir the meal along).
>
> In four sessions we worked with about 120 children from Years 2–6 and with about 20 teachers. It was one of the most exciting and rewarding teaching days of my life.
>
> I worked in role with Molly and we worked on a story of a girl who trips and tears her cloth of dreams. Questioned about the story, the 7 and 8 year olds said if you tear your cloth of dreams then they disappear and that to have your dreams disappear is the saddest thing that can happen to anyone.
>
> So as a group we made a new cloth of dreams (on a very large piece of cloth and [*sic*] fabric crayons). That cloth is so full of joy and brightness and colour. They made it to help the little girl in the story. A young girl who had lost family in the quake, drew herself flying on a unicorn through the land of everything that is good. Her teacher said later it was the first time in three days back at school she had seen her living in the moment, totally absorbed by the possibilities of something new.

> Then, enrolled as dream makers we drew up the ingredients for good dreams. We poured them into a cloud bowl (They decided it needed to be that big). We put in joy, love, belief (which they decided was heavy so we had to roll it in). One girl had a 'teaspoonful of light in the darkest tunnel.' I asked her how we would put it in. She said, 'We can sprinkle it in and then the light can go through everything.'
>
> Everyone without asking then leaned into the bowl and we sure could see it in there. We wrapped Molly up in the cloth of dreams we had made and as she fell asleep and dreamed again her found dreams, we congratulated ourselves for being able to make happy endings to stories. (It was then I saw the teachers in tears … ) At the end they came up and hugged Molly and I and thanked us for what we had done. Of course it was the children. …
>
> (O'Connor 2011)

The workshop had progressed without any pre-planned ending. There was simply the wonderful pretext, and the question of what they thought losing your dream cloth meant. They had shared this with us through a series of freeze frames which showed the young girl as sad, angry, worried. The pedagogical intent was simply to provide a means for the children to reconsider their futures with hopes and dreams repaired. The word earthquake was never mentioned, there was no desire to retell the quake stories, but instead to begin the process of thinking about how to repair something in your life when it has been broken.

The recipes created that day by the children were rich in metaphor and also in practical advice. They demonstrated that children didn't need to be taught or given a list of what they needed to do in the next few weeks. They had the list already themselves. The traditional TIE approach of using actor-teachers 'to mediate between the young people and the world they inhabit' (Big Brum Theatre 2011) meant that the moment of beauty was co-created in a place of terrifying uncertainty and shaken possibility. The great gift of the teaspoon of light was that 'for a time at least, it actually felt as we would like the world to feel' (Winston 2009: 44).

The next day we worked with teachers at a golf course. It was a beautiful sunny day and the clubrooms were totally unscathed (as was, surprisingly, much of the city). It was hard to reconcile the images of people playing golf with the knowledge that only metres down the road there were damaged buildings, bodies still trapped under rubble.

The teachers that day all carried the grief of their own stories from what had happened and what was still happening. Yet they were focusing on the job ahead, what they were about to do when the children returned to their classrooms. The Ministry of Education had sent a two page advisory to Christchurch schools. Most of it talked of the importance of hygiene matters and in particular about washing hands. The Minister of Education reminded teachers that literacy and numeracy would be even more important and that, at senior secondary level, teachers would have to work hard to ensure the national assessment tasks could still function. There was a simmering resentment at the comments. More palpable was a sense of people with an overwhelming desire to help, to do something meaningful with their children and an accompanying tentativeness and caution about what that might be.

Schools in New Zealand, like so many other parts of the world, are 'futures focused'. They are, as Dorothy Heathcote once remarked, rehearsal rooms for a future that never arrives (Heathcote 1984). Combined with the dulling impact of national strategies on literacy and numeracy, measured regularly against national standards, the everyday inadequacy of what we do in schools becomes startlingly obvious at a time of crisis. Teachers in Christchurch wanted to help their children make sense of their world now, not engage in the soul-numbing business of schooling for future employment. They wanted to find safe ways to talk about the present and reconsider new futures, unimagined only weeks before. The teachers who came to our workshop recognised the potential of the arts to do exactly that. They were interested in a pedagogical approach to provide opportunities for their children to create alternative aesthetic statements on dreams that had been lost. They came seeking ways to create classroom work which focused on hope-filled possibilities rather than on reimagining the terrors of the quake. The teachers that day saw the process we were using as an antidote to the darkness of current educational orthodoxy in the New Zealand context. Simply working with a powerful story and allowing children to find the answers to deep and important questions, to create moments of beauty and moments of awe (Heathcote 1984) seems more radical now in an increasingly conservative school environment than in the 1960s and 1970s when TIE started.

As we flew back to Auckland that night, the news of the quake and tsunami in Japan had broken. Our flight home was again full of uniformed men and women. Now they were headed to Auckland to catch international flights to Japan. I was overcome by their bravery and wept on the plane at the thought of the scale of their heroism.

By the time we got back to Auckland the Dean had sent my original email across the university and it had bounced around the globe. In the week after my return Molly and I gave a seminar about the work and it was made into a pod cast, which was then put on YouTube (O'Connor and Mullen 2011).

Over 600 people downloaded the clip in the first 48 hours and by March 2012 there had been over 2,000 downloads. It has attracted considerable interest across the world. People started emailing, telling me they were showing it to their undergraduate and postgraduate classes. I grew increasingly uncomfortable about the growing 'hero narrative'. Yet I was also deeply conflicted in that I also understood that the offering of the teaspoon of light had inspired many fellow educators. I began to sense a reassurance inherent in the work that, despite the deadening approach to teaching and learning involved in constant assessment, schools could still be places where the unexpected could happen, places where moments of beauty might be recognised and celebrated. For a community of scholars and teachers who engage in educational theatre on a daily basis, in the gloom of the everyday, the story of our work in Christchurch seemed to reaffirm their commitments and their beliefs about the value of their work. For other educators who didn't know of this pedagogical approach and its charms, the work was inspiring and elevating.

In the weeks after our initial visit Ginny told me that children in schools were using the dream cloths as a metaphor to talk about what was happening to them and their city. (From the February earthquake the city was rocked by a further 5,000 aftershocks to the end of 2011.) They were asking questions such as:

'What if you can't stop looking at the place where the tear was and you can't dream?'
'What if the dreams are still there but they have lost their colour?'
'What if the thread that fixed the tear doesn't work any more or all the time?'

These questions demanded a different aesthetic approach, a new way of working that would shift from the largely experiential and process drama[2] form of the first workshop. As both a dance and drama educator Ginny had ideas about how we might create small pieces of dance that allowed a more embodied approach to solving the problems the children were posing. We had more time to plan for the return visit so Ginny and I worked on an idea of a drama that brought the dreams off the cloth and embodied them in movement phrases.

This part of the project became a transitional phase away from the teacher-in-role led process drama we had created in our initial visit to a more traditional TIE project where the children responded in role to a small piece of theatre.

The short performance we used as a pre-text has a little girl now waking, distressed that her dreams have vanished from her cloth. Enrolled as dream makers the children devise ways of embodying the dreams and making them move so that the little girl can return them to the cloth. Two months after our initial visit we returned to Christchurch. We worked with nearly 250 children and managed to workshop eight versions of the story over two days. We would teach the drama for an hour, reflect on what happened in a twenty-minute break and then reinvent the process with the next group.

I've never played improvisational jazz, but I imagine it feels like our teaching did in those sessions. We had a strong motif and we seemed to riff off each other as we tried new approaches, slight variations on the teacher-in-role, added or removed tensions, framed things slightly differently or extended or shortened pieces of work. It was truly exhilarating, playing with what was in front of us, rather than towards something. The opportunity to play with the aesthetic and pedagogic possibilities was enabled by the loose funding framing under which we operated. Because there weren't tightly prescribed pedagogic outputs required, nor any formal reporting requirements, we found ourselves free to work completely focused on the theatre-making we were engaged with. Our primary focus on the aesthetic, however, meant that we created powerful moments of learning for the children.

## Full transition to Theatre in Education

Following what I considered the success of the second series of workshops, I was determined to make the work available as widely as possible across the city. I wanted to replicate the open-ended nature of the arts making and saw that the best way to do this would be to create an easily reproducible piece of TIE that could be staffed by local artist-teachers. Such an approach would mean that the programme would more rightly belong with the Christchurch community. It would build on the initial work that had also engaged with local artists.

A full TIE tour working with actor-teachers would change and shift our improvisational work into a more structured programme that would combine the original work with our new movement-inspired piece. I had often trialled TIE programmes as smaller-scale process dramas, relying on a teacher-in-role approach rather than a scripted performed pre-text (O'Connor and Nichol 2001; O'Connor 2005), and I knew the process of translating the work we had begun in the second phase into a fuller TIE project was fairly straightforward. The long and unenviable task of seeking funding for the project began.

Over those months further, and some large, aftershocks were keeping Christchurch in a state of unease about its dream cloth. Approaches to the local Christchurch Office of the Ministry of Education involved showing them the YouTube video about our original visit. A bureaucrat commented that she didn't see the educational value of the work and that maybe it was 'only therapy' and not suitable for supporting into schools. Perhaps any relationship with government would have meant, just as it did in China, that the programme would need to alter the way it worked if it was going to be able to continue. Of course the demands in China were politically motivated; in New Zealand it was about what counts and doesn't count as worthwhile in an educational context.

If the project had had neat plans, with easily identifiable and measurable goals, linked specifically to narrow curriculum guidelines, it might have gained the Ministry of Education's support. Yet by introducing these pedagogic constraints, it would have changed the aesthetic of the programme. At one level I was relieved *not* to get the money. I was worried that I would have had to teach something, have a check list of learning intentions to tick off, and some curricular guidelines to work with. They would not have been as offensive as the ones demanded in China but they would have radically altered the work and its possibilities.

The bureaucrat's comment about therapy demands some attention. The comment demonstrates the confusion many have between drama therapy and the therapeutic qualities and potential of drama making. Unlike the dismissal of the work as 'only therapy' by the bureaucrat, drama therapists from around the world on seeing the YouTube clip claimed the work as drama therapy. I remain unsure as to how to deflect or challenge their obvious delight and pleasure in the work. In a moment of true Kafkaesque bureaucracy, my appeal to one of the relief organisations set up to deal with the quake told me that my application could not progress because schools had not identified a need for TIE. In an irony not lost on myself I found myself defending the work on therapy grounds – that it was helping kids traumatised by the ongoing quakes. Despite thirty years of work in educational theatre I was struggling to provide reasons for the work, knowing that funders were not necessarily interested in the moments of aesthetic beauty I was attempting to create across the city. And beyond the powerful and deeply moving story of the teaspoon of light I had no evaluation of the work, no hard evidence to suggest that what was on offer was of any value. I became truculent and obsessive in my demands for money. Thinking of those brave men and women in uniforms on the plane with whom we flew on our first day, there might simply be more important things to spend money on than a TIE programme.

Approaches to corporations fell on deaf ears except for Norcross Print, the company that does all the print work for the University of Auckland, which gave us in-kind support. Finally, applications to UNESCO and the Mental Health Foundation of New Zealand released monies for the establishment of the *Teaspoon of Light Theatre in Education Company.* UNESCO and the Mental Health Foundation funding arose out of my previous track record in doing similar work and their own understandings of the value of TIE in those situations. The key decision-makers in each organisation were also from Christchurch. The power of the story of the teaspoon of light offered in the days immediately after the quake created a significant emotional impact that obviated the usual need for hard (quantifiable) evidence.

Ginny Thorner took over management of the project as well as being an actor-teacher in the programme. We spent three days devising the programme to combine the initial process drama and transitional workshops and to reshape the narrative and aesthetic so it could be easily reproduced three times a day for two actor-teachers. A song was written for the pre-text performance which the children would use later in the programme. Two identical dream cloths were made, one of which was then torn. A dream box, lists of instructions for dream makers and uniforms were also made. As with the earlier drama work the TIE team would be in role as dream makers. Now they would work for a company called the *Teaspoon of Light Dream Makers Company* who work on cases of torn and damaged dream cloths.

In the TIE programme the children are enrolled as helpers to the company and their first in-role job is to work with a young girl called Sarah whose cloth is torn. Ginny doubles in role as Sarah's mother and as the Head Dream Makers Top Assistant, who desperately needs help with the case of Sarah's torn cloth. Fortunately a set of instructions is found inside the dream cloth box that sits at the end of Sarah's bed. For much of the initial part of the drama the work has to be done with great care and quietly so as to not disturb the sleeping Sarah. This part of the drama consists largely of huddles of very quiet six-year-olds unfurling and inspecting the dream cloth, analysing the dreams and working out ways to help as they tiptoe across the room.

Dramatic tension is added by the need to complete the job before the sun rises. The instructions ask the children to make a repairing potion to fix the tear and then place the dreams into the potion for the repair to work. When Sarah unexpectedly wakes up, the children allow her to help them sort through the problems. Sarah's role allows the actor-teacher to ask a range of seemingly naive questions about how to help people with trouble dreaming. The questions, however, challenge and deepen the children's commitment to the drama and also challenge their ideas about what helps. The instructions then ask the children to remove the dreams from the cloth and bring them to life. Each performance sees novel ways to take the dreams off the cloth and embody them. For example, children use dream maker ungluing machines, or they are skipped off the cloth, and in many cases very specialised powerful gloves are worn to wipe the dreams directly into the body. The assistant dream makers usually quickly take charge of the whole operation and organise Sarah to go back to bed, often using the song they heard Ginny sing in the opening piece of theatre. When Sarah is reluctant and wants to stay awake, the children often reprimand her, now playing the roles of concerned adults who know better and they reassure her no doubt with the very words they hear their own parents say when they are woken at night with earthquakes.

Just before Sarah goes to sleep, Ginny reminds the children to add the teaspoon of light to the dream box. Asked what the teaspoon of light might contain, the children often suggest things such as happiness, love, hugs, knowing your parents are across the hall and memories of good times.

The programme ends with everyone out of role except for the sleeping Sarah with her dream cloth returned to the box. Ginny asks if the children are happy to leave the story there. Every time the children want to see whether or not the dream makers had fixed the cloth. As audience, now the children watch Sarah ever so carefully unfold the cloth, which, with a little theatrical magic, is revealed to be fixed. Gasps of delight and incredulity that they had repaired the cloth are reminiscent of children at pantomime performances.

In a period of eight weeks, *Teaspoon of Light* was presented fifty-three times as a ninety-minute interactive programme with 3,000 6- to 10-year-olds in the most damaged parts of Christchurch. The TIE piece is a huge development from the original process drama work created within days of the quake. The theatrical devices of the torn and fixed cloth, the surety of the scripted performance and the tied-down sequencing of conventions has at one level narrowed the work. There are fewer aesthetic and pedagogic choices to be made by the actor-teachers as they work. The open-ended teaching of the second phase of work had to be tempered by a less flexible approach to ensure three programmes a day could be rolled out over a sustained period. The planned ending of the cloth revealed as mended constrained the options that could be taken to get there. However, each day a totally new programme is created because of the genuine and open-ended in-role questions the dream makers ask. Movement patterns are different every day, ways of removing and embodying dreams are different. But every day, as it was in the very first workshop, children become active arts makers, and active learners in a crumbling world.

We have begun to evaluate the work so that it might be easier to gain further funding to continue it as the earthquakes continue to rumble. Ginny keeps a research journal that documents each day. It records student reactions and comment, teacher responses and her conversations with her fellow actor-teacher and myself. A video team recorded three programmes and constructed thirty-minute and twelve-minute documentaries. They captured moments of highly engaged, excited children helping to repair torn dreams. An early analysis of the videos is providing a deeper understanding of what is working in the programme, and beginning to show the beauty of the work and therefore its teaching potential.

In April 2012, UNESCO agreed to further funding after a presentation of the video documentary to the National Education Sub Committee in Wellington, which includes people who understand deeply the nature of learning. In this video a boy offers cups of love to make the magic thread to fix the torn cloth. Ginny, in role, asks how many cups. The boy replies, with steely resolve and a surety that comes with real expertise, that six cups are needed. For ten minutes after screening the video the group of educators discussed this moment. The manner in which the boy could so convincingly answer the question, and his ability to use and manipulate the metaphors inherent in the work, hooked them. The committee saw that the work could resonate beyond earthquake zones and recognised that here was a way of working with children that was rich and powerful. I have a sense that much of the decision to commit further funds was based on seeing the evidence in one child's response to a genuine question asked within the drama.

The early stages of the research are telling us that working with children in the aftermath of deadly earthquakes, and in the ongoing wake of thousands of aftershocks, requires a commitment to an interlinked aesthetic and pedagogic intention which provides an opportunity to reimagine the world that shifts and moves beneath them. In the comments we receive from teachers, from our own observations of how readily children who have been severely hurt by the quakes engage in helping others with torn dreams, there is a growing understanding of the importance of working to reposition children within their own narratives. It requires structuring work that focuses on some of the core issues created by the quakes without addressing them directly. The distancing theatre devices used in the *Teaspoon of Light* project enable children to explore the issues without overloading their emotional engagement in the work.

The role of helping someone who has lost her dreams, rather than creating a narrative that reinforces their own position as victims, has begun to enable some children to reframe and make sense of what is happening to them. Rather than a rehearsal room for a future that is now so very uncertain, the project provides the possibility for becoming an actor in a changed world. It can be easily argued that a teaspoon of light is vital in places all over the world and not just in areas of natural disaster. Darkness takes many shapes and forms. The hope implicit in this work, the same hope that informed the creation of TIE as an art form, needs to be sprinkled so 'it can go through everything'. The programme remains true to the radical pedagogic origins of TIE, of creating an open-ended decision-making, problem-solving enquiry for children to explore issues of significance and become actors in and on the world.

Aesthetically, as the children create beautiful images of dreams brought back to life, or sing in unison to make Sarah go back to sleep, or watch with rapt attention the unfurling of the repaired cloth, they are involved in potent theatre: potent theatre as education.

## Notes

1 Learning Through the Arts organises conferences and professional development for teachers in the arts in the Canterbury region.

2 By process drama, I mean a form of whole class improvisational theatre-making often involving the teacher in role alongside the students. The theatre making is not intended for an external audience but for the aesthetic pleasure and learning experience of the participants.

## Works cited

Ackroyd, J. (2000), 'Applied Theatre: Problems and Possibilities'. *Applied Theatre Researcher*. www.gu.edu/centre/atr (accessed 26 April 2012).

Big Brum Theatre in Education Co. (2011), 'Artistic Policy 2011', www.bigbrum.org.uk/resources.html (accessed 26 April 2012).

Blackburn, J. (2000), 'Understanding Paulo Freire: reflections on the origins, concepts and possible pitfalls of his educational approach'. *Community Development Journal* 35, pp. 3–15.

Denborough, D. (2008), *Collective Narrative Practice: Responding to individuals, groups and communities who have experienced trauma*. Adelaide: Dulwich Centre Publications.

Dewey, J. (1916), *Democracy and Education*. New York: Macmillan.

Dunn, J. and Stinson, M. (2000), *The Dream maker*. Brisbane: Queensland Curriculum Documents.

Heathcote, D. (1984), *Collected Writings on Education and Drama*, ed. L. Johnson and C. O'Neill. London: Hutchinson and Co.

——(2006), Preface to J. Carroll, M. Anderson and D. Cameron, *Real Players? Drama, technology and education*. Stoke on Trent: Trentham Books, pp. i–iv.

Lankshear, C. and Lawler, M. (1987), *Literacy, Schooling and Revolution*. London: Falmer Press.

O'Connor, P. (2005), *The Lost Bag: Mental Health Resource for Years 7 to 10*. Auckland: Mental Health Foundation.

——, ed. (2010), *Creating Democratic Citizenship through Drama Education: the Selected writings of Jonothan Neelands*. Stoke on Trent: Trentham Books.

——(2011), 'Christchurch'. Email. (10 March 2011).

O'Connor, P. and Mullen, M. (2011), Online seminar at www.youtube.com/watch?v=jznOhFrSvJY (last accessed 8 June 2012).

O'Connor, P. and Nichol, J. (2001), *Natural High: Mental Health Resource for Alcohol and Drug Education*. Auckland: Mental Health Foundation.

O'Toole, J. (2009), 'Writing Everyday Theatre: applied theatre, or just TIE rides again', *Research in Drama in Education: the Journal of Applied Theatre and Performance* 14.4, pp. 479–503.

Prentki, T. and Preston, S., eds (2009), *The Applied Theatre Reader*. London: Routledge.

Winston, J. (2009), 'Beauty, laughter and the charming virtues of drama', *Drama Research: International Journal of Drama Education, Preview* 1, pp. 38–47.

# INDEX

[Theatre companies are listed by country.]

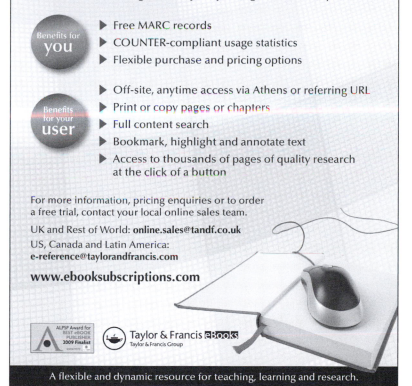